THE BRITISH NARROW GAUGE RAILWAY—No 4.

NARROW GAUGE RAILWAYS IN SOUTH CAERNARVONSHIRE

by

JAMES I. C. BOYD

with drawings by J. M. LLOYD

THE OAKWOOD PRESS
LINGFIELD, SURREY
1972

To the Memory of Tom Davies
Last Engineman of the Old Order on the Festiniog Railway; sometime on the Welsh Highland Railway.
A patient teacher and devoted Railwayman whose enthusiasm inspired this book.

PRINTED AND BOUND IN ENGLAND BY
HAZELL WATSON AND VINEY LTD
AYLESBURY, BUCKS

CONTENTS

Note. Miscellaneous tramways in Caernarvonshire are collated in the Appendix to Volume 2 of this work ('Narrow Gauge Railways in North Caernarvonshire') together with sections on Spooner & Co., Tickets, Narrow gauge/Standard gauge transfer wagons, De Winton & Co. Union Ironworks.

Note on track diagrams and signalling arrangements

These have been compiled by the Author using field work, photographic and a limited quantity of official material. The latter is frequently misleading, as it usually denotes 'intent' rather than accomplishment. All drawings are original and based on these sources; this is brought to notice as drawings in this Series are not copies from official sources open for public inspection.

THE BRITISH NARROW GAUGE RAILWAY SERIES

by the same Author

No. 1. THE FESTINIOG RAILWAY
(in two volumes)

No. 2. THE ISLE OF MAN RAILWAY

No. 3. NARROW GAUGE RAILWAYS IN MID-WALES

No. 4. NARROW GAUGE RAILWAYS IN SOUTH CAERNARVONSHIRE

*No. 5. NARROW GAUGE RAILWAYS IN NORTH CAERNARVONSHIRE
(*Penrhyn, Padarn, Nantlle, Snowdon Mountain, etc.*)

*No. 6. ENGLISH NARROW GAUGE RAILWAYS

Publications on Scottish and Irish Narrow Gauge Railways are proposed within the Series.

*THE NARROW GAUGE RAILWAY MANUAL
(*A non-regional history and technical reference book to the narrow gauge railways of Great Britain and Ireland*).

* Titles in preparation

The spelling of place names is based on that commonly used in Bradshaw's Timetable, allowing for changes in Bradshaw's spelling and alterations in the names of stations etc. Where railway systems had no passenger service and Bradshaw cannot be quoted, the customary spelling used by railway historians has been adopted. Early maps frequently mis-spelt Welsh names, and official documents (usually of English origin) are disastrous in this particular. Official changes from Anglicised to more Welsh forms of spelling have occurred over the period covered in the book, e.g. Carnarvon to Caernarvon and more recently, Port Madoc to Porth Madog etc., etc., and care is necessary in identifying some smaller places, especially as names are often duplicated within a comparatively small area.

AUTHOR'S NOTE

Railway history has traditionally been presented in the form of Company History. This is convenient for the chronicler and tidy for the reader, but it is basically misleading and makes for insipid reading. There is much more to be said for presenting railway history as a regional study and not to confine it by artificial commercial boundaries.

There is a certain danger that the history of the Festiniog Railway (which forms a part of this Series), will be read in isolation because of its prominent position. In the Appendix to the Second Volume of its History, a much-abbreviated summary of the Festiniog's surrounding neighbours will have led the broader-minded to realize that the Festiniog Railway was but one thread in a tangled skein, the more interesting because it was one of the oldest and strongest strands of that skein.

The other strands, some even older and often much smaller, are also full of legend and interest; in fact in many respects they are more so. Without their existence—or threat of existence—the Festiniog would have become lazy and lifeless. So now the opportunity is taken to study the remainder of the pattern in greater detail, avoiding, it is hoped, over-emphasis on each individual undertaking, but showing how it stood up both against and alongside its contemporaries. By these two further volumes on the narrow gauge railways of Caernarvonshire, the whole narrow gauge picture in North and Mid-Wales becomes complete.

Unfortunately the regional boundary method does not permit a convenient assemblage and has not been too rigidly applied in consequence. Thus the first volume, dealing with South Caernarvonshire, takes in also a part of North Merionethshire. In this will be the railways with which the Festiniog had to live. The northern part of Caernarvon will be covered by the second part, dealing with some railways without whose earlier existence the Festiniog Railway would not have come into being.

James I. C. Boyd.

Colwall, Herefordshire,
December, 1971.

INTRODUCTION

For many people, the railways of Caernarvonshire simply consist of that line which clings to the north coast connecting Conway and Holyhead as part of the route of the 'Irish Mail'. Some others knew about the standard gauge lines from north to south and along part of the county's south coast, and that was about all. For the esoteric there was a bonus of fascinating little railways—most now a memory —which mapmakers seldom drew, because the system appeared and disappeared between Editions! And being non-passenger-carrying lines, railway timetables ignored them. Many were private, some were pioneer, and all are part of an age which has disappeared very quickly since the Second War.

The origins of these railways lay in the mineral resources of the county. These are so prodigious that more narrow gauge railways were built in Caernarvonshire than any other county in the Kingdom. For the terrain and the job, the small-gauge tramway was ideally suited. The most important of these resources was slate; in some places it had been worked for over 300 years before the coming of railways. Of the lesser railway-users, certain minerals were carried by rail, but often they were mined erratically over the years by successive owners or lease-holders, so that there was no continuity. For instance, one landowning family is said to have simply 'poured money down holes in the ground' in the expectancy of fortunes from below the earth's surface. Some of the more barefaced promotions which were publicly financed, made great promise of their potential and sometimes built railways to carry it away; all too often they went into liquidation within the next decade. The problem with minerals and their associated tramways was that they went through intensely profitable periods (usually the result of political and economic pressures of the times), but they were highly sensitive to slump. The tramways connecting these speculative ventures are among the most ephemeral in the country. Only human memory recorded them, and those who dared record these memories in print were often contradicted by the next raconteur.

The predecessors of rail transport in this part of Wales included the horse or mule carrying a pannier along a specially built path over the rough mountainside. A later development was to enlarge the path into a very rough road and use the traditional Welsh farm sledge. This was widely used in all places and seasons where wheeled transport was impracticable. The next development, if required, was the building of a McAdam road, and the landed proprietors were foremost in providing good roads through the mountains, mainly for their own promotions. These same proprietors followed their road-making activities by building 'Iron Railways' (as they were often termed in these parts) when it became clear that whilst a horse might haul a road wagon along a new road quite easily, that same horse could haul a greater tonnage over iron rails and moreover, right out of the workings and down to the sea coast and a ship's side.

It is possible that certain early tramways were initially laid out as sledge-ways and were used as such, probably having rails laid on them at a later stage. This was certainly true in some quarries, notably Dinorwic, where man-carrying sledges descended the inclines in formidable fashion.

An account of sledging in the Llangynog slate quarry in the early 19th century is revealing: '. . . slates . . . are brought down the steep declivity of rock in sledges containing about 5 cwt. each, with extreme danger to the persons engaged in this arduous task. When the sledge is loaded, and drawn to the edge of the declivity, a conductor sits upon it, passing over his shoulders a rope which is fastened at each extremity to the front, and also being assisted with a pole. Then raising his feet from the ground, he begins his descent by a narrow winding path, guiding the sledge by opposing his feet to the projecting points of the rock . . . governing its velocity by pressing firmly with his feet upon the ground and sustaining the weight of the carriage by the rope which passes over his shoulders . . . sometimes the guide . . . instead of sitting on the front of the sledge, descends backwards . . . when in danger of being overpowered . . . by the sledge, slipping the rope over his head, detaches himself from the carriage and throws it sideways over the precipice, regarding only his own preservation.'

All of which suggests that the advent of balanced-inclined tramways, even with all their attendant risks of cable breakages etc., must have been welcomed by such 'guides' (as the account calls them) 'who expose themselves to inevitable destruction'.

Every user of mineral workings faced the problem of transport. Little of his products was used locally and most had to be shipped. Slate went to many overseas markets as well as England and Ireland, and copper and other metal ores to South Wales for smelting. Water was the cheapest form of transport and even inland waters would be used for part of a load's journey if available, the cost of trans-shipment being considered unimportant. The coming of the tramway, with its flexibility, cheapness and penetrating capability soon opened up workings which hitherto had lacked development for their inaccessibility, and some remote tramways came into being.

The county had only one important port, Caernarvon. Pwllheli was also used, but was not so convenient. Artificial ports came into existence during the railway period, among them Portmadoc, Port Dinorwic and Port Penrhyn, all within twenty years of each other. Later the coast was to be dotted with shipping points where quarries on the hilltops along the coast ran tramways onto jetties and ships could load at most stages of the tide. Indeed, in neighbouring Denbighshire a jetty with tramway from the Llandulas Lime Quarry on it, had been built as early as 1822. In the context of this book, Caernarvonshire looked to the sea and the railway or tramway formed an integral part of the route.

The railway systems which resulted from this demand were very personal and parochial. Those which did not develop until the age of the steam locomotive were often too late for the trade they intended to serve. The slate industry was already declining in the 1880s and generally continued so from that time onward. Other minerals enjoyed intermittently good times. Usually, it was the oldest-established lines which had the longest lives and lasted until the nineteen-sixties. There were cases where a line which had been faithful to horse-power remained so to the end of its days.

The narrow gauge railways of Caernarvonshire have, (save one which is quite untypical, and a few short mineral lines which enjoy a lingering death), passed into memory. Walking along their mountainy courses today, it is hard to imagine the intrigue, high hopes and lost causes which surrounded most of them. Money was made and lost in a big way in this still very unpopulated region. After the Second War there came a time when hopes were high, but the expected boom in slate and tourists never came. Ultimately the remaining slate lines closed down and more recently, some of the largest slate quarries in the world have gone under the hammer.

Caernarvonshire has some of the finest scenery in the world and yet—at least at the time these lines are written—no narrow gauge railway of the type which flourishes under 'preservation' auspices, runs entirely within the county. This is not to make out a case for the establishment of one, but in a county which did more for the birth of narrow gauge railways and their establishment throughout the world than any other, it is ironic that the few passenger lines struggled hard and died early. Certainly at the present time when expansion in narrow gauge tourist railways is manifest, some native Welsh are still recalling the Welsh Highland Railway débâcle, so it seems that, even today, authority in Caernarvonshire is divided on the merits of passenger narrow gauge railways. Which, considering all that has passed within its boundaries, is a pity.

THE EMBANKMENT TRAMWAY

(*Gauge* 3 ft.)

Used in the construction of the Embankment or Cob at Traeth Mawr, between 1808 and 1811, and retained thereafter for maintenance purposes. Disposed of before building of Festiniog Railway over Embankment, and materials possibly disposed of to local users, including the Tremadoc Tramway.

Length: app. 1 mile as completed; double track.

The story of the Great Embankment (or 'Cob') and its place in the history of North Wales has already been fully published. In dealing with its designer and builder, W. A. Madocks, Elizabeth Beazley's 'Madocks and the Wonder of Wales' concentrates on its conception, construction and aftermath. Using some of the same material, Dr. Lewis has enlarged upon the railway aspect in 'How Ffestiniog got its railway'. Finally, the tramway in relation to the Festiniog Railway and other railways which entered Portmadoc, is adequately covered in 'The Festiniog Railway' Volume 1. It is therefore unnecessary to repeat the background save that for good order's sake the tramway should be mentioned here as being the second to be built in South Caernarvonshire.

The danger of consulting the above-mentioned works is that having regard to Madocks' remarkable genius and buoyant enthusiasm for everything he did (which is fully brought out) it might be concluded that he was engaged in some pioneer effort. The work, and the tramway used to build it, was truly remarkable but not unique; it was more difficult as being done in a then very isolated part of North Wales.

Reclamation work had been done in the Dee Estuary by Nathaniel Kenderley & Co., following an Act of 1734 for improving the navigation of the river to Chester, and passing through Saltney Marsh. This was completed in 1737. A new canal was formed and 800 acres of new land was appropriated by the Company for their own use on the north side of it. Between 1754 and 1790 further land was reclaimed which ultimately became Sealand. Another 2,000 acres was added under another Act of 1778. At Golvtyn (Golftyn) the Irish Coal Co. erected a large quay and pier at the mouth of the New Dee Channel. Here in fact, was the immediate predecessor of Madocks' schemes for reclamation, canal, town and port, not more than 50 miles from his Penmorfa Estate, purchased in 1798.

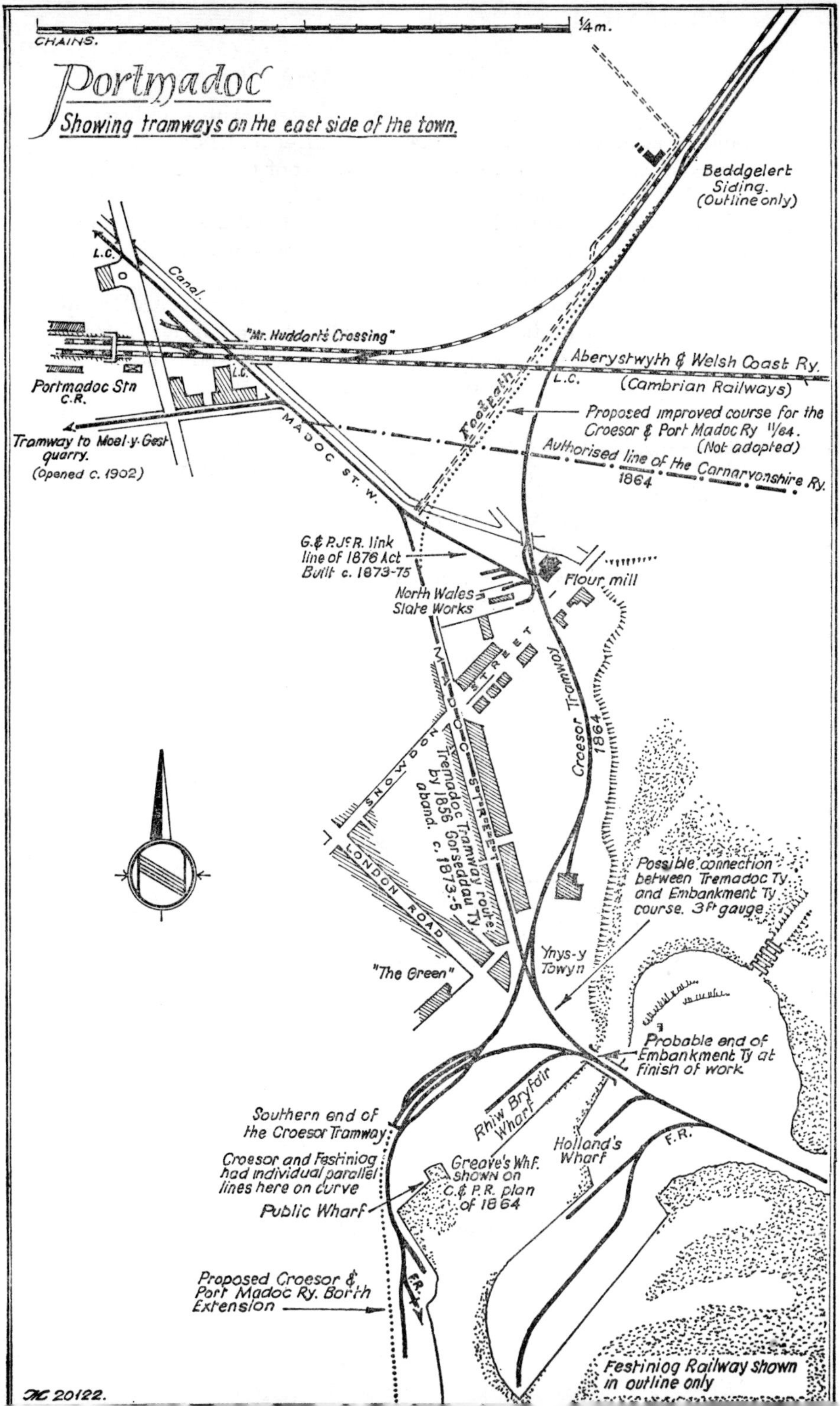
CHAINS.
¼m.
Portmadoc
Showing tramways on the east side of the town.
Beddgelert Siding. (Outline only)
L.C.
Canal.
"Mr. Huddart's Crossing"
Footpath
Aberystwyth & Welsh Coast Ry.
(Cambrian Railways)
L.C.
Portmadoc Stn C.R.
Tramway to Moel-y-Gest quarry.
(Opened c. 1902)
Proposed improved course for the Croesor & Port Madoc Ry 11/84.
(Not adopted)
Authorised line of the Carnarvonshire Ry. 1864
MADOC ST. W.
G. & P. Jc. R. link line of 1876 Act Built c. 1873-75
Flour mill
North Wales Slate Works
STREET
MADOC STREET
Croesor Tramway 1864
SNOWDON
LONDON ROAD
Tremadoc Tramway route by 1856 Gorseddau Ty. aband. c. 1873-5
Possible connection between Tremadoc Ty. and Embankment Ty course. 3ft gauge
"The Green"
Ynys-y Towyn
Probable end of Embankment Ty at finish of work
Southern end of the Croesor Tramway
Rhiw Bryfair Wharf
Holland's Wharf
F.R.
Croesor and Festiniog had individual parallel lines here on curve
Greave's Whf. shown on C. & P. R. plan of 1864
Public Wharf
Proposed Croesor & Port Madoc Ry. Borth Extension
F.R.
Festiniog Railway shown in outline only
JKC 20122.

Madocks' first experience in reclamation came with two dykes he built to enclose parts of this estate from river and tidal flood; the second dyke, the James Creassy Embankment of 1800, is said to have had the assistance of a wooden railway to bring the soil etc. with which it was built, from the hills surrounding, but the source of information is somewhat open to doubt. This sea wall was lightly made, not using rock or solid material at all.

Madocks' ambition was far greater than this; he proposed to enclose the estuary of the river Glaslyn by building a barrage between the shores of Caernarvonshire and Merionethshire, and build a road along it to connect the two counties. His first interest was in communications; the reclaimed land was a secondary matter. He was anxious to promote Porth Dinllaen (he had given £600 towards the cost of a pier there) as the seaport for Dublin, and such a road would lie on the direct London–Porth Dinllaen route; more importantly for him, his new town of Tre Madoc would lie on it too. He acquired the right to build the embankment at his own expense under an Act of 1807 (47 Geo III Session 2 Cap. 36) which vested any sands reclaimed in him and gave him an annual rent of 1/5th of the marshlands reclaimed. With only the first few hundred yards on the west bank in Caernarvonshire, he proposed to extend the bank from the rocky outcrop of Ynys-y-towyn to a point near Penrhyn Isa farm on the Merioneth shore, nearest to where rock might be found for infilling. To carry materials from quarries at Ynys and Penrhyn, he built a double tracked tramway which ultimately extended the full length of the work and into the stables, yards and workshops and quarries at each end.

The idea for such a tramway may have originated with the 1800 bank, if such a tramway had in fact been used there. On this occasion he would doubtless be guided by his friend Benjamin Wyatt, agent to Lord Penrhyn; Wyatt had designed a number of buildings in the vicinity of Lord Penrhyn's Bangor Estate.

Madocks' first mentions the tramway in correspondence of January 1808; it was at work in the following March. The stone quarried from opposite shores was tipped from horse-drawn wagons into the rapacious sands. The track was carried beyond the stonework on 'stilts' (piles) covered by a wooden platform; as the arms of the great bastion gradually closed together, so the tramway crept forward and its use intensified to frenzied proportions as time and money ran out, and the gap between the solid matter grew less and less, while the force of water grew greater and swept away all the materials thrown into it. At this time 600 wagon loads of stone were discharged into the breach on a good day, and there might have been more but for a chronic shortage of horses. The gap was closed in July 1811 and official opening took place on 17 September 1811.

The vast cost, met from Madocks' own pocket, bankrupted him. Inventories of the site were prepared by his creditors and vary in their content. It seems there was about a mile of track (2 miles double line) valued by one at only £370. The number of 'small waggons' on the site varies between 20 and 40, but all agree there were both old and new to be found. One list included a 'caravan' and a Bathing Machine.

With the work done, part of the tramway was taken up, possibly sold to meet creditors' demands. Evidence suggests it saw further service locally. Then in the following February a storm broke down the Cob and a great hole resulted. So appalling was this tragedy to all in the neighbourhood that there seems to have been an extraordinary effort by all concerned to repair it. The tramway was replaced with some difficulty, but was probably never completely put back. When the Cob had been repaired in late 1814 the track was, despite pressure from Madocks' creditors, allowed to lie undisturbed in case an emergency should require its use again. Possibly its materials ultimately found their way into the Tremadoc Tramway which, allowing for part-disposal in the 1811–14 period, would just about account for what was available when the track was hurriedly relaid. What had been Penrhyn Cottage on the Merioneth side, was enlarged into workshops, stables and offices and in May 1811 took the name of Boston Lodge after Madocks' Parliamentary constituency. The premises later became the Festiniog Railway's Works.

Of the permanent way materials, little is known. Dr. Lewis suggests that with the Wyatt connection, they may have been of the same pattern of 'Round Rails' invented by him and used on the Penrhyn Railway which had opened in July 1801. On the other hand it may equally have come through Lord Penrhyn himself who was familiar with an idea put forward by Richard L. Edgeworth of Co. Longford for reclaiming Irish bogland in 1787, and which Edgeworth admitted in 1810 to having been adopted on the Penrhyn Railway. By 'Round Rails', oval rails were meant, and to suit them, wheels with a concave rim were provided. This will be examined in a section dealing with the Penrhyn Railway in Volume 2; although there are gaps in knowledge on the first materials there, accounts of it to date have not accurately described it. Lewis says that wooden sleepers were first used, but this is not so; such were replacements for the cast-iron sill connections introduced about 1811. If the Embankment Tramway track is likely to have been very similar to that on the Penrhyn in 1801 (and there is good reason for suggesting it) then it had oval rails of cast iron, laid crudely into cast-iron chairs which were bolted through slate or slab sleepers. This was not an efficient track; the Penrhyn pioneer rail was soon replaced by a different section in lengths of 4 ft. 6 ins. which did not wear the wheel treads hollow—a state of affairs which would have affected the embankment wagons with their intensive usage. The simple chairs had no means of securing the oval rails either; the rail rested in a form of plain saddle and stayed there by its own weight.

The rails and chairs must have been removed ultimately from the Embankment when the Festiniog Railway was laid on the site in due course. If the Tramway was laid with slab sleepers they would have been available for re-use and this would predetermine the gauge of the purchaser's track. The Tremadoc Tramway is known to have been of 3 ft. gauge and, when extended to serve the Gorseddau Quarry, continued of that gauge. It was not converted to 2 ft. until the Gorseddau Junction and Portmadoc Railways Act sanctioned the conversion. If the Tremadoc Tramway used Embankment Tramway redundant materials including stone sleepers (if used), then the Embankment Tramway could have been to 3 ft. gauge. If however, Penrhyn experience was followed in the matter of gauge, a nominal 2 ft. gauge would have existed; this would logically suggest that (as distinct from individual blocks) some of the numerous slab sleepers used under the early Festiniog track might have had their origins in the Tramway.

The rails and some of the wagon wheels came from Jones of Wrexham, perhaps from a foundry of Edward Jones of Tuttle Street in that town and to provide ready-to-run wagons, some were purchased from South Wales.* Madocks records that the wagon bodies were mainly built by local carpenters; perhaps this was before the day of the sheet-iron sided wagon or the ability of local industry to build them.

The Embankment under construction, with a scene of the tramway at work, was incorporated in a drawing 'The Embankment, Traeth Mawer . . . In the autumn of 1810', by H. W. Billington. Though proportionately inaccurate, the detail of the wagons is probably fairly accurate and shows how little contractors' stock has changed in 150 years. The wagon shown has inside bearings for the axles (the wheels are likely to have been loose on them anyway, and secured by a wedge holding a collar in place at the axle-end), a wooden frame and body, and has a drop side door. Other detail in the picture suggests the wagons could swivel round on the frame.

* Lewis, p. 3. (But Beazley, p. 142, maintains the rails were cast at 'the famous Brymbo works near Wrexham' in which Madocks had a holding. They went by road and canal to Chester, thence by sea.)

TREMADOC TRAMWAY pre-1845–*c.* 1895

(*Gauge* 3 ft.)

Incorporated by Act: None.
Opened: Mineral traffic; before 1845.
Closed: Absorbed by and became a portion of, the Gorseddau Tramway 1855.
Length: app. 1 m. 30 ch.

GORSEDDAU TRAMWAY

(*Gauge* 3 ft.)

Incorporated by Act: None.
Opened: 1856–7. Used existing portion of Tremadoc Tramway between Portmadoc and Tremadoc.
Absorbed by and became part of Gorseddau Junction & Portmadoc Railways under Act 35/6. Vic. Cap. 155 25 July 1872.
Length: 8 m. 5 ch.
Capital: None; constructed privately.

GORSEDDAU JUNCTION & PORTMADOC RAILWAYS COMPANY

(*Gauge* 2 ft.)

Incorporated by Act: 35/6 Vic. Cap. 155 of 25 July 1872.
39/40 Vic. Cap. 137 of 13 July 1876, increase of capital etc.
55/6 Vic. Cap. 44 of 20 June 1892, rates and charges.
Opened: Goods and minerals; 2 September 1875.
Closed: Braich-y-bib to Gorseddau Quarry about 1875, Cwm Trwsgl to Cwm Dwyfor by 1884. Remainder by 1892.

Registered Office: St. Clement's House, London, E.C.
Length: Gorseddau Tramway section: 8 m. 1 fur. 1½ ch.
Cwm Pennant extension: Braich-y-bib (Old Junction) to Mine: 5 m. 1 fur. 1½ ch.
Total: 13 m. 2 fur. 3 ch. (Only 11 m. used from 1875.)
Capital: 1872 Act. £20,000 in £10 Ordinary shares. £6,666 in Debentures (= ⅓ capital).
1876 Act. £10,000 additional capital in Ordinary. £3,333 additional Debentures (issued as £800 Loan @ 6%+£5,800 Loan @ 8%). Meeting of 22 September 1876 sanctions issue of 1,000 First Perpetual Preference Shares (5%) @ £10 each—£1,400 issued December 1876 +£1,650 in 1877+£2,100 in 1885=£5,150 @ 5%.
Cost per Mile: £2,750 to 1876.

History

The origins of what was ultimately to become the Gorseddau Junction & Portmadoc Railway lay firstly in a canal and secondly in two earlier tramways. The canal would have remained a mere land drain had it not been for the imagination of one who 'canalised' the drain in order to landscape his creation of Tremadoc, and the tramways came into being because of the existence of nearby Embankment Tramway materials which were no longer required for their original purpose.

William Alexander Madocks has already come to notice in a previous chapter on the Cob Tramway. He had come into the district in 1798 after purchasing the Penmorfa Estate, (Penmorfa was described in 1800 as a 'wretched village') and lived at nearby Tan-yr-allt, overlooking the then sea-washed Glaslyn Estuary. He conceived a model village (as it was then deprecatingly named) to enhance his own importance, to satisfy his whims and improve the view from his residence! The name Tre Madoc or Tremadoc was given to it and building began in 1805. It stood 3 ft. below low water mark. A large woollen mill, finished in 1800, lay within the town, and with 60 looms, was larger than anything similar in North Wales. Madocks conceived boldly . . . as with the Mill, so later with the Cob. One of his characteristics is still perpetuated in the district at Port Meirion by Clough Williams-Ellis; he was fond of architectural whimsy and decorated Tremadoc with follies and other romanticisms, even the Public Convenience. He had a weakness for having ships within his vision, and to improve the appearance and businesslike atmosphere of the town, built a short branch from the main land-drain nearby, right into the town. This drain, known as Y Cyt (or The Cut—the Lancashire vernacular for a canal is apparent) was the fruit of an earlier land reclamation scheme and its water passed through the 1800 embankment by means of the Great Sluice and so into the Glaslyn.

Madocks formed a 'Bason' at the top of his new branch, alongside London Street (now Church Street) and arranged for it to be filled with boats so as to impress his London and Dublin friends when passing through.* The drain thus became a canal. It was easy on the eye as well as having a limited commercial application.

The Bron-y-gadair Copper Mine, owned by Samuel Holland Senr. of Liverpool used it, as water transport was the only means of getting the ore out to sea-going vessels.† The mines in this district however, were very prone to flooding and in 1836 Holland sold out to the Cambrian Mining Co. who, though they installed a 12 h.p. steam engine to pump out the workings, had to cease when they were drowned out in 1844.

West of the town at Llidiart Yspytty, was a small ironstone mine which had been worked from at least the 1820s; records of its tonnages through Portmadoc Harbour in the 1839–40 period have survived. Clearly the canal was of limited value to this mine for, at an unknown date, (but before 1845 as it is shown on Portmadoc Harbour Improvement Plans of that date) a tramway was laid down on the west bank of Y Cyt to connect the mine and Portmadoc Harbour. Materials formerly used by Madocks in the tramway built for the construction of the Cob may have been utilised for a second time for this line; these had been partly disposed of after the work was finished though it is on record that part of the tramway was kept for maintenance purposes at least. We have seen that the Cob Tramway may have been of 3 ft. gauge; the new Tramway certainly was of that gauge and was owned by Martin Williams of Bryn Gwyn, Denbighshire. The lessee was John Williams and the occupier John Hayward.

Despite the building of the tramway, the town continued to provide the canal with some traffic. In its heyday, the waterway could accommodate vessels of up to 120 tons and astonishingly, despatched a steamboat for New York in 1830! Ultimately it fell into disuse and today has reverted to the drain it was designed to be. Inspiration for building it is said to have come from Madocks' visits to Talgarth, and seeing the Brecon Canal nearby.

The Tremadoc Tramway—as it is convenient to call the Llidiart Yspytty line—is first recorded on the Portmadoc Harbour Plans of 1846 where it is shown as making its way southwards along Madoc Street, Portmadoc, crossing London Road on the level and curving round the west bank of the Glaslyn to the Outer Harbour. It is presently impossible to say if the 2 ft. gauge Festiniog Railway, opened

*** In 1970 the site of the 'Bason' became a Housing Estate.**

† See chapter on Festiniog & Blaenau Railway for references to Holland.

in 1836, or the Tremadoc Tramway was first on the scene, but if the latter was the case, then there must have been mixed gauge lines on the west bank of the river. Being almost level for its entire length, the Tremadoc line is likely to have been horse-worked in either direction throughout its life. Its wagon stock may have been supplied locally and may not have differed much from 3 ft. 6 in. gauge wagons on the nearby Nantlle Railway, of which there is a Portmadoc-built example in the Narrow Gauge Railway Museum, Towyn. But this is conjecture, as is the nature of the track materials; perhaps both track and wagons came from the Embankment Tramway; or perhaps in the surviving Nantlle material we may have much of the character and features of this early system.

With the fortunes of the iron mining ventures running out, the Tremadoc line became less well used and without Parliamentary authority the Bangor & Portmadoc Slate & Slate Slab Co. Ltd. approached the owners and arranged to extend the line by means of wayleave and a reversing neck and junction beside the Llidiart Yspytty Mine.

The Bangor & Portmadoc Slate & Slate Slab Co. Ltd. (hereinafter called the Bangor Co.) came into being because Richard Morris Griffith of Bangor had intended to lease the distant slate quarry at Gorseddau* to Henry Van Uster in 1853. (He was later connected with the nearby Hendre-ddu slate and slab quarry near Dolbenmaen, 1861.)

A draft was drawn up by a Bangor solicitor whose name (though less well known than C. E. Spooner as a promoter of narrow gauge railways), crops up continually at this time in South Caernarvonshire railway and quarry matters. He was Hugh Beaver Roberts, of Plas Llandoget, Llanrwst. This proposal fell through, but Robert Gill of Mansfield and John Harris of Darlington (the Company) took up a lease for 63 years. Edwin Dixon was appointed quarry manager. In May 1855 they did what the Bryn Eglwys Quarry at Abergynolwyn was to do ten years later when they built the Talyllyn Railway as an outlet to the sea coast; they planned a tramway to Portmadoc. The Talyllyn has passed its century, but the Gorseddau was not so lucky. At least the Bangor Company managed, with the help of the course of the old Tremadoc Tramway, to have part of the line working by 1856 and in 1858 the annual average output of the quarry was quoted as 1,338 tons of roofing slate (Ref. Geological & Mineral Statistics of Great Britain 1858). In terms of tramway traffic, this

* *Gorseddau*—'a place where on a great copped heap of stones, sat the Druid whilst he instructs the people'.

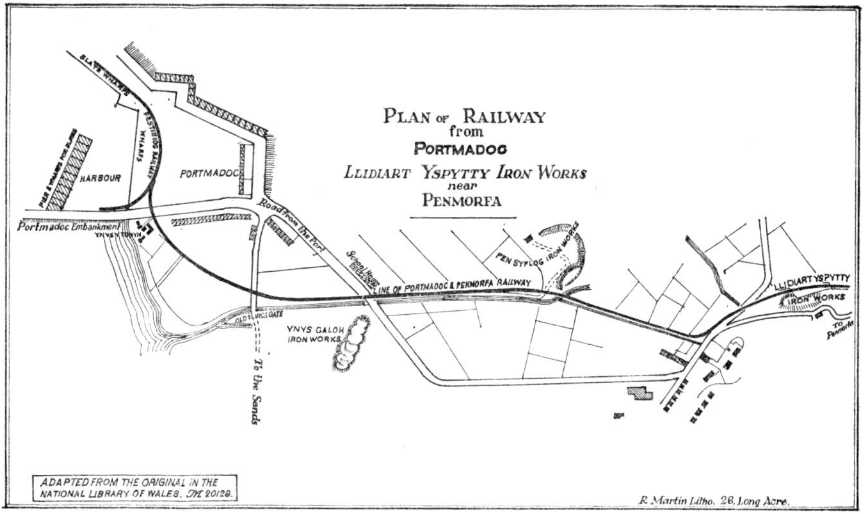

meant about four or five 1 ton loaded wagons passing down the line each working day.

The 'Caernarvon & Denbigh Herald' for January 1857 records: 'An accident which might have terminated fatally, occurred last week on the line of railway between the Gorsedda Slate Quarry and Port Madoc, which is now nearly completed, and the fences of which are in course of construction. Wagons loaded with stone are running down for this purpose. The incline on the railway being very great, the utmost caution is required in breaking the wagons. Some slight obstruction occurring on the road, the run was nearly stopped, and during this time the hooks connecting the wagons together became unfastened; the two first wagons got detached and then the speed was enormous. Happily no human being stood in its way, but the constructor's horses were working lower down the road, and could not be reached . . .' (and one was killed).

Above Tremadoc it served other concerns, and to keep gradients to a minimum, it reached Gorseddau by a circuitous route through Hen-efail. Even so, west of Tremadoc severe inclinations of 1 in 23 and 1 in 25 were involved. Luckily this was mainly against empty wagons returning to the quarry and horse-working was used over the whole system.

The 3 ft. gauge of the Tremadoc line was also retained, though the materials used for the track of the extension are not known. Slate wagons and a 'Passenger Carriage' were supplied by Boston Lodge and there was an exchange of letters between C. E. Spooner of the

Festiniog Railway and the Bangor Co.'s Manager, E. S. S. Dixon, concerning wagons, sizes and design, in April 1857. Since the line had no Parliamentary authority and no public service was envisaged, presumably the Carriage was for the private use of the management.

Under an arrangement with John Priestley of Ty-uchaf-cwmystradllyn dated 31 December 1857 regarding a lease of his land for the tramway, it was agreed that Priestley's servants and agents be given 'full and free liberty at all seasonable times on one day in every week at his or their option and on the days of holding horse and cattle fairs at Portmadoc, Tremadoc and Penmorfa, after the construction of the said tramway or railway, of using so much of the same as shall be in and upon the hereby demised premises with his and their own trucks for the conveyance thereby of corn and other crops stock and produce of the said farm . . . and of timber coals, lime bricks tiles and other materials . . . for the purposes of the same farm and for rebuilding and repairing . . . etc'.

The land was to be rented from Priestley for 63 years from 15 March 1853 at an annual rental of £2; the tenants agreed to fence the land alongside the line and to provide within six months of opening the track, at their own expense 'a siding extending at a proper and convenient angle from the said tramway or railway'. At a level crossing on the same premises, gates were to be provided and a pencilled note has been added in the margin of the draft lease, 'I think it would be a hardship upon the lessees to be bound to watch the gates constantly by night'!

In the outcome Priestley seems to have come out of it very well; not only was he permitted to use the tramway which crossed his own lands, but on one day a week he could use the whole line to Portmadoc (or elsewhere) with his own 'trucks' '. . . with full power to make use of the horse or other locomotive power for the time being employed in conveying slates or other minerals or goods by the said Robert Gill and John Harris etc.'.

Lease of the line would terminate if Richard M. Griffith re-entered the Gorseddau Quarry. The lease was again drawn up by H. Beaver Roberts of Bangor.

It should be added that Priestley did not sign the lease which gave him his once-weekly right until at least early 1858; he would not commit himself to any one day saying he was 'requiring full and free liberty' to use the line. The actual lease has not survived, but presumably traffic could not use the full length until reconciliation, on which Priestley agreed to use it on a 'Horse and Cattle fair days' basis, was arrived at. Priestley seems to have been astute enough to believe his land could be surrendered on his own terms. He had already pre-

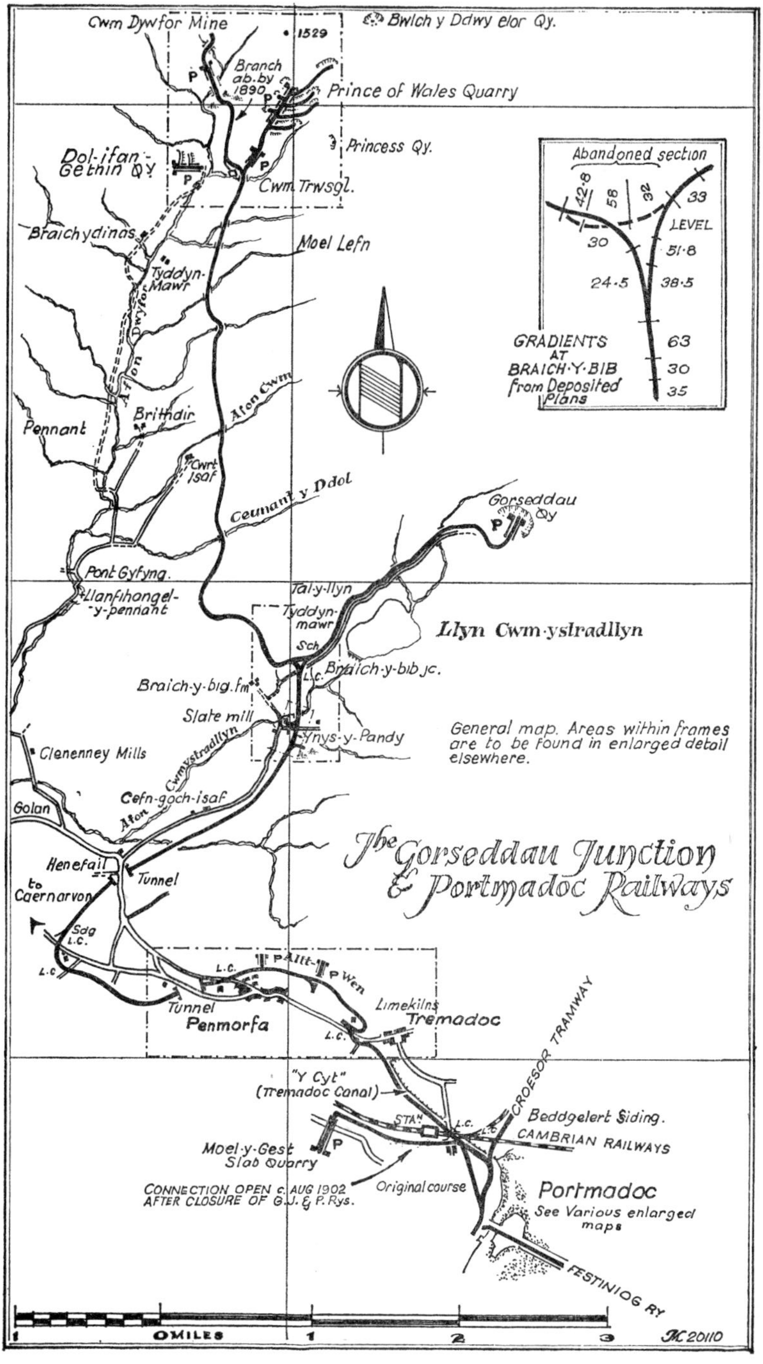
Cwm Dywfor Mine
Bwlch y Ddwy elor Qy.
1529
Branch ab. by 1890
Prince of Wales Quarry
Princess Qy.
Dol-ifan-Gethin Qy
Cwm Trwsgl.
Braichydinas
Moel Lefn
Tyddyn-Mawr
Afon Dwyfor
Pennant
Brithdir
Afon Cwm
Cwrt Isaf
Ceunant y Ddol
Gorseddau Qy
Pont Gyfyng.
Llanfihangel-y-pennant
Tal-y-llyn
Tyddyn-mawr
Sch
Llyn Cwm-ystradllyn
Braich-y-big.fm
Braich-y-bib jc.
Slate mill
Ynys-y-Pandy
Clenenney Mills
Afon Cwmystradllyn
Cefn-goch-isaf
Golan
Henefail
to Caernarvon
Tunnel
Sdg
L.C.
Allt-Wen
Tunnel
Penmorfa
Limekilns
Tremadoc
"Y Cyt" (Tremadoc Canal)
STAN
CROESOR TRAMWAY
Beddgelert Siding.
CAMBRIAN RAILWAYS
Moel-y-Gest Slab Quarry
CONNECTION OPEN c. AUG 1902 AFTER CLOSURE OF G.J. & P. Rys.
Original course
Portmadoc
See Various enlarged maps
FESTINIOG RY
Abandoned section
42·8
58
32
33
LEVEL
30
51·8
24·5
38·5
63
30
35
GRADIENTS AT BRAICH-Y-BIB from Deposited Plans
General map. Areas within frames are to be found in enlarged detail elsewhere.
The Gorseddau Junction & Portmadoc Railways
0 MILES 1 2 3
JC 20110

vented the building of another railway to Portmadoc because he set his sights too high (see p. 116).

It is unlikely that sufficient track material from the Embankment Tramway was available for the extension to Gorseddau, but perhaps ex-Festiniog Railway discarded track materials were used beyond Tremadoc whilst the original equipment in 3 ft. gauge survived below. By the 1850s, they must have been becoming somewhat careworn. The provision of new slate wagons suggests the existing stock was probably too old and unsuited to the new traffic. It is evident that the tramway was to become a slate carrier and its former traffics had dwindled away.* To this end a small modification was made to arrangements in Portmadoc; by 1863 a slate wharf had been built for the use of the Gorseddau Slate Co. (sic) on a wharf on the north corner of the Sluice Bridge (near the present Glaslyn Foundry) so giving the Madoc Street route direct access to it at the south end of the street. By this means the Gorseddau owners had independent wharfage at Portmadoc without passing over or alongside Festiniog metals on the south side of London Road. It could be suggested that this line was on the site of a link between Cob Tramway and Tremadoc Tramway, but this is pure conjecture.

A second tramway now came on the scene, making the third railed access to Portmadoc, all for the same purpose. The Croesor Tramway (see Part 4) was building in 1863 and like the Gorseddau line had been built without statutory consent; it was opened in August 1864 and came into the town from the north-east, using the Creassy land-reclamation embankment for the latter part of its route. Being of the '24 inch gauge' it had no physical connection with the Gorseddau. However, it made an acute angle crossing on the level with it on the north side of London Road (later High Street) before making for those same west bank wharves to which both the Tremadoc and Festiniog lines had at first aspired!

The Portmadoc railway scene was not to remain in this form for long. Already there were plans for various lines of standard gauge in

*D. E. Bick, the authority on Welsh Metal Mining, gives locations for iron ore mining in the Tremadoc district as: a. 1⅓ m. northwest (Tyn-y-llon) b. 500 yds. west (Llidiart Yspytty), c. ½ m. south (Pen-syflog), d. ¾ m. southwest of the town (no rail connection). The second location was the most important and lay within the curve formed by the later tramway to Gorseddau Quarry. The junction at this mine, shown on the First Edition O.S. Map of 1888, is marked 'Gorseddau Junction' and the line beyond as 'Gorseddau Railway'. In all these locations the iron ore was largely obtained by open quarrying but work had ceased by 1860. The site at Yspytty is still comparatively clear, together with traces of an adit. Tyn-y-llon and Pen-syflog are also easily found. Lead too was being mined at Gêst, Penmorfa, in the 1850s.

the district, mainly linking points along the coast. These plans took shape when the Aberystwyth & Welsh Coast Railway opened between Barmouth and Portmadoc and on to Pwllheli on 10 October 1867.

This Company, although under the terms of its Act to have working arrangements with the Festiniog, Croesor & Port Madoc Railway (as it had become) and the Gorseddau Tramway, was faced with an arrangement at Portmadoc which it had also faced between Machynlleth and Dovey Junction . . . it was obliged to cross a rail tramway of earlier date by means of a crossing on the level—a state of affairs quite unacceptable to the A. & W.C. (later the Cambrian Railways) Board. The last-named crossing (at Derwenlas near Machynlleth) was ultimately to be rendered inoperative because by reason of the opening of the Cambrian line, the former tramway was made uneconomic.* The position at Portmadoc was doubly frustrating! Here the Cambrian faced crossing two tramways on the level within a matter of 330 yards and in physical circumstances where it was impossible for anyone to build a bridge without going to an expense which was quite unjustified. The Cambrian was in no doubt of its liability to provide sufficient safeguards to its trains at these crossings, at its own expense. Nor was it in doubt as to which of the three lines was the senior, and does not appear to have questioned the elderly status of the Gorseddau line. With the Croesor, which had preceded the Cambrian by only a matter of a few years, the position was different and the Cambrian attempted to blackmail the Croesor into accepting some liability for safety expenditure at the crossing.† As neither of the tramways enjoyed legal substance at the time, there are no plans of the actual arrangements at each crossing when the Aberystwyth & Welsh Coast line was opened; to judge from evidence available, the Cambrian put trap blades into each side of the tramways' crossings and interlocked them with signals on its own line only. A hut was provided for a signalman at each railway's point of intersection. These arrangements were to last for the full period of the Croesor as a horse-worked line—and were little improved when the Croesor became the Welsh Highland Railway and took on the status of a Light Railway; but the Gorseddau crossing was short-lived in this form.

On 8 November 1871 public notice was given of intention to apply to Parliament for an Act for a new railway of length 5 m. 11 ch. 'on a gauge of 2 feet' and also to purchase the 8 m. 11 ch. tramway of

* Ref. 'Narrow Gauge Railways in Mid-Wales', p. 29 (Oakwood Press).

† See p. 99 for detail.

the Bangor Co., 'from Gorseddau Slate Quarry . . . to a certain slate yard in Portmadoc . . .' (then being voluntarily wound up* and to relay it 'with new rails'. The Bangor Co. did not have legal entitlement to all lands passed over by the tramway and the Act would remedy this. On 22 February 1872 the Cambrian petitioned against the Bill and was followed by Mr. E. Breese and the Ynyscynhaiarn Board of Health the day after; however, on 23 April the owners of property along the proposed route petitioned in favour of the line. Certain copies of the plans had 1871 Edition O.S. maps correctly attached to them, and these had been carefully overprinted to show the railway as if already in existence. The implication of this might be sinister, but at least showed strength of purpose! The title was to be the Gorseddau Junction & Portmadoc Railways. The spelling of Gorseddau had reverted to that used locally for the slate quarry of that name, and the locally fashionable habit of putting 'Railways' in the plural may be noted. On 25 July 1872 (35 and 36 Vic. Cap. 155) an Act authorised the adoption and subsequent maintenance of the

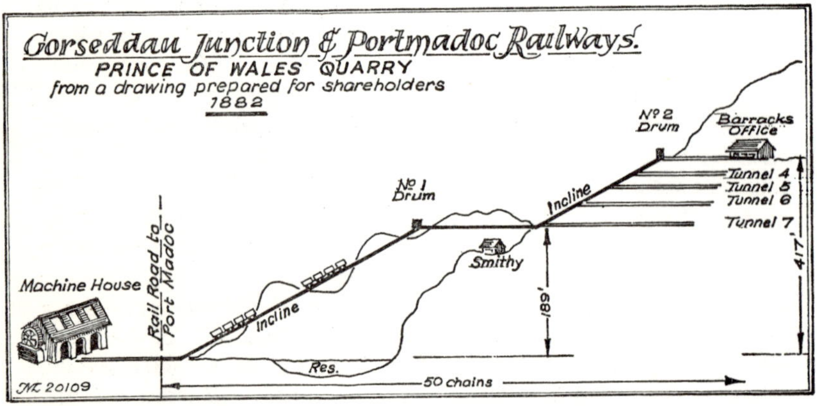

existing railway from the Gorsedda (sic) Slate Quarry to Portmadoc and for the building of an extension from the existing line at Braich-y-bib to Blaen-y-pennant. The gauge was to be 24 inches. Three years were allowed for the building: 3d. per ton mile would be charged for private wagons plus 1d. if the Company's wagons were used for slate or copper ore carriage. Permission was granted to use the Croesor Tramway between Portmadoc Gas Works and the end of that line on the wharves, and a junction was duly made with the

* The Bangor Co. was in voluntary liquidation April 1870 and under supervision of the Court in July 1870.

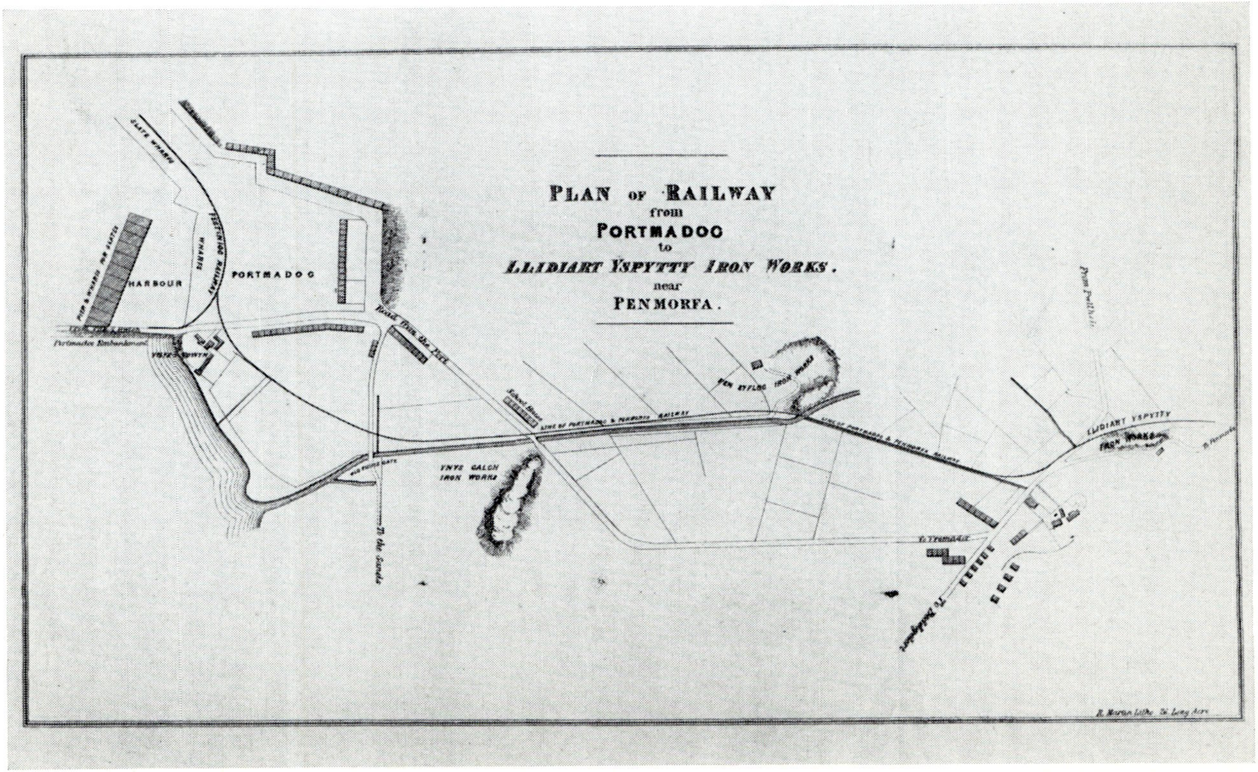

The Tremadoc tramway, as shown on an undated plan in the National Museum of Wales.

Reproduction of H. W. Billington's drawing of the Embankment Tramway in 1810, showing quarrying and stone wagons, the incomplete 'Cob' and Ynys-y-towyn at its far end. From a copy in the Caernarvonshire Record Office.

J. I. C. Boyd

'Railway Terrace', with the site of the line in front running eastwards towards the foot of the Penmorfa escarpment. 1971.

J. I. C. Boyd

Ynysypandy Slate Mill from the south-east, showing high level line into first floor of mill and low level beneath the retaining wall to the left. 1971.

J. I. C. Boyd

Cutting north of Ynysypandy Slate Mill, with river bridge. Looking towards Braich-y-bib Junction, quarter mile to north. 1970.

Cwm-dwyfor Copper Mine branch; 33 ft. cutting west of Cwm Trwsgl Slate Mill, 1970.

D. L. E. Boyd

Site of 'Mr. Huddart's Crossing', Portmadoc, looking north-west over G.W.R. towards Tremadoc. This was the course of the Llidiart Yspytty tramway. 1944.

J. I. C. Boyd

tramway opposite the Portmadoc Flour Mill, for which the Croesor charged tolls for the length of track run over.

There were to be working arrangements with the Portmadoc Croesor & Beddgelert Tram Railway Co. Ltd. (the Croesor Tramway) and Cambrian Company. The promoters were the New Prince of Wales Slate Co. Ltd. and their Engineer was Richard James Davids of Caernarvon. James Stewart, later a director of the Railway, was Chairman of the New Prince of Wales Company and also connected with the Cloddfarlon or Penbryn Quarry, Nantlle; a locomotive at the latter quarry carried his name. J. Maw, another director, was also on the board of the Dorothea quarry there. The title of 'New' was adopted by the promoters as they intended to buy both the Prince of Wales and the Bangor Companies' quarries, both in liquidation as it happened! The existing Prince of Wales quarry up at Cwm Trwsgl had not of course, at the time, any railway connection.*

The matter of the existing Gorseddau Tramway's course down Madoc Street had been the subject of a letter to Edward Breese (solicitor to the Tremadoc Estate) and Thomas Harvey, solicitor who was to become the Chairman of the Railways Company. Harvey, writing on 23 November 1871, says he had commissioned Davids the Engineer to point out that they intended to purchase the line exactly as laid down and they must therefore prepare notices and plans on the subject as it existed and not add in any alternative lines. He adds 'we have no intention whatever to use Madock Street but to arrange with you for a junction with the Croesor in the manner suggested . . . we can only show what we apply to purchase and we can only purchase what the Gorseddau possess *or use* . . .'

This clearly did not satisfy the Estate as they petitioned against the Bill.

The Act was a sequel to an Agreement of 20 April 1872 between the New Prince of Wales Co. and the G. J. & P. Rlys. Co. This sold the Slate Co. to the Railways Co. for £5,000 in cash, a deposit of £500 to be paid on the incorporation of the Railways Co. and the balance six months afterwards. If however, the Railways Co. put down £2,000 after depositing the £500, they might commence rebuilding their line at once, regardless of incorporation. An Estimate of £6,756 6s. 8d. was given for the work. George Gray, Secretary of

* In fact the original Prince of Wales Slate Quarry Co. Ltd. was hopelessly insolvent and in voluntary liquidation by early 1868. (See *The Law Times* Reports Vol. XVIII, p. 77, 21 Mar. 1868.) It was established in 1863 with £50,000 capital of which £45,000 was paid up, and with Thomas Harvey as Manager.

the Railways Co. was also Agent for the Slate Co. A maximum number of 25 men was employed in the quarry in 1885, so the concern was not a large one.

The position of the original Tramway, built partly by wayleave, was regularised by the Act; at Blaen-y-pennant the new line was to divide into two branches, the westerly leading on a falling gradient for one mile to the foot of an incline serving the Cwm Dwyfor Copper & Silverlead Mine. The easterly branch rose up an incline to the existing Prince of Wales slate quarry. According to the Returns of 1875, only 11 miles of the line was by then being operated, which possibly confirms that the old tramway between Braich-y-bib and Gorseddau quarry was not being worked. 'The Bangor & Portmadoc Slate & Slate Slab Co.' (before Vice-Chancellor Sir R. Malius at Lincoln's Inn, 23 April 1875) was already in voluntary liquidation.

The junction for the extension at Braich-y-bib entailed yet another reversal in order to gain the new line, and there must have been a loop line to enable the engine to run round its train. This procedure would have to be done twice in a journey from Portmadoc. The Act provided for locomotives, passengers and goods traffic, and anticipation of the latter, mainly in agricultural produce, was very keen.

On 19 September 1872 'The Times' reported that subscriptions had been invited for the balance of 2,000 shares in the Railways Co., 1,126 at £10 each being offered.

The existing permanent way was lifted, and the whole line relaid in more robust materials which were clearly purchased from the same source (and were much of the same pattern) as had been used for the Croesor track. Local foundries were the suppliers of chairs. The new 1867 crossing over the Cambrian was re-furbished, the traps in the Gorseddau line being extended on the north side into a siding, the narrow gauge gated and both gauges signalled. Oddly, the signal box controlling the crossing was on the east side of Y Cyt and not beside the tramway. It was the property of the Gorseddau.

Among other working arrangements was one with the Hafod-y-llan Slate Co. whose office and wharf was in front of the Festiniog Railway's Harbour station.

In view of the reduction of rail gauge sanctioned by Section 4 of the Act, running powers were given between the other railway users of Portmadoc Harbour, and the old 3 ft. gauge Gorseddau Slate Co.'s wharf was abandoned.

Apparently construction, reconstruction and re-equipping was a somewhat slow business. Between the Act of 1872 and the opening on 2 September 1875, over three years were taken for the changeover, and even then only mineral traffic was to begin on that date.

A little tragi-comedy was enacted over the land of one G. H. Owen (owner of the Ymwlch Estate) whose property to the extent of 1 acre 16 poles was on the route of the new Pennant line. Owen did not wish to sell his land to the Company; they offered to treat on 16 July 1873. Correspondence dragged on until February 1874, but meanwhile the contractors entered his land in the autumn of 1873 and started work. The Company, getting no further with Owen, applied to the Board of Trade for a valuation; Owen wanted £80 for the land and the Railway had refused to pay it. A Bond for £51 12s. od. was then paid into Court by directors Thomas Harvey (Solicitor) and James Stewart (Wine Merchant) to secure the purchase money. The matter dragged on, not for months but for years, the land ultimately being conveyed on 24 November 1888, by which time the railway had almost ceased business; in fact on 8 July 1887 Owen's solicitors wrote to him : 'We understand the company have ceased working and have now no funds and fear that there is but little prospect of the Bills you refer to being paid'. In 1888 he received the £51 12s. od. paid into the Court fourteen years earlier . . . and nothing more.

The deviations from the authorised 1872 course were at Braich-y-bib Junction and in the streets of Portmadoc. At the former place the north side of the triangle was officially abandoned when a junction of 9 chains 5 links was put in to give direct access to Blaen-y-pennant. At the latter the route along Madoc Street was abandoned and a new line of 9 chains 45 links from the south side of the Cambrian crossing to meet the Croesor near the Gas Works, was put in. To give some idea of the traffic using this second section, 295 tons passed over Croesor metals on its way to the wharves in October 1875 and in ensuing years, hundreds of tons of flour for Watkins & Williams of Clenenny Mills at Brynkir went back up the Gorseddau from the Flour Mill.

The Cambrian was much inconvenienced by having two level crossings in the vicinity and intended to rid itself of both if possible. It proposed a junction between the Gorseddau and Croesor lines north (instead of south) of its metals, and though the Act provided for such a connection, nothing was done. It would have entailed a third reversal for Gorseddau wagons to reach the Harbour. A trans-shipment siding was built instead (Section 14) which passed over Y Cyt bridge alongside the Cambrian, but on its north side and eastwards in front of the Gorseddau signal box to terminate a few yards further on at a stop block. At a later date it was extended to make an end-on junction with the Croesor's spur from the Beddgelert Siding, so nominally at least, meeting Cambrian wishes for a junction north of its line. This by no means spelt the end of usage of the Gorseddau's own crossing; it had been agreed that if the Gorseddau would provide the

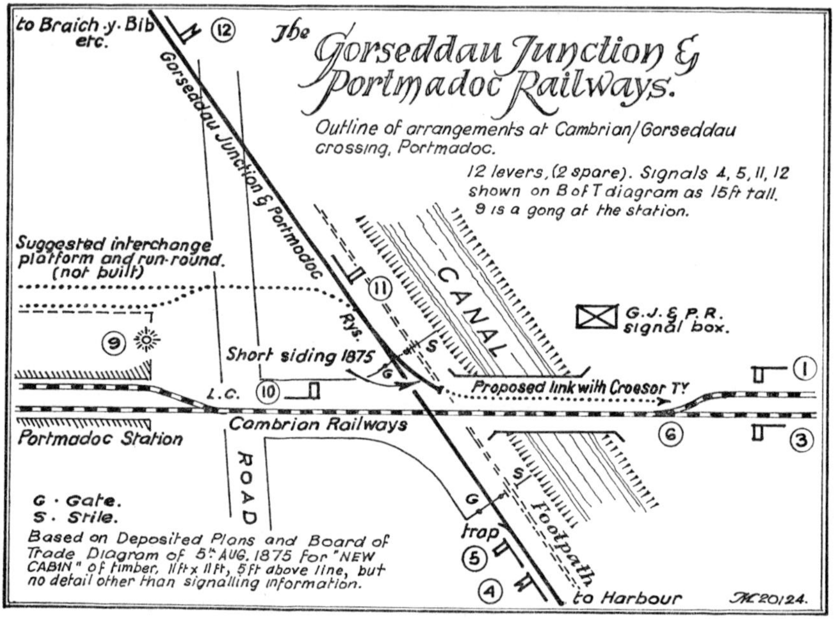

land for the above-mentioned exchange siding free of cost to the Cambrian, the Cambrian would make no toll over the crossing. Free use of the crossing thus continued, but the exchange siding took more and more traffic as the Cambrian enjoyed a dominant role at the crossing and it was operated to suit their convenience. Their legal right to do this was established when, for the purposes of the 1872 Gorseddau Act, the existence of the old Gorseddau Tramway was officially ignored. There thus existed the curious state of affairs whereby the Cambrian, the incoming railway on the scene, was given priority of traffic and forced the original railway to provide a signal box and man it for traffic which was subordinate to the Cambrian's!

This was not the end of the affair. Under a later scheme of 1879 it was suggested that by means of a trailing junction in the Gorseddau line Portmadoc-bound trains would terminate north of the crossing and reverse over the street into the north side of the Cambrian Portmadoc station. Here a new standard/narrow gauge platform would be built with sidings and locomotive run-round, the latter terminating behind the Cambrian engine shed.

In the fullness of time, the Cambrian was relieved of the Gorseddau without any effort on its own part.

'The Times' of 17 December 1875 made mention of the Directors' Report stating that 'the line was fully opened for goods traffic on 2 September last'. Up to 30 June the land and works had cost considerably more than was estimated and it was necessary to apply to Parliament in the ensuing session for further capital powers. 'New properties were being developed along the line of route and new sources of traffic had been discovered'.

By arrangement between the two companies, Gorseddau trains began to use Festiniog tracks in the Harbour area during 1875.

The Act forecast in the 1875 Report was duly obtained (39 and 40 Vic. Cap. 137 of 13 July 1876), the principle features being:

1. It regularised the position of two lengths of line where the Engineer had diverted outside the limitations of the 1872 Act.
2. Authority was given to construct a siding at a cost of £81 15s. 7d. in the parish of Ynyscynhaiarn (namely the Cambrian exchange siding already noted) and to use a portion of the Festiniog Railway giving access to the west bank of the Glaslyn (namely, between its termination on the Public Wharf and the Sluice Bridge).
3. Permission was given to raise additional finance.

There was some alteration to the awkward junction at Tremadoc where the original steep extension connection was 'improved', leaving a reversing neck with a 2½ chain curve on a gradient of 1 in 23! The Act gave powers of abandonment to the sections superseded by these alterations, which were just about sufficient to take it from the horse power era into the steam age. So it was that on 10 July 1874, the Cambrian Railways' goods train delivered a steam locomotive to the Beddgelert Siding, and this load, together with a quantity of chairs, was taken up the line. At this late stage, the new engine must have been a useful asset in completing the railway, but it might have been a shock to the promoters if they could have foreseen that its useful life would not exceed the next four years! It is difficult to see just why a locomotive was obtained at all; if the traffic was to be all that was promised, it was too small for such a heavily graded line. Its water capacity would have meant frequent stops if it was intended to work the whole route in one journey. Perhaps it was intended that horses should do the work, the engine being used as a stand-by when business was brisk. This was exactly how events turned out.

At the Board Meeting on 22 September 1876 it was said that since opening 'A fair amount of traffic had been obtained. The Directors however believed arrangements were now about to be made for the more vigorous working of some of the undertakings on the line of route by which the traffic would be very much increased . . . believed the line would be the means of speedily developing the whole of the district through which it runs. They regretted they had to apply for further capital . . . for these purposes for the complete equipment of the line and the construction of the mile and a half branch railway not yet made it would be necessary to raise £6,000 or £7,000.' A shareholder asked why the prospectus had said the line could be made for £15,000 and it had already cost £29,000. Now they asked for more. The Chairman said the money was for a further extension of the line not contemplated when the prospectus was issued. Great miscalculations had been made, particularly as to the price paid for land. ('The Times' 23 September 1876).

The next half yearly meeting to be reported in the press was mentioned in 'The Times' on 22 October 1877. 'The non-completion of arrangements referred to in the last report' was referred to. The quarries had provided unfavourable traffic returns; the Company could not declare an Ordinary Dividend and had been compelled to postpone payment of the Debenture Interest. The usual glib hopes were expressed by the Chairman, who added that £31,583 had been spent on the railway, being a rate of 'only £2,746 per mile'.

Certainly the westerly arm of the line at the head of Cwm Pennant was a futile scheme. This farthest reach of the track was described in the preamble : '. . . To commence at Blaen-y-pennant in a field called Llanfawr the property of G. A. Huddart and 23 chains south of the Cwm Dwyfor Copper & Silverlead Mines Company Limited's Blacksmith's Shop and terminating at Braich-y-bib at a junction with the existing tramway in a field called Gors-uchaf, 42 chains north of the Weighing Machine House of the Gorseddau Company'. This Weigh House stood at the junction of the branch into the Gorseddau's slate mill.

The mine at Cwm Dwyfor had opened some time after 1840 and before the railway was conceived, rejoiced in the name of the Dinas Great Consols Mine. Names of such ventures were frequently changed as the financial collapse of one undertaking was succeeded by another under a new title, all with the intention of attracting fresh public money in the speculation. In the year mentioned, the mine amalgamated with the nearby Moel Hebog Mine, one mile off the new railway's course near Cwrt-isaf. Dinas Great Consols was useless from the start and Hebog was equally so! Though the ore struck was very rich, it turned out to be iron and not copper as expected. It became the Cwm Dwyfor Mining Co. to meet this unforeseen event, but on 4 November 1868 changed to the Cwm Dwyfor Copper & Silverlead

Mining Co. Ltd., the title given in describing the approach of the new railway to serve it.* No sooner had rail connection been achieved, than the concern got into difficulties. A visit to the workings will show how incomplete were mine, incline and railway works even when final abandonment took place. A little mining was done in 1877 when thirteen men below and four men above ground produced five tons of *lead* ore. Work was suspended again, but carried on in a small way between 1883 and 1887.

The C.D.C. & S.M. Co. Ltd. worked on land leased from the New Prince of Wales Co. The latter was the dominant feature of the Pennant valley within the context of this study, being linked with the Railways Co. and, in the absence of other users of the line, providing the railway with almost all its mineral traffic. When the slate quarry failed, the railway fortunes fell to zero. The Railways Co., as has been seen, were ever hopeful that fresh sources of mineral traffic might develop. They never did. The C.D.C. & S.M. Co. Ltd. liquidated in 1876, its assets being bought by a concern of the former title, the Cwm Dwyfor Mining Co. Ltd. in 1877. Our old friend James Stewart was on the Board and the faithful G. J. Gray was Secretary. Formed with a capital of £10,005 (a peculiar sum) the investing public had already been persuaded by 1878 to part with 18s. 9d. for every 20s. share they had taken up. Not surprisingly there were insufficient funds for this venture too, and it sold out such equipment as it had to the Cwm Dwyfor & Brynarian Mines Co. Ltd. in 1882. During all these changes of ownership, the railway traffic continued to dwindle throughout the period, and evidence of work around either mine or slate quarry was on a very limited scale.

The highest train mileage is recorded in 1876 (3,533 miles) and assuming the full out and return journey of approximately 20 miles is taken as a measure of distance, this made the equivalent of about 180 return workings in (say) 265 working days of the year, assuming full journeys were not made on Saturdays. On this day and mileage basis a full journey would operate on two days out of three, but when mileages fell significantly in later years, once a week was sufficient.

The New Prince of Wales Company succumbed in 1880, having no further capital available to exploit the works. A last appeal for finance was accompanied by the innuendo that if only their probings in the Trial Shaft would strike the 'Glanrafon Vein'—that same vein which

* 'The Times', 2 Aug. 1871: 'A prospectus has been issued by the Cwm Dwyfor Copper & Silver Lead Mines Co. Ltd. with a capital of £12,500 in shares of £1 to develop a mining property in North Wales.'

was worked by the Glanrafon Quarry over the mountain and to the east, and served by the North Wales Narrow Gauge Railways—all would be well. A new company, reverting to the title Prince of Wales Slate Co. Ltd. took over the remnants in 1881; Charles Baron of the Railways Co. was on the board, but Stewart had disappeared. Gray, inevitably it seems, was appointed Secretary. The prospects of the quarry were highlit in a report by Thomas Williams of Bryn Croesor and Manager of the Croesor New Slate Co. Ltd. in 1882. The new concern, with a pitiful output over the railway, was soon appealing to shareholders over Gray's name, to take up the balance of 10% 3-year secured shares in order to drive a horizontal adit and prove the slate by means of cross-tunnelling recommended by Williams. It was no use, and even the Railways Co. 'went to ground' in 1882–4 and no Returns were made. In fact, from 1881 slate traffic over the line virtually ceased.

By 1882 the Company was in such financial difficulty that the Cambrian Railways asked for a Receiver to be appointed. Formal request was made on 23 January 1883, but it does not survive among the Chancery Decrees & Orders for that year so cannot have been effective.

The Company ceased to render financial reports in 1886.

Under the Railway Rates & Charges No. 6 (Festiniog Railway & Etc.) Order of 1893 (55 & 56 Vic. Cap. 44) 20 June 1892, new rates and charges for the Gorseddau were brought into force as from 1 January 1893. The Portmadoc Croesor & Beddgelert Tram Railway Co. Ltd., North Wales Narrow Gauge Railways and Festiniog Railway were included also. It was of little help to the Gorseddau whose last mileages had already been recorded.

The Gorseddau Quarry's rail link from Braich-y-bib which had been shown on earlier editions, was removed from the Ordnance Map of 1885. Nor was the Cwm Trwsgl to Cwm Dwyfor link shown any more.

The Slate Company was wound up in 1899 and removed from the Stock Exchange Register.

Bradshaw's Manual for 1902 states simply 'No recent returns have been received' and the Stock Exchange Year Book for the same year says 'Debenture is in arrear and working of the line suspended. No figures have been furnished for Board of Trade returns of 1897 onward'.* Even in 1920 the title of the Company still appeared in the latter publications reading 'Not working and no returns available'!

* In truth, no Returns were made for 1894 and subsequently.

The last full Returns issued 1893 show:

Expenditure on Capital Account £31,560
Issued: £19,995 Ordinary Shares
£ 2,100 5% Preference Shares
£ 800 in Loan @ 6%
£ 5,800 in Loan @ 8%
Debentures = $\frac{1}{3}$ capital

It would seem that at the rebuilding period, the section between Braich-y-bib and the Gorseddau Quarry was not rebuilt—at least a descriptive article of June 1875 stated that the branch had not then been tackled, and it is quite possible that with the lessening traffic over it, the most economical way would have been to retain the old materials and gauge, and trans-ship at Braich-y-bib. The line seems to have escaped attention during its lifetime and only one contemporary article exists; permutations of possibilities should find no place in factual history, but with the Gorseddau there is ample material for the imaginative mind!

There was fortunately a brief article published in 'Engineering' (11 June 1875) but without illustration. It differs from the evidence which survives in a few particulars, and it could have been supplied by the Bangor Co. rather than have been a first-hand field account. At this time the line had just opened for public traffic and was awaiting inspection of signals at the Cambrian crossing. The gauge is given as 1 ft. 11½ in. From the port the line was level to Tremadoc and then rose to 810 ft. in just under 6 miles. The ruling grade of 1 in 25 pertained for considerable lengths, but eased to 1 in 152 elsewhere. There was a summit level of nearly two miles, followed by a fall of 1 in 70. At the topmost end the line was almost level. The sharpest curve was 2 chains radius. In addition to developing the mines and quarries already named, agriculture and adjacent peat works were to benefit; there were no alternative roads. Details of the right of way, track and motive power followed (these are dealt with later). The article states that gravity working was carried on one way, with locomotive power the other—this seems unlikely over much of the line, which was unfavourable for this type of working. Reference is also made to locomotives in the plural, but the concern only owned the one and this featured in all the returns. No assistance or co-operation was received from the local landowners when building the line, which cost '£2,500 per mile'. The Engineer for the railway construction had been George Wilson M.I.C.E., 22 Parliament Street, Westminster.

No dividend was ever paid: in the Stock Exchange Year Book for

1881 it stated, 'In 1877 the payment of the debenture interest had to be postponed. Nothing further has transpired . . .'. It never did.

The Route described: Portmadoc to Gorseddau Quarry

Because of the uncertainty of the extent of the Gorseddau line in times past, it is easier to describe the line's course from its wharf at the north-east corner of the Sluice Bridge, Portmadoc. There would have been only limited accommodation here as the site was small. Immediately behind it the tramway would have been crossed, after 1864, by the Croesor Tramway. Originally, as the two lines were of differing gauge, this meant a simple acute crossing of rails in the roadway. The Gorseddau line, virtually level within the town, then made its way up the east side of Madoc Street, which at the time of the tramway's building, would certainly not have been skirted with housing as it is today. At the top of the street the track turned north-westward and made a straight course behind the town along what is still a piece of undeveloped and uninteresting ground. The route is now a footpath, and within the past ten years has been excavated by the writer at various points between the standard gauge crossing to the west and the later site of junction with the Cambrian to the east. This proved that this section of line was never properly lifted; almost all sleepers and chairs were intact though rails had gone. At the time of inspection, the track had been buried about nine inches by the footway. The north-east edge of the site is bounded by the erstwhile Canal and beyond this were allotment gardens.

From about 1902 there was retained a section just short of the Cambrian Crossing. A branch tramway led westwards along Cambrian Street, over the main road and then beside the Cambrian goods yard to the Moel-y-gest Quarry who owned and worked it, latterly with their own locomotive. (The Gorseddau line from this concern's junction, along Madoc Street West to the junction with the Croesor at the Flour Mill, remained in use for Moel-y-gest purposes after abandonment of the Gorseddau proper.)

The former Cambrian Railways' crossing is now reached and today is crossed with the aid of stiles in the boundary fences, and a foot crossing on the site of the old line. Within a few yards, still using the west bank of the canal, the line crossed what is now Avenue Road, with the standard gauge level crossing at hand to the south, and the Queens Hotel on the left hand. The tramway passed between the Hotel and the canal bank. Thirty-three chains from the Cambrian crossing was a short branch to the west to serve the Pen-syflog Ironstone Mine—still a prominent rock outcrop. This was followed by a stone bridge over the Afon Oer. Continuing in flat country of little note, and still on the canal side until within a few yards south of Dublin Street, 15 chains west of the Tremadoc town centre and 1 m. 20 ch. from the Sluice Bridge it curved into the southern edge of Dublin Street and ran beside it for two chains. Turning slowly right it crossed the road on the level at the point of a fork between Criccieth and Caernarvon roads, and ran in behind a wall bordering the north edge of the Caernarvon road. Some indication of the flatness of the land may be gained from a nearby Bench mark showing slightly under 13 feet.

The terminus of the original tramway to Llidiart Yspytty Mine was now reached. Though clearly marked with the earthworks of former rail access, it is now too overgrown to pick out all the detail. From the Deposited Plans it is shown that the new railway, extended from here, did not use the full length of the first tramway as a reversing neck, and that the layout at the mine was probably unchanged despite the coming of the extension. Access to the mine was made by a back shunt from the end of the old tramway, up a steep incline still visible from the nearby road. Thus there were, in effect, two reversing junctions from the line running beside the Penmorfa road; the more easterly route climbed up a shelf at 1 in 23, and turning anticlockwise, completed rather more than a 180 degree turn by means of this 2½ chain curve—a formidable obstacle to train working! By the time the line had rounded the bend, it was several feet above the level at which it had crossed Dublin Street, and below it to the left hand, lay the site of the Mine. One spur of the mine tramway passed under the new line to reach the workings; the adit entrance has been filled in. Ahead now stretches the Gorseddau Railway, as the O.S. 1884 Sheet labels this length. It is interesting to note two features still visible at this site; firstly as to how the line carried itself up through a cutting behind the school, and secondly, how use of it could have been made for the nearby limekilns, both of which existed here before the extension was built; though a difficult piece of line to operate, it is ingeniously surveyed and built. The route ahead was not easy. Now with the flat lands behind it, the course was forced to run between the foot of a craggy escarpment, Allt Wen, and the Penmorfa road and village below. The road, in fact, climbs to a point where, at the west end of Penmorfa village, it can pass over the tramway. Allt Wen is one of several similar ridges in the neighbourhood, and seen from afar, they resemble waves of hills with their crests in the breaking position. The face of Allt Wen was in fact broken with scree in many places so the tramway was part-built on an embankment through the debris at the bottom of the ridge. In parts the foundations of the line were boulders which had fallen years before; since the closing of the line, sections have been covered by later rock falls. The wooded climb is still severe, 1 in 25 continuing for this section.

Signs of early inclines and workings into the face of Allt Wen will be seen at Cae-crwn and, a few yards further west, where the Penmorfa Quarry was served. Both quarries had spur connections to the tramway. Here (2 m. 10 ch.) there is a small row of cottages still named 'Railway Terrace', a title they seem to have acquired at the time more of the closure of the tramway than whilst it was working! The tramway is now running almost westward and leaves the foot of Allt Wen for the upland meadows beyond Penmorfa. It crossed a minor road on the level and then came back to the main Caernarvon road beside its northern edge, a quarter of a mile west of Penmorfa. Gradually the road climbs above the level of the tramway which dropped into a cutting beside the highway. About here both are 164 feet above sea level and at this site was Tyn-y-llon Mine, the most distant quarry of the local group which mined for iron ore.

The County Council made use of the available railway route to widen the road here in 1966–7, and in doing so destroyed the east mouth of the stone tunnel which took the line under it. The west mouth may still be partly discerned, but the blocking of the bore took place over thirty years ago. The bore dimensions are: height 9 ft. 6 in., width 10 ft., and length approx. 25 yd.

The course now runs parallel but to the south of the road, much of it along a tree-lined embankment which takes it to Glan-byl Farm and to cross a minor road on the level immediately beforehand. There

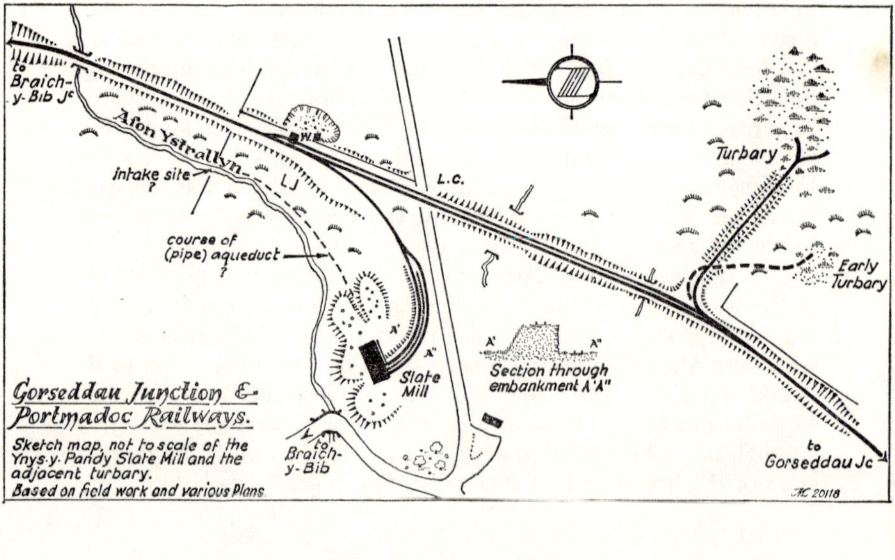

is now a short run of a few yards before the Caernarvon road is crossed on the level once more, but between the last two road crossings, farming has partly obliterated the site; on this length too, the tramway has changed direction from westward and now faces north-east. There follows another straight section of about half a mile—an unusual feature in this sinuous line—mainly over a low embankment. At the beginning of this earthwork, and alongside the Caernarvonshire road crossing was an agricultural siding 20 yards long (3 m. 50 ch.).

The land each side now is marshy and the ordered fields begin to change their style into upland sheep-farming country. The straight length ends with a deep cutting and a well-preserved stone-built tunnel (bore : height 9 ft. 6 in., width 9 ft., and length approx. 26 yd.) at Hen-efail under the old Caernarvon road. The railway is now at a height of 459 ft. and 4 m. 20 ch. from the Sluice Bridge.

Climbing out of the bridge cutting, the scenery changes immediately. Ahead stand the bare uplands of Caernarvonshire, the rounded foothills near at hand and more spectacular peaks rising to 2,000 and more feet beyond. On a sunny day this cycloramic sweep has a colourful beauty which is never forgotten, but all too frequently the uplands are blanketed down in a wet mist off the sea and the magic of this view is so completely lost that it cannot be imagined. So up into this bleak country, with the surrounding land becoming more wet and scrubby, pressed the railway to the Gorseddau Quarry, now on the western flank of the foothills. On this length, the route is wet and gorsey until at about 5 miles the ancient Meini Hirion standing stones are passed on the right hand.* The cutting here then widens and for the first time, the line doubled. The track on the east side then branched off at a junction and its route over the mountainside can easily be followed as it cuts its way through the rough moorland in a straight line and through an ever-deepening cutting. In about a quarter of a mile the branch ends in a shallow depression of considerable extent, the remaining vestiges of the turbary which featured in early descriptions of the line.† Owing to the natural tendency of peat to be unstable, the levels have obviously filled up with new growth and the original arrangements have lost their definition.

* Meini Hirion or Menhirs is the accepted Welsh for Long Stones, either a single standing stone or more, e.g. a stone circle. This example is thought to be pre-Bronze Age and was probably the traditional way of honouring the dead. There is a collection of stones with an identical name near Penmaenmawr..

† At this time coal was expensive and not commonly used, having to be imported from Flintshire or Lancashire. Consequently most homesteads had access to a turbary.

At the beginning of this branch, and almost immediately after its junction with the main line, may be traced the route of a still earlier line to the south of the later one. This track passes through the cutting of the newer line at its west end and may be followed for a short distance to a depression in the ground where there were once the original turbary workings. The impressions of sleepers in the soft

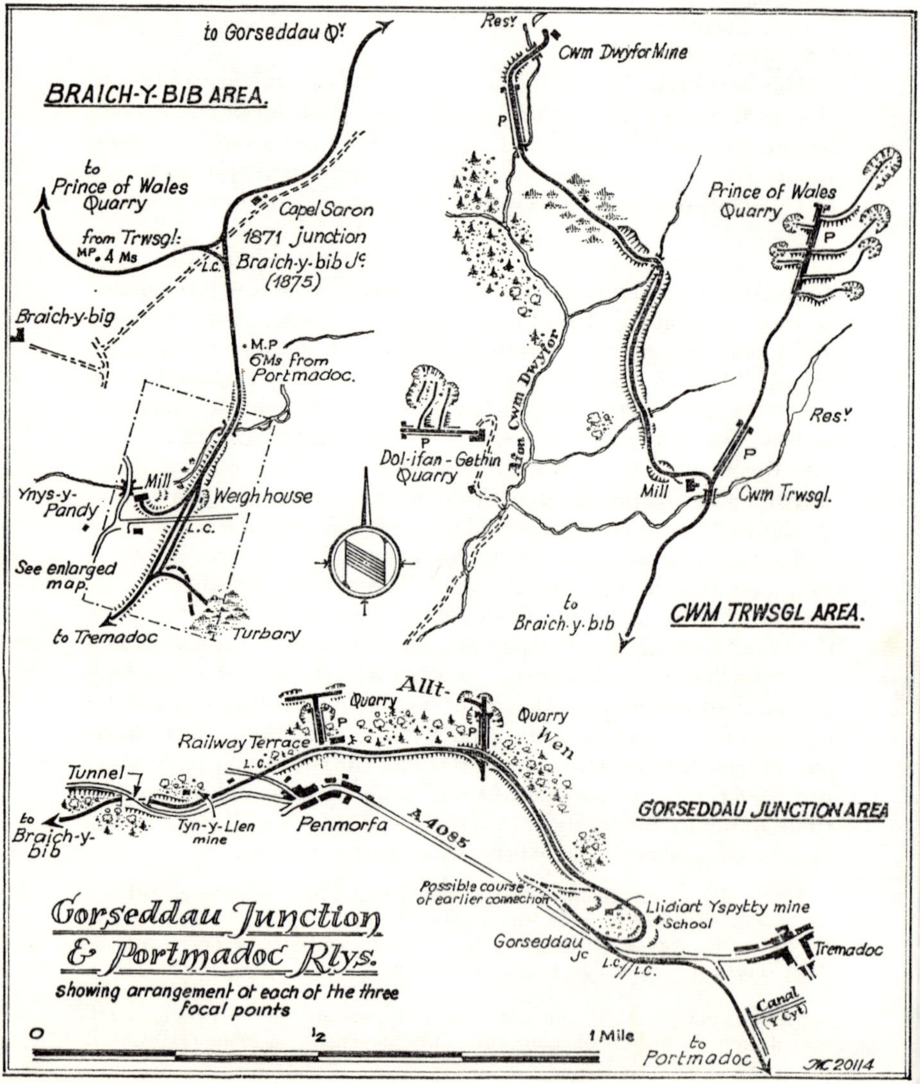

ground along this long-abandoned course, are remarkably clear.

Returning to the main line again, the double track extends over an embankment carrying a large culvert beneath, passes through walls where once was a level road crossing and continues as a double line past what was formerly the slate yard of Ynys-y-pandy with its weighing machine, rubbish sidings etc., all now hardly traceable (630 ft.). Double line becomes single again beyond the yard's precincts. To the left a remarkable ruin dominates the scene. This is the old slate mill of the Gorseddau Quarry (said by some to have been a tannery, this is unlikely).

The Gorseddau Quarry was unusual. Instead of work being carried out on the stone within the quarry precincts, it was brought here to be sawn and split. This building, with its water power and suitability, was clearly considered preferable to anything the company might build near the workings. The junction into it faces the quarry and a branch line curves away to the west, and supported by a high stone wall on its southern flank, enters the building by the first floor, so to speak. A second line, outside the wall, entered at a lower floor. The machinery was driven by two wheels at different levels, one at right angles to the other. Both are within the building and the water for the larger one falls down a vertical shaft below the access tramway to drive the undershot wheel which lay 'athwart' the structure. After passing under the wheel, the water was led out through a tunnel mouth on the lower side of the mill, and so into a valley alongside to rejoin the Afon Cwm-ystradllyn. The building itself is of considerable interest to the industrial historian, and is ornamented in a style rare in a slate mill! The roof was taken off in 1905 and said to have been the finest in the district.

The north end of the yard outside the mill is marked by the site of the Weighing Machine House, a building used as a reference point in the Plans of 1875. After passing northwards through a cutting, another short straight length ensues and the Cwm-ystradllyn river crossed by a stone-piered bridge with 15 in. square timber spans. A short run brings it to the site of the 'New Junction of 1875' or Braich-y-bib (also known as Braich-y-big). The line is now 690 feet above the sea, and having entered a section where the gradients are subject to Statutory Plans, it is known that the rise from Hen-efail tunnel has involved an almost continuous pull of 1 in 67/51/38/27/38/52, luckily only against empty slate workings. The junction is 6 m. 10 ch. from the Sluice Bridge.

Ignoring the new line to the head of the Pennant Valley for the time being, the course of the older Gorseddau line may be followed over a road crossing and sweeping eastwards above a minor road, as it climbs up behind the now derelict schoolroom and chapel (Capel Saron). The initial gradient of this section is known : 1 in 21½/32/34, and so on almost as steep as far as the quarry. Of course, this line was always worked by horses and as has been stated, is unlikely to have been reduced from its original gauge of 3 ft., laid in what may have been Cob Tramway materials. (A piece of fish-bellied rail in use as fencing along here, and found by the writer in 1946, does nothing to confirm that any fish-bellied track of Nantlle or similar type was used up here. There is widespread use of rails in fencing, roofing etc. and it may not be indigenous to the district.) The vista is now wild and bleak; below is the former Llyn Cwm-ystradllyn, now a reservoir. Ahead is the re-entrant at the top of which the extensive working of the Gorseddau Quarry dominates the view; behind and above climb the rocky sides of Moel Hebog (2,568 ft.) whose summit is out of sight. The tramway has now had a slab-built ledge constructed for it, and there being no other route, has become a roadway of sorts. For the last mile the ledge curves eastwards and then south-eastwards before, at the eight-mile point, describing a half circle to end its journey at the foot of the long incline which divides the workings almost into two equal parts and takes the upper galleries, served by the tramway, along ledges over 1,000 feet high in the slopes of Fridd Uchaf. It was abandoned before the turn of the century, and extensive investigation of the workings over 25 years ago revealed nothing which would make the somewhat little-known Gorseddau Quarry line give up any more of its secrets!

The Route described: Braich-y-bib to Cwm-dwyfor Copper Mine

The area of the triangular junction at Braich-y-bib is clearly marked in the patch of ground bounded by stone walls to the south of the road to the Gorseddau Quarry. Although more overgrown than it was, the three sides of rails may be followed. The southern junction of 1875 is the last one; the first access to the Pennant valley extension (The Gorseddau Junction and Portmadoc Railway proper) of 1871 was by means of a line which trailed into the Gorseddau Tramway and which would oblige a short section at least to be re-gauged for use as a headshunt. The section off the new line, and down to the 1871 junction, fell at 1 in 34/42/58/32 before becoming level for a short stabling length. The newest (west) side of the triangle was empowered by the 1875 G. J. & P. R. Act and this short section inclined upward from Braich-y-bib at 1 in 24/30/108/42/34. Beyond the north-west junction there was a level crossing* and the line

* Col. Yolland, inspecting for the Board of Trade, was in favour of the level crossing being replaced, but was overruled by the House of Lords' Standing Orders Committee (6 July 1876).

climbed upward at 1 in 34, passing over the flank of Braich-y-cornel and through the 700 ft. contour. The sharpest section of curve from the new junction was 3 chains 50 links. Mileages were now officially measured from Cwm Trwsgl; the new junction was 4 m. 20 ch. from there.

As the shoulder of land is crossed, the line takes a long slow bend to the north and falls at 1 in 50 for a furlong. Between the four-mile point and 1 m. 6 ch., the course is level, being a somewhat monotonous contour-hugging northward drive towards the valley head at about 825 ft. The route is mainly a levelling of the hillside which here is not steep. Here and there are shallow cuttings, and where streams are crossed, embankments are used with small stone culverts in the bottom. The Pennant valley below, is entered high on its eastern flank near Caer-fadog. In the valley below to the south-east lay the estate of Brynkir, with its tower-topped hill. Here between 1809 and 1910 lived a family closely linked with the narrow gauge railways of the district from the time of Madocks at Tan-yr-allt. Nearer lies the hamlet of Llanfihangel-y-Pennant, and beyond both, there are glimpses of golden sands and the sea. It would have been a wonderful vista had a passenger service ever operated. Instead, the line passes an occasional derelict farmstead and there are numerous slate tips on the far side of the valley marking Dol-ifan-gethin, Chwarel-y-plas, Hendre-ddu and Moelfre Slate Quarries. The spoil tips of Gilfach Copper Mine lie below. All these had internal tramways, but all are now abandoned. Gilfach's large water wheel was a feature of the district. Above Cwrt-isaf, the Afon Cwm-llefrith is crossed. This was once bridged and the approach embankments are the largest on this section. One mile to the east, nearly 1,500 feet up in the rocks of Moel Hebog, was the Moel Hebog Mine, an offshoot of the Cwm-dwyfor Mine and if anything, even less lucky! Apart from a rough path, there was no connection with the outer world in general or the G.J. & P.R. in particular. Above Brith-dir Mawr another stream is crossed and beyond here the level section ends, the line falling the rest of the way to Cwm Trwsgl at 1 in 76, a very unhelpful arrangement. There are a few shallow cuttings as Cwm Trwsgl is approached, and in certain sections the marks of where the sleepers have lain would suggest the line has only recently been lifted. There is a stone embankment and culvert over the Afon Cwm Trwsgl and short level section to the tramway.

To the left stands the roofless building of the Prince of Wales slate mill, with its wheelpit alongside the Trwsgl stream. Ahead, though somewhat obliterated due to the instability and wetness of the ground, climbs the lower incline to the Prince of Wales Quarry.

The exact layout here is impossible to trace, but the plans show a level crossing between the main tramway as it swings west behind the slate mill en route for Cwm Dwyfor, and the foot of the line coming off the lower Prince of Wales incline as it made its way into the mill. If the Prince of Wales line is followed, there are remains of the drum at the head of the lower incline. There is then a quarter of a mile of near level tramway and a second incline is entered. From this spine-like incline, fingers extend on either side; these were tramways, their boundaries flanked by piled rubbish as each made its way to levels in the mountainside. There is abundant evidence that although extensive, the quarry did not produce much slate throughout its life. Its situation is impressive; that is about all. Looking south, the rock-strewn slopes on the left sweep up to Moel Hebog directly ahead; the shallow bowl of the Pennant valley falls slowly to the hills which prevent a direct view of the mouth of the Glaslyn estuary, but allow glimpses of light on mountain and horizon down the length of Cardigan Bay. To the right the Pennant valley has narrowed considerably and a prominent feature is the Dol-ifan-gethin slate quarry opposite with its steep incline and three parallel tramways near the summit. At the foot of the incline nestle the remains of the slate mill, barracks and workshops.

Returning now to the main line at Cwm Trwsgl slate mill; the railway curves to the left and passes behind the end of the mill building. Within this curve may be seen the site of three tracks each entering the mill building by its own separate arched entrance. The water wheel would have driven a shaft running the length of the mill, at right angles to the tramways entering the building. The three lines were carried right through it to tips on the west side. To the south and east of the mill stand five of six slab pillars which carried an aqueduct with water for the overshot wheel. The spent water was conducted by a short sluice back into the Trwsgl. The Plans show a connection from the west side of the mill back onto the main line again, but earthworks do not confirm the building of the connection. The railway now has to pierce a rocky bluff by means of a curved cutting, 33 ft. deep and with 9 ft. width clearance at track level. At its further end the line is running due north along an 8 ft. 6 in. formation ledge, as here the mountainside is steeper than formerly. Cwm Trwsgl farm lies immediately below the line and was the most northerly habitation on this side of the valley. The Plans give this section of line a 'Level' indication but in fact the course continues to fall to the foot of the Cwm Dwyfor Mine incline. The valley is now quite narrow, but more attractive, and is wooded on the other side. An immense amphitheatre of mountain, its summit rounded and uniformly shaped, cradles the end of the valley. There is no footpath to the north; exit from the valley is from the end which the railway entered only! Over this northern ridge whose highest point is 2,408 ft., lies the Drws-y-coed Valley which runs due east and west, and from whose western end the Nantlle Railway emanated. From this position on the Gorseddau Junction line, there is and never has been reason for communication over this impressive barrier, there being no col to make it practicable. Ahead, the line can be seen clinging to the eastern slopes, disappearing for a short stretch into a re-entrant to the right, and then proceeding along its ledge to the bottom of the clearly-defined final incline. There are three fillings where streams are crossed, and the largest of these in the re-entrant has been almost entirely swept away by spectacular landslide of water and rock. Traces of the permanent way are not so clear and the ground is more marshy; chairs and pins have been found here so confirming that the same track materials were provided throughout the system. Shortly before the incline a remote stone building is passed though its connection with the railway is unclear. The final double-tracked incline is not steep and the drumhouse is curious having separate passages for each track.

The incline lifts the track from 740 to 915 feet, its foot being almost exactly a mile from Cwm Trwsgl. At the incline top, it leads ahead towards the smooth bowl at the top of the valley. In front lie spoil tips in disarray, the remains of wheelpit, engine house, processing floors and barracks. The track curves eastward over a low embankment and after crossing the infant Dwyfawr (the correct spelling of the corrupted Dwyfor) it forks; a very short spur runs into the blacksmith's shop and the other, hardly longer, disappears into what must have been a loading bank. On a higher level and beyond stand various heaps of variegated rock spoil, their composition and colour revealing the complex geological variety of these rocks. Clearly the mine was built with adequate capital, its buildings and tramway works being soundly contructed of a dark grey stone which must have been brought here for the purpose. As at Cwm Trwsgl, there are the remains of stone piers to carry water to the overshot wheel. Once more, and as with the Croesor tramway, the lasting impression is of the immense amount of labour and money which was poured into a railway to connect this lonely spot with the sea. In the case of the Croesor, the subsequent output of slate probably justified the effort . . . in the present example, the result must have been quite disastrous.

In passing, it should be emphasised that it was likely to have been this mile from Cwm Trwsgl which showed weaknesses in the new permanent way provided by the G.J. & P.R.; at first the sleepers were spaced at 2 ft. 9 in. intervals; from impressions along the foundations of the Cwm Dwyfor branch, the sleepers have been reduced to 2 ft. intervals. Had copper or iron ore been carried in any quantity, insufficient support on this boggy length would soon be evident. What is not known is whether it was the output which was destructive—which seems unlikely—or simply the provision of heavy stone for the erection of the mine's buildings.

Permanent Way

Such information as is available or conjectured concerning the track of the Llidiart Yspytty Ironstone Mine Tramway, and the extension of this line from Tremadoc to the Gorseddau Slate Quarry at

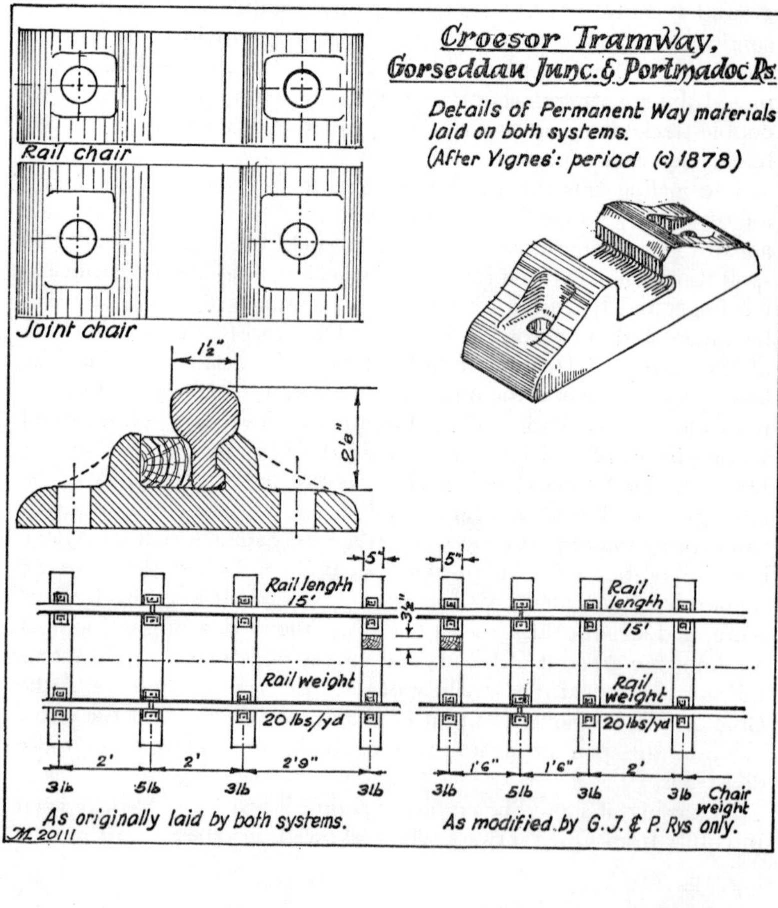

Ffridd Uchaf, has already been given on p. 26 and nothing can be usefully added.

The first precise description of Croesor and Gorseddau permanent way is that given by Vignes in 1878. The ancestry of the T section rail carried in chairs as used by the Croesor when building in 1862–3, is still an open question, but Vignes confirms that Croesor and Gorseddau materials were identical in the mid-1870s. The original supplier of rail and chairs was probably a Portmadoc foundry.* It is convenient to repeat the material dimensions for the opening of the Croesor Tramway in August 1864 and the Gorseddau Junction & Portmadoc Railways in September 1875. Despite the eleven years intervening, the Railways Company had not seen fit to introduce a heavier specification, even though the Croesor line was built for horse haulage and the G.J. & P.R. had powers to work with locomotives and carry goods and passengers from the start. This was because there was already a surfeit of this material available locally. And from this one may question whether the G.J. & P.R. aimed to build its line at the cheapest possible initial cost and relay if traffic warranted it? It seems hardly likely that as late as 1875 they intended to work all their traffic with motive power light enough to use 20 lbs. rails without damage. The gradients and curves of the new railway suggest a speculative element in the whole undertaking. So the new Gorseddau Railway came to be laid in 15 ft. length wrought-iron T rails weighing 20 lbs. per yard. These were carried in supporting cast-iron chairs of 3 lbs. and butt-jointed in larger chairs weighing 5 lbs.† having 4 in. length plain fixing pins. At first, iron wedges keyed the rail in the chair; later wood was used. The wooden sleepers were nominally 4 ft. long and the formation 8 ft. wide. In practice sleepers of any suitable length were used and the formation was wider in places. Sleepers were 5 in. wide × 3½ in. deep and spaced at 2 ft. 9 in. centres except at joints where the adjoining spacing was 2 ft. The gauge was precisely as the Croesor, 24 in.

At the time of Vignes' visit, all the old tramway had been converted to the narrower gauge in this material. All that is, save '3 Km.' which on 1 January 1877, 'remained to be converted'. This was presumably the section between Braich-y-bib and the Gorseddau quarry.

* The T section rail with bulb on one side of the foot was not confined to North Wales. Specimens of an almost identical section were found in autumn 1971 on the site of a tramway on Congleton Edge, Cheshire, stated by Baxter to have closed after about 1809. Baxter also refers to 'oval bars' on the Congleton line; perhaps the T section was of later installation? ('Stone Blocks & Iron Rails'. B. Baxter, p. 174).

† 'Engineering', 11 June 1875 gives 5 lbs. and 7 lbs.

Clearly, the new trackwork with its evidence of thrift, was not satisfactory. The costs involved in maintenance of works and way for the years 1875–78 support this. The rails were found to be too light for many of the sharp curves, which though few in number, were very restrictive. Some were under 2 chains radius. On such places, the locomotive was spreading the gauge. There were also problems of holding the rails in gauge during summer when the butt-joints did not take kindly to the expanding rails. Accordingly the sleepers were closed in to 1 ft. 6 in. intervals each side of joints and 2 ft. in the running line. Thus each rail was supported in nine places. Vignes emphasises the additional problems and cost of this revision and states the track is still only suitable for light traffic, which apparently, was all that the railway carried, fortunately!

Ballast was obtained by blasting rock, taken from the line of construction, into small pieces which gives it the appearance of slate rubble. It is laid about 6 in. deep.

Civil Engineering

The line was built through a difficult terrain. Between Penmorfa and Braich-y-bib where no official gradients have been documented, the average rise was 1 in 152. Having regard to the difficult country, heavy engineering works were avoided and construction costs reduced. Operating costs were much enhanced, of course. Embankment sides were sloped to 45 degrees and cuttings in rock were given vertical faces. Bridges and aqueducts were built up in rough stone blasted from the site. Some were laid loose, and others part-mortared.

Train Working

The sources of traffic were stated to include *lead* from Cwm Dwyfor, peat and slates from Gorseddau and Prince of Wales quarries. Slab tombstones were a particular feature of it! Vignes commented that certain traffic came Down to Tremadoc by gravity and that men pushing a single wagon were not unknown. 'The locomotive was only used to bring back the empties or to take loads to areas served by the railway' (which is a little ambiguous!). It would seem that the locomotive was used only when and where necessary, and only up to 1878. Thereafter it was stored. Croesor accounts show flour and corn traffic between Portmadoc and Clenenney Mills, near Henefail.

Local tradition maintains that quite a brisk passenger traffic was carried unofficially. The present Brynkir Mill's owner's grandmother took mill products to the nearby short tunnel at Hen-efail where the train would pick her up and take her to Tremadoc for the market there. Another woman walked to and from Caernarvon for provisions for the quarrymen and caught Up trains to the quarry from the same point. She would sell groceries to the quarrymen at Ystraddlyn. It is also said that on the Down journey, the horses rode in a Dandy at the rear of the train, Festiniog Railway-fashion. This cannot be confirmed.

Locomotive and Rolling Stock

There is the evidence from Festiniog records (p. 19) concerning the supply of slate wagons and a passenger carriage from Boston Lodge. As this took place before the G.J. & P.R. Act, they would be for 3 ft. gauge and possibly such stock was not suitable for conversion to narrow gauge. On 1 January 1878 Vignes gives the stock returns as: One Locomotive; 15 Wagons suitable for slate or goods—by 1885 reduced to 7 wagons—together with additional wagons owned by the quarries and some hired from the Festiniog Railway.

The 15 general purpose wagons would be similar to those used throughout North Wales and probably resembled the two-plank fixed side wooden wagons on the Croesor Railway. The slate wagons owned by the quarries may have been of Boston Lodge or other local build having wooden slat sides and marked in some way to show ownership. If the passenger carriage survived, it was not taken into official stock.

There was one locomotive, a vertical boilered four-wheeler built by De Winton & Co., Union Iron Works, Caernarvon. A contemporary source gives its dimensions as 20 in. diameter driving wheels, 4 ft. wheelbase, 6 in. × 12 in. cylinders, and boiler 5 ft. 6 in. × 2 ft. 9 in. diameter (these would be the measurements over cladding); heating surface 100 sq. ft. 'The boiler was pressed to work at 130 lbs. but would be capable of carrying a higher pressure'; ¾ ton of fuel was carried and 180 gallons of water. Tanks on such engines varied in size. The Weight in Working Order was 4½ tons and Tractive Effort 2,150 lbs.

According to Birmingham Locomotive Club records* the engine rejoiced in the name of *Pert* and was supplied new to the Prince of Wales Slate Quarry Company. The Portmadoc Croesor & Beddgelert Tram Railway Company's accounts contain a debit entry for the Gorseddau on 10 July 1874. 'To use of siding in unloading loco engine 10s.'. (This was the Beddgelert Siding). When traffic ceased after 1894, it was placed out of service 'near Tremadoc' (probably on

* 'Industrial & Independent Locomotives & Railways of N. Wales'. (1968) p. 15.

the Ironstone Mine spur) before going to Messrs. Owen, Isaac & Owen, dealers of the Vulcan Foundry, Portmadoc. It is possible that it became the second of three similar engines which worked at the Coedmadoc Slate Company's quarry, Glodd-fa'r-Glai, Nantlle, when that quarry re-opened in 1896. This undertaking liquidated at the end of December 1908 and the equipment was auctioned at the end of the following March.

Whatever may have been the fate of *Pert*, she can hardly have been much worn when her duties on the Gorseddau line were over. A contemporary account of her working on the line said she was quite suitable for negotiating the sharp curves, light enough to treat the track gently and sufficiently powerful for the steep gradients. Clearly, she was not overloaded! On test the engine would haul 20 tons including its own weight, or 20 loaded wagons up 1 in 25. (Braked wagons were 15 cwt. and unbraked 13 cwt. tare.)

Signalling

The only signalling on the whole system was in G.J. & P.R. days at the Cambrian Railway's crossing. There had been two crossings here on the same spot. The original was replaced and inspected by Col. F. H. Rich for the B.O.T. who reported on 18 August 1875 that no traps had been put into the Gorseddau line to protect the Cambrian. Rich refers to the 'Cambrian signalman's permission' (to use the crossing) as if the adjacent box was their property. Unfortunately, Cambrian records do not enlighten, but the signal box was intended to be Gorseddau property. It cannot be proven that all features on the Deposited Plans were carried out, but the diagram included shows the full arrangements, to which have been added the 1879 proposal for the interchange platform and run-round at the Cambrian station. The Plans do not show the Down Home Cambrian signal, but one would have been provided. In Cambrian records the crossing is known as 'Mr. Huddart's'.* The Gorseddau trap point on

* The Huddart family bought the Brynkir estate in 1809 and held it for about 100 years. The Hall was demolished after the First War and held German P.O.W. during that war. Purchase was made by Captain Joseph Huddart, Elder Brother of Trinity House who, after siting the South Stack Light, reported on Holyhead Harbour and surveyed the maritime side for an Irish Mail route via Holyhead. His son, also Joseph, became High Sheriff for the county and was knighted at the opening of Telford's Menai Bridge by George IV in 1826. The family played a great part in South Caernarvonshire and North Merionethshire during the Industrial Revolution. Brynkir passed from Sir Joseph to George Augustus who died in 1885; he was co-patentee with Spooner of the rail fishplate device which bears their names (ref. Festiniog Railway Vol. 1 p. 103). His eldest son was the Rev. Dr. G. A. W. Huddart, prominent in Festiniog Railway affairs and anxious to find management for that line

		1875	*1876*	*1877*	*1878*	*1879*	*1880*	*1881*	*1885*	*1886*	*1887*	*1888*	*1889*	*1890*	*1891*	*1892*	*1893*	*1894*
Cost Works and Way		£186	88	65	16	4	—	9	5	2	4	5	6	4	4	—	—	—
Cost Loco power		65	24	40	15													
Cost Carr/Wag maint.		2	3															
Traffic expenses		44	111	203	82	96	96	96										
Legal expenses		—	100	—	—	13												
Loss on working		414	512	545	404	354	232	255	48	47	43	45	51	49	29	28	28	?
Merchandise	Tons	324	1042	1270	856	649	443	329	—	39	—	4						
Minerals	Tons	381	733	318	345	371	157	184	—	—	46	93	31	21	20	—	—	—
Train mileage		2050	3533	2701	1658	2239	1347	1350	—	60	440	221	248	80	60	—	—	—
Locos		Returned as One throughout period																
Wagons		15		1875–81					7		1886–93							

Comment on the above:

Cost of Works and Way	Figures suggest track etc. incomplete when traffic began.
Loco costs	Loco used for four years only; thereafter stored as it was returned throughout the above period. Returns state 'Freighters using own horses' after 1880.
Carr/Wagon costs	Presumably charged in Quarry Accounts after first two years?
Traffic expenses	Little reduction after horses replaced locomotive. Possibly charged to Quarry Account after 1885?
Loss on working	These much reduced in second period. Mineral traffic possibly charged to Quarry Account?
Tonnage carried	Merchandise exceeds mineral traffic in first period, but falls to nothing in second (or is not returned). Zenith in 1876, thereafter line appears to have been only used occasionally.
Wagon Returns	Figures suggest 15 wagons of first period were for merchandise traffic and half were disposed of in second period. Quarries' own wagons used for mineral traffic.
No Returns made 1882–4	(Railways Company under threat of proceedings for not furnishing same.)

the north side of the crossing was extended to form a short siding, and had the Gorseddau–Croesor link been built, this siding would have extended alongside and over the Cambrian bridge to cross the Canal and run up into the Beddgelert Siding, Croesor tramway. According to Cambrian records, Mr. Huddart's crossing had been lifted by 1892. 'The Cambrian Railways' p. 98 mentions that 'the Gorsedda trans-shipped some slate traffic to the Cambrian *north of the crossing*'. If this is so, it must have been done by means of the short siding already mentioned, and presumably a Cambrian siding would have been built for loading. Of this there is no trace today.

Vignes has some supplementary information about this railway crossing : the operating of it was to conform to Clauses 9–12 of the Railway Clauses Act 1863; and there were to be mutual trans-shipment arrangements at a Goods Station by the crossing—probably by means of the short siding just mentioned—and the operation of the crossing was to be controlled by the Cambrian (a state of affairs which would command no surprise !).

---

which would develop the tourist trade at a time when the standard gauge was siphoning off the slate trade. The family was a large holder of Festiniog stock etc. and may be said to have financed the line in a liberal way from its earliest days. The estate's lands included parts of Criccieth, Penygroes, Penrhyn, Portmadoc etc.

GORSEDDAU JUNCTION & PORTMADOC RAILWAYS (& GORSEDDAU TRAMWAY) Mileages

Miles from Sluice	*Chains Bridge*	*Location*	*Gorseddau Tramway*	*G.J. & P. Rlys.*
0	0	Tramway Wharf	Zero Point	—
0	40	Portmadoc	Crossing with Cambrian Rlys.	—
1	50	Tremadoc	Reversing neck	—
5	53	Ynys-y-pandy	Slate Mill	—
8	10	Gorseddau	Slate Quarry	—

Miles from Cwm	*Chains Trwsgl*	*(including variations on official distances due to different points of origin.)*		
4	53	Ynys-y-pandy	—	Slate Mill
4	20	Braich-y-bib	—	New 1875 Junction
0	0	Cwm Trwsgl	—	Slate Mill
0	30	Prince of Wales Qy.	—	Foot of second incline.
1	14	Cwm Dwyfor Mine	—	End of line at Mine.

Directors (Quorum 3 Directors)

1873 Charles James FOX James STEWART of London (Wine Merchant) James MAW Thomas HARVEY of Brixton (Solicitor).
1876 Herbert C. MAUDSLAY James STEWART Rev. Logan LOGAN Thomas HARVEY.
1883 James STEWART of London E.C. Charles BARTON of Wincanton Rev. Logan LOGAN of Bournemouth.
1896 Charles BARTON of Wincanton Rev. Logan LOGAN of Bournemouth (One seat unfilled).

No Director other than Barton had any other railway directorships. He was of the Gloucester & Dean Forest Rly.

Secretary throughout above period: George Joseph GRAY, St. Clement's House, London, E.C.

The Seal of the Company shows the strong influence of Robert Fairlie's double engine but does not imply the Company's commitment!

FESTINIOG & BLAENAU RAILWAY CO. LTD.

(*Gauge* 1 ft. $11\frac{3}{4}$ in.)

Registered as a Company under the Limited Liability Act of 1862: 7 August 1862.

Absorbed by standard-gauge Bala & Festiniog Railway 13 April 1883 under powers given to Bala & Festiniog Railway by the Great Western Railway Act 43/4 Vic. Cap. 141 Sections 63–6 of 6 August 1880.

Opened to all traffic: 29 May 1868.

Converted to standard gauge: April–September 1883.*

Opened standard gauge: 10 September 1883.

Closed standard gauge: Passengers 4 January 1960; Freight 27 January 1961

Registered Office: Melbourne House, Llan Ffestiniog.
From June 1868 Duffws Blaenau Festiniog (later, a second office in Portmadoc).

Length: 3 m. 40 ch.

Maximum Gradient: 1 in 58.

Minimum Curve: 6 chains.

Maximum Speed: 12 m.p.h. – under Sealed Undertaking.

Capital: £20,000 in £10 Ordinary Shares.

* After gauge conversion, the L.N.W.R. was to be permitted to use the line under Section 65 of the G.W.R. Act 1880, but such powers not to be granted until L.N.W.R. physically connected with F. & B.R. ('The Blaenau Railway') which it never was, as the Festiniog Railway owned the connecting and intervening land!

THE MERIONETHSHIRE RAILWAY

(*Gauge:* Mixed)

Incorporated:	34/5 Vic. Cap.	72	29 June 1871.
Other Acts:	39/40	77	27 June 1876 Extension of time.
	42/3	53	3 July 1879 ,,
	45/6	16	19 May 1882 ,,
	50/1	108	12 July 1887 Abandonment Order.

Registered Office: 2 Westminster Chambers, Victoria Street, London, S.W.

Capital: £80,000 in £10 Ordinary Shares.

Loans: £28,000

Time for completion: Railways Nos. 1 & 2—Five years.

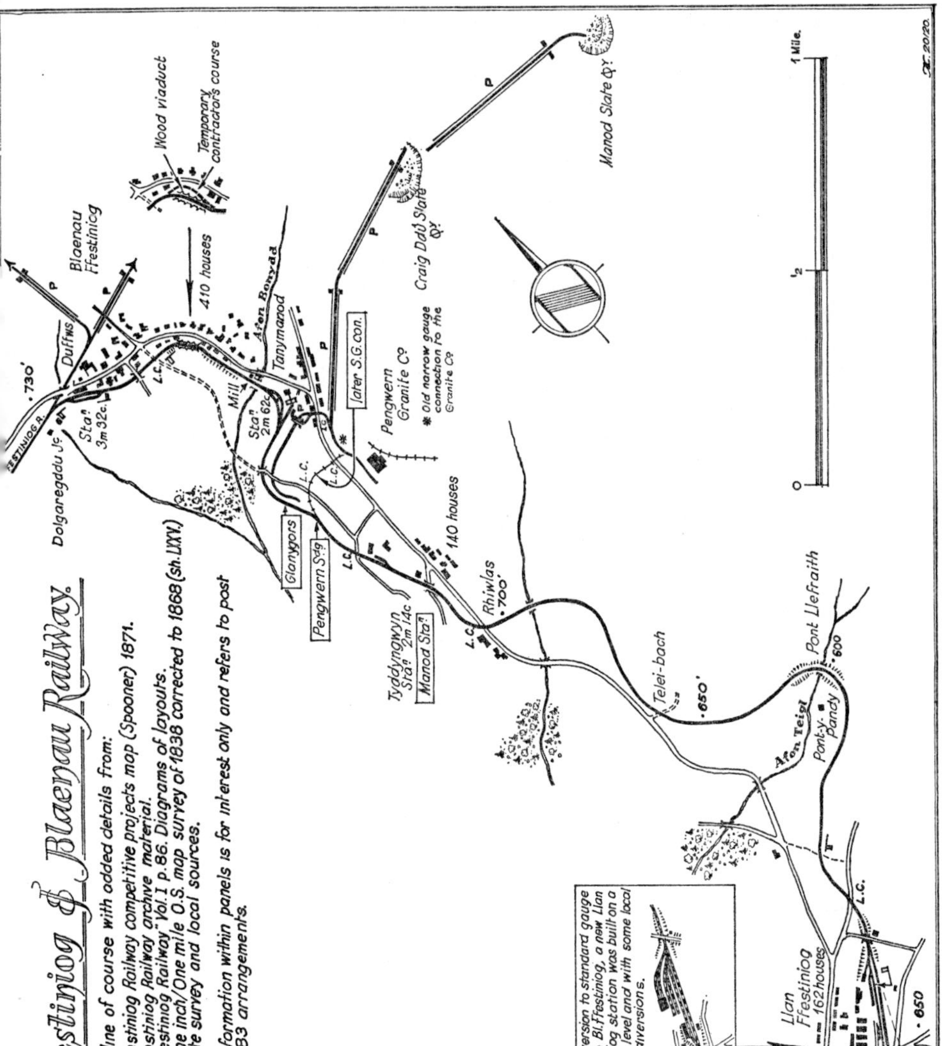
Festiniog & Blaenau Railway.
Outline of course with added details from:
Festiniog Railway competitive projects map (Spooner) 1871.
Festiniog Railway archive material.
"Festiniog Railway" Vol. I p.86. Diagrams of layouts.
One inch/One mile O.S. map survey of 1838 corrected to 1868 (sh. LXXV.)
Site survey and local sources.
Information within panels is for interest only and refers to post 1883 arrangements.
On conversion to standard gauge (Bala) to Bl. Ffestiniog, a new Llan Ffestiniog station was built on a higher level and with some local road diversions.
Dolgaregddu Jc.
Festiniog R.
Sta.n 3m 32c.
·730'
Duffws
Blaenau Ffestiniog
410 houses
Wood viaduct
Temporary contractor's course
Afon Bowydd
Mill
Sta.n 2m 62c
Tanymanod
later S.G. con.
Pengwern Granite Co
Old narrow gauge connection to the Granite Co
Craig Ddu Slate Q.y
Manod Slate Q.y
Glanygors
Pengwern S.dg
140 houses
Rhiwlas ·700'
Tyddyngwyn Sta.n 2m 14c
Manod Sta.n
Telei-bach
·650'
Pont Llefraith
·600
Afon Teigl
Pont-y-Pandy
Llan Ffestiniog 162 houses
Chap
·650
0
½
1 Mile.

History

The original quarries which opened in the neighbourhood of Blaenau Festiniog were, so far as the important ones were concerned, all connected to the Festiniog Railway by 1860. Slate quarrying had developed however, to the east and south of the town, extending southwards as far as Llan Ffestiniog, a large village some three miles away from its industrial namesake, Blaenau Festiniog. Llan Ffestiniog remains today quite unchanged by a century and a half of slate quarrying in the neighbourhood. It was the most southward point of the extent of the 'catchment area' from which the quarries drew their labour, and though having itself no connections with the slate industry, it marked the boundary, so to speak, of the quarrying 'dormitory' area which surrounded Blaenau to east and north.

Quarries east and south of Blaenau had no direct rail access to the Festiniog, at that time the only railway in the vicinity. Whilst the advantages of having a rail outlet to Portmadoc and the sea and, from 1872, an interchange connection at Minffordd with the standard gauge Cambrian Railways, were undeniable, the reality was greatly diminished by the then hopelessly overburdened state of the Festiniog Railway. This line still displayed most of the shortcomings of its 1836 horse tramway origins. Its track was primitive, its course was winding, and though the gradient favoured loaded trains, these were still worked by horse-and-gravity system over the single line of rails.* The proprietors of the line were keenly aware of the wrath of the quarry owners, the bottlenecks on their system and the delays to traffic at the collection points in Blaenau (of which there were two, one at Dinas and the other at Duffws), and at the quayside at Portmadoc. To be fair to them, slate output had grown to such an extent that they had been unable to meet its transport. They were actively engaged in laying more robust permanent way, in eliminating the more unsatisfactory sections of the tramway period, in finding a successor to the rustic horsepower and building more and larger slate wagons. But they were at full stretch. As if to make the position worse, a railway which was to be in essence an extension of the Festiniog, was incorporated under the Company's Act on 7 August 1862, to link Blaenau and Llan Ffestiniog! It lay just outside the Caernarvonshire boundary and shortly it will be recorded as having aspirations with a projected Merionethshire Railway: these systems find a place under the current title in view of their relations with the Festiniog Railway's south Caernarvonshire Portmadoc outlet.

It should be stressed that appearances proved to be deceptive. The Festiniog & Blaenau Railway was designed, it was true, to make a

* For full detail of the Festiniog position at this time see 'The Festiniog Railway Vol. 1', pp. 23–31 etc. etc.

physical junction with the Festiniog's terminal at Duffws and then extend as a continuation but under an independent concern for the 3½ miles (officially quoted as 4 miles of single line) to Llan Ffestiniog. It must have been abundantly clear from those promoting it, (who had not been on the best of terms with the Festiniog) that there was more to it than first appeared. The local landowners were to donate the land where the line was to pass through their property. All major civil engineering works were to be built in anticipation of conversion to 4 ft. 8½ in. gauge as and when necessary. Great care would be taken when laying out reverse curves to make these transitional and avoid any straight connecting sections; the maximum curve would be 6 chains against the 2 chains on the Festiniog. (It was intended that the steepest grade should be 1 in 100, but compulsory deviations almost doubled the steepness).

The prospectus issued in September 1866 stated:

Capital £10,000 in 1,000 shares of £10 each. Deposit £1 per share. The calls after the first to be made at intervals as required.

'This Company has been formed for the purpose of making a railway from Festiniog to the Quarry District at Blaenau and there forming a junction with the existing railway to Portmadoc.

The Promoters of the Company are the land-owners, quarry proprietors and other persons interested in the prosperity of the neighbourhood.

The length of the proposed railway is about 3½ miles and the estimated cost is £10,000. A survey has been made and a line selected which combines good gradients with facilities and cheapness of construction. It commences by the village of Festiniog, passes by Cornel-y-wal and Bethania and terminates by a junction with the existing railway at a point a little to the West of the Dol-y-garreg-ddu Station.

Enquiries have been made as to the existing goods traffic between Festiniog and Portmadoc by the different routes and the result has satisfied the Promoters that the proposed railway will when opened command a very large traffic in goods.

The passenger traffic will also be very great. A railway is now in course of construction from Llanrwst to Bettws-y-coed and active steps are being taken to make a new turnpike road from there to Blaenau for which purpose an Act of Parliament has recently been obtained. When these improvements have been carried out and the proposed railway made to Festiniog a line of country unrivalled in its beauties will be opened out to Summer Visitors and the number of Tourists passing along the route will be immense. The local passenger traffic will also necessarily be very great as it is intended to run cheap morning and evening trains for the convenience of workmen.

The traffic between Portmadoc and Trawsfynydd and the upper portion of the parish of Maentwrog will be secured to the proposed railway by improvements in the turnpike roads leading to those districts from Festiniog.

Looking at the cheapness of the line and the traffic that may be calculated upon the Directors anticipate that the capital to be expended will yield a high rate of dividend to the shareholders.

A large proportion of the capital has been already subscribed by the Promoters and the balance is now offered to the people of Festiniog and the neighbourhood generally. It is intended that the line shall be made by and for the benefit of the inhabitants of the district.

Applications for shares may be made on the following form and addressed to the Secretary, Robert Griffith at Melbourne House, Festiniog or to the Bankers, Casson & Co., Festiniog.

Applications for shares must be sent in before 20th October 1866.'

There followed a simple Application Form and the notice also appeared printed in Welsh.*

A resolution of 11 January 1868 increased the capital to £20,000, shares to be offered to existing holders in relation to their holdings. The Directors were authorised to borrow up to £1,000. On 22 March 1868 the Board was permitted to borrow up to £2,500 for buying rolling stock.

A glance at the list of promoters showed that they contained the principal complainants regarding the Festiniog's monopoly of coast-bound slate traffic and that they were among the biggest users of that line. As in later years in South Wales, when dissatisfaction and monopoly produced the strikingly militant Barry Railway, so here, sixteen years earlier, industrialists were tired of the shortcomings of the Festiniog route, and a line to connect Blaenau and Llan Festiniog was a cunningly contrived scheme; at this distant date, it is impossible to guess if the Festiniog board really appreciated what was in the wind. In any case, the Festiniog Company was fully engaged with its own problems, and in view of the fact that they hoped to introduce steam locomotives (and passenger working) very shortly—the former came about in October 1863—they probably thought little more than that this new extension to their line was an event they could willingly accommodate if steam power lived up to its promise.

Samuel Holland of Maentwrog and London was the moving spirit

* Ref. Brit. Trans. Hist. Records. Ref.: PROS. 1.

Surviving tracks at the junction of Welsh Highland Railway and a stub of the Gorseddau line, formerly the later connection between Gorseddau and Croesor systems. Portmadoc 1944.

J. I. C. Boyd

Train, believed to be at Duffws, about to leave for Llan Ffestiniog. This picture was found behind a Football Team photograph in the G.W.R. station, Blaenau Ffestiniog.

J. I. C. Boyd collection

Engineering

Engraving from 'Engineering' 15 April 1870, of Manning Wardle's engine for the F. & B. Rly.

J. I. C. Boyd

View south towards Tan-y-manod, with temporary course of original railway on left, and G.W.R.-period viaduct on site of former wooden structure on right. 1970.

J. I. C. Boyd collection

Tan-y-manod station, looking north towards Duffws, with double-armed semaphore signal.

L. T. Catchpole collection

No. 2 and train posed at Llan Ffestiniog in the 1870s.

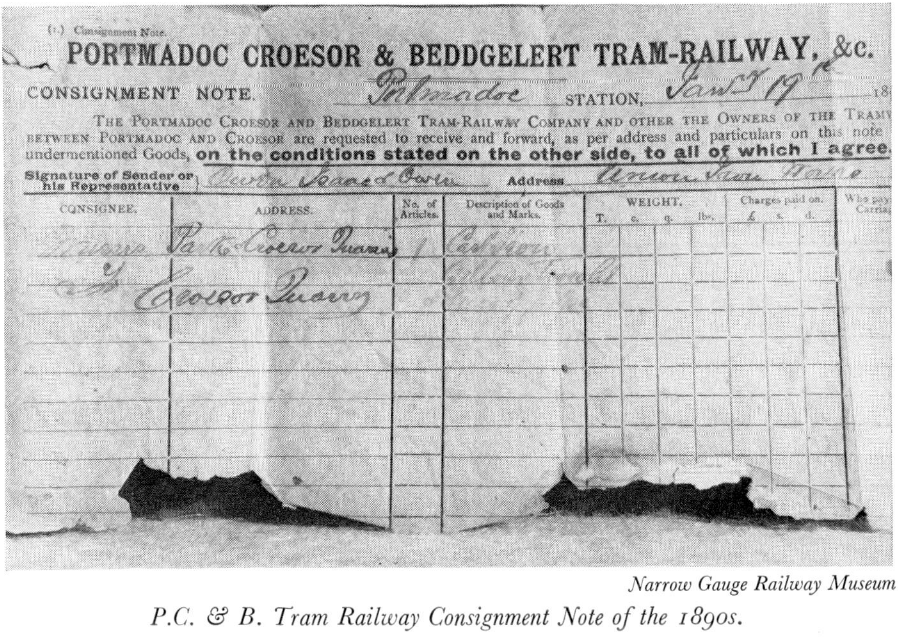

(1.) Consignment Note.

PORTMADOC CROESOR & BEDDGELERT TRAM-RAILWAY, &c.

CONSIGNMENT NOTE. ______ STATION, ______ 18

The Portmadoc Croesor and Beddgelert Tram-Railway Company and other the Owners of the Tramway between Portmadoc and Croesor are requested to receive and forward, as per address and particulars on this note the undermentioned Goods, **on the conditions stated on the other side, to all of which I agree.**

Signature of Sender or his Representative ______ Address ______

CONSIGNEE.	ADDRESS.	No. of Articles.	Description of Goods and Marks.	WEIGHT. T.	c.	q.	lbs.	Charges paid on. £	s.	d.	Who pays Carriage

Narrow Gauge Railway Museum

P.C. & B. Tram Railway Consignment Note of the 1890s.

Aerofilms

Portmadoc from the south, and the Glaslyn estuary. The intersection of standard and narrow gauges at the site of Portmadoc New station(s) in upper centre, the Croesor/Welsh Highland course leading off top right, the Gorseddau course past the Queen's Hotel at upper left and the Festiniog Railway Harbour station (lower right) are clearly visible.

in the F. & B.R. venture. He was later to become Member of Parliament for Merionethshire, and at the time his quarry's tonnages over the Festiniog were excelled by no other owner. His brother Charles of Liverpool, another active railway director, had a son, Charles Menzies Holland, who also joined the board. C. M. Holland was a civil engineer living in Wallasey, Cheshire. Other initial directors were quarry owners William Davies, Capt. T. H. Wynne, George and John Casson and Robert Roberts. Morgan Lloyd, Q.C. M.P., of Beaumaris and London and owner of an extensive estate on the south side of the Vale of Ffestiniog completed an influential picture. The official description was 'for a line from Diphwys on the Festiniog Railway to Festiniog, Merioneth'. It was to be of single line and to 1 ft. 11¾ in. gauge, a quarter of an inch more than the Festiniog figure. Capital was eventually £80,000 in £10 shares. The offices of the Company were at first in Melbourne House, Llan Ffestiniog, where the Manager and Secretary were housed; these offices as well as that of auditor were all filled by persons named Davies! In June 1868 it moved to Duffws terminus and there was also an office in Portmadoc.

C. M. Holland, though not termed Engineer to the undertaking, was given the task of building the line and equipping it. During the early 1860s he seems to have had something of a roving commission as he was engaged in superintending the building of a line from London to Croydon,* during which he occasionally went over to Messrs. George England & Co's works to review progress on the new locomotives for the Festiniog Railway, then building there. When the first locomotive trials took place at Portmadoc, he was in charge of one of the two engines. Holland had recently taken full credit for the Festiniog engine design, by letter to the editor of 'Engineering' from Essex Chambers, Manchester. Perhaps this is one reason, among others, why progress in building the new line was somewhat tardy.

Whilst the Festiniog was busily occupied firstly in introducing new motive power and, on 6 January 1865, starting a passenger service, the F. & B. bided its time patiently until the F.R. was in a position to cater for extra traffic and to see how the new power behaved over a period. Even with the slow progress of the works, and the problems of a viaduct at Tan-y-manod, locomotives for the new line were not ready for the opening on 29 May 1868. Between then and 31 August following trains were worked by the Festiniog Railway under contract.

C. M. Holland had advised the B.O.T. as early as 13 November 1867 that the line was ready for inspection, but nothing was then done. In May 1868 he wrote asking the B.O.T. to write to him at his

* Ref. Diaries of Samuel Holland.

London address: they replied that they could only reply to the Secretary of the Company.

At a meeting with the B.O.T. Holland discussed the position of a Railway Company not incorporated by Act of Parliament, and it was concluded that for B.O.T. purposes the Company should be treated as though it had been.

On 28 May 1868 Holland wrote to the B.O.T. urgently, asking for the line to be inspected by Friday of that week (its own locos presumably even then not being available for the service) 'as it is all-important to so small a concern to open their line before the close of this week and avail of the Whit Monday traffic'.

This letter conflicts strangely in date with the Official Inspection date and one must conclude it was made without Holland being aware of it, for Captain H. W. Tyler inspected and reported to the Board of Trade on 26 May 1868:

> 'This railway has been constructed for about 3½ miles, between the town of Festiniog and a junction near Blaenau with the existing line to Portmadoc, on a gauge of Two Feet or, more accurately, 1 ft. 11¼ in. in the clear. It has been made without Act of Parliament, but consent of the landowners, and it will be largely used by quarry workmen and others interested in the slate quarries. It is intended to run cheap trains morning and evening for the workmen. A considerable traffic in goods is also expected.
>
> The steepest gradient is 1 in 58. The sharpest curves have a radii of six chains.
>
> The permanent way is laid with rails of (here is denoted flat-bottomed section) section weighing about 38 lbs. to the lineal yard and secured by dog spikes to transverse sleepers. The sleepers are of larch averaging 4 ft. 9 in. long, by 8 in.×4 in. and are 2 ft. 4 in. apart at the joints and 2 ft. 7 in. at the intermediate spaces, from centre to centre.
>
> There are nine bridges over or under the railway, which appear to be standing well, and which are constructed of masonry, brickwork and timber. Certain symptoms of movement are however, visible in a cattle creep 2 m. 65 ch. from Festiniog, and in some of the retaining walls. These points should be carefully watched. There is a viaduct at three miles from Festiniog, originally constructed with four spans of 80 ft. each, covered by lattice girders of timber, resting on masonry piers and abutments. The girders having been constructed without camber, and applied to the viaduct in curved form, considerable deflection showed itself when they were erected, which has been partially obviated by the addi-

tion of intermediate trestles, reducing the spans to 40 feet. Halving the spans, and reducing also the load by half, these intermediate piers have quadrupled the relative strength of the girders. But the viaduct is not even now, with a view to permanent stability, in a satisfactory condition. I have therefore recommended that the intermediate trestles should be strengthened, that corbels should be added over them, and that covers should be added on the joints of the timbers forming the lower booms of the girders. The weight, however, to pass over the viaduct will be comparatively slight, the engines weighing only about eight tons each, and the trucks when loaded about $2\frac{1}{2}$ tons each.

I inclose a certificate signed by the chairman, under the seal of the company, stating that these works will be carried out, as well as that some improvements, which I have also recommended, will be made at the junction near Blaenau; and I am of the opinion that the sanction of the Board of Trade may, upon these conditions, be given to the opening of the line for public traffic.

A certificate should, however, also be given in regard to the working of the single line which is, I understand, to be conducted upon the train-staff system; and I have requested that this should be forwarded to the Board of Trade. This portion of line is, I am informed, to be worked under agreement by the Festiniog (to Portmadoc) Company, pending the completion of certain rolling stock which has been ordered for the Festiniog and Blaenau Railway.

Before closing this report, I think it only right to remark, as I have already done to some of the directors personally upon the spot, upon the question of speed, as connected with lines of this description, because I have observed a tendency to run undue risk in this respect.

I only consented to recommend the Board of Trade to sanction the opening of the railway to Portmadoc on the express condition that the same restriction should be borne in mind on the present occasion. These little railways, on a very narrow gauge, and neither constructed nor maintained with the same degree of perfection as a first-class passenger railway, may be worked with safety at slow but are not at present fitted for a speed of more than 10 or 12 miles an hour; and it is necessary, not only that such a rule should be laid down, but that the directors should by watchfulness and by a series of fines prevent their officers and servants from employing them at higher speed. Those who work them from day to day, finding how great a degree of safety is attainable upon them, are too apt to increase the speed of the trains; and they may do this for a time with impunity; but they will in doing so meet sooner or later with very disastrous consequences, unless they are checked in this respect, and prevented by the exercise of authority from exceeding the strict bounds of prudence; and they will thus also bring discredit upon a system which is very convenient in this particular district, and which may under proper control be worked with safety and efficiency.'

The conditions imposed by the Captain included:

1. The removal of certain facing points near the Blaenau terminus of the line, and also opposite the main junction signal box at that point.
2. The removal of the main junction semaphore signal and to reposition it at or nearly opposite the junction between the Festiniog and F. & B. Railways.
3. The said junction points be fitted with locking apparatus and until this is done, be locked between the passage of trains and subjected to a speed of 3 miles an hour.
4. That the viaduct at 3 miles be strengthened as suggested.

On 5 June 1868 the Board informed the Company that there was no objection to opening for public traffic; nevertheless, the passenger service appears to have commenced on 29 May!

At the start, the new line was worked so closely in conjunction with the Festiniog that 'it would almost have seemed to be a branch line of that concern' (see specimen timetables p. 90). Later,

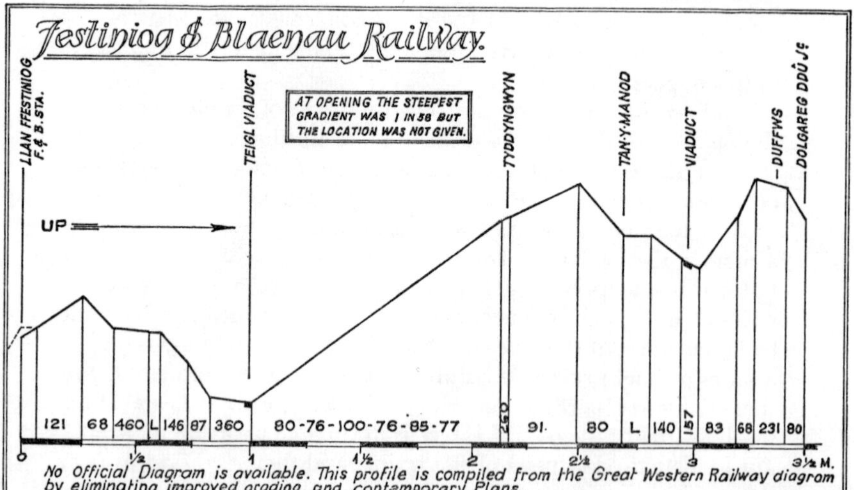

No Official Diagram is available. This profile is compiled from the Great Western Railway diagram by eliminating improved grading, and contemporary Plans.

the opposite was true; it had become a fierce competitor. During 1870 the Festiniog closed its Dinas terminal to passenger services and all trains ran to Duffws.

One of the causes of friction between Festiniog and F. & B. Railways was the slate rates. In 1864 the Festiniog offered lower rates to quarry owners in exchange for an agreement to use their line exclusively for the next fourteen years. Holland's and Greaves' quarries were among others which contracted to pay 2s. 6d. per ton. In 1871 the Festiniog made a contract with the Welsh Slate, Copper & Lead Mining Co. at 2s. 1½d. a ton but over an increased period of thirty years. When these terms were offered to the other quarry owners, they refused to accept them, pointing out that under the Regulation of Railways Act 1873, railway companies could not make unfair contracts between customers. Holland and Greaves took out an injunction against the Festiniog, claiming parity with other contract holders whom they maintained were being better treated. In February 1876 the Railway Commissioners granted an injunction against the Festiniog Railway. By the date of opening of the F. & B., the 2s. 6d. per ton contract had only run for four years out of fourteen. Even by that time, the motives of the Festiniog had become suspicious.

First public evidence of plans afoot for yet another new railway appeared in 'The North Wales Chronicle' for Saturday 28 January 1871 and was almost a word-for-word copy of the prospectus for a new railway: 'We understand that Standing Orders have been complied with as regards railway communication between Festiniog village and Talsarnau . . . it is proposed that the railway shall be constructed on the same gauge as the Cambrian and form a junction with the Festiniog & Blaenau Railway at about 300 yards distant from Festiniog village and then run to Hendre mur . . . through the valley of Felenrhydd-fawr and just above the waterfall down to within about 600 yards of the Pile Bridge over Waeth Bach estuary on the Talsarnau side, and form a double junction with the Cambrian Company's line.'

'The North Wales Chronicle' of 29 April 1871 also refers to a public meeting in the Market Hall, Blaenau Festiniog, to support a new railway to the town. This plan to tap the slate quarries and quit the Festiniog area (not the only one in which the Hollands were interested) received Parliamentary approval on 29 June 1871 as the Merionethshire Railway. The scheme was not only to rob the Festiniog Railway of traffic from Blaenau almost completely, but in part to give it to the Cambrian Railways, not at Minffordd—for which purpose the Festiniog Railway had to be traversed—but at Talsarnau, farther south along the Cambrian coast line.

This was not all of Samuel Holland's interests. He was also urging extension of the standard gauge westwards from Ruabon on the Shrewsbury–Chester section of the G.W.R. This had reached Corwen by May 1865 by means of the Llangollen & Corwen Railway; Bala by April 1868 (the Corwen & Bala Railway); and was being extended westward again by the Bala & Dolgelley Railway Act of 30 June 1862, the latter having suspended plans to thrust southwards by means of a line to Machynlleth and Aberystwyth. In this district it was Holland the Member of Parliament for the county at work, rather than Holland the quarry proprietor!

He now became associated with the formation of the Bala & Festiniog Railway, nominally independent but like all the foregoing lines, to all practical purposes under the Great Western umbrella. The B. & F.R. was to build a standard gauge line from a point short of the original Corwen & Bala Railway terminus south of Bala town, and extend up through the mountains on a spectacular route to make an end-on junction with the tiny but now strategic Festiniog & Blaenau Railway at Llan Ffestiniog. South of where Maentwrog Road station was later to be sited, there was to be another triangular junction with the Merionethshire Railway's line. The completion of these lines would have given slate an outlet from Blaenau to the south east; Holland had thrown in his hand with Paddington. As an alternative, it might be worked to the coast at Talsarnau, and taken by the Cambrian Railways thereafter. In the event, the standard gauge connection to Llan Ffestiniog was completed and the Merionethshire Railway proved to be unnecessary; powers to build lapsed in 1885 when it was allowed to die a natural death. The threat of it had played its part.

The period of the F. & B.R.'s narrow gauge existence, and the constant threat that a Merionethshire Railway would materialise, was evidently a source of concern to the Festiniog Company. Among Festiniog records, unfortunately undated, are drawings for a mixed standard and narrow gauge railway from Llan Ffestiniog into Blaenau with plans for a mixed gauge station on the site of the F. & B.R. Duffws terminal. Here the Festiniog would have entered from the west and the mixed gauge led off from the east. The mixed gauge line was shown on the site of the later standard gauge run-round loop and the narrow gauge only at the platform face, suggesting through working of minerals but passenger services worked by the Festiniog and F. & B.R. jointly. Perhaps this was one of the mollifying schemes conceived at the time. Trans-shipment facilities are absent; perhaps these were retained at Llan Ffestiniog.*

* See 'The Festiniog Railway', Vol. 1, p. 131 for details.

The heady wine of slate traffic figures had not only reached Paddington. The London & North Western Railway was always ready to fight the G.W.R. in the Principality. In January 1879 it too found its way into Blaenau Festiniog and opened to traffic on 22 July (though not before the seeds of a Great Western outlet from the town had already been planted). This line was to give J. W. Greaves at least, an outlet for his slate to the north, and other quarries including Holland's under its successors, came to use it. In the Festiniog & Blaenau story however, it plays no part; but as another narrow gauge project in south Caernarvonshire, it is related in Part 5.

It is convenient at this stage to examine in a little more detail, the Merionethshire Railway proposals, and then the Bala & Festiniog's successful birth. Firstly, the Merionethshire.

The F. & B.R. had only been working for three years when this scheme was given Parliamentary approval. The intentions of the rival factions were immediately clear. They threatened to build a 'mirror image' railway of the Festiniog which, instead of making its way westwards along the north side of the Dwyrd valley to Portmadoc, would wind its way westward along the south side and make a triangular connection with the Cambrian Railways just east of their Talsarnau station. At Llan Ffestiniog there was to be an end-on junction with the F. & B.R. Completion of the Festiniog 'image' was finalised by adopting the same gauge (given in the Act as Two Feet) and providing for exchange facilities near Talsarnau. The jargon of the Act simply described the line as intending 'to construct a junction between the Cambrian and Festiniog Railways' of length 10 miles.

There were to be three sections. Railway No. 1 was 3 m. 1 fur. 8 ch. 35 links in length from a junction in the parish of Ffestiniog with the Festiniog & Blaenau Railway, and terminating in the parish of Maentwrog in the plantation of a farm called Hendre mur—(the property of Morgan Lloyd, a director). Railway No. 2, 6 m. 7 fur. 8 ch. 5 links, was from a junction with Railway No. 1 at Hendre mur and terminating in the parish of Llandecwyn in a junction with the Cambrian Railways. It was stipulated that both Railways 1 & 2 should be built simultaneously, and that one should not be opened before the other. They were to be worked as one railway by the owning company. Railway No. 3 was simply the short curve forming the south connection at Talsarnau junction.

The Act also required the Company to run a train every morning of the week save on Sundays, from the junction with the Cambrian to the station at Llan Ffestiniog calling at all stations, and a similar daily return working. The outward journey was not to be made after 7 a.m. and the return not before 6 p.m., as might be most convenient.

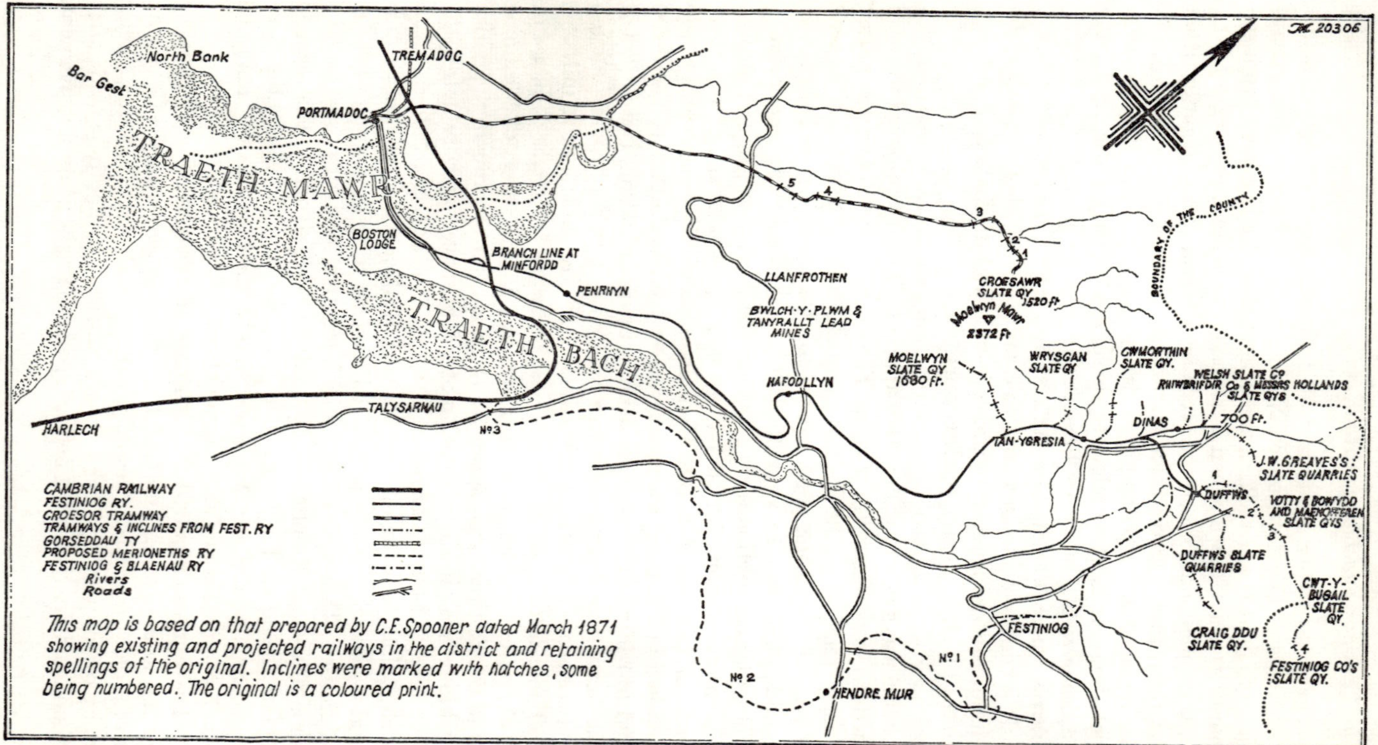

This map is based on that prepared by C.E. Spooner dated March 1871 showing existing and projected railways in the district and retaining spellings of the original. Inclines were marked with hatches, some being numbered. The original is a coloured print.

Quarrymen and labourers 'having daily occupation at the quarries in the parish of Ffestiniog . . . must be carried at fares not exceeding ¼d. per mile . . .' If during any period of three months less than 100 persons availed themselves of this service, the Board of Trade might allow the Company to discontinue it on application, but might re-instate it by order, under certain conditions. The Company might issue weekly tickets only for this service.

Arrangements might be concluded with the Cambrian and Festiniog & Blaenau companies.

As regards ownership of land and the interests of the promoters, it would seem that all landowners involved were earmarked to serve on the Board of seven directors save one. He was William Thearsby Poole through whose land ran Railway No. 2 for the last 5 chains before its junction with the Cambrian. Protection here was given to him by limiting the amount of deviation from the planned course.

Capital was £80,000 in £10 shares with loans up to £26,600 authorised.

Many of the names associated with the F. & B.R. reappeared—the Chairman was Samuel Holland, M.P. and though nephew Charles (then of Manchester) was not a director in this case, he was designated Engineer* in collaboration with J. W. Grover, M.I.C.E. of Westminster (then acting for the Hemel Hempsted & L.N.W. Railway). John Casson, J.P. (Banker) and Morgan Lloyd, M.P. (Barrister) were on the board of both lines, and additionally the Merionethshire included William Casson, J.P., Hugh Owen, A. A. Robinson and J. H. Foulkes, J.P., a Wrexham industrialist. Foulkes and Owen were directors of the Duffws Casson Slate Co. and Robinson had been a slate merchant. The offices were in Victoria Street, Westminster, initially, then moved to Oswestry and latterly to Pâle, Corwen, where the son of A. C. Sherriff (M.P. for Worcester), a director of the Bala & Dolgelley and many other lines, lived. According to who was holding office of Secretary, so the address of the Company's headquarters was changed! One of the auditors was the redoubtable James Frazer the younger, who included in a large portfolio of similar associations the Portmadoc, Croesor & Beddgelert Tram Railway Co. Ltd.

A bill lodged for the 1873 session of Parliament covering a railway between Bala and Festiniog (and with that title) referred to a proposal of working agreements and interchange of traffic between such a line and the Festiniog and Blaenau & Festiniog (sic) railways but when in fact the Act was obtained, reference to arrangements with the Festiniog did not appear! With the likelihood of much improved facili-

* He resigned the position in September 1871.

ties open to the F. & B. and the same promoters being involved, it is not surprising that no actual construction work was begun on the new Merionethshire Railway; the Bala & Festiniog plans included a triangular junction with the Merionethshire Railway south of Llan Ffestiniog which would thus have had such a junction at each end of its line. On the Merionethshire, the section between Duffws and Llan Ffestiniog was to be of mixed standard and two foot gauge, using three lines of rail. The Enquiry of 23 March 1871 before the House of Lords Select Committee had emphasised the company intended to take the standard gauge up inclines right into the Festiniog quarries if necessary!

Although the Merionethshire obtained further Acts on 27 June 1876 extending time for completion to 29 June 1879 and another on 3 July 1879 extending to 29 June 1882 and finally on 19 May 1882 allowing until 29 June 1885, these were simply a method of buying time until the position *vis-à-vis* the G.W.R. (or Bala & Festiniog Railway) and Festiniog relations had been resolved. As no work had been done by 29 June 1885, Merionethshire powers automatically lapsed. An Act for abandonment was obtained on 12 July 1887.

Secondly, the Bala & Festiniog scheme may be examined in more detail.

The G.W.R. thrust westwards from Ruabon had taken place through nominally independent companies which the G.W.R. worked and later absorbed; the progress westwards was marked thus—

Vale of Llangollen Railway.	Ruabon to Llangollen. Act of 1 August 1859. Opened to passengers on 2 June 1862.
Llangollen & Corwen Railway.	Llangollen to Corwen. Act of 6 August 1860. Opened on 1 May 1865.
Corwen & Bala Railway.	Corwen to Bala. Act of 30 June 1862. Opened on 1 April 1868.
Bala & Dolgelley Railway.	Bala (junction station with C. & B.R.) to Dolgelley. Act of 30 June 1862. Opened 4 August 1868.

As from 4 August 1868, the G.W.R. worked over the whole route as a branch line from Ruabon; on 29 May previously, the little Festiniog & Blaenau Railway had opened. The Bala & Festiniog was planned to bridge the gap between them.

By 21 December 1872 a Bill had been lodged 'for railways from Bala to Festiniog and Blaenau' and for 'working traffic and other agreements with the Great Western, Vale of Llangollen, Llangollen

& Corwen, Corwen & Bala, Merionethshire, Festiniog & Blaenau and Festiniog' railways with powers of some of those companies to subscribe. The Act was passed on 28 July 1873 for a line between the Corwen & Bala at Llangower Junction to Festiniog, of length 22¼ miles and in mixed gauge. The companies ranging westwards from Ruabon were invited to subscribe, as was the Great Western. Working arrangements were confirmed with the G.W.R. and Merionethshire.* The directors were an influential lot including Sir Watkin Wynn, M.P. of Wynnstay, Ruabon (industrialist etc.), Samuel Holland, M.P., John Robertson of Pâle (a director of all lines between Ruabon and Dolgelley), William H. Darby (the iron-master of Brymbo), Sir Daniel Gooch (of the G.W.R.), and William Wagstaff (director of all local lines, also of the Much Wenlock and certain Somerset railways). If businesses as today were valued by management potential, then the Bala & Festiniog was a strong team!

It was not long before the Bala & Festiniog Railway showed additional teeth. A scheme to extend westward from the south-west corners of Duffws station, traverse the north side of the Market Square and cross the open portion of ground opposite where the L.N.W.R. and Festiniog Exchange stations were to be sited, would have run roughly parallel to the Festiniog main line westwards out of Blaenau Festiniog. Then turning north-westwards, the line would have crossed the Festiniog immediately east of the Glan-y-pwll level crossing and continued northwards along the site of where the Festiniog Deviation Line of 1899 was laid. A Plan dated 1873, showing this proposal, underlines the aspirations of Holland and his associates to tap Hollands' and Greaves' quarries independently of the Festiniog.

Arrangements between the Bala & Festiniog Company and the Merionethshire were interesting. The Merionethshire's line between Llan Ffestiniog and a point where it crossed the Maentwrog–Trawsfynydd road at Hendre mur† was designated their Railway No. 1. This section of line was to enjoy reciprocal running powers for Merionethshire and B. & F.R. alike; the equipment, staff etc. to be of similar status. The B. & F.R.'s line was to connect with the cerned, as no construction had begun. Section 49 of the B. & F.R. Act Merionethshire at Hendre mur and for these last four miles of the

* But not the Festiniog Railway, which receives no mention in the Act. On the other hand Bradshaw's Manual of 1873, recording the incorporation etc. of the B. & F.R., states that arrangements *had* been concluded with the Festiniog.

† This approximates to the present end of the Blaenau-Trawsfynydd line spur as currently truncated near the nuclear power generating station.

M.R. to Llan Ffestiniog, a mixed gauge was to be laid. This would allow M.R. narrow gauge trains working east into Llan Ffestiniog and B. & F.R. trains working west to the same destination, to use the same set of mixed gauge rails.

Of course, all this was hypothetical so far as the M.R. was conrefers to that railway as 'running parallel to the Railway No. 1 as authorised by the Merionethshire Railway Act 1871' and not having powers to impede the M.R. from completing that length. Nor did the Act relieve the M.R. from any obligation to which they were liable to construct and open Railways Nos. 1 & 2 simultaneously; nor were they permitted to use their running powers on Railway No. 1 until Railway No. 2 had been completed.

In practice the two concerns intended that Railway No. 1 should not only be 'parallel' but to save expense, they should use the same formation and set of tracks. Mixed gauge trackage is so rare in the British Isles, that these proposed arrangements have been given in some detail; mixed narrow and standard gauge did not of course, ever come into existence on this length, but it is believed to have been used temporarily between Llan Ffestiniog and Duffws during gauge conversion.*

It is now convenient to return to affairs on the Festiniog & Blaenau Railway. The 1877 accounts show that during 1876 some heavy additional expenses had to be borne, especially by the Locomotive Department. In the same year the practice of running mixed trains ceased and goods/mineral trains ran separately. Train mileage increased by almost 30% and for the time being at least, it seemed that the promoters should be well satisfied with their success, even if the extraordinary figures for passenger traffic eventually turned out to be a once and for all phenomenon and were possibly boosted by development at Holland's and Rhiwbryfdir Quarries which had been reentered by Oakeley after the lease expired.

Possibly influenced by increased traffic, the change of mind of the L.N.W.R. and the now-approaching *standard gauge* railway of that Company from the north and the promise of the standard gauge Bala & Festiniog Railway from the south-east, the directors of the F. & B. did some quick thinking. Their relations with their narrow gauge neighbour the Festiniog, were not of the best and their own existence had sprung from lack of cordiality. To be sandwiched between standard gauge schemes and out of tune with the line to which they physically attached was unhealthy.

* Mixed gauge locations on other Railways have included: Ravenglass & Eskdale Railway, Welshpool & Llanfair Railway, Larne Harbour, and Londonderry Harbour.

Besides the somewhat uncomfortable position just described, there was the problem of financing considerable sums for refurbishing the line, which had taken some severe punishment since the opening. The obvious channel was through Holland himself and his position on the Bala & Festiniog; the outcome of some astute lobbying was that an Agreement was reached on 15 July 1876 whereby (a) the F. & B.R. was purchased by the B. & F.R. for £14,000, (b) shares in the B. & F.R. would be taken up by the F. & B.R. and (c) three years would be allowed to complete the purchase. Meanwhile the B. & F.R. would pay interest at 5% annually on £14,000 pending completion of the purchase.

There followed a Directors' Meeting of the Bala & Festiniog Railway at Paddington on 11 July 1876. The minutes state 'Arrangements with the Great Western Railway Company were discussed and specially the necessity of a subscription contract before the time of compulsory powers expired. The following subscriptions were arranged:

Great Western Railway Co.	£100,000
Llangollen Company	42,000
H. Robertson	28,000
Parties on behalf of the Blaenau & Festiniog (sic) to subscribe for (on the understanding that they are to be released hereafter to the extent to which that sum should exceed the value of their property under agreement with them)	12,000
Mr. Holland & Merioneth landholders	8,000
	£190,000

On 3 August following another meeting took place, considering especially the heavy costs recently borne by the Festiniog & Blaenau. Among those in attendance (not a director) was Henry Robertson, M.P. (who had promised to subscribe as above) who said he had been applied to with reference to the 'working of the Blaina and Ffestiniog railway and that he had instructed the Secretary and Manager to continue the present staff and mode of working under the discretion of Mr. Holland until further notice'. The Chairman added that 'Mr. Kelley would be instructed to examine and report as to the future working of the railway'. 25 October next saw another meeting. Messrs. Kelley and Chapman sent in a report on the F. & B. line, of its estimated revenue and expenditure. By then its track had got into a poor way and '10 Tons of rails and 600 sleepers were required for immediate repairs'. A purchase was authorised. Mr. Kelley was in-

structed 'to make such arrangements as may be necessary for putting the working arrangements of the line in a satisfactory state including obtaining indemnities in case of accident from the workmen carried over the line at low fares'.

From 28 February 1878, when the first sets of 'F. & B. New' and 'F. & B. Ltd.' accounts appeared, they were published separately but mounted together and got up in the same manner. F. & B. New had no Capital Account; F. & B. Ltd. had no entries under heading 'Working Stock' but under the same heading F. & B. New was said to possess '2 Engines, 2 Tenders, half a 1st Class Coach, half a 2nd Class Coach, 3 2nd Class Coaches, 20 Workmen's 'carriages' and 7 Goods Wagons'—little if any of which agrees with the B.O.T. Returns for stock made by the Company that same year! Whilst some explanations is that the figures were pure accountancy only, it could be that the two engines and tenders were Festiniog property—or was this a deliberate error to allow non-existent tenders to be written-down in the end-year accounts? If the motive power was Festiniog, perhaps on hire, had the F. & B.'s original engines been taken out of stock or 'forgotten' conveniently? Fortunately it is not essential to have answers to these intriguing reflections.

The principal income of the F. & B. Ltd. was the £700 'By interest received on part of the purchase money to be received in cash'. F. & B. New's Revenue Accounts are similar to those of a Company operating a railway and include such items as Maintenance of Way and Works. Griffith Griffith Davies, Manager of the F. & B. New, certified that line and rolling stock was in good order.

Accounts of this type appeared again in 1879, 1880 and 1881 but nowhere is the legal status of F. & B. New defined.

Payment of debts incurred by F. & B. Ltd. were recorded in a special book and from the time of the founding of the 'twin companies', the records have survived. A wage account for August 1876 lists the following employees: 1 Fitter, 1 Driver, 1 Master,* 1 Porter, 2 Platelayers, 1 Manager, 1 Secretary.

One may properly ask if a fireman or guard was employed or did the fitter drive and the driver fire when there was little to do in the workshop? Perhaps the porter doubled up as Guard? All this seems highly unlikely. The wage bill was £43 5s. 11. and was paid by cheque drawn on the North & South Wales Bank by the 'Trustees of the Bala & Festiniog Railway Co.'.

Connection with the G.W.R. is also clear from 1877 items; for example an account of 13 March from Paddington for putting a new set of brass tubes in a locomotive (obviously at Llan Ffestiniog and

* Station Master?

not at Swindon!) for a cost of £8 8s. 6d. This item was paid by the Bala & Festiniog Railway Company. In the following November the G.W.R. sent an account for supplying 2,000 card tickets, possibly due to the heavy demand on tickets for that season. There was also a bill for 'Nov. 1 & 2; To Mr. Kelley's travelling expenses to Barmouth and Blaenau to meet Mr. Spooner relative to signals'.

A Board Meeting of the Bala & Festiniog agreed to spend more money on the F. & B.R. when it met on 3 April 1878. Another 10 tons of rails were taken and the fencing was to be renewed in iron wire. The stations got a budget of £25 for repairs.

Mr. Kelley reported on an arrangement with the Festiniog Railway. This was on the basis of using each others wagons, four Festiniog to one F. & B. The F. & B. had not been playing the game and the Festiniog had given notice to end the arrangement. Worse, they had rubbed it in by proffering an account for hire of wagons up to December 1877 of £18 11s. 5d. Kelley was authorised to make the payment and patch up the quarrel with the Festiniog as best he could, as the use of Festiniog 'trucks' was essential to the F. & B.

There had clearly been complaints about the spartan nature of F. & B. passenger stock and it was agreed that estimates be obtained 'for enclosing the existing carriages'. There was a shortage of it too, and it was agreed that two new 3rd Class carriages be sought. The existing carriage stock was to be repainted.

In the outcome the G.W.R. supplied the new fences and fixed them for £150 and in July 1878 purchase of one 1st–2nd Class composite coach for £90 and one 3rd Class for £65 was authorised, suggesting that the earlier decision had been amended.

From 1 June 1879, maintenance of the F. & B.'s track was given to the G.W.R. at least in part, as they submitted an account for the subsequent six months' work of £95 10s. 0d.

On 26 October 1880 Mr. Breese, Solicitor to the F. & B.R., wrote to the Secretary of the Bala & Festiniog reminding him that the time for completing their purchase of the F. & B. had now expired and asking if they were now in a position to close the deal. The B. & F.R. manoeuvred round this question by referring it to their legal advisers, and matters dragged on, complicated by queries as to interest upon calls on certain shares. The last available B. & F. Minutes referring to the matter are dated 3 February 1881 and it was settled on 24 February.

During 1882 the F. & B.R. were using Festiniog wagons for their own needs and these were charged by weight. The Festiniog also charged the cost of working the junction at Blaenau at £66 per annum, plus costs of any repairs; Spooner refused to share the cost.

A Festiniog account of 14 July 1880 reads 'To use of engine to work the traffic; £1 0s. 0d.' but no period is given.

Work on the new railway's difficult terrain between Bala and Llan Ffestiniog took its time; but under an agreement of 27 March 1879, it was to be worked by the G.W.R.* Even before this, it was clear that the time for completion under the original Act was insufficient; another Act of 16 April 1878 extended the time to 28 July 1881. The official record of 1882 no longer records 'mixed gauge' but 'narrow gauge', probably to distinguish the G.W.R. connection and to use a term so often made to distinguish it from the two gauges of the G.W.R., the standard (or 'narrow') and the broad! Under the Great Western's Act of 6 August 1880, the B. & F.R. (with which the G.W.R. was associated) received power to absorb the Festiniog & Blaenau Railway and on 23 May 1882 it was resolved that the F. & B.R. Co. Ltd. be wound up voluntarily. William Davies of Ca'er-blaidd, Festiniog, was appointed Liquidator. He was able to report that his work was completed on 21 April 1884. On 13 April 1883, the little F. & B.R. became vested in the Bala & Festiniog, so finally becoming to all intents and purposes, part of the Paddington empire.

Out on the ground, so to speak, the 22-mile new railway from Bala opened to Llan Ffestiniog on 1 November 1882, but not until further powers were granted for an extension of time. Conversion of the remaining 3½ miles of two foot gauge, for which most of the necessary civil engineering had been done when the F. & B. was built, was completed by 10 September 1883. It makes interesting speculation as to how services were worked over this short distance during conversion or whether they were suspended completely for eleven months. Possibly the long-considered mixed gauge came into its own at last, but not for the purpose nor on the section that the original promoters intended! Although the new standard gauge line almost obliterated its predecessor, it had now to provide for the carriage of slate; in one respect this presented no problem as it could be carried in open wagons. In another, and with special reference to loading arrangements at Tan-y-manod station, 'pick-a-back' type wagons had to be built to carry the loaded narrow gauge wagons. The G.W.R. was not the first main line company to adopt this system at Blaenau Festiniog; the London & North Western had adopted it for their traffic north through the Conway Valley. Both companies built their own narrow gauge wagons for the traffic, and as with the Festiniog Railway, offered them to the quarries for use within their workings. Details of

* In that year the G.W.R. asked the Festiniog Railway to work the F. & B., but they declined. They required track and exchange facilities at Llan Ffestiniog which the G.W.R. would not entertain.

G.W.R. and L.N.W.R. narrow and standard gauge wagons and workings will be found in the Appendix to Volume 2. On opening of the standard gauge over the F. & B. trans-shipment wharves and goods shed were provided between G.W. and Festiniog railways, together with a dock for off-loading the 'pick-a-back' wagons.

The Route described

(Generally speaking, the district through which the railway passed has changed little over the last one hundred years. Although Llan Ffestiniog, Manod and Blaenau Festiniog have grown, the basic nucleus of these places already existed by the mid-1860s. The route of the railway in the 1970s presents in general, a similar appearance to that of the 1860s. The re-gauging of the line, and the improvement of structures etc. by the Great Western Railway, together with the levelling of extreme gradients carried out in the years before the First War, swept away some of the civil engineering of the first railway. The course of the line between Duffws and Llan Ffestiniog is still occupied by a single line of track used for access to the Nuclear Power Station at Trawsfynydd. The section of line between Llan Ffestiniog and the present terminus at Trawsfynydd is almost exactly on the course of the proposed Merionethshire Railway, never built.)

The railway was laid through undulating country, lying between 600 and 700 ft. up the upper east side of the Vale of Ffestiniog. To its west side the ground fell steeply into the Vale, and to the east there was a less steep rise towards the twin summits of Manod Mawr (2,166 ft.) and Manod Bach (1,575 ft.) which overlook the town of Blaenau Festiniog. The first two miles of the journey were through rugged upland country, largely treeless and often rocky.

The terminus station at Llan Ffestiniog lay just to the south-west, but some 30 feet below, the later standard gauge station. It was at the junction of the Dolgelley and Bala roads, the latter having been diverted south round the end of the station—and diverted even further when the line was linked up to form a continuous standard gauge branch. Opposite the station was a toll house and adjacent was built a chapel (still standing) with inscripion 1868, the year of the opening of the Festiniog & Blaenau line. When the standard gauge station was closed, a brick kiln embodied in its embankment was discovered beside the old narrow gauge station site; this is now a garage. From the terminus, the line climbed (gradient unrecorded) to the existing bridge at the north end of the standard gauge yard. The alteration in course and gradient between the two lines under this bridge is still perceptible.

It may be mentioned that the Dolgelley road forms in part the old

Roman highway of Sarn Helen, which now accompanies the railway for a very short distance to the north-east. It connected Roman Forts at Kanovium (Conway) and Tomen-y-mur (near Trawsfynydd). Near here is the site of the Graves of the Men of Ardudwy, a spot which may be picked out from the line. Legend has it that the local men of Ardudwy, tired of their own women, raided the Vale of Clwyd; after capturing a number of women, they set off for home. The men of Clwyd pursued them over the mountains and overtook them just outside Llan Ffestiniog where they were slaughtered. Apparently the women were not best pleased about this and not wishing to return with their own men, drowned themselves in a near-by lake, now a reservoir. The existence of the gravestones does not seem to have been officially vouched for during the last one hundred years!

Returning to the more material matter of the former terminal station, although outlines of the property survive, no track plans exist. There was a long wooden building with slate roof along the east side of the station; this appears to have done multiple duties as locomotive, carriage and repair shops. It is believed there was a small additional building used for station office, store and passenger shelter. Siding accommodation included a coal siding and possibly a wharf for slate loading, the latter being unconfirmed.* Certainly the G.W.R. received sufficient slate here to build a slate transfer shed (latterly owned by the Manod Quarry) in addition to a goods shed.† There was no platform. Signalling was of simple form; a common post just inside the station limits served to admit incoming trains and as a starter. Like early Festiniog examples, there were two arms on either side of the top of the post. These were worked by hand levers on the post at the foot.

The line climbed from the terminus in a slightly north-easterly direction and passed under a small road bridge (not the existing one) to climb a short distance at 1 in 121. After a level crossing (now an underbridge), it curved more easterly and began a fall at 1 in 68 which eased to 1 in 460 and then became level for a little time. The track now ran along the south edge of the Afon Teigl valley, the prominent feature being the dome of Manod ahead and the rough upland country to the east. Beginning a semi-circular sweep anti-clockwise, the fall began at 1 in 146, increasing to 1 in 87 and then 1 in 360. Here there was an embankment and the Teigl was crossed by a curved stone bridge. The railway had fallen about forty feet since Llan Ffestiniog and this was the lowest point on the line (1 mile).

* The official G.W.R. diagram of 1923 shows a double-road building marked 'Slate Shed'.

† In F. & B.R. days, Morgan Lloyd's Drum Quarry sent slates here by cart.

Rounding up from the bridge there was a cutting followed by a stiff climb along the north flank of the Teigl valley in short lengths between 1 in 76 and 100; behind, the line could be seen swinging in a great curve back towards Llan Ffestiniog and ahead, but to the west, the wooded Vale of Ffestiniog fell towards the open sea beyond, so much in contrast with the present surroundings of the line. The original starting level of the line was now reached, but climbing continued, now in a northerly direction on a high embankment and

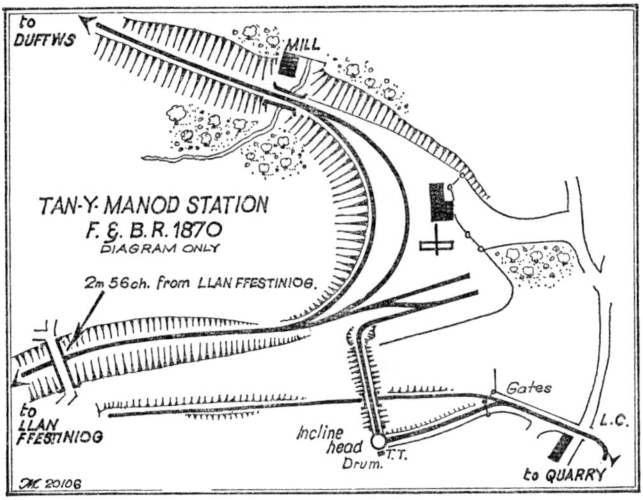

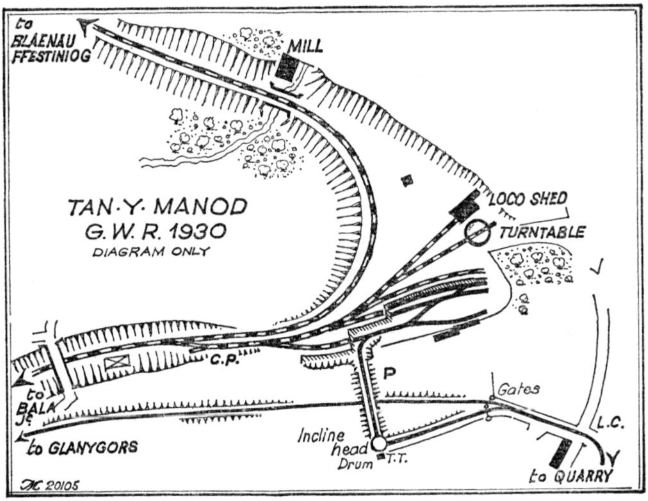

somewhat above the Llan Ffestiniog–Blaenau Festiniog road, past the hamlet of Telei-bach and with another slight curve to follow the contour of the hill, the line crossed the road on the level at Rhiwlas and left the open country behind (2 miles). From here into Duffws, housing and quarrying changed the whole picture. Groups and clusters of whitewashed small dwellings huddled wherever rock outcrop or contour permitted. The track passed over the Maentwrog road and the grade eased to 1 in 260 momentarily for Tyddyngwyn station, named after a large (for those times) residence nearby. There was no loop here, but probably a short siding, with a small building (2 m. 14 ch.).

In standard gauge times—and much more recently at that—a standard gauge branch was put in just beyond this point to serve the Pengwern Granite Quarry. Its course is still very clear. It crossed the main street to reach the granite bins and immediately beyond the site of this siding there lie the remains of its predecessor—high and low level standard gauge exchange sidings where they met a narrow gauge branch from the granite quarry. This installation does not date from F. & B. times of course, but the point where the narrow gauge branch crosses the street and dives under the Tan-y-manod slate quarry incline, is probably an alteration in arrangements which followed the conversion of the F. & B. from narrow gauge.

These two sets of standard gauge granite sidings were on a rising gradient of 1 in 91. It brought the former F. & B. onto a steep promi-

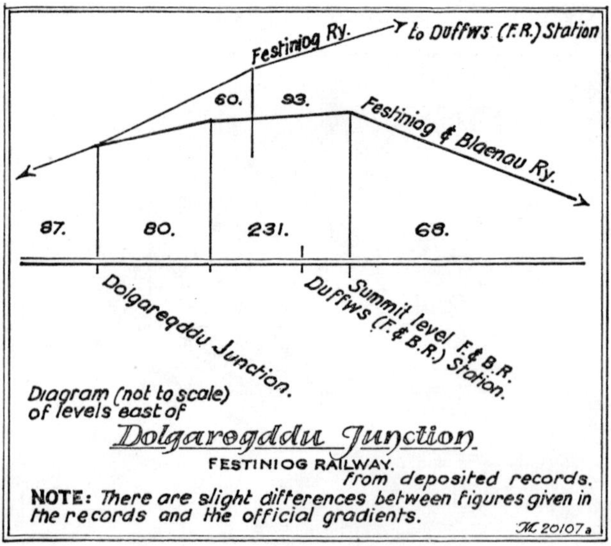

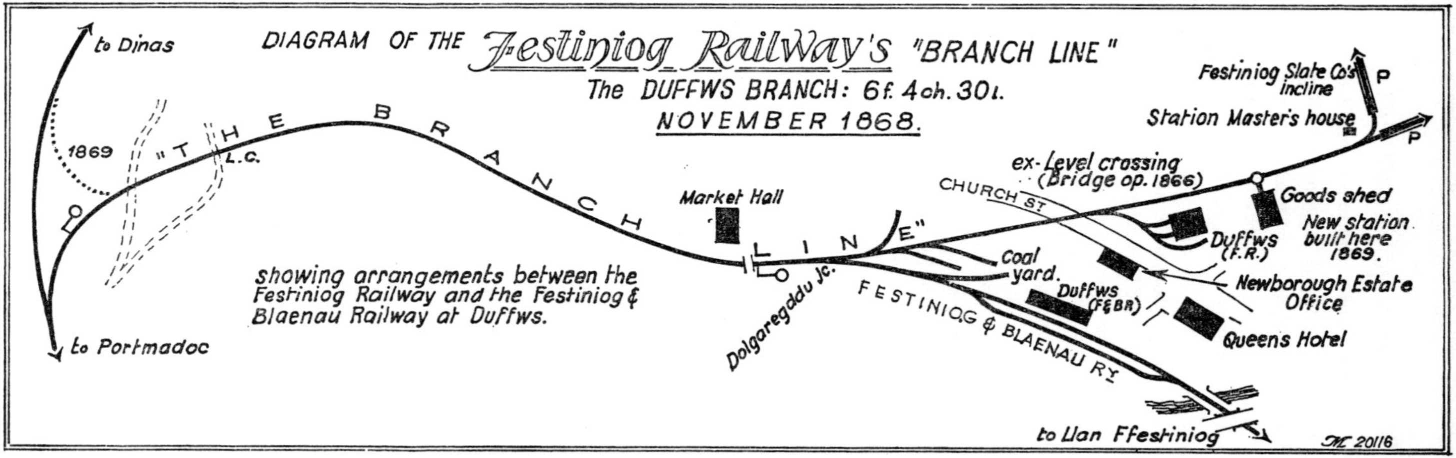
DIAGRAM OF THE Festiniog Railway's "BRANCH LINE"
The DUFFWS BRANCH: 6f. 4ch. 30l.
NOVEMBER 1868.
to Dinas
to Portmadoc
1869
"THE BRANCH LINE"
L.C.
showing arrangements between the Festiniog Railway and the Festiniog & Blaenau Railway at Duffws.
Market Hall
Dolgaregddu Jc.
FESTINIOG & BLAENAU RY.
Coal yard.
Duffws (F&BR)
CHURCH ST.
ex-Level crossing (Bridge op. 1866)
Duffws (F.R.)
Newborough Estate Office
Queen's Hotel
Goods shed
New station built here 1869.
Station Master's house
Festiniog Slate Co's incline
P
P
to Llan Ffestiniog
JIC 20116

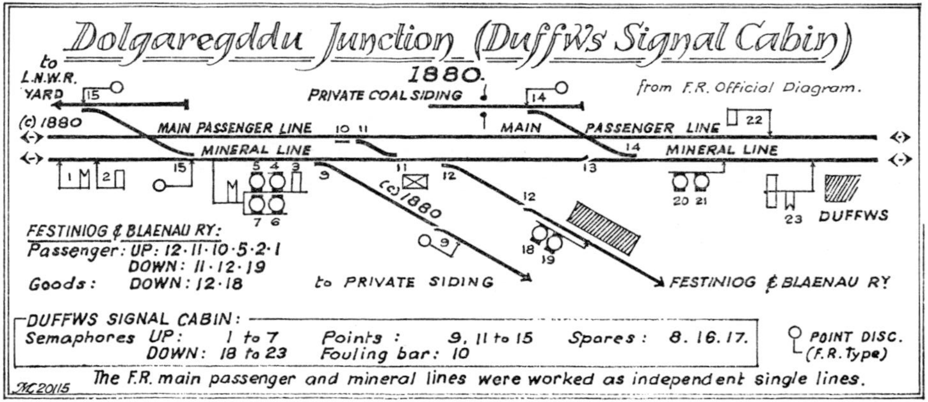
Dolgaregddu Junction (Duffws Signal Cabin)
1880.
from F.R. Official Diagram.
to L.N.W.R. YARD
(c) 1880
PRIVATE COAL SIDING
MAIN PASSENGER LINE
MINERAL LINE
MAIN PASSENGER LINE
MINERAL LINE
(c) 1880
DUFFWS
FESTINIOG & BLAENAU RY:
Passenger: UP: 12·11·10·5·2·1
DOWN: 11·12·19
Goods: DOWN: 12·18
to PRIVATE SIDING
FESTINIOG & BLAENAU RY
DUFFWS SIGNAL CABIN:
Semaphores UP: 1 to 7 DOWN: 18 to 23
Points: 9, 11 to 15
Fouling bar: 10
Spares: 8. 16. 17.
POINT DISC. (F.R. Type)
The F.R. main passenger and mineral lines were worked as independent single lines.
JIC 20115

nence overlooking the valley of the Bowydd, which fed below into the Vale of Ffestiniog. From this excellent vantage point the whole of Blaenau Festiniog and its quarries can be embraced, and the translation of Blaenau into 'valley' becomes quite obvious. The clockwise curve of the line continued before it fell under an occupation bridge at 1 in 80 to level out on a reverse curve on which Tan-y-manod was sited. In doing so it exchanged a cutting on the hillside for embankment construction. Tan-y-manod was the largest intermediate stop. There was a long loop, a wooden building on the east side together with double-armed signal, and sidings accommodation. On the south side was a slate wharf and connection leading to an incline which climbed to nearby road level and at its summit, a track therefrom led over the road by a level crossing. Here was a reversing neck and by means of two inclines 1,326 yards long, a tramway reached Craig ddu Slate Quarry and, by means of a third, Manod Slate Quarry. (The lease to build a tramway up to the 'New Craig ddu Slate Coy. Ltd.' from Glangors Inn, is dated 31 December 1865.) These were the most important slate feeders to the F. & B.R., and it would seem that the station loop at Tan-y-manod was used more as a slate wagon storage siding than for passing purposes. (The importance of this interchange point was not dimmed with the coming of the standard gauge. Wharfage and interchange facilities were provided on an even greater scale by the G.W.R. who also had a locomotive shed and turntable on the site of the F. & B. station premises. It was between here and Blaenau that the G.W.R. ran pick-a-back flat wagons carrying narrow gauge slate wagons.)

On leaving Tan-y-manod, the Afon Du-bach was crossed on a stone arch containing also, a mill leat. For the remaining distance into Duffws the line was mainly on intimate terms with the backs of houses on the west side of the main street which tumbled down beside the railway in untidy fashion sometimes to sprawl below it. Their intensity grew as Duffws was neared. The railway was obliged to pick its way between housing and small side streets, very much the intruder. Various forms of construction were involved, mainly using earthen embankment and some considerable slab walling on the west side to shore it up.

Just north of the Afon Du-bach bridge, an awkward fall in the ground had to be crossed. Presumably the Engineer, working on the principle of least expense, decided that a cheap viaduct rather than filling would be better. There thus arose the wooden spanned bridge, 320 ft. long with timber girders mounted on masonry piers, about which the Inspecting Officer was none too happy and which doubtless contributed to delays in opening the line. In order to reduce these and to connect either side of the bridge, a temporary railway was laid down along a shelf on the steep slope below the west side of the main street. The quality of work here was, of course, much inferior to the permanent work but oddly enough this temporary length remains as the only memorial on site of the old narrow gauge section, and may still be inspected. All other work was swept away when the route was rebuilt for standard gauge, including the feature which a Paddington-directed railway would not tolerate, the wooden bridge. In its place an eleven-arch stone viaduct arose.

North of the bridge, permanent and temporary F. & B. courses merged and a westward curve continued. Then followed a short length of line which must have proved most expensive. On the route at the present day there first comes a road crossing (gated) followed by a deep cutting taking a reverse curve through the edge of the town. On this section are three overbridges carrying streets; one is a stone arch and two are wrought-iron spans with ornamental railings, the latter supplied by Brymbo Ironworks in 1882 (the year of conversion) as their inscriptions prove. The middle bridge is the stone one and on the only site of an overbridge shown on contemporary maps of the F. & B.R. The present arch is not the original. The streets flanking it, and for which the Brymbo bridges were used, did not exist in 1868 but may have come into being before the F. & B. was converted. Lest it might be concluded that the Brymbo bridges were exclusively used in converting the F. & B. section, this is not so, as they are to be found in other locations on the Bala line and on other railways of North Wales, notably in Flintshire. They would seem to have been a standard product of the foundry. Beyond the last of the three bridges, the deep cutting's sides are now walled, and in the cutting bottom is the summit level. As for gradients, there was a fall from Tan-y-manod of 1 in 140 and 1 in 187, then a sharp pull up to Duffws at 1 in 83 and 68. The summit (720 ft.) was just before Duffws station through which was a downgrade of 1 in 231 (3 m. 32 ch.). On entering the station the Afon Bowydd was crossed on a low span.

Duffws was a stone building, suitably semi-pretentious enough to house the Company's offices! That was about all, there being no platform, but only a run round loop and, beyond the station, a single siding for coal. A lane ran up beside the station towards the Queens Hotel to reach the main street; across and over on the other side was (for the first year or two anyway) the even more primitive station of the Festiniog Railway.

Westwards from Duffws, the F. & B.R. fell at 1 in 80 for about ten chains to Dolgaregddu Junction, where it merged with the Festiniog's 'Branch Line' (3 m. 40 ch.).

A feature of 1878 was an apparent increase in trackage reflected by the much larger Works and Way expenses for that year in the Returns. The First Schedule, made up annually for the Board of Trade, sheds a little light on this. Up to 1874 the Schedule had not been returned; in 1875–6 the railway stated it had one connection with a passenger line, one with a goods line (presumably the same one, i.e. with the Festiniog Railway) and the main line made junction with sidings at four other points. B.O.T. regulations had been complied with at five of these six and one point was fitted with locking. There were no safety points. In 1877 whilst the junction point remains, no less than thirteen points made junction with the running line, suggesting that nine other sidings had been laid in during the year to cope with traffic. These seem to have been controlled by fourteen ground levers having no locking.

The Second Schedule was first returned in 1874 and in that year the length of line was given as 4 miles. Thereafter it shrank to '3 m. 60 chains' for the remainder of its narrow gauge life. In fact, it was somewhat less than this!

Permanent Way

The Board of Trade report regarding the Inspection of May 1868 is one of two sources of reference concerning the Railway's track. Vignes' account appeared ten years later. The Inspection Report unfortunately does not specify the type of rails used in words, but uses a small drawing which if taken literally would mean they were of conventional flat-bottomed type. The date on which these rails were first used in North Wales is not known, but possibly the Talyllyn of 1865 was the pioneer of them, and even then its Engineer, James Swinton Spooner of the Portmadoc family, appeared uncertain of their behaviour and put the rail into keyed chairs. Perhaps then, if the B.O.T. Report is taken on its face value, we may conclude that the F. & B.R. was the first passenger-carrying, locomotive-hauled, narrow gauge railway to be laid in what became a conventional form, using dog spikes to hold the flat bottomed rails to wooden sleepers. The predecessor of this type of track was the T-bottom-flanged rail held in chairs used by Gorseddau and Croesor, to name two of many users and, in view of recent discovery, probably in mid-Wales on the Corris, Machynlleth & River Dovey Tramroad when opened in 1859, but not copied by its neighbour the Talyllyn seven years later.

Details of the track as inspected in 1868 have already been given. The weight of rails (38 lb. per yard exactly as quoted by C. M. Holland to the Board of Trade) was another point of similarity with Talyllyn. If this rail is the curious section of flat-bottomed material still to be found as anchorages in the present standard gauge section

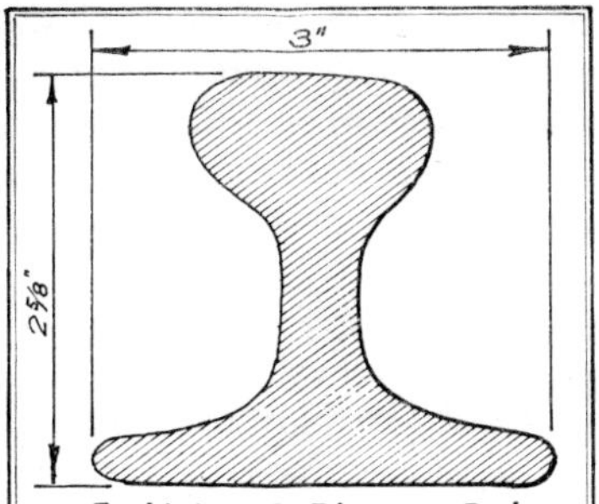

Festiniog & Blaenau Railway.
Section of rail unearthed on the course 6'II'71.

embankment on the F. & B.R. route, then it was unique to the Railway. (See drawing above.) By 1878 Vignes said the track was 'similar to the old Festiniog Railway track material save for certain replacements in more recent years'. He describes the rails as being 18 kilos per metre (about 39 lb.) with fishplated joints. These may have been the flat-bottomed rails just described, or something else. At this period the Festiniog was dispensing with its Phase Three track as quickly as possible. It was not standing up to the steam locomotive working over it. Introduced first in 1846, it had parallel section rails (the first forms had had fish bellies) in wrought iron, 21 ft. long and weighing 30 lb. per yard. In 1868 Holland specifically stated the gauge of the F. & B. was 1 ft. 11¼in.—'similar to that of the Festiniog Railway . . . (the rails upon the Festiniog Railway weighing 32 lb. per yard)'. In 1852 the same form of rail had been strengthened up to 42 lb. per yard and both weights of this rail were in use on the Festiniog main line until 1868 when double-headed wrought-iron rails were first laid. The Phase Three rail was of T-bottom-flange type once again, but much heavier than Gorseddau or Croesor specimens. Chairs held by iron pegs to wooden sleepers were used; by 1868 the iron keys had given way to wooden ones. If these two accounts, ten years' apart, are accepted, then clearly the flat-bottomed track first installed did not stand up to usage and in 1878 in particular, the B.O.T. Returns show an exceptional rise in costs of Works and Way—possibly a most necessary injection of new (second hand) material into the track? (Recently the Author found a 'Phase Three' Festiniog chair on the present standard gauge site of the F. & B.R.; this proves nothing, but its existence at this late date and so far from the old Festiniog Railway or from a quarry which might have used it in its tramway, adds a little bit of intrigue to the little we know.)

The original Festiniog four-wheeled engines worked regularly over the F. & B., especially in its latter years. They would not take kindly to track of a type which by then would no longer be in use on their parent line. The F. & B.R. engines, with their extra axle and a 5 in. shorter fixed wheelbase, would not be at such disadvantage.

Signalling

Where positions are known, these have been mentioned in the description of the line. Vignes states there was no signalling nor method of working the single line by staff; instead, the One Engine in Steam system was in force. Vignes was obviously wrong about both! The semaphores were of the Festiniog variety having double arms at the top of the post. The F. & B. types were more sophisticated as the red and green lenses and the attendant lamps were fixed lower down the post in the manner of the times. Hand levers which could be pinned through small quadrants at the foot of the post, worked the arms. Painting was conventional for left-hand running at the passing loops. The posts were surmounted by an iron finial and from the limited evidence available it is possible that the equipment was supplied by Messrs. Saxby & Farmer of Kilburn, London.

Train staff working was insisted upon by the Board of Trade inspector in 1868 though admittedly the 1878 Passenger Timetable could be covered by one engine alone.

*Locomotives**

No.	*Name*	*Type*	*Builder*	*Works No./date*	*Sold or Scrap*
1	*Scorcher*	0–4–2 ST	Manning Wardle	258/1868	1883
2	*Nipper*	0–4–2 ST	Manning Wardle	259/1868	1883

'Engineering' for 15 April 1870 contains the following article:

> 'We publish . . . an engraving of one of a pair of tank locomotives constructed by Messrs. Manning Wardle & Co. of Leeds, for the Festiniog & Blaenau Railway . . . which forms an extension of the well-known Festiniog Railway. It is worthy of notice here that although Messrs. Manning Wardle & Co. have never supplied any engines for the Festiniog line itself, they were the first locomotive builders who got out complete designs for engines to work on that railway . . .'

It would be out of place here to go into detail concerning the introduction of steam locomotives on the narrow gauge in these islands. It is sufficient to summarise by saying that C. M. Holland, nephew of Samuel Holland Jnr., director of the line and engineer

* Official Gauge 1 ft. 11¾ in. Gauge in Locomotive maker's catalogue and 'Engineering' 1 ft. 11¼ in. Gauge in Vignes' survey 1 ft. 11½ in. exactly (sic.).

to the Merionethshire Railway appears on the evidence to have been responsible for much of the design of the first two-foot gauge engines, which began work on the Festiniog Railway in August 1863. These engines were built by George England & Co. of Hatcham, London, their geographical advantage being that Holland was then working nearby on the London to Croydon Railway and could visit England's to supervise the work. Clearly however, other manufacturers had submitted designs* and in fact that of Manning Wardle, received on 7 November 1862, was the *last* of twenty nine submissions.

Of Manning's previous experience, their Official List gives a 3 ft. gauge engine as being the first to leave their works in 1859; nothing of lesser gauge appears until the entry for the F. & B. engines which, with charming unreliability states that they were built to the order of the 'Ffestiniog Railway Co.'. They were delivered new to 'Ffestiniog'. (Manning's were later to build a number of even narrower gauge engines, for in 1871 they supplied the first of a series of four-coupled saddle tanks for the 1 ft. 6 in. gauge railway at Woolwich Arsenal.)

Whilst the first Festiniog engines were small for the gauge, the F. & B. examples were little larger. For some reason their width was restricted to a maximum of 5 ft. 6 in. and may have been due to lack of certainty on the part of early designers as to how 'top heavy' a saddle-tank engine full of water might be on the narrow gauge! Free of any inherited limitations on loading gauge, it is difficult otherwise to see why F. & B. stock was so small—it would not appear that there was any intention to work it through over the Festiniog proper.

No record exists of the paint colour but it is suggested they were in Indian Red with double lining in yellow. The engine number was carried on the bunker panel in paint and oddly, maker's plates do not appear on any illustration. After delivery, the names *Scorcher* and *Nipper* countersunk on brass plates, were fixed to the flat sides of the saddle tanks.

The chimney was the slender elongated form of the maker's standard pattern; there was no footplating at all save in the cab and bunker. Frames were inside as was the Stephenson valve gear. The smokebox door was of the flat, horizontally hinged type covering the lower part of the box and flanking the smokebox sand boxes were fitted after delivery. Beneath the beams at each end was a plough-shaped device to clear obstructions from the rails. Coal was carried

* A full list is shown on p. 380 of 'The Festiniog Railway', Vol. 2, together with other notes on early Festiniog locomotive deliberations, on adjoining pages.

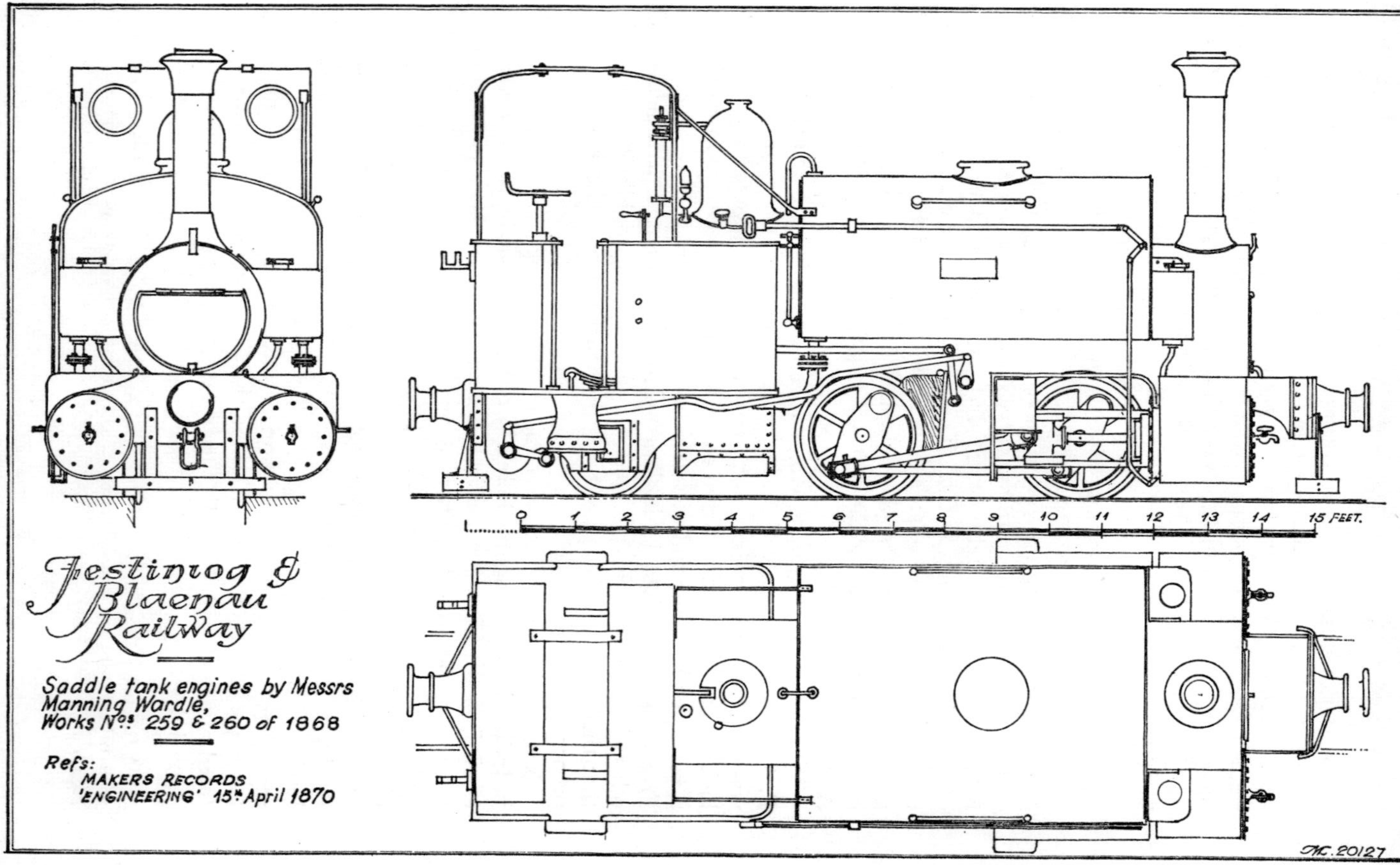
Festiniog & Blaenau Railway
Saddle tank engines by Messrs Manning Wardle,
Works Nos: 259 & 260 of 1868
Refs:
MAKERS RECORDS
'ENGINEERING' 15th April 1870
0 1 2 3 4 5 6 7 8 9 10 11 12 13 14 15 FEET.
M.C. 20127

in pocket bunkers before the front cab sheet and braking was limited to a handbrake working wooden blocks on the driving wheels only (not the front drivers). The rear wheels were carried in outside bearings in the main frame plates but given adequate sideplay for curves. The outer firebox, as usual with the makers, was of larger diameter than the boiler and carried the dome.

The springs from the Salter safety valves, on top of a large brass dome cover, were carried through the front cab sheet in the customary way. The rear protection was a separate cab sheet, the overturns of each sheet being connected by two stiffening members over which a canvas sheet might be thrown in bad weather. *Nipper* was modified in this respect, the turnover from the back sheet being removed and the stiffening members cut back short to the extent of the front turnover. Both engines had stiffening stays fitted to the front sheets after delivery. A step alongside the motion bracket was fitted each side to enable the fireman to reach the tank filler, at the same time. Between the cylinder and the motion bracket, a cover plate was fitted to protect valves and motion. All springs were laminated, the rear pair projecting considerably up through the cab footplate across the entrance openings.

Overall length was 18 ft. over buffers; width 5 ft. 6 in.; driving wheels 2 ft. 3 in. diameter (Manning Wardle's own pattern with boss-type counterweight and having only four spokes); trailing wheels 1 ft. 6 in. diameter; wheelbase 4 ft. 1 in. + 4 ft. 9 in.; outside cylinders $8\frac{1}{2}$ in. × 14 in. at 3 ft. 5 in. centres. Tractive effort 3,853 lb.; boiler pressure 120 lb.; boiler 6 ft. 11 in. × 2 ft. 5 in.; tubes 92 of $1\frac{1}{2}$ in. diameter; grate area $4\frac{3}{4}$ sq. ft.; total heating surface $284\frac{1}{2}$ sq. ft.; water capacity 300 gallons; weight empty 8 tons; in working order 11 tons. (Holland had estimated $8\frac{1}{2}$ tons.)

Tradition has it that as traffic grew, work became too heavy for one engine and they were often used as a pair. This was Festiniog practice at the time. Festiniog engines helped out when required. By the time of gauge conversion, boiler pressures were down to 80 lb. which would not help! Neither engine came into G.W.R. stock, both being sold or scrapped about 1883.

Passenger Carriages

In 1878 there were six passenger carriages, two 3rd class being new that year as already noted (but not agreeing with the numbers shown in Statutory Returns). There was another of unknown type, possibly a special vehicle for the use of the Board and others. The public vehicles were built by Ashbury Railway Carriage & Iron Co., of Belle Vue, Manchester, and were quite similar to the four-wheelers built by them for the initial public service on the Festiniog Railway. (Details of the Festiniog specimens are scanty as they were all out of use before 1914, though some bodies went over to the Welsh Highland Railway for use as shelters at Halts. Nantmor had two.) For comparison, dimension are shown for both varieties :

	Festiniog & Blaenau	*Festiniog*
Length over body (not couplings etc.)	11 ft. 6 in.	9 ft. 9 in.
Width over body (not handles etc.)	5 ft. 6 in.	5 ft. 0 in.
Height rail to roof (except lamp)	6 ft. 6 in.	6 ft. 9 in.
Wheelbase	5 ft. 0 in.	5 ft. 6 in.

The later vehicles for the F. & B.R. were longer and wider in the body, but slightly less high. Holland made a point of reporting that they were an improvement on the F.R. design whose latest carriages were raised 1 ft. 3 in. above the rails in order to clear the wheels etc., whereas the F. & B. carriages 'are lowered to within 9 inches of the rails and the wheels are recessed . . . under the seats . . . thus affording more stability . . . and headroom'. They both had standard Linley oil lamps in the roof, projecting 6 in. The Festiniog had the longer wheelbase but in the F. & B.R. examples, three doors instead of two were provided and from the drawing it will be seen that though the wheelbase was shorter, the seats were almost contained within it. The seating arrangement was unusual, there being no seat against each end wall. The drawing shows one of the three all 3rd coaches; the fourth had two 2nd class flanking a central 1st. The 3rds were plain wooden interiors, but the upper classes had upholstery proportioned as to class. The mixed vehicles had double small side windows, the thirds a single small pane, due to full partitions in the mixed class and none in the thirds. Unlike the earliest F.R. vehicles, the bodies were lower slung like later F.R. types; for this reason the wheels projected through the floors, accounting for the arrangement of seats whereby these were used to encase the wheel boxes and through the floors of which lubrication was done. Laminated springs and grease boxes were fitted. There were no brakes; at each end was a large central buffer with screw coupling and hook below. Dimensions corresponded with F.R. standard, for obvious reasons. The bodies were low enough to dispense with footboards and station platforms.

The oil lamps were arranged with two for the mixed class, and one for the thirds, but the latter may have been so insufficient as to cause at least one of the all-thirds to have two lamps fitted later. There were no end steps for access to the roofs.

The carriages were painted in a single colour livery (unknown) with 'First' etc. in gilt lettering under each door drop-light.

Besides the classified passenger vehicles, there were nineteen Quarrymen's coaches which Vignes describes as 'very similar to those on the Festiniog Railway, but without roofs'. Presumably it was these which the Board agreed should be 'enclosed' in 1878. That is all we know of them. At the time of the building of the F. & B.R. the Festiniog was still employing a very primitive type of quarrymen's vehicle; the earliest form was converted from an outside framed open wagon having springless inside bearings. Probably the F. & B. stock consisted of such ex-Festiniog Railway open coaches which had been displaced when that line introduced a similar pattern which did not

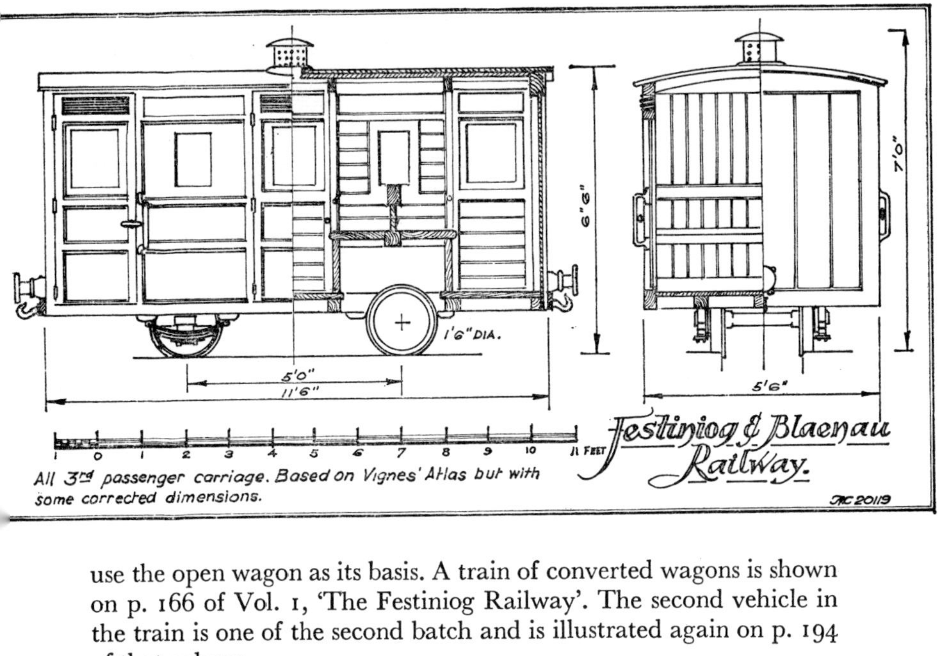

All 3rd passenger carriage. Based on Vignes' Atlas but with some corrected dimensions.

use the open wagon as its basis. A train of converted wagons is shown on p. 166 of Vol. 1, 'The Festiniog Railway'. The second vehicle in the train is one of the second batch and is illustrated again on p. 194 of that volume.

Slate and Goods stock

Holland's 1868 Report to the Board of Trade mentions that 'The waggons are precisely similar to those used on the Ffestiniog Railway —their length from hook to hook is 7 ft. 6 in.—the width 3 ft. 3 in. and height from rails 3 ft.—when fully loaded they weigh $2\frac{3}{4}$ tons and empty $12\frac{3}{4}$ cwt.' (these were frame-sided). 'A few of the largest size coal waggons weigh when fully loaded $3\frac{3}{4}$ tons and when empty 15 cwt.'

Vignes remarks that goods traffic is carried in Festiniog Railway wagons if destined to run over that line. For F. & B. internal use only, he also describes their own wagons as 'similar to those on the Festiniog Railway'. Here again, the Festiniog was undergoing a period of great improvement in wagon stock, and probably the stock Vignes saw was indeed Festiniog-built and was sold as obsolete to the F. & B., for whom it would be completely suitable.

What was the fate of the F. & B. stock when gauge conversion came? Did any stock go back to the Festiniog or would the Great Western simply sell it for scrap? It would be helpful to think that in the F. & B. some explanation might be found for the curiously small coaches (7 ft. 8 in. × 5 ft. 4 in. high and only 4 ft. 6 in. wide) which during the 1930s were being whittled down to skeletons on the Festiniog lineside, where they had been in use for years as gangers' huts. Their origin is still unknown, but they do not conform to F. & B. descriptions unless Vignes did not see all their quarrymen's stock!

Finally it may be assumed that shed accommodation was found only for the classified passenger coaches and the rest lived their lives in the open.

Directors

A list of original directors is given : there were few changes during the life of the enterprise. John Vaughan and J. W. Greaves joined the Board at an early date in place of Capt. T. H. Wynne and George Casson.

The Board at the time of the September 1866 prospectus was :

			Shares held
George Casson (Chairman)		Festiniog	?
Samuel Holland	Glanwilliam,	Maentwrog	50
Capt. T. H. Wynne	Nerquis Hall,	Flintshire	?
John Casson	Blaenydelos,	Festiniog	30
Morgan Lloyd	5, Chester Terr.,	London	50
William Davies	Bryllewellyn,	Festiniog	20
Robert Roberts	Tyhwyntirbwch,	Portmadoc	10

Solicitor

Edward Breese, Morfa Lodge, Portmadoc 10

Secretary

Robert Griffith, Melbourne House, Festiniog

Engineer

Charles Menzies Holland, Liscard Vale, Wallasey 10

Bankers

Messrs. Casson & Co. Festiniog

Offices

Melbourne House, Festiniog.

(Figures following indicate number of £10 shares taken up, where known.)

The Seal of the Company was a roundel containing the name of the Company encircling a Shield on which appeared a rampant goat.

A commentary on the Company's originator and moving spirit, Samuel Holland, is to be found in the Minutes of the Select Committee, re the Festiniog Railway Bill of 1869, sitting on 6–9 July 1869. This was shortly after the F. & B.R. had opened to traffic. The issue in discussion was the Festiniog charges for carrying goods to Blaenau; the rates were condemned by all the opponents of the Festiniog's proposed Bill. It was agreed that in comparison with other Welsh railways, they were high. Samuel Holland was cross-examined and his remarks were typical. His appearance was not entirely to his credit however. Reading between the lines, one may visualise the apparently public-spirited benefactor whom everyone locally knows is revelling in the occasion, for he is likely to benefit from the publicity and probably materially if the examination goes in favour of the opponents. His manner and speech were pompous, and he took up cudgels on behalf of the people of Blaenau Festiniog by complaining that fuel and foodstuffs which had to come from Portmadoc by train, were unreasonably charged for so doing. However, Mr. Michael, counsel for the promoters of the Bill, was a match for him.

Mr. Michael obtained information from Holland concerning the rates paid to quarrymen in general and his own men in particular. The cost of living had been rising and there had been much complaint among the men regarding the low wages. Holland had no intention of increasing wages if he could, and was brought to the point of admitting that his principle interest in the Festiniog rates was to keep them as low as possible with a view to keeping the cost of living down and avoiding labour problems in his own quarry. In short, he was made out to be more fearful of a cut at his own pocket than concerned for the welfare of the local workpeople.

Thrust and counterthrust were typical of these Enquiries, but there is nothing to suggest that Holland was any worse or better than other contemporary employers. In his defence it may be added that all the quarry owners complained of the dictatorial agreements which they had been forced to draw up with the Festiniog Railway, but which almost all expired about the period of the proceedings.

Shareholding

The promoters of the railway put great store by the way in which local people might participate in the ownership of the railway, with what degree of success may be judged by extracts from the Annual Returns:

31 Dec. 1867	976 issued to 110 holders. 44 of these were Quarrymen, most holding only 1 or 2 shares.	
27 May 1874	1148 issued to 110 holders.	
	Samuel Holland	215 shares
	Mrs. Casson	120 shares
	All others:	less than 70 shares
23 June 1879	Similar to above, but:	
	Samuel Holland	290 shares

Timetables

FESTINIOG RAILWAY and FESTINIOG & BLAENAU RAILWAY February 1878

DOWN									
Portmadoc	6.00**a**	7.00**b**	8.40	10.45	1.00	—	3.20	5.00	—
Duffws	7.17	8.15	9.55	12.00	2.15	—	4.38	6.20	—

DOWN									
Duffws	7.40A	—	10.00	12.10C	2.20	3.45	5.00A	B6.22B	8.00B
Tan-y-manod	7.43	—	10.03	12.13	2.23	3.48	5.03	6.25	8.03
Tyddyngwyn	7.46	—	10.06	12.16	2.26	3.51	5.06	6.28	8.06
Festiniog	8.00	—	10.20	12.30	2.40	4.05	5.20	6.42	8.20

a Mondays only.
b Except Mondays.
A Workmen's Train; times of departure variable.
B Runs on Saturdays only.
C Leaves 10 mins. later on Saturdays..

UP	*X*								
Festiniog	—	—	8.30	10.30	—	3.05	4.20C	5.30B	7.15B
Tyddyngwyn	—	—	8.40	10.40	—	3.15	4.30	5.40	7.25
Tan-y-manod	—	—	8.43	10.43	—	3.18	4.33	5.43	7.28
Duffws	—	—	8.50	10.50	—	3.25	4.40	5.50	7.35

UP									
Duffws	6.12**a**	7.12**b**	8.55	11.00	1.15**c**	3.35	5.15	—	—
Portmadoc	7.15	8.15	10.00	12.05	2.25	4.40	6.22	—	—

X Blank column headed *X* for the purpose of A above, for working empty stock and engine Festiniog to Duffws, or for workmen's train, as required. Times not publicly advertised. [Author's Note.]

B Runs on Saturdays only.
C Runs 10 mins. later on Saturdays.

a Mondays only.
b Except Mondays.
c Low fare carriages attached on Saturdays.

Festiniog Railway: For the period during which the Duffws-Llan Ffestiniog line was narrow gauge, the Festiniog Railway appears to have reversed its previous 'Up' and 'Down' directions to comply with Festiniog & Blaenau Railway directions. In the period before and after this phase, Festiniog Railway 'Up' referred literally to up-gradient working from Portmadoc, and vice versa.

	1873	1874	1875	1876	1877	1878	1879	1880	1881	1882
Cost of Works and Way	£137	243	218	302	363	895	376	429	384	250
Cost Loco power	326	459	519	447	814	690	469	489	558	620
Cost Carr/Wag Maint.	—	9	13	9	148	362	68	88	152	143
Profit (Loss) on wkg.	456	360	497	604	910	(334)	571	545	687	461
Merchandise Tons	3510	3462	4550	4257	7823	6022	4044	8950	17702	9177
Minerals Tons	2685	3085	3968	4625	5700	2284	1820	3012	2420	9393
1st Class passengers	886	744	745	714	1350	905	807	954	903	654
2nd Class passengers	1255	1324	1514	1490	2297	2185	1678	2396	2085	1802
3rd Class passengers	35851	42309	48409	54498	82365	59723	49614	48753	48736	45537
Mixed Train mileage	13782	13728	13728	13936	—	—	—	—	—	—
Passenger train mileage	—	—	—	—	24184	14820	14617	13524	13510	13009
Goods train mileage	—	—	—	—	415	312	376	377	390	350
Locos		Returned as Two throughout period								
Carriages	4	4	4	4	6	6	6	6	25	23
Other carriages		Returned as One 1873–1879						—	—	—
Merchandise wagons	7	7	7	7	5	5	5	5	3	1
Other wagons		Returned as Nineteen 1873–1880							—	—

Comments on above: Quarrymen's Open carriages ultimately taken into stock and shown on Returns from 1881.
Peak costs and peak traffic come in 1877–8; loss on working for latter year results.
The Continuous Brakes Return to the Board of Trade for 1879 states: 'Two passenger train Engines. Twenty-five carriages for use on passenger trains made up of six carriages and nineteen "other wagons".' None fitted with continuous brakes.

CROESOR TRAMWAY

(*Gauge* 2 ft.)

Incorporated by Act: None.

Opened: Goods traffic: 1 August 1864 but possibly carrying traffic over completed sections twelve months earlier (see text). Goods and mineral line only.

Office: That of Proprietor, H. B. Roberts. (Probably his residence.)

Capital: None, private undertaking constructed under wayleave.

CROESOR & PORT MADOC RAILWAY COMPANY

(*Gauge* 2 ft.)

Incorporated by Act: 28 & 29 Vic. Cap. 295 of 5 July 1865 and to make Extension.

Registered Office: Caernarvon.

Length: 4½ miles (also officially given as 1¼ miles in error).

Capital: £25,000 in Shares and £8,330 in Loans (issued £15,000 and £8,000 @ 5½% loan).

Promoted to maintain the existing section of Croesor Tramway between Portmadoc and Carreg-hylldrem, and to extend to Borth-y-gest.

PORTMADOC, CROESOR & BEDDGELERT TRAM RAILWAY COMPANY

(*Gauge* 2 ft.)

Incorporated by Act: 42 & 43 Vic. Cap. 171 of 21 July 1879. Change of name and authorised to construct branch.

Act: 55 & 56 Vic. Cap. 44 of 20 June 1892: Rates and Charges.

Registered Office: 99 Gresham Street, London, E.C.

Length: 5 miles (official).

Capital: £23,000 in Shares and £7,650 in Loans.

Capital per mile: £5,700.

Promoted to absorb the Croesor & Port Madoc Railway by giving it a fresh title and taking its powers. Additional powers for new line Llanfrothen–Beddgelert (3 m. 7 fur.) over period of five years. No work done. New line to be titled 'P.C. & B.T. Railway Company's Beddgelert Extension' with capital to be kept separately.

Company into Receivership: 1882.

Powers sold to Portmadoc, Beddgelert & South Snowdon Railway:

Act: 1 Ed. VII 262 of 17 August 1901.

Closed: By embodiment of part into Welsh Highland Railway. No official closure date for remainder of tramway though all out of use by 1936. Unofficial usage continued over these sections until about 1955. A few sections extant 1971.

History

Outside the Blaenau Festiniog area, and with the exception of the big Glanrafon Quarry near South Snowdon, which was later to be served by the North Wales Narrow Gauge Railways, the quarries at Croesor came to be the third largest employers of labour in the area. On a small scale, quarrying was being done on a site at Croesor (or Croesawr), the head of a valley east of Portmadoc, by 1840, and this became worked by the Croicer Valley & Portmadoc Freehold Slate Co. Ltd. which went out of business shortly afterwards. By 1861 there were two undertakings working there, the Croesor Fawr Slate Quarrying Co. Ltd. (formerly the Croesor Slate Quarry Co.) and the Upper Croesor Slate Quarry Co. Ltd. These two were almost working in one another's pockets for in September 1865 the Upper Co. granted the Fawr Co. permission to dump rubbish on its land.

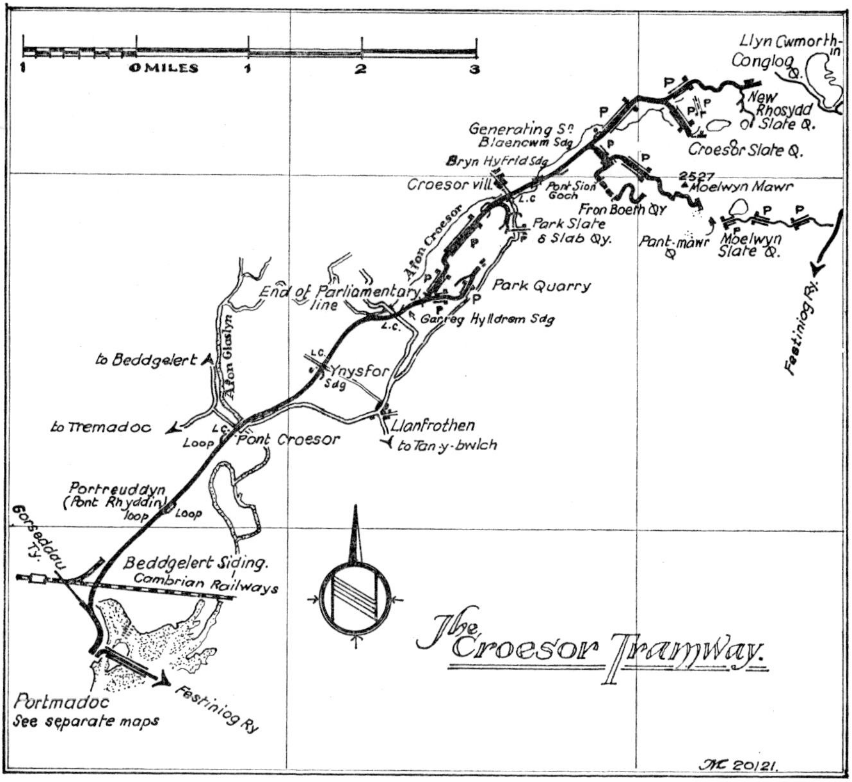

The two companies amalgamated after H. B. Roberts gave a new company, Croesor United Slate Co. Ltd., a lease to search for slate on the land of Croesor Fawr farm. Croesor United entered business in mid 1866 with a capital of £160,000 and a formal lease of Upper's property was assigned to it on 1 August 1866. Upper's champion was Hugh Unsworth McKie who like Roberts, appears later in connection with other local enterprises, and not surprisingly, was also a director of the Croesor & Port Madoc Railway. Development of the quarry took place in 1868–9, a contract with Beaumont, Appleby & Ashwell of London being placed for cutting the shafts and tunnel. James Wyatt, former agent to Lord Penrhyn's quarry, was Managing Director from 1865. From 30 June 1867, T. H. Wyatt was Chairman and McKie Manager & Secretary.

Progress on the site was not favourable, and a private report was placed before the Board which said it might be hoped that better slate would be found below the present level of working; by then 110 men were at work. Debentures had to be issued in 1870 to meet continuous development costs, for the slate vein 'of paying quality' had still not been reached. It was a time of great anxiety and the directors reported it would be necessary 'to stop everything unless further measures are forthcoming' i.e. more capital was put up. Underground, they were hampered by a 'chert band' of hard rock. The Machine Tunnelling Co., now holding the contract for the work, made slow progress and in June 1872, the slate vein not having been reached in the Trial Shaft, the Machine Tunnelling contract was terminated and the Diamond Rock-boring Co. took over. In the November the Board appealed for more money; water could not be pumped out quickly enough, but by June 1873 the shareholders made it clear they had subscribed enough and the directors decided to wind up voluntarily and re-constitute the concern as The Croesor Slate Company. Some of the detail of this period is worth recording.

Even before the United Company was formed, McKie had reported that he could not make a good report of the existing slate chambers—there had been excessive rain. Samuel Holland inspected in November 1866 and said the present slate quality would not pay its way. They must go deeper to prove the rock. In June 1868, C. E. Spooner inspected. The machinery was always short of power and overheated the shaft. The water pouring into the workings was lifted into wagons by bucket and carried away, as £700 was needed for new pumps. McKie complained in January 1872 that the diamond borers were too weak for the rock, and then without consulting him, the Board removed all the machinery from the valley. McKie, now Consulting Engineer to the Mine, 'although deprived of the last prop he had to support his family', offered his resignation. He added, 'There has been the most reckless and wasteful destruction of plant.'

Auction of the quarry was attempted in April 1875 and the Croesor Slate Company never really began work. A second attempt to sell was made in July 1875.

The undertakings all failed because of heavy costs; Penrhyn slate cost 1s. 2½d. a ton to produce, Croesor 10s. 9½d. Whereas at Penrhyn in June 1868 the output was 9,000 tons a month, Croesor only produced 226 tons. It need not be added that Croesor United's traffic contribution to the new tramway was miserably small.

On 9 December 1875 the Croesor New Slate Co. Ltd. took over.* Edward Breese the Portmadoc solicitor to the Festiniog & Blaenau Railway was Chairman and there was more impressive talent and wealth on the Board. Thomas Williams of Bryn Croesor was made Manager; he had been Manager of Lord Penrhyn's quarries. (Throughout there is evidence of personnel moving from one concern to another in this fashion.) John Francis of Portmadoc was Consulting Engineer.

With a capital of £45,000 they took over the workings, manager's house, eight quarrymen's cottages, workshops etc. together with a railway which linked the quarry with 'the Croesor & Port Madoc line' and it was estimated that each ton of slate would be carried from the quarry to Port Madoc wharves (sic) for less than 3s.

The other major quarry in the neighbourhood was worked by the Rhosydd Slate Quarry Co. Ltd. formed about September 1866 working a quarry previously owned by the Rhosydd Slate Co. and opened about 1857.† It had some Festiniog quarry directors on its board which included George A. Huddart with his Pennant Valley and Festiniog Railway connections. The capital was substantial for those days, (£200,000) and they took over the small existing quarry which had already built a 'Branch Railway and Incline' by June 1864 to connect it to the new tramway. They were working the same vein as Lord Palmerston's Welsh Slate Co. in Blaenau Festiniog. The railway works had cost £2,500 and arrangements had been made with the Croesor Tramway to carry output for the next four years on to Portmadoc quays for 2s. 10d. per ton, reducing to 1s. 10d. per ton as traffic increased. Until the railway had opened, opening up of the quarry had been seriously hampered. A report showed that the cost

* Croesor New went out of business in December 1882; purchased by S. Pope of Llanbedr 7 July 1883. Became part of Park & Croesor Slate Quarries Co. Ltd., formed 21 August 1895. Closed 1930. Wound up 8 February 1931.

† The prime mover for the original Rhosydd Quarry project was said to be C. E. Spooner.

of these competitive rates over the Croesor & Portmadoc Railway was £5,000, but how this came about is not stated; it certainly made a mockery of the alleged cheap terms of carriage! The local Bangor paper was quite cynical in its report of the new railway connection . . . 'The Croesor Slate Quarry—Railway to Portmadoc. Among the many signs of "progress" which may be witnessed in this district . . .'. Like newspaper errors of the present, it gave the quarry the wrong title too.

At Rhosydd there were then five galleries, and tunnels of 550 yards and 700 yards. Output was soon 2,000 tons a year and it was recommended that some land taken be sold off to another user. Here too, C. E. Spooner sent in a full report with elaborate directions as to working the quarry in the future.

The Croesor Tramway was the second railway undertaking of size in the locality to be built without Parliamentary authority.* By the mid 1850s, trial levels for slate at the upper end of the Afon Croesor valley (about seven miles from Portmadoc and in a valley which even today is bleak and remote), were showing promise and exploitation by means of a railway from Portmadoc was considered. Throughout the district rail communications were proving their worth and to make the venture as economic and expeditious as possible, it was proposed to connect Portmadoc with the Croesor area workings in two distinct undertakings, the first given authority for its progress between the quays and Carreg-hylldrem by means of a series of wayleaves, the second being a continuation eastwards from there on land already leased to quarry owners, thus making it virtually a private tramway. Proof of the potential of such a railway was easily to hand. The figures for slate shipments from Portmadoc from the Croesor Quarries without rail communications on the one hand, and from the Gorseddau Quarry with its new tramway on the other, spoke for themselves. They were : (in tons)

	Croesor	*Gorseddau*
1856	414	226
1857	497	478
1858	533	1006
1859	70	1338

Carreg-hylldrem is in fact, a rocky eminence just to the west of Llanfrothen village and above the roadbridge crossing the Afon Croesor, known as Pont Carreg-hylldrem. In the Portmadoc area, connections were made with the already-existing Gorseddau Tramway. The builder and owner of the portion constructed under wayleave was Hugh Beaver Roberts (who has already come to attention),

* The first being the Gorseddau Tramway (see Part 2).

a solicitor practising in Bangor and at that time Chairman of the George Hotel Company, Bangor, and the Cwt-y-bugail Slate Company of Festiniog (which he sold on 17 April 1876). The line was built between 1862–4 to a gauge contemporarily quoted as '24 inches' and also as 'slightly greater than that of the Festiniog Railway'. The track was of primitive type similar to that at first used on the Festiniog Railway and only suited to horse, gravity or manpower—at that time even the Festiniog had done no more than contemplate self-propulsion for its trains. The rails were of wrought iron, 20 lbs. per yard laid in small chairs on wooden sleepers; extended details are given later. Writing twenty years later, Vignes says that horsepower was the mainstay but that horses were hired not owned; this was in keeping with the original Festiniog practice.

Construction was made easier at the Portmadoc end of the line by using James Creassy's reclamation embankment built in 1800 for William Madocks. Where the availability of this useful dyke ceased east of Portreuddyn a new embankment was built to Pont Croesor, where a wooden bridge was thrown over the river; in later years the bridge was well-remembered for its deplorable condition, so that later it was necessary to rebuild it completely to carry the Welsh Highland Railway of the early nineteen-twenties.

The Creassy embankment was the second of two works built in an attempt to reclaim the west side of the Glaslyn valley from the sea. It was over two miles in length and varied in height from 11 to 20 feet, and was a simple dyke of seasand covered by sods of turf to bind it, costing £2,800 excluding ancillary works. For about half of its length it ran outside of but parallel to an even earlier embankment said to have been built by William Wynn of Wern but which had only been a partial success. It was considered so fragile from the first that only sheep were allowed to graze on it. The Wynn embankment is mentioned because it is often taken to be an abandoned railway earthwork and one recent writer has erroneously described it as that being utilised by the Croesor Tramway.

The third, or 'Great Embankment', or Cob, is widely known and of course was a later work built for William Madocks and its seaward side is used by the Festiniog Railway to this day. Confusion between the contruction of the second embankment and the Cob comes in a letter from Madocks' agent's grandson writing in April 1900 which says '. . . The material was carried from the surrounding high ground in trolleys which ran upon wooden rails and sleepers . . .' without specifying which of the two 'Madocks' embankments was meant. However, there is no doubt that here The Cob is being described under construction.

Much of the western end of the route of the Croesor Tramway was similar to a course proposed by 36-year-old James Spooner in his 1825 plan for a Moelwyn and Port Madoc Railway; this line would have headed for the slopes of the Moelwyn massif by means of an almost straight route to carry it up on to the col between Moelwyn Mawr and Moelwyn Bach by means of a succession of long levels and inclines. In the event, the east end of the Croesor Tramway and its extensions were built on a somewhat similar theme in an adjacent valley to the north-west, involving some splendid locations and occasional civil engineering quite on a par with the Festiniog Railway. C. E. Spooner, though not Engineer to the project, was engaged as surveyor and laid out the course and civil engineering features.*

Because the Croesor Tramway proper went no further than Carreg-hylldrem, it is important to note that official references to later developments do not in fact involve the tramway above this point, but the *whole undertaking* has always been known loosely as the Croesor Tramway. Beyond Carreg-hylldrem is the Croesor tramway, a subtle distinction especially as even today, the 'Croesor Tramway' is shown on maps † as the part-surviving section eastwards from Carreg-hylldrem—portions of which still exist—whilst the Croesor Tramway as such and which has been correctly deleted from some modern maps, was demolished finally between August 1948 and the following August!

A Deed of Mutual Covenant dated 1 October 1863 between the Rhosydd Slate Co. Ltd., and Roberts, by which Roberts granted the quarry a wayleave to build the tramway and incline from its property to the main tramway previously mentioned (a useful controlling factor enjoyed by Roberts beyond the confines of the Tramway proper) was based on a rate of 2d. per ton, reduced to 1d. per ton. This agreement expired on 25 March 1906 but was then extended until 1921 and the rate was restored to 2d. A rate for carriage was also made in an Agreement of 1865 between the Croesor & Port Madoc Railway (a statutory successor to the Croesor Tramway) and the Aberystwyth & Welsh Coast Railway (later the Cambrian Railways) which concern planned initially to build its own independent branch to Portmadoc Harbour, but in the event, obtained running powers over the Croesor & Port Madoc Railway from its level intersection with it at a rate of 1d. per ton. The Croesor & Port Madoc Railway was given reciprocal powers into Portmadoc (standard gauge) station, 'if the Abersytwyth & Welsh Coast Railway carried

* Select Committee Minutes, House of Commons, 6–7 July 1869.

† Even the official Railway Clearing House Junction Diagram book being guilty of the error!

Croesor & Port Madoc Railway traffic from there to local wharves'.* This arrangement would have involved a mixed gauge line.

Had the Croesor & Port Madoc Railway been extended along the north side of the Aberystwyth & Welsh Coast Railway into Portmadoc station it would have had to cross also the Gorseddau Tramway on the level (the A. & W.C.R. obtained powers for and built a level crossing) but in any case, there seems to be no evidence that the powers were acted upon.†

The first load of slate came from Rhosydd on 1 August 1864; 4 wagons of 7 tons 8 cwts. The second load was run on 3 August on behalf of the owner's own quarry, the Croesor Slate Company, 7 cwts. 'iron materials' at 2s. 10d. per ton. The first slates from the same quarry were on 17 August being 3 wagons containing 4 tons 1 cwt. at 2s. 3½d. per ton. The 'second Croesor' quarry must have been sending traffic by the October and a ledger entry reveals that traffic had been conveyed earlier in the year, though probably the line was not open all the way; it may be assumed that 1 August was significant only in that the whole tramway opened for business on that day. In October an entry read 'Deals & Boards conveyed for Mr. Thos. Williams about January last. 1 Ton. Rate 2s. 10d.'. These went to the Croesor Fawr Slate Quarry Co.

On 24 October 1865 the small workings of Gerynt Slate Co. began to use the tramway. Besides the Croesor Fawr, there was the Croesor Bach Slate Co. who bought rails to build a tramway in 1864. Of the small quarries up at the top of the valley, little more was heard.

A good example of Up traffic in the first year was to Mrs. Edmunds, Park Farm, and included coal, a wheel, oats, hayseed and flour.

Rhosydd sent down 284 tons of slate in the first month of workings and almost 200 tons a month for the remainder of the year. In the same period a good business in Up coal haulage began. This was dropped at Carreg-hylldrem, Cwm and Rhosydd, some of it going to the quarrymen's barracks.

Over the Tremadoc Estate a toll of 2d. for sundries and 3d. per ton for slate was levied. The early years show good husbandry; hay con-

* 'The Cambrian Railways', p. 78 (Christiansen & Miller).

† (The nub of the case would seem to have been a bid by the A. & W.C.R. (Cambrian Railways) to encourage the C. & P.M.R. to work its traffic into the Cambrian station at Portmadoc and thereafter close the C. & P.M.R./Cambrian level crossing. Under such an arrangement the Cambrian agreed to carry C. & P.M.R. traffic to the Harbour, thereby placing the C. & P.M.R. traffic at the tender mercies of the Cambrian. The bait was not swallowed by the C. & P.M.R. !)

veyed at a charge of £1 14s. 0s. and 'Old wire sold £2 5s. 6d.'. Rhosydd received £23 1s. 3d. for slates broken in transit; Bryn-hyfryd Cottages, near the Siding of that name, were let out to provide income.

Between opening and 1870, new works and 'relaying' (a surprising feature for a railway only six years old but perhaps enduring an amount of wear and tear) account for considerable sums being spent in materials, larch sleepers, chairs and rails. The Festiniog Railway was the source of this material—obviously second hand. The tramway was also able to 'lend' rails to the Gorseddau in 1869 '30 bars @ 6d. = 15s.'. Chairs were cast and supplied by J. Henry Williams & Sons, Portmadoc in 1874.

In the first nine days the six employees were paid by the day but after that the carriers (hauliers) received 6d. or 3d. per ton and the brakesmen (on the inclines) 3s. 4d.–4s. 6d. per day. The two platelayers got 3s. 4d. and 3s. 8d. a day and in November 1866 were provided with capes!

There was a good exchange of traffic between Croesor and Gorseddau when, from 1875, the latter made junction with the Croesor at the Gas Works. Flour traffic onto the Gorseddau was the largest item, but falling traffic hit the Gorseddau and the last wagon load was in April 1879. At the end of 1883 the Croesor wrote off £26 5s. 6d. owed by the Gorseddau as a bad debt.

Contemporary records* show that the Tramway was officially opened throughout for mineral traffic on 1 August 1864. The year of the opening was to give problems later to its successor, the Welsh Highland Railway. This arose from a rail level crossing formed when the Aberystwyth & Welsh Coast Railway was extended to Pwllheli and was obliged to cross the Tramway on the level on the east side of its Portmadoc station. (The Coast Section was opened to traffic between Barmouth and Pwllheli on 10 October 1867.) The successor to the Cambrian Railways, the Great Western Railway, imposed a charge on all Welsh Highland Railway movements passing over this crossing with their metals. This came to dispute in 1925, so in the same year steps were taken to find 'an oldest inhabitant' who would be prepared to make a sworn statement 'in exchange for a pound of tobacco'. Robert Morgan, then 80, made the following statement . . . 'I can remember, before the Cambrian Railway was done, crossing the Croesor Railway with the horses, drawing timber at Llyn Bach. When Mr. Jones, the Manager of the Croesor Railway, came to me and asked on whose authority I was drawing timber over his railway,

*Railway Year Book, 1911, quotes the above date – the only 'published' source to be found as yet.

I remember telling him it was the contractor's order'. Morgan also recalls that traffic on the Croesor was done under contract at this time. It was necessary to obtain more than one sworn statement, but because no other witness could be found, the idea was not pursued. As there is no doubt that the Croesor Tramway was first on the scene and the A. & W.C.R. was obliged to cross its path, there seems little enough validity in the Great Western's charge—in fact, the reverse would have been the lawful position.

Owing to the light traffic which the Croesor carried, though it was the subject of successive Acts of Parliament, no major improvements were necessary. A report by Major Spring for the Festiniog management in 1921 shows that much of the original construction survived at that time. The track was still the original material 'and most of the sleepers are rotten'. The rails and chairs were of cast-iron, some keys being of wood and others of iron strip. Wider chairs were used at joints and the chairs held to sleepers by iron pins. Pointwork was very primitive, of 'quarry type' (sic) and without switch blades. The bridge over the Glaslyn at Pont Croesor, previously mentioned, was of eight 25 ft. wooden girder spans carried on slate rubble piers. By 1921 it was very faulty. All traffic was horse-drawn.

With the likelihood of the Aberystwyth & Welsh Coast Railway extending northwards from Barmouth to Pwllheli along the coast, plans were drawn up by C. E. Spooner and an estimate prepared for the conversion of the Tramway proper into a public railway with powers to extend at the western end to the seaside village of Borth-y-gest and northwards to Beddgelert.

This stated:

'CROESOR & PORTMADOC RAILWAY BILL

The objects of this Bill are to incorporate "The Croesor & Portmadoc Railway Company" with a capital of £25,000 in £10 shares and £8,330 by loan, to empower them:

To maintain the Railway, length 4 miles 3 chains on a two-feet gauge, from Carrig Hylldrem, near Llanfrothen, to Portmadoc, constructed by Hugh Beaver Roberts Esquire, and intended to be vested in the Company by this Bill;

To take lands for the improvement of that Railway, and to adapt it for passenger as well as other traffic;

To make an extension Railway, length 1 mile 19 chains, also on the two-feet gauge, from the termination of the former line at Portmadoc, to Borth-y-gest;

To increase the gauge of the Railways from two feet to three feet, with the approval of the Board of Trade.

(Observations). It appears to be a question whether Parliament has hitherto sanctioned the conveyance of passengers on Railways on a gauge so narrow as those which are the subject of this Bill, viz., two feet, without imposing some restrictions as to the speed at which passengers can be conveyed.

In the case of the Corris Railway, near Machynlleth, authorised in 1858 to be constructed on a gauge of 2 feet 3 inches, the use of steam power and the conveyance of passengers were prohibited. An Act of 1864 removed the former prohibition, but restricted the rate of speed to ten miles an hour, and it continued the prohibition against the conveyance of passengers. The last mentioned restrictions, however, it is proposed to remove by the ABERYSTWYTH & WELSH COAST RAILWAY (No. 1) Bill of this Session . . .

Board of Trade James Booth'
March 1865.

The suggestion of increasing the gauge to 3 feet may have two-fold implications : (1) it might have been thought easier to find agreement in the matter of passenger traffic and (2) physical connection with the Gorseddau Tramway might be established in Portmadoc.

By Act of 5 July 1865 (28/9 Vic. Cap. 295) authority for a Statutory Company was obtained to 'maintain the existing tramway . . . and extend to Borth-y-gest with the title Croesor & Port Madoc Railway', thus regularising the existence of the Croesor Tramway as well as permitting its conversion to a public railway and of standard gauge if necessary. The cost was estimated at £14,960. Perhaps the most significant pointers were that H. B. Roberts and H. U. McKie were on the Board (the former as Chairman), C. E. Spooner * was its Engineer, and locomotive haulage was authorised—in the same year when the Festiniog Railway had been operating locomotive-hauled passenger trains since 6 January—and in fact, agreements with that Company and the Cambrian Railways were arranged. The southward extension to Borth-y-gest was to be completed within four years and of mixed gauge to be shared with the Coast Railway, (a point described as being between Trwyn-penclogwyn and Borth, by Vignes) but was never carried out in any form. As for the Croesor & Port Madoc Railway, it was destined to remain simply a new title and the existing Tramway continued its duties without alteration or extension. In the Act, the official length of the Croesor line is mistakenly given as 1¼ miles. Roberts is quoted as Chairman and his brother,

* Spooner was by now virtually *the* consulting engineer for narrow gauge projects. In 1867 he was invited to advise the Belfast & Co. Down Railway on conversion to narrow gauge.

Arthur, of The Towers, Mold, was also a Director, as he was also of the Mold & Denbigh Junction Railway (authorised 1861). Of the five directors, at that time only Arthur T. Roberts had other railway interests; the Company's Registered Office was in Caernarvon and its official underestimated mileage was repeatedly quoted. A capital of £63,980 was authorised and £25,000 in Ordinary Shares and £8,330 in Loans issued.

Under a Statutory Mortgage No. 1, sealed on 23 June 1870 in the presence of Hugh Beaver Roberts, the Croesor & Port Madoc Railway Company mortgaged its undertaking to Mary Elizabeth Littledale to secure repayment of £8,000 at 5½%.

A sequel to this came ten years later when on 15 September 1880 Evan Morris of The Priory, Wrexham, wrote to Edward Breese pointing out that the purchase of the above mortgage would give control of the Croesor & Port Madoc Railway to the purchaser, the borrowing powers of the Company being limited to £8,330.

It was February 1879 before any attempt was made to broaden the horizons of the Croesor & Port Madoc. In that month a circular from Robinson Bros., Mansion House Chambers, 11 Queen Victoria Street, London, E.C. invited investment in the Company. This was headed 'A remunerative Home Investment may be accrued in the CROESOR & PORT MADOC (TRAM) RAILWAY COMPANY' and offered at a premium, £25,000 in £10 shares carrying '5 per cent *guaranteed* £10 fully-paid-up Shares in the Company . . .' The offer continued: 'An Act of Parliament was obtained a few years since by five gentlemen, and the necessary land having been purchased, the CROESOR AND PORT MADOC (Narrow gauge) TRAM RAILWAY was completed, and opened for Mineral Traffic only. The entire Share Capital of the Company has hitherto been held by the above-mentioned five persons only, who have not, up to the present time, parted with a single Share. Although the Act of Parliament authorised the use of Steam and the conveyance of Passengers, the Proprietors have hitherto worked the line by Horse power, and been content with the returns of the carriage of the Mineral traffic alone.

The Tramways Corporation, Limited, having deposited plans in Parliament this Session, for powers to construct an important extension to Beddgelert, as a branch of this line, the CROESOR AND PORT MADOC COMPANY, have entered into a Three Years' Working Agreement with the Corporation to prove Passenger Cars, to develop and work the existing Line by *Steam* as part of their extended system, paying for the use of the line a rent equal to a Dividend of five per cent. on the existing Share Capital.

At the end of three years the Shareholders will have the privilege of both lines being amalgamated on an equal basis.

We are of the opinion, based upon the returns of the adjoining Festiniog Line, referred to below, that at the termination of the stipulated period, the Passenger traffic will have developed on both new and old Lines to such an extent that future Dividends will be much in excess of the present *guaranteed 5 per cent* and . . . likely to increase . . . The proposed Extension will pass along the most frequented route, and through the most attractive and romantic scenery of North Wales, including the Pass of Aberglaslyn to the celebrated village of Beddgelert, at the foot of Snowdon. When this Extension is completed, arrangements will be made with the Cambrian Railway for the joint use of their Station at Port Madoc . . . One of the principal advantages of the present line is that it possesses the monopoly of running through the Town to the Harbour and Wharves of Port Madoc, and having a junction with the Cambrian Railway* conveys at present all goods to and from the Harbour for that Railway'. There follows a glowing account of the prospects together with references to Festiniog dividends of 12½% . . . 'must fill many a shareholder's heart with envy' etc. etc. and the brokers strongly recommend the shares compared with Bank, Gas Shares and Foreign Stocks of the times!

No work having been undertaken under Croesor & Port Madoc Railway auspices, another Company obtained an Act which absorbed it and its powers. This was the cumbersomely-titled Portmadoc, Croesor and Beddgelert Tram Railway Company (Act of 21 July 1879 42/3 Vic. Cap. 171) to which Lefevre & Co. (and later Spooner & Co.) were the Engineers, and H. Beaver Roberts was later Secretary. Once again, no new work or any outward change revealed the existence of another new Company, and the tramway continued to exist in its original form. The unbuilt line to Beddgelert was officially referred to from this time onwards as the 'Portmadoc, Croesor & Beddgelert Tram Railway Company's Beddgelert Extension', an impressive title indeed even had anything contributed toward it. The immediate goal was Beddgelert, but the ultimate target was the North Wales Narrow Gauge Railways terminus at Rhydd-ddu.

The Portmadoc, Croesor & Beddgelert Tram Railway Company was given 5 years to complete its works together with the branch to Beddgelert. Under the Act, the capital of the Extension was to be kept separately; it was £23,000 in Ordinary Shares and £7,650 in Loans or Debenture Stock. Working arrangements with the Cam-

* The Beddgelert Siding.

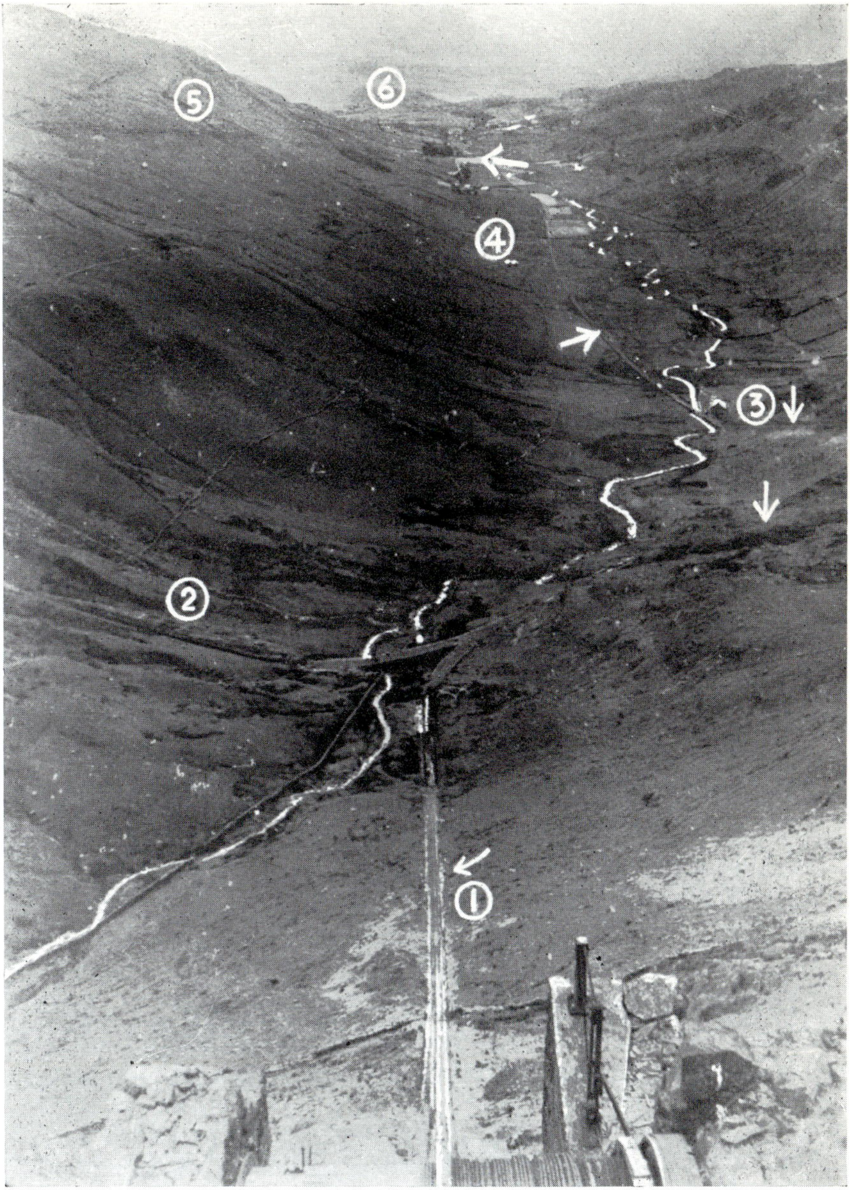

R. W. Kidner

Croesor valley looking down from the Rhosydd Incline drum, towards Portmadoc, 1934. Tramway shown by arrows (1) Incline to New Rhosydd quarries (2) Incline to Croesor quarries (3) Incline at Blaen-y-cwm with Power Station at foot (4) Pant-mawr quarries' Incline (5) Summit of (4) (6) Parc Inclines with Glaslyn estuary and Portmadoc below.

J. I. C. Boyd

Three-way stub point with cast frog sections and selecting lever with catch-handle, outside tractor shelter, Croesor Quarry. 1948.

R. W. Kidner

Entrance to New Rhosydd adit, 1934. The train is headed by a 'gripper car' and the endless cable may be seen lying between the rails; it reversed around a wheel behind the photographer.

Trackwork with movable blades and diamonds at Blaen-y-cwm, and Croesor Quarries wagon. 1940.

J. F. Bolton

Baldwin tractor used for Croesor tramway service, in Boston Lodge after receiving number.

Real Photos Co

Parc & Croesor braked wagon; Tre-saethan. 1946.

J. I. C. Boyd

J. I. C. Boyd

Cast frog unit with raised wing rails at Pant-mawr Incline junction. 1968.

J. I. C. Boyd

Standard form of T-bulb rail joint in main tramway. 1968.

J. I. C. Boyd

Varieties of chair found in locations at Lower Parc Incline (left to right; carrying, joint and Festiniog horse-period) 1948.

R. W. Kidner

Croesor Quarry showing overhead wiring and slab trollies 1934.

Kellow's electric mine locomotive, probably the first in the world, and slab trollies in Croesor Quarry about 1902. The hydro-electric installation was built in 1900.

J. I. C. Boyd collection

J. I. C. Boyd collection

Beddgelert Siding's exchange and stock yard, with Croesor line in foreground (a section not relaid by the P.B. & S.S.R). Standard gauge Cambrian Railways' wagons at rear. 1910.

R. W. Kidner

Pant-mawr cable drum and incline, looking down on to Croesor Tramway below. 1934.

J. I. C. Boyd

Remaining portions of Croesor main line at Blaen-y-cwm, showing Power Station (derelict) and rail-less incline beyond. 1968.

Blaen-y-cwm Power Station and incline foot, with Festiniog wagons in siding. 1941.

W. H. Tate

J. I. C. Boyd collection

New Rhosydd Incline (foreground) with a 'run' of that quarry's wooden framed slate wagons at the foot. Slab platform in centre foreground. Croesor quarry incline and river bridge in distance, with Croesor rubbish tips on skyline. c. 1885.

Parc & Croesor slate wagons with remains of stencilled markings on sides; standing on main tramway near Blaen-y-cwm. 1946.

J. I. C. Boyd

S. H. P. Higgins collection

Looking towards Croesor village from near top of Upper Parc Incline, with Cnicht rising in the distance. c. 1929.

J. I. C. Boyd

Civil engineering works on the South Snowdon Quarry tramway, between the top incline and quarry, west Snowdon. (This quarry, though unconnected with the Croesor, used that line for deliveries to Beddgelert Siding.) 1970.

brian, Gorseddau and Festiniog lines were outlined. The Company was based on London with Registered Office at 99 Gresham Street, and only James Fraser (a director of the Corris Railway) had any other railway directorships.

The link between the new Portmadoc, Croesor & Beddgelert Tram Railway Company and the proposal of early 1879 to work the new line with its intended Beddgelert Extension by the Tramways Corporation, is not completely clear. It would seem that the five original proprietors of the Croesor & Port Madoc were able to dispose of their interests and of the five, only Hugh Beaver Roberts continued in office, not as a director, but as just mentioned succeeded E. F. Tremayne as Secretary. Working by the Tramways Corporation, with subsequent amalgamation, did not materialise either, though the link with tramway interest was retained through the Chairman of the new undertaking; he also held the Chair of the Preston Tramways Company. Four of his other five directors' interests seem to have been purely speculative; certainly they had no known railway influence.

The new Company issued a prospectus in October 1879, three months after formation, and invited purchasers of 1st Preference Shares at £10 each paying 6% which was of course, the Extension Capital. The accompanying propaganda ran very close to that used by the earlier Company in the previous February, and was clearly copied from it. Junctions with the Festiniog and Gorseddau Railways were mentioned additionally, and having repeated the statement about monopoly of traffic to the Harbour and *proposal* to arrange with the Cambrian for joint use of their station, reference is made to the rapid development of Llanberis since the L.N.W.R. opened a branch thereto. The extract from *The Times* giving the same figures concerning the Festiniog is quoted, and telling how it was practicable '*to make a large profit on a moderate outlay*'.

The main and additional points of interest were :

1. The Beddgelert Line was to be built by a Contractor who had consented to allow interest at a rate of 5% per annum during the period fixed for construction upon all payments made in respect of shares (perhaps an arrangement based on the experience gained in the lamentable affairs of the neighbouring North Wales Narrow Gauge line only a few years previously).
2. W. H. Lefevre's (Engineer) Estimate & Report of the same month maintained that the line 'connected with the entire railway system of England' (which was partly true but involved break of gauge of course). There were 14 small slate quarries excluded from his esti-

mate of gross income which totalled £8,325 per year and would show a profit of £4,612 10s. 0d.

3. The current rate of cartage was 8s. to 10s. per ton to Portmadoc.
4. The opening of the L.N.W.R. extension into Blaenau 'had opened up a large tourist and passenger traffic to Portmadoc wanting to be conveyed to Beddgelert'. (One envisages the queue at the non-existent booking office).

As just mentioned, the promotion failed to attract public imagination or money in sufficient amount to justify a start on the Beddgelert Extension, and the ghastly lesson of the nearby North Wales Narrow Gauge Company was sufficient in itself to daunt the promoters—it lost £1,893 in 1879.

A further statutory mortgage of the undertaking as it now existed was given to James Cholmeley Russell on 19 June 1882 in the amount of £330 at 5%; Russell had become Receiver to the North Wales Narrow Gauge Railways Company on 13 December 1878.* The same year Mary Elizabeth Littledale, whose principal and overdue interest on her own £8,000 mortgage was to amount to upwards of £10,000 by 1901, put the Portmadoc, Croesor & Beddgelert Tram Railways Company into Receivership for the remainder of its days. In consequence of this, the proposed transformation of the Tramway was postponed for many years to come. No new work was begun under the P.C. & B.T.R. Act.

The astonishing feature of these successive failures was the drive behind them and one wonders why the apparently inconsequential Croesor Tramway should be considered to be of such strategic and bargaining importance. As has been commonly instanced throughout history, the vision of the Croesor forming part of a railway to link north and south Caernarvonshire was the dream of one man, Charles Easton Spooner, then Engineer to the Festiniog Railway. It was he who created the bullets which, with his strong local connection, he hoped others would help him to fire. In this he was only partially successful, and when in later years the vision became reality it was too late, and the reality was a failure.

By the early 1870s the standard gauge railway map of Caernarvonshire was becoming complete. Spooner had recently enjoyed two triumphs on the Festiniog Railway; firstly passenger trains had been

* In view of the 1880 correspondence between Breese and Morris referred to above, and Russell's position on the N.W.N.G.R. Co., it might well be his mortgage on the Croesor & Port Madoc Railway was an attempt to purchase control of that line 'via the Back Door'. Did anyone try to buy out M. E. Littledale? (!)

introduced with statutory backing, and secondly, steam traction had proved itself. The critics had been made to eat their words and Spooner, riding the crest of the wave, was now looking beyond the purely local horizons of the Festiniog Railway. He was concerned about the ambitions of the Cambrian, Great Western and London & North Western Railways in the neighbourhood. The Cambrian was looking north and east towards Beddgelert (their proposed route would parallel the Croesor for the first part of its way). The L.N.W.R. was already in Bettws-y-coed and planned to extend to Blaenau Festiniog by means of a narrow gauge extension authorised by Act of 18 July 1872 as the 'Bettws and Festiniog Railway', 12 miles long of 2 ft. gauge. Under the L.N.W.R. Act of 28 July 1873 that company was given powers to use portions of the Festiniog Railway at Blaenau Festiniog and to enter into arrangements with the Festiniog company. The L.N.W.R. intended in fact, to debouch from a tunnel (still in use by British Rail) at Blaenau, form three running lines and make an end-on junction with running powers on the Festiniog's Dinas branch. Apart from this real threat to Festiniog monopoly, powers had been obtained for a Merionethshire Railway at the instance of quarry owners who wanted an outlet from the Blaenau district independent of the Festiniog Railway; this railway would have been partly in mixed gauge and would tap the Festiniog where it hurt. The ground which had for so long been the bastion of the Festiniog was about to be infiltrated. Spooner had cause for concern.

In reply to the clouds on his horizon, his answer was firstly to baulk the Cambrian's bid to reach Beddgelert and Caernarvon by a branch line from Portmadoc and secondly, to divert the attentions of Euston by containing the L.N.W.R. in the Conway valley. Already that Company had taken over the Caernarvonshire Railway (to which Spooner had been Engineer) and being now linked with the Cambrian at Afon Wen was to obtain running powers into Portmadoc itself. To achieve a diversion, Spooner's plan was to project a new narrow gauge line northwards from Portmadoc via Beddgelert and thence to Caernarvon, so linking the important slate ports of Caernarvon and Portmadoc whilst at the same time giving interchange for all types of traffic with the standard gauge at these ports. Such a line would deter the London and Oswestry-based companies from extending their empire into territory which, while of vital interest to the Festiniog Railway, interested Spooner more personally in respect of his private affairs and his connections with the local slate industry. His first personal thrust came through plans for the North Wales Narrow Gauge Railways project of 1872. Not all of this ambitious scheme came to be (see Part 6) but ultimately a narrow gauge line was built from Dinas on the L.N.W.R.'s Caernarvon–Afon Wen line (the former Caernarvonshire Railway) towards Rhydd-ddu or South Snowdon. It opened to Quellyn Lake for all traffic by 15 August 1877 and was a highly unsatisfactory compromise, as it reached neither Caernarvon in the north nor Beddgelert in the south, but it did have the merit of tapping most of the more important slate quarries in the neighbourhood, (such as they were).

At first, this new line had opened to Quellyn on a goods-only basis, and within three days of this event, Spooner produced a master plan in which he hoped to interest the Board of the Festiniog Railway. He entitled this 'A Project to secure Railway connections with the Festiniog Railway at Portmadoc by a connecting link with the North Wales Narrow Gauge Railways at Rhydd-ddu on the 2 feet gauge, the latter forming a junction with the Caernarvonshire Railway near Caernarvon. Also a line to Snowdon.' In the ensuing statement he wrote: 'It is daily becoming more apparent that what with the threatened Lines of the Railways between Bala and Festiniog and the Merionethshire Railway in junction with the Cambrian Railway near Minford; and also the L.N.W.R. Line in course of construction from Bettws-y-Coed to the Blaenau Quarries at Duffws, that a considerable quantity of Festiniog traffic will be absorbed, not only in respect of slates and goods, but the passenger traffic will to some extent be reduced . . .' (here he draws attention to the compensating traffic which he hoped the L.N.W.R. would produce for the Festiniog Railway) . . . 'It is the passenger traffic which is the most remunerative to your Company and obvious that steps should be taken to increase the traffic . . . The mode for increasing and maintaining the traffic of your own line is in your own hands to mature. What is now required is to grasp the opportunity and give such encouragement as will allow others to construct the proposed connections. The following table is an approximate maximum estimate for the construction of the lines of railways shown in red on the sketch plan;

(a)	4 miles of Croesor Railway 2 feet gauge to be purchased ($3\frac{1}{2}$ miles to Junction)	£13,000
	Relaying of Croesor Railway	8,000
(b)	$9\frac{1}{2}$ miles from Junction of Croesor Railway near Ynsfor to Rhydd-ddu via Beddgelert	45,000
(c)	4 miles of line from Rhydd-ddu (at Junction with the North Wales Narrow Gauge Line) to Snowdon on the Rigi system	28,000
		£94,000

After setting out this idea in full, Spooner adds expenses for surveys, Parliamentary expenses, engines and stock with an estimated capitalisation of £104,000 in Ordinary Shares and £34,666 in Debentures. The estimates of traffic for systems (a) and (b) involve 120,600 passengers per annum at 1¼d. per mile. Especially revealing is that the project envisages the construction of the new link by persons unconnected with the Festiniog Board, and that the Estimate furnishes sources of traffic then obtaining (about 1875).

Croesor Slate Company	1000 tons of slate per annum
Rhosydd Slate Company	5000 tons of slate per annum
*Hafod Llan Slate Company	16,000 tons of slate per annum
Pant-Mawr & Geraint	720 tons of slate per annum
Goods, Coal, Lime, Timber	4000 tons per annum

On the rack line to Snowdon summit, estimates were based on the experience of the actual Rigi line in Switzerland, opened in 1871. 55,000 passengers per annum were *anticipated*, the final net revenue for the whole system being calculated at £9,958.

(The House of Commons Sessional Papers of 1872 (3) p. 11, had already published a projected 'Snowdon Railway' for making a line from Llanberis to the summit of Snowdon with a capital of £30,000, loans of £7,500 and of intended length 4 miles 16 chains).

Spooner points out that working expenses would have to be lower than those on the Festiniog Railway as traffic would be mainly passenger and therefore costly to work. Only a small stock of mineral wagons would be required. His intention was that a separate company would build these railways and provide the rolling stock. The Festiniog Railway would operate the line and supply maintenance at (say) 60% of gross receipts (. . . 'or some other mode that would succeed in securing parties to raise the necessary capital to construct the lines proposed'). His estimate of actual profit to the Festiniog Railway was £1,992 per annum and that much traffic would originate from around Caernarvon and Beddgelert to pass south over the Festiniog, and then forward again by the L.N.W.R. In this respect, Spooner anticipated the circular tour which was to become such a feature of North Wales resorts' holidays with a zenith between the World Wars. Alas, when his dream became a reality, holiday makers found that the round trip from Llandudno and back via Blaenau Festiniog, Portmadoc and Dinas Junction entailed longer than they were prepared to give to a day on holiday, and the section between Portmadoc and Dinas became notorious for slow running, bad timekeeping and missed connections at Dinas for the North Wales coast.

* Not on the Croesor tramway network; slate loaded on to Croesor wagons at Pont Croesor. The proper title is Hafod-y-llan.

A feature of Spooner's tourist proposals was that traffic would pass from and to the then narrow gauge Festiniog & Blaenau Railway, and he ends by adding '. . . hence making a circular tour either way through the most attractive and beautiful parts of North Wales. The public are precluded from this district for the want of it' (i.e. the new railway link). He felt that 40,000 extra passengers per year would travel over the Festiniog and that new L.N.W.R. and G.W.R. lines now building would bring in 'swarms of tourists who would want to avail themselves of the ascent by rail at so much less cost, time and fatigue' (here he refers to the Snowdon rack line). He reminded his directors that half Festiniog profits came from passenger sources and urged them to consider the advantages should the lines be built. 'I beg therefore to submit for your serious consideration the above scheme to improve your property. The mode I propose is to take such steps as to ensure the lines (a), (b) and (c) being constructed (not at your own cost but at the expense of a separate and independent company, such as would ensure to your company a continuously increasing revenue in perpetuity) which in the present critical and uncertain position of your company is so desirable and such as would give you a foothold of a new and good district by the same gauge line as your own'. (30 May 1877.)

The Spooner project has been referred to in some detail because it forms the basis for most of the narrow gauge development in South Caernarvonshire. Although possibly appropriate at the time, it became less so as time went by. It is now impossible to trace why the Festiniog directors did not rise to Spooner's suggestions—possibly relations between Board and Engineer were simply commercial and the Board had no wish to feather the nest of an employee who clearly had ambitious intentions further afield and had already demonstrated them. There was also the perennial question as to the future of the slate industry seen against the economic background, the growth of labour unrest among quarrymen and a lack of local enterprise. Suitable sources of capital were likely to have been deeply committed as it was, and the recent failure of the N.W.N.G. Railways' ambitious plans conceived by Spooner, could not have encouraged the Festiniog Board to commit itself to further unproven enterprises where others had failed.

Throughout these negotiations, C. E. Spooner wore two hats, so to speak. He was of Spooner & Co., Engineers to the Portmadoc, Croesor & Beddgelert Tram Railway Company, and also Secretary to the Festiniog. Perhaps because of this, H. B. Roberts took over negotiations. These lapsed largely into an informal exchange of letters between Festiniog Directors (in Drogheda, Somerset and London) who replied via Spooner to Roberts' attempts to build the Beddgelert line. The five years permitted for the work was nearing its end when Roberts proffered a 'Heads of Agreement' scheme to the F.R. Board on 15 February 1883. In short, this proposed that the Festiniog should manage, equip and maintain the P.C. & B.T.R. Co. in perpetuity, the receipts to be divided equally between them and the F.R. The Portmadoc Co. was to build its line to Pont Aberglaslyn and bring the Croesor section up to passenger standards. As a second phase, it would extend to Beddgelert and in these two stages, the F.R. would take over responsibility. Two F.R. locomotives and three passenger trains, forty slate wagons etc. were estimated as required for this work.

This final carrot did not attract the donkey in the least. The F.R. Board was not interested; it had problems enough of its own. Firstly, they wanted to see the Portmadoc Co.'s line finished before they would discuss things. They called the scheme premature, the reward not nearly adequate enough, and no detail could be considered until construction was complete. To the P.C. & B.T.R. Co.'s suggestion that a physical junction between the two railways in Portmadoc be made at the joint expense of the two Companies, the F.R. Board replied they would not incur any further expense on their own line.

Although this outright refusal to be involved brought the matter to a close, Spooner made one more personal effort to interest his Board and show them the advantages of a tactical line to Beddgelert, not only to ward off standard gauge competitors but also to link eventually, with the N.W.N.G. line at Rhydd-ddu. The F.R. were not drawn by this either, and clearly no support was to come from elsewhere. The almost identical Welsh Highland Railway scheme of 1922 was therefore nothing more than another re-hash of the P.C. & B.T.R. Company's plans, and perhaps on 1 June 1923 the day of Welsh Highland opening, Spooner could be allowed a last laugh . . . from the grave.

So it was that whilst for the time being at least, the Croesor line did not materialise into the vital piece for completing the jig-saw-puzzle map of the county, it continued to feature in fresh proposals. The first was the Beddgelert & Rhyddu-ddu Railway of 1889 with Engineers Charles Minns and John S. Lawrence. This would link the south end of the N.W.N.G.R. with the Croesor line over much of the 'Tram' route of 1879 save that it used the west side of the Glaslyn valley. Plans were deposited but nothing further done. Under the Light Railways Act of 1896 a scheme was dated 1898 with the title Portmadoc, Beddgelert & Rhyddu-ddu Railway and was strictly a re-hash of the 1889 plan except for changes in course. Thomas

Roberts & Sons of Portmadoc were the Engineers. Powers were sought to work over the Croesor Tramway between Parc and Portmadoc and for this section of the Tramway to be embodied in the new undertaking. A new branch was to be built from a point north of the Croesor/Cambrian level crossing to pass along the Cambrian's interchange siding and terminate on the site of the former Gorseddau Junction & Portmadoc/Cambrian crossing just east of Portmadoc station. An alternative title for this scheme was to be the Portmadoc, Beddgelert & Snowdon Light Railway.

Proposals for building standard gauge lines, some involving the use of the Croesor Tramway are now summarised below:

Carnarvon, Beddgelert & Port Madoc; Carnarvon, Pen-y-groes & Pwllheli Direct Railways. (Session 1864–5). Engineers: H. J. and J. W. Gridlestone. A route over much of the later Welsh Highland Railway. Also a coastal line over the Lleyn to Pwllheli with a branch to tap the Tal-y-sarn Quarries in the Nantlle Area. This scheme did not directly involve the Croesor line.

Beddgelert Railway. Plans deposited 30 November 1865. Engineers: Ordish & Le Feuvre, London. A line from Llyn Gwynant, through Beddgelert and thence along the west bank of the Glaslyn to Portmadoc. (Not involving the Croesor directly.)

Portmadoc & Beddgelert Railway. (Session 1881–2). Engineers: Ordish & Le Feuvre. A line from a junction with the Cambrian Railways at Portmadoc using the Croesor route to Pont Croesor and then an adjacent but parallel course, eventually reaching Beddgelert, partially on the planned course of 1866—see above. Clearly a tactical scheme to draw local narrow gauge interests—a ruse in which it succeeded.

The Land Register accompanying the above shows the lessee of the Weighing Machine and Platform of the Beddgelert Siding, Portmadoc, to be Thomas Savin, the lessee of the Aberystwyth & Welsh Coast Railway. The land surrounding the Siding was part of the Tremadoc Estate (Francis William Alexander Roche).

Portmadoc, Beddgelert & Snowdon Light Railway. (1897). An alternative title for the scheme described previously, but revived under the Light Railways Act of 1896. Formal application never made.

It may now be seen that this simple tramway of limited intentions formed the subject of various strategic schemes for over 35 years; some of these reached an advanced stage but none altered the physical appearance of the line. It remained a horse-worked tramway straddling the dykes of the Traeth Mawr and threading the upper valley with an isolated pair of rails which looked so improbable in such an expanse of mountainscape. Ultimately it became a part of yet another scheme to link Rhyddu-ddu, the terminal of the North Wales Narrow Gauge Railways, and Portmadoc.

On 17 August 1901 the Portmadoc, Beddgelert & South Snowdon Railway was incorporated (1 Edward VII Cap. 262). Under an Agreement previously reached (18 March 1901) the Tram Railway Co. had agreed to sell its interests to that new railway conditionally upon it receiving Parliamentary authority. So on 30 June that year, the Croesor under the mantle of the Portmadoc, Croesor & Beddgelert Tram Railway Company Limited, sold its powers to the new owners for £10,000. On the assumption of the Russell mortgage, the original investors lost all their capital.

The last entry for the Company appears in the Stock Exchange Year Book for 1901 when John Edward Jones, 16 Bank Place, Portmadoc, was Receiver. The position summarised therein was for an authorised railway of 9 miles of which five had been built. £20,000 of the authorised £48,000 in £10 Shares had been raised; Loans of £330 @ 5% and £8,000 @ 5½% had been made against the power to raise £15,980. All the capital was held by Hugh Beaver Roberts. No dividends had been paid for the past year. The two mortgagees were currently J.C. Russell and Henry William Assheton Littledale.

On the ground, so to speak, the staff employed at the end of the Tram Railway Company's life included 2 clerks, 3 horse drivers, 2 men on the track and 2 'miscellaneous'. These made a total of 9 men, 'no boys' (sic). From previous records this suggests that one horse and driver was employed between Portmadoc and Parc, and the other on the top level in the Croesor valley.

From the 1901 move, it might have seemed that the Croesor line was on the brink of bigger things and that at least some evidence of its new ownership would become tangible without delay. Not at all. With thirty-six years of life behind it, another two decades were to pass before the plans of its new masters came to maturity, and by then, even they had gone out of business under that title!

Having shown that the history of the line was more marked by paper work than track work, more by tactical moves in the office than outward signs along the railway, it is fitting to look as deeply as the meagre records will allow into the tramway as it was worked (almost without change of system) from 1864 to about 1920.

Firstly it must be said that its owners conceded it had a two-fold purpose and the accounts were divided accordingly. The line was divided into two operational units; between Portmadoc Wharves and the Beddgelert Siding, and between the Beddgelert Siding and the quarries to the north-east. The former was the 'Siding Traffic', the latter the 'Croesor Traffic'. The key to this system was the opening of the standard gauge and the connection to it via the exchange Beddgelert Siding, which continued to be of prime importance even after Festiniog Railway slate traffic began to enjoy its own private trans-shipment yard with the Cambrian at Minffordd, opened in 1872.* And it must be added, that even after this date, Beddgelert Siding continued to trans-ship large tonnages of slate, possibly due to the fact that Minffordd was congested. Luckily for the Croesor, its route from Portmadoc wharves, over the Cambrian to the Siding, was a goldmine financially. Ex-Festiniog slate, carried by Festiniog trains, was taken forward from the Harbour station throat, and onto the quays. Here, it would be collected by horse and taken back over Croesor metals through the streets to the Siding. Consignments of Cambrian-borne goods were off-loaded at the Siding and taken down to be loaded into ships along the same route.

Secondly there was the importance of the Flour Mill traffic, the consignees being the Portmadoc Steam Flour Mill Company. The Mill was beside the tramway between wharves and Cambrian crossing and though the haul was short, tonnages were high and most of the flour was shipped out by sea. A much smaller but useful quantity was carried in the days of the Gorseddau line, from Clenenney Mills by that railway. Croesor income from this source was small, the journey being so short.

Before the opening of Minffordd yard, all Festiniog locomotive and other coal due for carriage up the Festiniog, was trans-shipped at Beddgelert Siding, taken to the wharves and left for the Festiniog Bottom Shunting Engine to marshal.

'Croesor Traffic' was off-loaded at Beddgelert Siding or continued to the quays. Coastbound traffic included slate and slab, but inland traffic was considerable in timber, foodstuffs, coal, manures, lime and occasionally track materials, ballast and machinery for quarries or repairing inclines.

The first wages were paid on 10 August 1864 for a working week of nine days. The Croesor appears to have used the tonnage method of costing and though at the start the hauliers were paid a daily rate, later it was done by tonnage as was payment for the hire of wagons. This began in May 1870.

Haulage was done by men who, as just mentioned, were paid by the tonnages hauled (e.g. 2s. 3½d. per ton for slate). They were obliged to find and feed their own horses, so relieving the tramway of providing motive power. In the halcyon days, two hauliers worked the

* An interesting side-issue being the objection of the Tremadoc Estate to the Minffordd yard scheme, due to loss of income from tonnage over F. R. and Croesor.

top level, two the lower. When David Hamfray* (the Manager at £25 per year) made one of his regular inspections, a haulier with horse would call for him at 'The Sportsman Hotel, Portmadoc', and the cost of the horse etc. was paid over and above the usual slate contract. H. B. Roberts made similar inspections each February and August. In the matter of wagons too, the tramway preferred to hire rather than own and left the quarry owners to provide their own. The Festiniog Railway appears to have been the most useful source for these, though clearly the demand fluctuated wildly and occasionally traffic was so low that no wagons were hired at all.† Latterly there was evidence of preference to hire from quarries on its own system, as both New Rhosydd and William Kellow are creditors for hire of slate wagons. Timber was carried on Festiniog bolsters, there being no one else who could provide them. Accountancy for these was somewhat lax as suddenly there appears an item in the books for 'Hire of Timber wagons—Three years' and then another for two years. When business was brisk wagons were hired from Rhosydd, Kellow and the Festiniog. Clearly the rates of carriage were long unchanged. On 21 March 1893 the Secretary told the Board of Trade, 'Our railway . . . has only a small traffic consisting of slate and the old rates that were in force prior to the passing of the Railway and Canal Traffic Act of 1888 are still extant as we were bound by agreements existing between the slate quarry proprietors and our Company.'

Clearly the two men working on the line were kept busy. The horses' hooves cut the sleepers and mentions of renewals appear frequently in the accounts. The Glaslyn Bridge must have given constant trouble from the start and was consistently under repair; in September 1877 materials for this, including hire of horse, cost £19 18s. 1d. In a Return to the Board of Trade of 1896, the bridge was said to be subject to monthly inspection and be in 'Good Condition'. Floods regularly breached the line; the sea cut through the embankment near the Flour Mill at times, and flood water damage was done to stone and earthworks. Embankment walling tended to slip and an extra buttress on the Croesor wall cost £3. To repair a breach made by the high tide cost 14s. 8d. including hire of horse for the day at 7s. In 1880 Wagon No. 60 (probably wooden and Festiniog property) caught fire; repairs cost £1 17s. 6d. 'Timber keys' for one year (1877)

* Homfray also audited the Croesor United accounts for £5 a year in his spare time!

† Example: In December 1889 only one Festiniog wagon was hired—for £1 6s. 8d.

cost £8 13s. 10d. and the Festiniog was paid £39 9s. for hire of wagons two years previously.

H. B. Roberts received irregular payments of varying sums of money, classified as 'dividend' but obviously based on what the kitty could bear; at first it was about £200 a year. There was one for £50 in February 1877 and amounts of £25 or £10 appear two or three times per year later on. In January 1882 he acted for the Company in opposing the Beddgelert Railway scheme, receiving £50 in fees. His last dividend was £10 in October 1881.

A temporary but interesting user of the line was the Hafod-y-llan or South Snowdon Slate Quarry. Their quarry was to be found at the end of a considerable tramway which included two inclines about one mile south of Snowdon summit. The tramway ended beside the road at Nant Gwynant and carts were used into Portmadoc from there. Between January and May 1875 and again between March and June 1881, the quarry off-loaded at the short siding by the Pont Croesor. This was done because the slate was to be carried by the Cambrian and trans-shipped at Beddgelert Siding. South Snowdon, though unconnected by rail with the Croesor Tramway, placed 1,600 tons of slate on the line in the early part of 1875, and was quoted in Spooner's Report of 1877. Although isolated quarries with their own railway systems will be considered in the second volume, this quarry is so closely linked with the Croesor that it must be taken as if it were physically connected with it. This it would have been had there been the opportunity. The quarry was owned by Allen Searell, a Devonian who had come to Wales to develop mining. He worked for copper at Sygun near Beddgelert and for slate at Cwm Orthin. He speculated at Hafod-y-llan, successfully, and at Cefncam, ruinously. He came to Beddgelert in 1841 and died in 1865 after which his son failed to make headway for long. The records of Hafod-y-llan are partially undated, but Searell was working there in the 1840s. An undated Specification (possibly about 1850) for a railway to Portmadoc quay was thwarted by the same personality as faced the Gorseddau during the 1850s, the landowner John Priestley. Searell intended to build a complete line too, but his successors had to make do with a truncated system which put the slate into carts at the edge of the Nant Gwynant valley. His specification included an 8 ft. wide horizontal loading gauge, which suggests he may have considered the then gauge of the Gorseddau, namely 3 ft. There were to be 'iron rails of a pattern approved by the Engineer, not more than 15 ft. long and to weigh not less than eighty pounds each bar . . . to be laid in iron chairs not exceeding three feet from centre to centre, none to weigh less than seven pounds . . . good sound stone sleepers 14 inches square by 8 inches depth . . . and the ends of each rail to be fastened in an iron chair etc. etc.'. Searell prepared an estimate for re-opening the quarry—which he had ceased to work some years before—in 1856 and Wyatt of former Penrhyn connections produced another in 1860. Searell clearly believed that without a railway outlet there was little point in spending money to develop the quarry, despite its potential. His papers refer constantly to the problem of getting land for the line and the many amendments required by the Turnpike Trustees. His death brought the proposition to an end, and when a public company put out a prospectus for 6% Debentures in June 1869 for the Hafod-y-llan (Snowdon) Slate Company Ltd., the only rail systems were to be additional ones within the quarry.

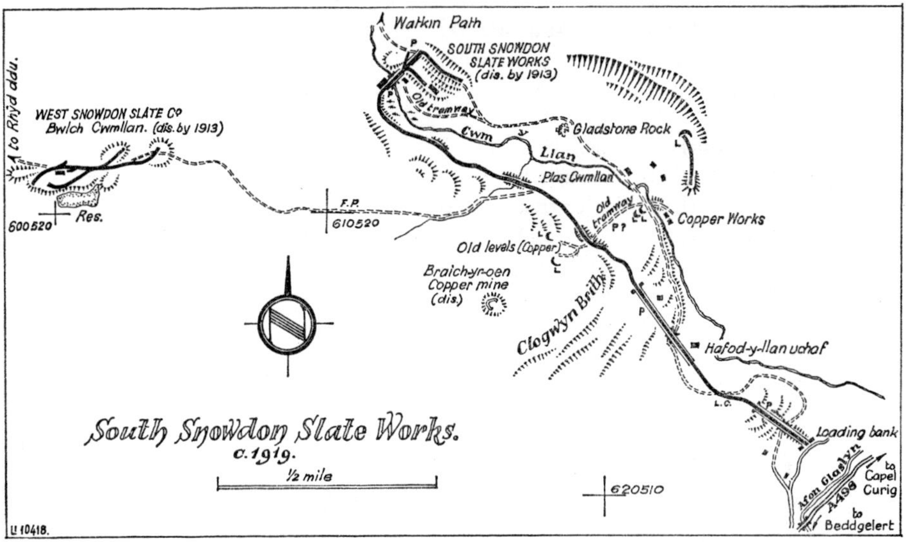

The new venture reflected the mood of the times. At Bryn Eglwys the proprietors were also in the Lancashire Cotton Trade. At Prince of Wales they were London Wine Merchants. Now it was rum; the Chairman was Mr. Lemon Hart and co-director was brother David. Other directors included the Rev. W. Kitching of Runnymede, Windsor—they were all Londoners otherwise. The Resident Engineer was none other than Hugh Unsworth McKie C.E., who of course was still in office at Croesor United. The Company had bought the business from Searell's son and obtained a 51-year lease. There was a barracks for 150 men and a 50 h.p. turbine for the machinery; £5,000 was reserved for building a tramway and inclines which were constructed almost at once. Output was put on the Croesor Tramway whenever a consignment had to leave the Beddgelert Siding by Cambrian Railways.

Another temporary user of the Croesor was the Glistening Valley Mining Co. of Penant (being the title on the folio in the ledger). The whereabouts of this venture is uncertain and if it was in the Pennant Valley, why did not the traffic pass over the Gorseddau? From the entry, one cannot tell if it *did* come over that line and the charge was simply for running over Croesor metals to Portmadoc. Perhaps by then there was no traffic on the Gorseddau? At all events the phase was short-lived; but between 12 January 1889 and 7 February, about 40 bags of copper ore were moved over the Croesor. (About 30 bags could be stowed in one wagon.) This appears to have been a healthy output and one wonders how such ponderous loads were accommodated by alternative transport afterwards . . . or was this simply a once-only consignment requiring part-Croesor transport?

A curt entry of April 1879 shows that the New Rhosydd Slate Co. repaid A. B. Roberts £200 in settlement of debt; this must have been money lent through the tramway business, but which Roberts of the two Directors is not clear. There would seem to be a clerical error but it carries the implication that loans from the Roberts' to New Rhosydd were not paid off until then.

In May 1877 571 tons of new ballast were purchased and by 1883 business was brisk enough to employ two hauliers on each section again. The upper one was then termed 'Croesor Valley & Inclines'. At this period the Festiniog charged 4d. per ton mile for hire of wagons.

After the concern became mortgaged and payments to H. B. Roberts ceased, there are annual entries for the remainder of the life of the business :

Williams & Co., Bangor	Use of Incline	£19	7s.	7d.
Williams & Co., Bangor	Use of Railway	82	4	3
H. Griffith & Son, Portmadoc		57	15	9
H. J. Robinson & Sons, 2 King St., Blackburn*		55	0	0

One, if not all of these payees were lawyers, probably collecting on behalf of the mortgagees and landowners.

Wagonwork, wheels, tyres, incline rollers and the like were supplied by Isaac Williams of Portmadoc. Two new wagons were supplied by them in June 1870 and again in July 1890 for £10 11s. 6d. and presumably re-sold as none ever appeared on Croesor Returns.

* Solicitors to the Portmadoc, Croesor & Beddgelert Tram Railway Co.

New wheel tyres were bought at the same time for £3. Other Portmadoc concerns to supply wire ropes, incline drums etc. were Owen Isaac & Owen, and J. Henry Williams & Sons. There was also a continual demand for yellow grease for the incline ropes.

Relationships with the Tremadoc Estate are outlined in some Instructions to Counsel prepared by solicitors Breese Jones & Casson of Portmadoc in about 1901 in connection with the preparation of a conveyance. The Portmadoc end of the tramway traversed Estate lands for about 2½ miles. The Estate was then the subject of a Chancery suit. F. W. A. Roche at the time of building the line was then an infant and a Mr. David Williams claimed to be mortgagee in possession of the Estate.* It was said that Williams had allowed Beaver Roberts to build the Tramway through the Estate without agreement being made as to terms of purchase. In 1868 the Court declared Williams to be mortgagee for about £100,000. In 1873 a Receiver was appointed pending Roche's majority, the mortgage being reduced to £82,000 by the sale of lands in 1893, the balance being re-invested in three new mortgages. When Roche's Trustees came into possession of the Estate they pressed the tramway into terms of settlement for the acquisition of lands and about 1883 it was agreed that an annual sum of £50 should be made over. No proper agreement was ever made, but the sum was paid annually. (The Estate's land was used by every railway in the vicinity of Portmadoc.)

In the matter of mileages, the Accounts have a pencilled note in the flyleaf:

Parliamentary portion of railway in Parish of Llanfrothen	180 chains
Private portion of railway in Parish of Llanfrothen	230 chains
	410 chains

The most distant incline at Blaen-y-cwm was damaged by New Rhosydd in late 1874 and cost them £16 13s. 7d. in repairs; it was provided with new rollers and wire rope in November 1890 at a cost of £43 11s. 3d. Owen Isaac & Owen supplied the rollers. Perhaps this was the last renewal?

The management was clearly interested in the welfare of its employees and in this respect could have been ahead of others in the locality. In August 1891 there was an 'Excursion Trip to Chester for

* F. W. Alexander Roche, born 1859, died 1875; grandson of W. A. Madocks and son of his daughter Eliza Anne.

the Railwaymen; 7 @ 4s. plus Dinner @ 10s. £1 18s. od.'. The following year a day out was arranged to Shrewsbury.

There is a domestic note in March 1888, 'Bag of Peas, lost in transit (Value 2s. 6d.).' The Gorseddau Railway left a bad debt of £26 6s. 5d.; in July 1887 there is a note against this entry 'thought to have ceased working and have no funds'.

Officially at least, that portion of the tramway beyond the length absorbed by Statutory Undertakings, still survives and has never been closed. This is the private tramway or Croesor Tramway proper. It was auctioned on 14 October 1936 and stated then to have been a substantial source of revenue to the Park and Croesor Estates. A Deed of 20 June 1871 contained reference to the carriage of goods but the 1936 auction particulars stated that 'no one had exercised the rights contained in that Deed for upwards of 20 years'.*

So oddly enough, it is the Croesor Tramway which in 1972, may still be seen in places in a form in which it has lain undisturbed for many a year. Its link with Portmadoc has come and gone, the last rails there being lifted in June 1949 as the final stage of the Welsh Highland Railway disposal. In the 1950s the private section was still operational; an ancient Ford farm tractor slewed its way uncertainly along the muddy formation straddling the rails and hauling three open wagons still showing 'Parc & Croesor' lettering faintly on their sides. Their contents were not slate however, but cow dung—which is precisely the type of local traffic that Hugh Beaver Roberts intended the tramway should convey when he started in business in 1864.

The Route described

The most southerly tip of the Croesor Tramway was at the rear of the Oakeley Slate Company's Wharf and close by the Public Wharf on the west bank of the Glaslyn, where at the time of its building, it would be closely inter-related with the Festiniog Railway's several lines and the various connections at Greaves and Rhiwbryfdir Wharves close by. Running northwards, it curved behind the two aforementioned wharf yards and crossed the foot of London Road (now High Street) at right angles and on the level. Coming up on its right hand would have been the Gorsedda (as it was then spelt) Tramway, which had also crossed London Road lower down and would then cross the Croesor line by a rail level crossing at an acute angle. Apart from mixed gauge trackage, there would have been no connection between the two tramways for until its own Act, the Gorseddau line was of 3 ft. gauge until at least 1872. These circum-

* See Narrow Gauge Railways in N. Wales (C. E. Lee), p. 60.

stances are thought to be the reason for sections 31 of the draft of the Croesor and Port Madoc Railway Act to have been worded: 'The existing and extension railways shall be made, maintained and worked on a gauge of *two* feet; Provided that, it shall be lawful for the Company at any time hereafter, with the previous approval of the Board of Trade, to increase the gauge of the existing and extension railways from *two* feet to any gauge not exceeding *three* feet' (the italics are in the original draft). When assented to, this section of the Act had been amended on Advice to enable the gauge to be increased to 4 ft. 8½ in. gauge.

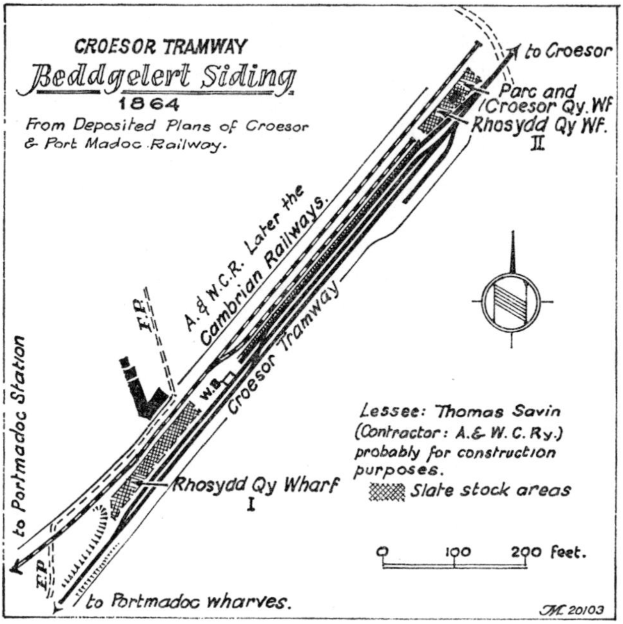

The tramway proceeded northwards (climbing at 1 in 228), passing out of the terraced housing and traversing a slow curve round the east fringe of the town and using what was to be, in 1864, the west shore of the Inner Harbour, formed by the Glaslyn above the Sluice Bridge. Turning slightly eastwards and now on level track, it entered the monotonous 'slob land' behind the town, a flat and almost treeless expanse where once the sea invaded. After a few yards of 1 in 924 a level crossing was then made with the Aberystwyth & Welsh Coast Railway (0 m. 39 ch.) on the north-west side of which an A. & W.C.R. siding came up alongside the Croesor and there was a high level interchange wharf with narrow gauge slate stockyard, weighbridge, sidings etc. From earliest times this was known as the Beddgelert Siding (loop 600 ft.), taking its name as was often the custom in North Wales, from the nearest rail point to a place rather than any acquisitive intent on the part of the owners.* Here the line fell for a short distance at 1 in 833 (and six chains beyond Beddgelert Siding, facing southbound trains was a short spur of uncertain age on the east side used for loading sand).

Running along the top of Creassy's 1800 embankment the tramway rose at 1 in 3,556 along an unremarkable route with little for company save for sheep and dyke as far as Portreuddyn (1 m. 49 ch.). At this point the Creassy work turned inland and the builders were obliged to build their own embankment for the next stage to Pont Croesor. As the Croesor line was worked by horsepower and loops were provided at regular intervals, here too, was the first passing place northwards from Portmadoc. There are the remains of a slab milepost just beyond the loop. (Loop = 180 ft.).

Now at marsh level, the line climbs only six feet above the surrounding land before reaching Pont Croesor (2 m. 25 ch.), a place remarkable for nothing at all save that here the tramway crossed the old road between Penrhyndeudraeth and Tremadoc (built as a short cut between the original Coast Road which, before land reclamation, ran inland to Pont Aberglaslyn to connect these two places) and the Afon Glaslyn—being the first road crossing of that river inland from Portmadoc's Britannia Bridge. To this point the river is tidal under certain conditions. The six foot of climb between Portreuddyn and here brought the line along the top of a low broad embankment at Pont Croesor, enabling it to cross the road there on the level and keeping it clear of Glaslyn flooding. Here and there original culverts remain, built of slab and unrebuilt in Welsh Highland times. Along the south side of this embankment, within tramway boundaries, was a substantial drainage ditch.

Seven chains before reaching Pont Croesor road crossing, a 110 ft. siding, its point facing Portmadoc, ran off tangentially on the north side of the track. Its usage is problematical as, although so close to the nearby road, there was only a footpath connection to it. Hafod-y-llan was among users of it.

On the south side of the road crossing which followed, there was formerly a gate across the rails; with the road to its right, the tramway now crossed the Glaslyn on the eight-span bridge already described. It then ran parallel to and somewhat higher than the adjacent

* A similar example was the L.N.W.R.'s Bryn Eglwys Siding, near Corwen.

road, one or two spans being inserted in the embankment to aid the clearance of flood waters. Slab piers and spans were used and may still be seen.

The line continued almost due north-east, curving very slightly eastwards, crossed a farm access road on the level and lost the adjacent road which swung away eastwards. The slow curve is now towards the north and all the way a very gentle upward inclination continues. The formation is a low embankment, just sufficient to keep the rails clear of the boggy surroundings yet at the same time, of substantial proportions. At 3 m. 30 ch. there was another access road crossing on the level where once more the tramway was gated but not the road—this was the practice throughout. To the left was the Lodge for Ynysfor, a large house standing in the grounds of Ynys Fawr (the name being a corruption) once a considerable island in the Glaslyn estuary, and easily recognisable as such today as it stands proud above the surrounding marshland. To the north-east is a much smaller 'island', named Ynys Fach (the names mean Big Island and Little Island; c.f. Great Island and Little Island, Lee Estuary, Co. Cork).

Occupying a similar position on the north side of the line, there was another 40 ft. siding on the Portmadoc side of the occupation crossing. Unlike Pont Croesor, this was conveniently placed as a loading point and was certainly used within living memory for the carriage of farm materials, manures etc. by tramway wagon.

Now follows a straight section, flanked by drainage ditches, as far as the later Croesor Junction (3 m. 59 ch.).* Though the surrounding land is flat and turbary, the line lay in a positive amphitheatre of hills, a magnificent situation for a line of rails and a vantage point which was to have all too short a life for those who could visit it by passenger train. Ahead and above, lies the valley above Croesor village, Cnicht to the left with its Matterhorn peak; to the right the twin domes of Moelwyn. Each side the hills rise to buttress this central picture, certainly one of the loveliest in North Wales. In summer the semi-circle of mountains rise from the old foreshore in varying shades of green and brown, backed by blue sky; in winter a cold clear day, the greens subdued and the browns almost black, with the inevitable mantle of snow coming down to within 500 ft. of sea-level, highlights the path of the old Croesor Tramway. Looking north-east from Croesor Junction, the various inclines and quarry branches stand out in a third dimension of snow and sun shadow; the great incline at the far end of the main line, and the shelf-like location of the Pant-mawr Quarry branch as it picks its way among the boulders along the

* Known locally by its original name of Erw Fawr.

flanks of Moelwyn. Imagination supplies a picture of how the slate from this remote place eventually came trundling down., past this same spot en route for shipment at the Port.

Before the coming of the Welsh Highland, there was nothing to mark what later became Croesor Junction. Today, with the wheel turned full circle, there is little either. Sheep, black Welsh cattle and jackdaws have it to themselves . . . and even when the 'proper' railway came, there was little interruption to their lives from that. Forging onwards, the tramway, still on an almost imperceptible embankment, turned clockwise through a quarter circle and made towards what at this point are correctly termed the foothills of Snowdonia, formidable as they look. Years ago, these same crags were cliffs above the shore. Today they overhang the old Coast Road which now the tramway ran alongside and under the lee of the great bluff of rock which was considered prominent enough a feature in the Act; Carreg-hylldrem. Shortly, the Coast Road—as it was—is reached, and crossed on the level; once again gates protect the tramway but not the road. Beside the line runs the Croesor, a tributary of the Glaslyn, and up its valley the tramway takes its course. Once over the road, a last short rise of 1 in 302 ensues. There was a peculiar double siding in similar position, both entering a stone shed used for warehousing. The track now reached the foot of the Lower Parc Incline (length 1,725 ft.) and the main line turned left for the incline foot. Ahead a branch ran level for a stretch, then rose by an incline, crossed the Afon Maegwyn and so up a second incline into the Park (or Parc) & Croesor Quarry. This working had opened as the Parc Quarries in 1866 and ultimately became part of Park & Croesor Slate Quarries Co. Ltd. which was formed 21 August 1895. It was meanwhile owned by James Staveley in the 1880s and employed about twenty men. William Kellow bought it and after May 1893 his son Moses—then proprietor of the Croesor quarry also, became Managing Director. Its storage sidings were dubbed by the Croesor management 'Moses Kellow Siding'. The quarry began using the tramway about 1878. Moses Kellow, a Merioneth County Councillor, appears to have owned and managed the concern until both Park and Croesor quarries closed in 1930, the last on the tramway to survive.

Apart from spoil tips and the remains of dressing sheds, there is little evidence of working today; the source of slate was underground. In 1921, Spring's Report stated this quarry was sending 80–100 tons of slate a year down to the Beddgelert Siding for the Cambrian.

Returning to the foot of the incline, there was a loop line in the main tramway (4 m. 50 ch.) and storage sidings for the Park quarry.* At the top of the Lower Parc incline was a short storage siding and an 'S' bend in the main line made necessary by the desire to make the tramway 'lift' into two shorter sections rather than one of great length involving much embankment work to keep it straight. The Upper Parc incline was 1,225 ft. long and its drum house at the summit was for years a prominent feature on the crest of the hill. From 19 ft. above sea level, the Lower Parc incline lifted the line to 275 ft. By the Upper Incline, the tramway was now above the 500 ft. contour. The short connection between the two inclines was less than 20 yards in length, but sufficient for operating purposes.† In 1949 all these works were complete though very overgrown; the track up to Croesor village began to disappear shortly afterwards. Now all is gone.

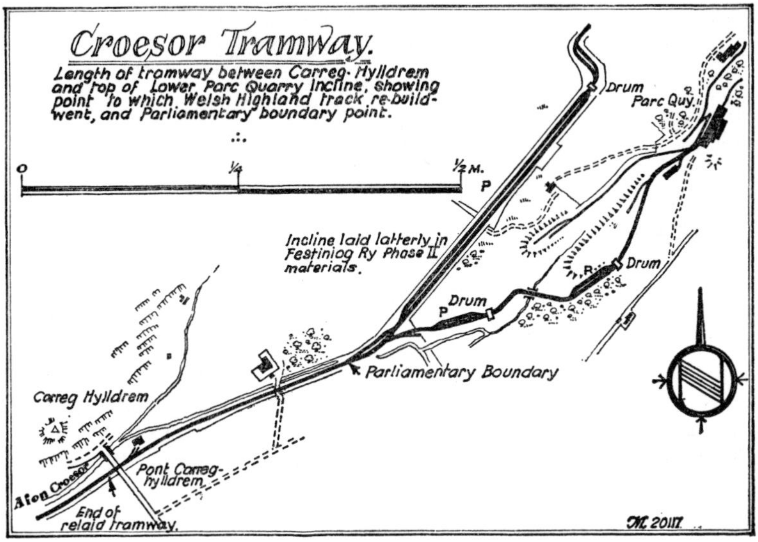

The tramway had now gone up and over the 'lip' of the upland plateau, and drove straight inland. There follows a fine drystone em-

* This point was the Parliamentary extent limit of the Croesor & Port Madoc Railway et. seq.

† Incline length figures quoted are taken from those given at the Auction of Park & Croesor Estates 14 October 1936. Sidings are quoted as being at 'Tresaethon, Brynhyfryd and at the upper terminus of the railway'. When the inclines were measured in 1884 by Thomas Roberts, C.E. of Portmadoc, he gave:

No. 1	Incline:	Blaen-y-cwm	693 ft.
No. 2	,,	Parc	1,140 ft.
No. 3	,,	Parc	1,716 ft.

bankment over 100 yards long being the principal work of its type on the system. Approaching the environs of Croesor village, there was another loop and a siding was thrown off to the right to serve the former Park Slate & Slab Quarries. The branch curved sharply south-eastwards and through a narrow cutting almost 25 ft. deep. Though not on the main tramway, it is the deepest cutting on the system. From the branch various sidings served the workings and one crossed the road on the level, stretched out across the valley and after climbing a short incline, served older workings long since closed. Both branch and quarry closed before World War One.

The main line now crossed the Afon Croesor by a bridge of three spans built in local material of slabs with stone piers. No wood or metal was used. Shortly it passes through the usual tramway 6 ft. gate, one of several on this upper section. As elsewhere, the gates were usually kept closed across the line, emphasising the original authority for building the line and the continuance of landowners' rights. Now followed an ungated road crossing outside Croesor village, a small hamlet which in recent years has been 'discovered' by sound and television, often connected with the pleasures of the promiscuous life which this remote place offered to those seeking concealment!

Onward again, with steeply upward-sloping ground to either side, the tramway ran beside the Croesor river along the upland valley which, even on a summer's day can be bleak. Almost treeless, it is rock strewn and sparsely populated with broken walls, deserted homesteads and farmhouses, a feature being the fencing of slates stuck end-downwards into the ground and wired along the upper ends. Mist, rain and wind are usually the companions of this place; even the lower fields are not cultivated and sheep graze there, straying up the steep slopes into boulders and gorse flanked pitches. Towering to the left stands Cnicht (2,265 ft.) and hidden to the right, the rounder Moelwyn Mawr (2,334 ft.) with their contrasting outlines. Once a telephone system flanked the tramway between village and the quarries. At Pont Sion-goch the Croesor is crossed again by a slab bridge. Here on the left is a level with an adit, its spoil being tipped between tramway and river; this was a loading point but there was no siding. From there the tramway ran almost straight, earthwork being confined to an occasional cutting and most of the line a simple embankment. The only excitement brought to this length was in 1949 when one of the quarry reservoir dams high above the valley head at Blaen-y-cwm, threatened to crack and was repaired. To reach the isolated spot a helicopter was used to carry cement etc. and the tramway embankment became a spectators' grandstand for the landing place in the adjacent field! Thus side by side were modes of transport almost a century apart. (Ultimately the helicopter crashed.)

Earthworks now vary up to ten feet deep, embankment work being 6 ft. wide, sufficient evidence that the works were built with increasing and heavy traffic in mind and quite suitable for steam locomotive traction. This straight length continues for about 1½ miles and at Bryn-hyfryd there was a short siding, entirely for agricultural traffic. The climb is steady all the way, but no dimension is on record and it is very slight; exceptionally, there is a short fall once or twice and sufficiently deterring to prevent the line being worked by gravity, however slight the general levelling may have been. Above and to the right the road to the Croesor Quarry (still in use but not as a quarry) climbs its solitary way, diagonally up the mountain face. En route it passes Bryn-hyfryd formerly the property of the tramway, but latterly the Croesor Quarry Manager's house whose last occupant was Moses Kellow, M.I.C.E., M.I.E.E., F.R.G.S., an engineer of very inventive mind. It was he who was responsible for the electrification of the quarry, and needless to add, Bryn-hyfryd was probably the finest all-electric house in North Wales before the First War. Kellow's main private customer was Lady Owen of Croesor Hall; he built a reservoir and fitted out the Hall's electrical supply, enabling her to dispense with all but one butler. Kellow invented a hydraulic rock drill, an electrical insulator made of slate, and his car included a float in an oil bath which gave automatic control with changes of level; this was tested on the quarry roadway. Croesor Quarry was among the most efficient of its time.

Shortly beyond this point was a junction to the right with a long incline which is still a predominant feature. The pointwork here was unusual; it was a special casting of bridge rails, one for each set of rails. The wing rails of the frog were raised into 'ears' which guided the outer faces of the wheels to prevent derailment; by this system, check rails were unnecessary. The tramway which this branch incline carries was laid in similar materials to the original tramway but was built about ten years later. The rail and chairs may have come from Festiniog surplus as a load of rails and chairs was invoiced on 11 October 1891. The incline was divided into two sections, with an 'S' connection between them; the upper section included an exceptionally steep length at the top. South-westwards from the summit there remains, despite rock falls etc. a fine example of drystone shelf construction into the Pant-mawr Quarry. This is a remote location and the works have been disused since the First War; little remains. A further short incline on to the col between Moelwyn Mawr and Moelwyn Bach ends in incomplete excavations. In these quarries all work was underground, and water-filled adits may be seen still with tramways submerged in them. Not all these are connected with the main tramway system. The more important adits have individual weighbridges at their entrances and are well preserved. They lie below the older Pantmawr workings and above the later Fron-boeth Quarry below.

Pant-mawr appears in the accounts between September 1877 and May 1892; it had been abandoned by 1916 and the tramway lifted by 1920. To reach the slate strata lower down the face a new tramway was built in the mid 1880s to serve the Fron-boeth workings. The top section of the lower incline from the main Croesor Tramway was continued up through the site of the drumhouse and a line led along a ledge southwards for a distance. It then turned sharply into the mountainside and by means of a tunnel somewhat over quarter of a mile in length, reached the hillside basin below the Pant-mawr workings. Whilst underground tunnels in connection with mining etc. commonly contain tramways, this tunnel is the main 'overground' example of its type in North Wales. At the south-east tunnel mouth are extensive spoil tips, mainly of granite however, which was used in the buildings. A two-stage incline doubles back up the hillside again and then runs parallel to but below the Pant-mawr branch above it. On the way it passes the Manager's Office and Dressing Sheds. The only other item which survives is a large Lancashire boiler probably used for water storage. As it would not have passed through the tunnel and is unlikely to have been erected on the site, the question of how it was brought here remains unanswered. The Fron-boeth Quarry lines were laid in more conventional flat-bottomed rails, and though they remained *in situ* for many years afterwards, work here stopped during the First War. It is a bleak place on anything but the best of days. Use of the Croesor tramway began about 1886.

Back on the main tramway and down below the aforementioned quarries, the tramway continues its unrelieved course for another half mile to the former Generating Station at Blaen-y-cwm, situated at the foot of a steep northern mountain barrier up against which the tramway has now come. There was once a loop and stabling sidings here, together with Station siding. Ahead rears up the Blaen-y-cwm Incline (835 ft.) which once carried both tracks and the supply pipeline to the Generating Station. This was the first of two inclines to carry the line up the face of the Bwlch-y-rhosydd ridge and the summit is over 800 ft. above the sea. There followed a spectacular section across the head of the valley by means of a mountain shelf carried on a rock wall and a bridge over the Afon Cwm-y-foel. Here there was another junction where the incline serving the Croesor Quarry rose steeply to the right, and at its foot, bridged the infant Afon Croesor. At the incline foot the Company first provided 'a hut for the horse' in December 1876.

The Croesor Quarry was the largest served by the tramway, being 1,600 ft. above sea level. Work began here about 1856 (and at the complementary Parc workings about 1866) and both were pioneers in hydro-electric power. By the building of reservoirs and the power station just noted, an output of 775 h.p. was obtained from turbines and two overshot water wheels. Alternating current was used throughout workings and mills and the half mile of main adit together with tracks outside were fitted with overhead supply wires to feed an electric locomotive, probably the first of its type. Built in the quarry workshops, it was of 30 h.p. The driver sat under the pillared-roof cab with pantograph above it and current was obtained from street-tramway type overhead cable suspension. To enable the loco to enter the workings it was both narrow and low; large headlamps were fitted at each end. The adit was near-level for some distance and then reached a vertical shaft to reach other levels. There are many natural sand-bottomed caverns and the surrounding rock is too hard even to take a scratch; a thin vein of white clay running through it cannot be removed if caught on the clothing!

Croesor Quarry was in the news as early as 1870 when a representative from 'Engineering' visited the site ('Engineering' 1870 (i) p. 405). The Croesor United Slate Co. had just abandoned hand labour and were using a diamond boring machine (on hire from The Diamond Rock Boring Co. Ltd., an American concern) instead. This was driven by compressed air obtained from a turbine worked by water supply to the Generating Station at Blaen-y-cwm, one of whose turbines was used for air compression. The whole rock drilling outfit was working in an inclined shaft and mounted on wagons; a tailrope was taken from thence, out through the adit mouth and a balancing wagon, suitably weighted, was fastened on its other end. The incline, apparently without beginning or end, is clearly visible on the mountainside below the Croesor workings and is commonly mistaken for an older tramway access to the quarry. The balance wagon carried a wooden tank; when the drill was down the shaft the tank lay under a mountain stream which when required, was diverted to fill the tank and draw the drilling rig clear of the face. At the balance incline foot a device automatically opened a valve and emptied the water tank. This work was begun in 1868 under contract with the Machine Tunnelling Company under the direction of John Vivian.

Work ceased in Croesor and Parc quarries in 1930. They were the last workings in the valley. After this there was spasmodic working and an occasional train on the tramway. More often it was a single wagon drawn by a horse and even in the early thirties, Welsh Highland trains were known to stop at Croesor Junction to attach a slate wagon in the rear. Sometimes a rail tractor from Boston Lodge worked to the foot of the Lower Parc Incline (heavier units were not allowed further than the Llanfrothen road level crossing as the track beyond here had not been relaid with flat-bottomed rail). No self-propelled units worked on the section above Upper Parc Incline.

During the Second World War, Croesor Quarry was requisitioned for storage purposes and continues to be used in this way. A much-improved road now serves the quarry but not the valley bottom along which the tramway runs. For this reason a part of this length still has track along it; in the early 1960s it was reasonably complete and a single wagon was used by farmers. A feature of the shorter inclines was that the horses transferred to different levels to pick up the wagons again; some formations were made wider to accommodate a horse-path. On most other tramways, horses were kept to their own levels.

'Train operation' within living memory has relied on horses being used without change from the foot of the Parc Incline, to the port. For this purpose horses were hired from Garreg Hylldrem, a farm near the foot of Carreg-hylldrem, as required. The largest and nearest village to this length of tramway was Llanfrothen and the inhabitants enjoyed rather a special relationship with the tramway. Llanfrothen's most convenient access to the tramway was along the rough but direct road to Ynysfor; at the level crossing there the siding was usually occupied by wagons used for bringing the necessities of the village within reach of road carts. Lime, coal and beer barrels came up from the port. Some of the more influential people of the locality would send word down to the siding that they intended to go 'to Port' the following day and for this purpose a wagon would be cleaned out; for instance, a mother would push her children in it not only the three miles to Portmadoc, but also the same distance back again. Even with the very slight descent to Portmadoc, it was said to be possible to coast along over much of the westward journey. (To these folk, Pont Croesor was a name brought in by the Welsh Highland Railway—Pont Reuddyn was its local name and Pont Croesor the bridge below Carreg-hylldrem.)

Returning now to the junction of the Croesor Quarry incline, there followed one of the most remarkable inclines of its type, New Rhosydd. It rose like Jacob's Ladder in a seemingly unending parabola to carry the line above the 1,400 ft. level. It was about 1,500 ft. long and at the summit was inclined at rather more than 1 in $\frac{3}{4}$, making ascent on foot almost impossible. It is a fine piece of civil engineering and its upper reaches are made from slate waste piled in an almost vertical tower. At the summit a rock wall forced the tramway to turn right along a shelf which is commonly swept by high winds as they rise up from the funnel-like valley below. Half a mile ahead is the abandoned New Rhosydd Quarry. Here in 1952 was a wilderness of dereliction with its broken barracks, mills and shed full of rusting machinery. Upturned wagons and dripping adits made a depressing environment; the main haulage adit was ⅔ mile long and wagons were moved along it by attaching them to an endless haulage rope. This is the farthest reach of the tramway. Just over the ridge beyond, into which New Rhosydd workings penetrate, are other workings which tunnel in from the south side and whose tramways are connected with the Festiniog Railway's branch system at Tan-y-grisiau.

In 1948 (when the Author made a full survey of the Tramway and its feeders), the track was in position from Carreg-hylldrem to the summit of the last incline, including the Croesor Quarry incline. At this time it was hoped that certain workings might be re-opened and the tramway re-used. It never was. The 'Slate Trade Gazette' of February 1911 had this to say '. . . The Croesor Tramway, 8 miles in length, serves the quarries to shipping at Portmadoc. There is 3½ miles of slate strata, and the mountains of Cnicht and Moelwyn are almost entirely slate. Croesor Quarry was opened in 1856 and Parc in 1866, the former producing roofing slate, the latter slate for manufacturing purposes. Both are underground and are complementary to one another. The Croesor Quarry is worked downwards in the usual manner, the Parc upwards to allow the spoil to fill the workings afterwards. The Croesor Quarries are 2,560 ft. above sea level.* Electricity is generated by water power for lighting and driving machinery. This was the first case of electricity being used in a slate mine for this purpose and also later for haulage and the underground drills etc. . . .'

The Croesor Tramway was the largest and longest of its kind and unique in North Wales. It was lengthy, remote and fascinating. It served quarries of interesting origin and up-to-date methods. Its lower length was the subject of many behind-the-scenes schemes and its upper length, no longer so cut-off from the outside world as in former days, is still out of reach of anyone without two good legs to gain it. Even today, there is still a little of the mystery and speculation which involved its progenitors over one hundred years ago. Other narrow gauge lines in North Wales were better known, but the Croesor deserves its unique place in rail transport history. It had a character unlike its contemporaries. Its quarries opened and closed in

* An exaggeration of 1,000 ft.

a barometric pattern of the economy: by 1914 only four remained at work—Rhosydd, Croesor, Pant-mawr and Parc.* The war closed Pant-mawr and the others remained to the slump of 1930.

Permanent Way

Writing in 1878, Vignes records that the track was exactly as laid on the Gorseddau Tramway, and the rails set to the same gauge. The rails were 20 lb. per yard in weight, though elsewhere they have been given as 15 lb. The rails were carried in iron chairs weighing 3 lb.; joints were made in wider chairs of similar pattern weighing 5 lb. Vignes describes the track as 'being like the original Festiniog Railway' which is a little misleading but accurate in general terms. The wooden sleepers were 4 ft. × 5 in. × 3½ in. deep at 2 ft. centres under joints and at 2 ft. 9 in. elsewhere. Fishplates were never used, only butt joints. Oddly enough, though in plentiful supply, slate or slab was never used for sleepers; its disadvantages were by then well known. Presumably the section of rail, a T section with a rib on one side of the lower edge, was copied from the Festiniog, although the section was quite different. This rail is of uncertain origin if one excepts the cruder forms in it which occurred among early standard gauge railways; a considerable mileage of it was used by the contractor operating over the unfinished sections of what was later to be the Welsh Highland Railway during the First World War. It is found sporadically all over North and Mid-Wales even as far south as the lead mining workings of Cardiganshire, but only the Croesor seems to have laid it as new material. The source of supply is not known and it does not usually appear as an available section in catalogues of suppliers. Unlike the flat-bottomed and bridge rail it requires the additional expense of chairs and keys, which would account for its unpopularity. The chairs were laid with the notch cast in them to receive the lower flange of the rail inside the track; the rail was secured in the chair by a narrow iron key (later wooden) driven in along the outside of the rail. There was clearly some variation in sizes as many rails had their bottom flanges cut away to make them fit the joint chairs. Two luxuries were permitted—double chairs were cast to take check rails, and double angled chairs were cast for frog crossings. Chairs were held to sleepers by iron pins. Detail variation in chairs occurs, the samples in the Narrow Gauge Railway Museum include a clean, well-shouldered specimen of later date.

The precise material used in the early pointwork is not known, but later points were built up from cast sections of left and right hand for

* Ref.: letter from Moses Kellow to J. Davies of 1 December 1914 re railway potential from Croesor quarries (N.L.W.: Davies Collection).

each running rail; the switch blade was pivoted and moved over a cast plate integral with the unit. The units had 'bridge section' rails with special sockets at each end to receive the T rail without recourse to a joint chair. At frogs there was either a cast piece socketed to receive T rails at each end and having a centrally pivoted bridge rail section in the centre, or a cast piece of conventional frog and wing rail type having raised wing rails which prevented the face of the wheels from running out of alignment. The former type of frog permitted a simple and single piece of trackwork forming an X to serve the purpose of a double slip without employing check rails or blades; there was a good example at the foot of Blaen-y-cwm Incline and another at Croesor Incline.

Away from the main running line, there was later occasional use of heavier T rail in heavier chairs of identical pattern as the old Festiniog track. These were purchased when obsolete on the F.R.

All rails were 15 ft. long, a common dimension of the early railway period. Oddly, Croesor, Conclog and Pant-mawr used a similar rail in chairs but contrived to manage without keys!

Motive Power and Rolling Stock

At no period during its life did the Tramway own any motive power. Horses were used from the first, and even these were hired under contract from farms. Thus there were no stables which featured beside many a similar line. The upper section never had self-propelled units along it though farmers were known to 'borrow' wagons and use them along the main line, hauled by a farm tractor straddling the rails. This was unofficial.

The section of the line between the wharves and Croesor Junction—though not in the period under review—became in part the southern end of the Welsh Highland Railway and in this form, steam locomotives and petrol tractors were used over it. But the short section of the former Croesor Tramway between Croesor Junction and Lower Parc Incline foot still remained faithful to the horse, though exceptionally, a tractor would make its way at least as far as the Llanfrothen road crossing. Some sources refer to this traffic continuing until 1937 and certainly an odd wagon occasionally passed, but regular slate haulage had ceased by 1930. In the first flush of enthusiasm, the W.H.R. borrowed the Festiniog's Baldwin tractor (purchased secondhand in 1925) from its shunting duties at Minffordd Junction from time to time, and used it to haul longer trains of slate wagons between Llanfrothen crossing and Portmadoc Wharves. This usage was very unpopular as it left Minffordd Exchange Sidings without motive power; from 1926 a Festiniog-owned

Austro-Daimler tractor began to make regular runs between Lower Parc and the wharves. It was light enough to run over Croesor rails which the Baldwin could not, and so more suited to the work. It was also tried on a passenger coach between Portmadoc and Croesor Junction (time 45 minutes for 3½ miles!), but when the slate traffic had dwindled away the tractor was pushed out of sight into the Boston Lodge Paint Shop in 1929, and never ran again ('Festiniog Railway', Vol. 1, p. 391).

Although strictly outside Croesor Tramway days, it is amusing to note a further example of Festiniog/Welsh Highland policy of the late 1920s. This was the nominal 'posting' (to use a military term in accordance with the Col. Stephen's regime then in being) of the Baldwin tractor. In 1937 Festiniog records note it as having been transferred to the Festiniog Railway along with other Welsh Highland stock and assets, and the tractor as having been formerly the property of the 'Croesor & Portmadoc Junction Railway'. This was simply a book transfer of doubtful legality, containing proof of illicit manipulation in that there never was a Railway of the name quoted, which was a corruption of the titles Croesor & Port Madoc Railway and Gorseddau Junction & Portmadoc Railways. Further, Festiniog accounts for 31 December 1925 show the tractor as a Festiniog purchase for £248 13. 4d. and the returns show an increase of one unit that year in the form of 'Petrol Tractor for Shunting'.

In practice therefore, the Croesor never owned any motive power, but in the quarries the position was different. According to a sales list of Croesor United Quarry Co. of September 1874, and another list of its successor the Croesor New Quarry Co. Ltd. of June 1883, there were probably two steam locomotives during this time, being the same two for the whole period. It can be assumed that both quarries had closed by 1881, and again in the 1890s; sporadic working is not uncommon, nor is successive ownership. Parc & Croesor Quarries were wound up on 8 February 1931 (having closed the previous year). Overhead wiring at Croesor was removed but the track left intact; in 1942 the premises were leased to Cooke's Explosives Ltd. who still use them—three Ruston & Hornsby Ltd. internal combustion tractors have been used there but none are now used. The two steam locomotives are believed to have been built by De Winton & Co. of Caernarvon and of their well-known vertical-boilered type. Their fate was that one was sold or scrapped and the other may have found its way to the Coedmadoc Slate Co. Ltd., Nantlle, in 1898. This company's quarry at Gloddfar-glai, Nantlle, is reputed to have received a De Winton about 1898 from Croesor district, the engine possibly having been built before 1874. It is assumed that the two engines at Croesor Quarry were disposed of after 21 August 1895 when Park & Croesor Quarries began business and the railway was electrified. The electric locomotive was cut up after the closure of 1930.*

The above-ground trackage in the Croesor Quarry was limited to the yard, which was of restricted size; the De Wintons were mostly therefore used underground as well as in the open—the adit was quite large enough to accommodate them. Otherwise the necessity for two engines is scarcely credible. Of all the quarries connected with the Croesor, only Pant-mawr would be deserving of a locomotive, but no record exists of one.

The slate wagons used over the tramway fell into four main types, the earliest being of the wooden-bar and cast-iron bobbin sided type so common in the district. Conversely to Festiniog practice, all wagons belonged to private owners, the Tramway having none of its own. Quite possibly many of these were built at Boston Lodge to Festiniog patterns, as Boston Lodge Works certainly produced wagons for other nearby lines. Later, small iron-framed wagons replaced the wooden ones. Both varieties held two tons of slate and weighed empty 10–12 cwt. (wooden) or 13–16 cwt. (iron). New Rhosydd preferred the frame type and an early view shows many wooden frame wagons in use. Whilst Park & Croesor used frame wagons they preferred sheet-iron sided wagons of which there were several variations. All were of fixed side and end type and those fitted with brakes were peculiar in that brake shoes worked on one pair of wheels only; the wheel on one side was braked from outside, and the wheel at the other end of the axle, from the inside. Brake handles

* Details of locomotives in these quarries may be found in 'Industrial and Independent Locomotives and Railways of N. Wales' (Birmingham Loco Club), 1968.

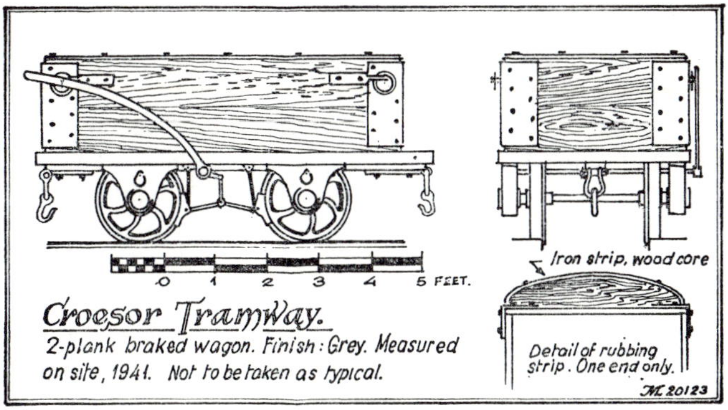

were pulled *up* to apply the shoes and these vehicles were distinguished by having horse-rings attached to the top-side strengthening rib, to which the haulage chain was attached. The fourth wagon variety was a wooden two-planked side and end wagon, again with fixed sides and ends. The owners are not positively identified.

Sheet-iron wagons were lettered with the quarry owner on the sides and the wagon number below; more recently this work was done in white stencilling but owing to extensive rusting, the iron-framed and planked wagons had lost all identification by 1940 when inspected—and worse, further investigation was made impossible at the time by the suspicions aroused in the local military by such necessary field-work!

All wheels were 1 ft. 6 in. diameter and other average dimensions (and colours) were:

Type	*Length overall* ft.	in.	*Width overall* ft.	in.	*Height overall* ft.	in.	*Wheelbase* ft.	in.	*Colour*
Wooden frame	5	3	2	7	3	2	3	0	Red oxide
Small iron frame	6	0	3	4	3	2	3	0	Dark grey & black
Sheet iron side	6	10	3	6	3	0	3	0	Dark grey & black
Wooden planked*	8	6	3	6	3	2	3	0	Red oxide

From the same work ('Festiniog Railway', Vol. 2, p. 405) is taken an example of a sample survey undertaken by the Festiniog Railway to ascertain how many of its wagons had 'strayed' from the parent system and were being used by quarries unofficially. This gave, incidentally, the stock of the quarries' own wagons. In 1928, only two Croesor valley quarries were involved:

Name of Quarry	*Quarry Wagons in working order*	*Wagons unfit*	*Total*
Rhosydd	30	24	54
Parc & Croesor	23	27	40

This high percentage of unusable wagons meant that both quarries had to hire wagons from the Festiniog. Of these many were retained illegally for internal use, the quarries not troubling to repair them at all, nor to pay the Festiniog for their hire!

A peculiar sidelight on this hiring was recorded in 1923; 14 ex-Welsh Slate Co. wagons had been sent to the Rhosydd Quarry. One day in April, six of these wagons came down the incline on to the Festiniog main line near Tan-y-grisiau—the Conclog Incline. As there was never a railway between these two points or between the quarries concerned, the matter was investigated and it was found they had been let down a mountain footpath, an unrailed distance

* A smaller 2-plank variety existed in dark grey: it was 6 ft. 10 in. long.

of almost two miles! The Welsh, like the Scots, were well known for sheep stealing; possibly this improved their fitness for a different purpose.

On quarry premises open ended sheet sided wagons were used for rubbish; early photos show long wheelbase flat wagons for slabs being drawn along the Tramway proper. Flat trolley types were used in the adits. Unidentifiable open wagons with outside framing (probably wooden) were used by Croesor Quarry, probably predecessors of the sheet-iron types. Possibly the best reference to local wagonry is the Festiniog list ('Festiniog Railway', Vol. 1, pp. 150–5). No wagons now survive on the tramway.

CROESOR TRAMWAY. Relation to later Welsh Highland Railway works where applicable:

Miles	*Chains*	*Location*	*Croesor Tramway*	*Welsh Highland Rly.*
0	0	Oakeley Slate Wharf	Zero Point	—
0	8	Foot Madoc Street	—	Connecting Junc. with Fest. R.
0	37	South Cambrian Rlys.	—	150 ft. loop. Corrugated iron station building. Portmadoc New Station (the first).
0	39	Crossing with Aberystwyth & Welsh Coast Railway		
0	42	Beddgelert Siding	600 ft. loop	Portmadoc New Station (the second).
1	49	Portreuddyn*	180 ft. loop	Loop removed 1/1924; not used.
2	25	Pont Croesor	110 ft. siding	Siding lengthened to 300 ft.
2	27	Pont Croesor (Halt: W.H.R.)		Corrugated iron shelter.
2	28	Pont Croesor	Rail crossing of Afon Glaslyn	
3	30	Ynysfor (Halt: W.H.R.)	40 ft. siding	Corrugated iron shelter.
3	59	Croesor Junction	Non existent	Loop ex Portreuddyn laid 5/1924. Corrugated iron shelter.
4	50	Foot Lower Park Incline	Parliamentary limit of Croesor & Port Madoc Rly. et seq.	

* In early 1880s also referred to as Pren-teg, probably because local slate quarry then used the name and the loop here. Connection was likely to have been by carts between quarry and tramway although a branch railway connection between the loop and the foot of the quarry incline is not impossible.

Iron bar rails with hooked ends, five feet long, and mounted on wooden sleepers, were found in Pren-teg Quarry in the mid 1960s and Croesor type track was lifted from the incline there in the late 1960s. The earliest record is 1858 when Thomas Chaffer & Co. were quarrying flagstone there.

Directors of Croesor & Port Madoc Railway (successors to Croesor Tramway)

Hugh Beaver Roberts (Plas Llandoget, Llanrwst)—also initial Director N.W.N.G Railways.

Hugh U. McKie (Hafod Tan-y-graig, Beddgelert)—also Engineer/Contractor N.W.N.G. Railways.

Arthur T. Roberts* (Coed Du, Mold, Flints.)—also Director Mold & Denbigh Junction Railway and Buckley Railway.

Richard M. Preston.

John Ormiston.

* Brother of H. B. Roberts.

Directors of Portmadoc, Croesor & Beddgelert Tram Railway Co. (successors to Croesor & Port Madoc Railway)

James Fraser Senr.* (London, N.W.)—Director until 1883—and also Director of Corris Railway, and Secretary of Halesowen Railway, Hereford, Hay & Brecon Railway, Wrexham, Mold & Connahs Quay Railway, Whitby, Redcar & Middlesburgh Union Railway.

Arthur Campbell-Walker (Major)—also Chairman Preston Tramways Co., and later, Chairman Brighton & District Tramways Co.

P. E. Neville (Hampstead).

J. Robertson (Finchley).

Hon. Archer Turner (Kew).†

E. R. Vyvyan (Cheltenham).

* Son of same name was auditor of the concern (and his other audits included Corris, Cambrian, Hemel Hempsted & L.N.W.R., Manchester & Milford, Navan & Kingscourt, Pembroke & Tenby, Whitland & Cardigan, Merionethshire Railways).

† Father was Sir Llewellyn Turner (Parkia, Caernarvon), Director of N.W.N.G. Railways.

The Railway Year Books of 1911 and 1914 gave the same entry; the Secretary and General Manager was J. E. Jones, and Registered Office at Bank Place, Portmadoc. 'No passenger traffic. Mineral traffic worked by horses in owners' wagons'.

	1871	1872	1873	1874	1875	1876	1877	1878	1879	1880	1881	1882	1883	1884	1885
Cost of Works and Way	£108	74	92	87	70	95	186	211	74	50	95	81	146	81	53
Cost Loco Power*	329	333	290	279	258	267	329	348	242	336	337	274	230	317	233
Profit/Loss on wkg.	354	55	97	17	30	5	56	79	82	115	97	137	(19)	181	34
Merchandise Tons	1575	1294	475	690	921	1694	1879	4630	4249	1471	3127	596	2361	2185	3286
Minerals Tons	25910	24904	21106	18815	16991	14952	18946	21195	15703	22263	22080	20104	12482	18615	10856
Goods train miles	6886	6326	5730	5096	5302	6014	6925	6260	5884	5302	5634	5321	5406	5634	4873

	1886	1887	1888	1889	1890	1891	1892	1893	1894	1895	1896	1897	1898	1899	1900	1901
Cost of Works & Way	£88	60	64	87	81	47	73	109	91	100	143	192	128	119	189	97
Cost Loco Power*	313	162	147	144	156	126	153	150	152	151	195	231	209	195	215	202
Profit/Loss on wkg.	95	85	72	30	59	62	65	60	107	107	93	131	154	123	43	91
Merchandise Tons	1800	1636	1949	1656	1994	1640	2652	8467	10705	13829	11051	16958	15942	11956	11155	11213
Minerals Tons	11195	6732	6332	5983	6332	5274	6250	6332	6418	5971	7690	9620	8786	8240	8811	7612
Goods train miles	3717	3087	3052	2925	3033	3030	2840	2844	2921	2736	2956	5173	4410	3950	4088	3910

Division denotes Croesor & Port Madoc Railway up to 1878; Portmadoc, Croesor & Beddgelert Tram Railway 1879 onwards.
No returns made before 1871. In 1870 Secretary states 'There are no shareholders consequently no accounts are published (private property)'.
* Note on returns: 'Cost of Horsepower, the haulage on the line being done by horses'.
Statement by Secretary: 'The Company have no rolling stock or locomotives. The haulage is done by horses and the wagons are provided by the persons using the railway'. (1871).

Traffic Expenses of £135 are shown for 1871 and 1872, but none thereafter.
Carriage and Wagon maintenance Expenses for 1880 are £57, the only year returned.
Stock Returns: One entry made in 1880 only showing eighty wagons (type not stated). Perhaps these bought secondhand from Festiniog Railway and re-sold to quarry owners as mineral tonnages rose to over 20,000 for the next few years; such an item does not however, feature in the Accounts but their purchase and re-sale may have been purposely omitted from the books.
Legal Expenses for years 1900 and 1901 (only) shown as £10 and £22.
In 1903 Returned as 'Purchased by Portmadoc, Beddgelert & South Snowdon Railway as from 29 October 1903 under Act 1 Edward VII c. 262 of 7 August 1901'.

THE BETTWS-Y-COED & FESTINIOG RAILWAY

In the north of Caernarvonshire the Chester & Holyhead Railway bestrode the coast, choosing for its course the narrow strip of upper foreshore for much of its journey between Chester and the Conway River. It had opened in stages, but ultimately the full route was opened on 18 March 1850 with the bridging of the Menai Straits completed. In 1856 the working of that railway was taken over by the London & North Western Railway and became vested in it in 1858. That same year a branch on the north-east bank of the Conway River was opened on 1 October by the St. George's Harbour & Railway Co., $3\frac{1}{2}$ miles long, to Llandudno; an intermediate station at Deganwy (from whence at a later date it was hoped to ship considerable loads of slate from Festiniog) was opened in April 1868. Trains for Llandudno started from Conway and the present-day approach to that town from the coast line was non-existent.

About 1860 the present Llandudno Junction was opened, and the Llandudno line junction re-sited to face Down trains. Into this same junction station (but in those days from the south-west and east shore of the Conway, and not as today) came the Conway & Llanrwst Railway whose $11\frac{1}{4}$ miles from the Junction to Llanrwst were opened on 17 June 1863.

The Conway & Llanrwst had had a far more interesting birth than this simple recital of dates might indicate, but as the line falls more properly into the north Caernarvonshire section, it will be found in its proper context of a proposed narrow gauge railway in Volume 2. Suffice to say that with none other than H. B. Roberts as solicitor for the promoters, a line was drafted on 28 February 1853 to run from the Chester & Holyhead at Conway. Nothing tangible transpiring, another plan for a line extending fifteen miles to Bettws-y-coed and described as 'Secondary System; Gauge 3 ft. 3 in.; Capital £45,000 in £10 Shares' appeared on a prospectus of September 1858 having such provisional directors as C. M. Holland of Liverpool and James Swinton Spooner of Beaver Grove, Llanrwst, to show it was no idle threat. The detail of these schemes, formed once more to bleed off the valuable slate traffic from Blaenau Festiniog, must await its proper place.

In 1867 the Conway & Llanrwst Railway was absorbed by the L.N.W.R. who extended it 3¾ miles to a new terminus at Bettws-y-coed (there are various ways of spelling the name) on 6 April 1868. The former Llanrwst terminal became the goods yard.

Only a short time after this, the North Wales Narrow Gauge Railways issued its prospectus which showed that Bettws was one of its objectives and would be reached from Capel Curig by means of the Llugwy valley. By this time the L.N.W.R. had formed plans of its own to thrust southward for twelve miles via the Lledr Valley, pierce the mountain wall north of Blaenau Festiniog, and tap the slate traffic at its heart. In order to make the line cheaply and to bring wagons of slate direct from the quarries into Bettws for transshipment, it intended to break the gauge there and build southward in 1 ft. 11½ in. gauge and make physical junctions with slate producers in Blaenau. There was also a deeper idea of obtaining running powers over the Festiniog and Festiniog & Blaenau lines. Thus the L.N.W.R. hoped to scotch Great Western Railway plans to attack Blaenau from the southeast by means of an ostensibly independent line striking northwest from Bala. The L.N.W.R. petitioned against the N.W.N.G. Railways bill in that the lands sought for building that line were required by their own Bettws & Festiniog Railway, but resolved the problem when joint ventures for a station in Bettws were agreed upon.

To put their schemes into practice the L.N.W.R. were empowered by two Acts of Parliament. The first was the 'L.N.W.R. (Additional Powers) Act of 1872' which as 35 & 36 Vic. Cap. 87 was assented on 18 July 1872, the relevant portion being: '. . . expedient that one of the railways by this Act authorised (hereinafter called the Bettws & Festiniog Railway) should be constructed on the same gauge as the other local railways with which it is intended to be connected. (Section 5. Para. 6) . . . The Bettws & Festiniog Railway (length 11 m. 7 fur. 1 ch.) commencing in the parish of Bettws-y-coed . . . and terminating . . . by a junction with the Festiniog Railway . . .' In Section 15 there is reference to 9 & 10 Vic. Cap. 57 (Gauge of Railways Act) which suggests that notwithstanding the contents of said Act. the B. & F.R. should be built and maintained to a gauge of 1 ft. 11¾ in., 'being the gauge of the Festiniog Railway . . . with which the B. & F.R. is intended to form a junction (or such other wider gauge etc.)' Under Section 16 it would be unlawful to run passenger trains without the consent of the Gwydr Estate between midnight Saturday and midnight Sunday. Section 17 suggests the rates for carriage should be 2d. per ton mile for slates in private owner wagons, or 3d. per ton mile for slates in L.N.W.R. (2 ft. gauge) wagons, plus an additional charge for trans-shipping at the break of gauge for traffic of all descriptions. The period for completion of the line was to be five years.

Further thought on the subject of connections at the Blaenau end of the line suggested that what was to be virtually an end-on junction with the north end of the Festiniog's Dinas branch there would only give the L.N.W.R. limited access to other quarries, and by the 'L.N.W.R. (New Works and Additional Powers) Act of 1873' which received Royal Assent on 28 July 1873—36 & 37 Vic. Cap. 201—the following is to be found among a hotch potch of bits and pieces; the preamble states :

> 'And whereas by the L.N.W.R. (Additional Powers) Act 1872 the Company was empowered to make the Bettws-y-coed and Festiniog Railway for the purpose of connecting their system of railways with . . . the Festiniog Railway Company . . . and it is expedient that the Company should be empowered to run over and use so much of the railways of the Festiniog Railway Company as extends from the junction therewith of the . . . B. & F.R. to the terminal station at Dyffws of the Festiniog Company.'

Powers were sought to purchase certain pieces of land on both west and east sides of the existing standard gauge Bettws terminus with the consent of Baroness Willoughby De Eresby (Gwydr Estate). It was intended that running powers over the east end of the Festiniog Railway should be subject to an agreement between the two Companies as to tolls etc., failure to agree being settled by an arbitrator appointed by the Board of Trade.

It has already been seen that the Festiniog & Blaenau Railway intended to link with the L.N.W.R. in the neighbourhood of Duffws, and had this taken place, there would have literally been a 'scissors movement' of the two narrow gauge companies across the tracks of the Festiniog. The matter caused great anxiety to Spooner and the Festiniog Board, and though details are outside the scope of the present account, the outcome was that the Festiniog agreed not to oppose entry of the L.N.W.R. into Blaenau so long as they did not interfere with the Festiniog's line into Duffws terminus; by this they meant the threat of L.N.W.R. narrow gauge trains running across their own tracks and down the Festiniog & Blaenau to Llan Ffestiniog would cease. Thus the matter was resolved, but it is an interesting speculation how matters would have gone had the Merionethshire Railway come into existence and the L.N.W.R. found themselves south-east of Blaenau. The interplay of Cambrian, Great Western, London & North Western, Festiniog, Merionethshire and Festiniog

& Blaenau interests, not to mention mixed gauge trackage, would have been good business for the lawyers and further work for Parliament. Some of these Companies could not live together elsewhere, let alone in company!

Returning to Bettws and the building of the new narrow gauge extension south of this terminus, it was intended that the station should be of mixed gauge, and shared with the North Wales Narrow Gauge Railways. At an early date work was started on the major civil engineering obstacle, the long tunnel at Blaenau—to narrow gauge standards. By 1876 it was reported that '. . . on the Bettws & Festiniog line the tunnel works were proceeding steadily and considerable progress had been made with the remaining portions of the railway'. The bridging contractor was a local man, Gethin Jones. Between Bettws and Pont-y-pant the track crossed the River Lledr by an odd stone structure, half wall and half viaduct of six small arches plus a large one, still locally known as Gethin's Bridge or Pont Gethin. Certain other work was done by Thomas and Robert Dougall, two Scots brothers both of whom may have had previous railway building experience in Russia which may have qualified them for the peculiar problems of the Lledr Valley where they ultimately settled and took to farming, near Dolwyddelen. The ruling grade was 1 in 47 to a summit 790 ft. above sea-level about 400 yd. from the Festiniog end.

Whereas work on the ground went ahead steadily, piercing of the tunnel began in February 1875 and became more difficult owing to the hardness of the rock. The contractor for this work failed, and the L.N.W.R., under William Smith, took over the work themselves. Smith was their Engineer for the Bangor District.

During this impasse there occurred the failure of the North Wales Narrow Gauge Railways General Undertaking (which would have terminated jointly with the L.N.W.R. at Bettws); there was a growing conviction that the stage was already set for the Festiniog & Blaenau Railway to be encompassed by the Great Western, and the visions of the L.N.W.R. (built to any gauge!) straddling the quarry district from north-west to south-east at Festiniog became a thing of the past, so Euston decided very wisely to revise its plans. G. P. Neele ('Railway Reminiscences' p. 230) puts it very simply: 'The line from Bettws-y-coed to Festiniog was originally intended to be constructed on the very narrow gauge adopted by Mr. Spooner for his "toy railway" from Festiniog to Penrhyndeudraeth, but in order to avoid constructing engines and vehicles of different gauge, the Directors decided on keeping to the 4 ft. 8½ in. gauge throughout. The change entailed considerable outlay as many of the curves and viaducts had to be re-arranged. The cost was especially excessive in the long tunnel near the terminus at Blaenau Festiniog. So much so that the Directors called for a special report on the expenditure.' Of the tunnel he wrote, 'The contractor long back had given up the work and the Company's own Engineer, Mr. W. Smith of Bangor, had the difficulty to contend with. The line was opened in July . . . but the slate traffic itself which was a considerable factor in the calculations of the probable receipts from the line was very slow in adopting the route by rail. The quay at Deganwy was in subsequent years arranged to suit this particular traffic, but has not been phenomenally successful.'* Neele ends by saying, '. . . As the terminus of the line at Blaenau Festiniog was but a short distance from that of Mr. Spooner's line, subsequently it was extended so as to be exactly opposite his station . . . a new means of inland communication to and from the slate quarries was given by the line to Llandudno Junction . . .'.

To complete the story of the initial invasion of Blaenau Festiniog by a standard gauge railway based on London, it should be recorded that the first L.N.W.R. station was at the south end of the tunnel mouth which was regarded only as a temporary terminal. Traffic began from here in January 1879.† Had the 2 ft. gauge line come about, it would have emerged from a tunnel at this same point and made a physical junction with a branch from Greaves' Quarry. Further, nearby it was to be connected with the Welsh Slate Co. by an incline. There was to be an engine run-round and an end-on junction with the Festiniog line.

The single line tunnel under Moel Dyrnogydd was 2 miles 206 yards long, the longest on the L.N.W.R. system. Neele describes the opening inspection very fully, the inspection of the tunnel being made on foot, followed by a carriage with its doors open on both sides propelled by an engine at walking speed '. . . the engineer's men having lanterns also showing the jagged edges of the tunnel . . .'.

The second station, about 300 yards south of the temporary one, was opened across the road from the Exchange station which the Festiniog opened there for the exchange of passenger traffic. It opened on 1 April 1881. The narrow/standard exchange sidings north of the L.N.W.R. permanent station were opened on the same day, also the Queen's Hotel (built by the L.N.W.R.) which having lost money, was later sold.

Whilst Neele was undoubtedly correct in summing up the failure of the L.N.W.R. to woo away the slate traffic (the pier at Deganwy was a White Elephant for many years, with its rows of narrow gauge

* See Volume 2 for details of L.N.W.R. stock for this traffic.

† Elsewhere given as June 1879 and the opening to passengers on 22 July 1879.

tracks on to which the Wolverton-built 'slate-truck wagons' were to discharge their cargoes) the threat of traffic being enticed away by cut-price rates was very real. Cambrian representative C. Lewis met C. E. Spooner in Portmadoc and they signed a Joint Agreement on 10 May 1881 headed 'Slate Rates and opening of the L.N.W.R. Bettws-y-coed line'. The L.N.W.R. had quoted an all-in rate of 14s. 11d. per ton for slate and 'to meet this unusual state of things' it was recommended that Cambrian and Festiniog together quote 14s. 9d. (including trans-shipment and loading) which broken down would mean 12s. 3d. to the Cambrian, 2s. 1d. to the Festiniog and 5d. for loading. It was further agreed that additional standard and narrow gauge trans-shipment sidings be provided at Minffordd. The rate and the work was duly carried out, and though quarry owners were continually complaining, they were conservative enough to continue, in the main, supporting the venture which they knew best.

If the prospect of Crewe-built 2-ft. gauge engines emerging from a 2-mile tunnel at Blaenau had finally disappeared, so had the hopes of the Directors at Euston that the order of things might change to their advantage.

NORTH WALES NARROW GAUGE RAILWAYS COMPANY

(*Gauge* 1 ft. $11\frac{1}{2}$ in.—also officially returned as 1 ft. $11\frac{1}{4}$ in and Two Feet)

Incorporated by Act: 35/6 Vic. Cap. 175 of 6 August 1872. Powers to build a 'General Undertaking'; a railway from Croesor & Port Madoc Railway (sic) to Bettws-y-coed, and a 'Moel Tryfan Undertaking' connecting Llanwnda with Beddgelert and Bryngwyn (two railways).

Act: 36/7 Vic. Cap. 72 of 16 June 1873. Powers to lease Moel Tryfan Undertaking to H. B. Roberts, etc.

Act: 39/40 Vic. Cap. 125 of 13 July 1876. Powers to abandon General Undertaking, etc.

Act: 48/9 Vic. Cap. 134 of 31 July 1885. Powers to extend to Caernarvon Harbour: separate undertaking.

Act: 53/4 Vic. Cap. 70 of 4 July 1890. Extension of time for works of 1885 Act, and alteration in capital arrangements, etc.

Act: 55/6 Vic. Cap. 44 of 20 June 1892. Rates and Charges.

Light Railway Order: 3 November 1900. Powers to extend line from Rhydddu to Beddgelert.

Agreement: 26 August 1904 with Portmadoc, Beddgelert & South Snowdon Railway. Powers of L.R.O. of 3 November 1900 to pass to P.B. & S.S.R. This ratified by P.B. & S.S.R. L.R.O. of 24 October 1906.

Light Railway Order: 6 June 1905. Powers to work line as Light Railway.

Opened—Goods:	Dinas–Quellan (sic) (Temporary Station), 21 May 1877.*
	Dinas–Snowdon Ranger, 1 June 1878.
	Dinas–South Snowdon (Rhydd-ddu), 14 May 1881.
	Tryfan Junction–Bryngwyn, 21 May 1877.*
	(*May dates also given elsewhere as June in each case.)
Opened—Passengers:	Dinas–Quellan (sic) (Temporary Station), 15 Aug. 1877.
	Dinas–Snowdon Ranger, 1 June 1878.
	Dinas–South Snowdon (Rhydd-ddu), 14 May 1881.
	Tryfan Junction–Bryngwyn, 15 Aug. 1877.
Closed—Passengers:	Tryfan Junction–Bryngwyn, 31 Dec. 1913.
	Dinas–South Snowdon, 31 Oct. 1916.
Closed—Goods:	Whole system run on an 'as Required' basis from 31 Oct. 1916.
	Purchased by Welsh Highland Railway (Light Railway) Co. as part of new system, 1 Jan. 1922.
Registered Office:	Parliament Street, London. (1873).
	60 Threadneedle Street, London, E.C. (1876).
	Dinas Junction. (1883).
	14 Dale Street, Liverpool. (1914).
Length:	Dinas Junction–Top of Incline, Bryngwyn, 5 m. 0 fur. 9 ch.
	Tryfan Junction–Rhydd-ddu, 7 m. 1 fur. 8 ch.

and officially returned as (1921):

Length of road,	12 m.	40 ch.
2nd track,		48 ch.
Total,	13 m.	8 ch.
Sidings,	1 m.	46 ch.

Maximum Gradient: 1 in 35.
Minimum Curve: $3\frac{3}{4}$ chains.
Maximum Axle Load: 4 Tons.
Speed Restrictions: 25 m.p.h. (mixed trains), (later 16 m.p.h.).
Cost per Mile: £10,434 (slight variations quoted).

Authorised Capital: Shares	1874–5 £150,000:	1876– £106,000
Loan	1874–5 £50,000:	1876–9 £35,300
	1880–1900 £50,000:	1901–1921 £54,000
	Further £20,437 created 1919 but not issued.	

Issued: Ordinary:	1876–1918	£65,975
6% Pref.	1876	£ 2,496
	1877	£15,150
	1878	£17,140
	1880	£17,340
	1881–1918	£17,390
	1919–1921	£96,000 *

Loan:	1876	@ 6%	£18,500		
	1877–9	@ 5%	£ 2,300	@ 6%	£19,700
	1880	Nil			
	1881–7	@ 4%	£ 2,800	@ $4\frac{1}{2}$%	£ 3,200
	1888–9	@ 4%	£ 4,400	@ $4\frac{1}{2}$%	£ 1,600

Debentures:	1880	@4%	£25,940	@5%	£ 3,123
A & B=4%	1881–4		£30,000		£ 3,123
C=5%	1885–9		£30,000		£ 3,463–3,563
	1890		£36,200		£ 3,563
	1891–2		£37,807		£ 3,563
	1893		£38,277		£ 3,563
	1894		£39,177		£ 3,563
	1895–1921		£39,477		£ 3,563

* *Financial position 1921:*	A Debentures	4%	£ 9,477	
	B ,,	4%	£ 26,060	—part repaid?
	C ,,	5%	£ 3,563	
	6% Pref. Shares		£ 17,390	
	Ordinary Shares		£ 66,000	
			£122,490	

Beddgelert Extension:	Authorised Capital:	Shares	£13,800
	(separate account)	Loan	£ 4,600

HISTORY

By the early seventies the time was ripe for what might be termed an 'explosion' of narrow gauge schemes in North Wales. The timing could not have been better. On the premier line of the time, the Festiniog, steam locomotives had shown their mettle; Fairlie's Patent double engine had come to the forefront, and passenger traffic was not only legalised but growing. New lines to quarries at Croesor and Gorseddau had been laid down, a small extension to the Festiniog's eastern end was now open, and plans were laid to extend the line out to Croesor by making a northwards branch which might ultimately link Portmadoc with Caernarvon. Charles Spooner's involvement lay directly or indirectly with each and every scheme; he was the 'common denominator'. Spooner's advocacies had never before appeared to be more correct. The menace of other railway invaders was still contained, even though it was not long delayed. As yet, there was nothing to show that Spooner had not been right all along the line, and that nothing succeeded better than success.

So it came about that a master plan to link almost all the larger places in North-west Wales by narrow gauge railway—and some of much less significance also—was born. This was to be a comprehensive, worked by a Company whose administrators (as far as possible) were either experienced or would be locally beneficial and influential. The railways proposed were not all connected, but all were to be of a gauge between 2 ft. and 2 ft. 9 in. Chief Engineer to the scheme was Charles E. Spooner, and Assistant Engineer Hugh Unsworth McKie, now of Tanyrallt, Tremadoc, a director of the Croesor & Port Madoc Railway.* The provisional promotional committee included Sir R. William M. L. Bulkeley, Sir Ll. Turner, G. A. Huddart and J. P. de Winton of the Caernarvon engineering works, and the four initial directors were Livingston Thompson (a director and past Chairman of the Festiniog), Sir Llewellyn Turner (a slate quarry owner and prominent local figure who lived north of Caernarvon), Hugh Beaver Roberts (a solicitor and director of the Croesor & Port Madoc) and James Hewitt Oliver who had no other railway connections.

Eight railways were proposed, but Parliament rejected application to make Railways Nos. 2, 3, 4, 5 and 8.† The full proposal was:

* McKie had recently resigned (1872) from the Croesor United Slate Coy. after a disagreement with the directors.

† This fact is additionally recorded in a footnote on the reverse of an Agreement between the Company and the Rt. Hon. Clementine Elizabeth Heathcote Drummond. Baroness Willoughby de Eresby (owner of the Gwydr Estate, Bettws-y-coed) 17 May 1872.

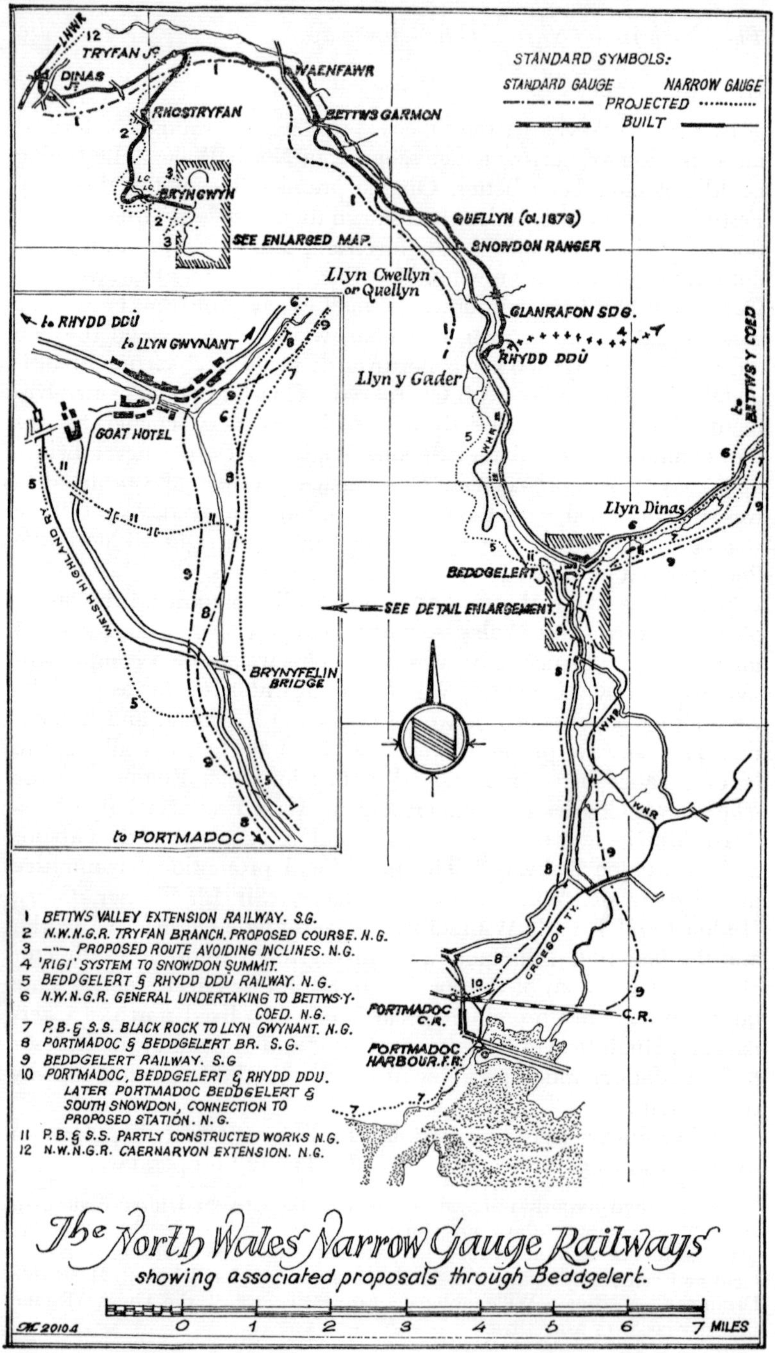

The North Wales Narrow Gauge Railways
showing associated proposals through Beddgelert.

No. 1 To extend from a Junction with the Portmadoc, Croesor & Beddgelert Tram Railway Company's proposed line to Beddgelert, thence to Pen-y-gwryd via Nant Gwynant involving reversing spirals of 2 chains radius. Thence to Capel Curig and Bettws-y-coed.

No. 2 From Bettws-y-coed, following alongside route of Holyhead–London road to a point three miles west of Corwen.

No. 3 From end Railway No. 2 into Corwen, terminating behind standard gauge railway station (G.W.R.).

No. 4 A short branch reached by reversing from Railway No. 1, to the L.N.W.R. standard gauge terminus of the line from Llandudno Junction, in Bettws-y-coed. (The L.N.W.R.'s line south of this point was to be of narrow gauge.)

No. 5. A branch from Railway No. 2 in the Lledr Valley, to Penmachno.

No. 6 A branch from Dinas, on the L.N.W.R. Caernarvon–Afon Wen line, to Bryngwyn, with an incline to the Moel Tryfan area slate quarries.

No. 7 An extension from Railway No. 6 to Rhydd-ddu, South Snowdon.

No. 8 A short line from Pwllheli (adjacent to the Cambrian Railways' terminus of that period) to Porthdynllaen, with the added possibility of joining up with the Portmadoc end of Railway No. 1, by either an independent line from Pwllheli to Portmadoc or by laying a third rail along the Cambrian Railways.

The Draft Bill went before a House of Commons Select Committee in early April 1872. It listed the subscribers as including Livingston Thompson, Sir Llewellyn Turner, Hugh B. Roberts and James H. Oliver and stated that they, plus three others, would be the first directors.

Objections had been raised by :

Porthdynllaen Harbour Co.	(Opposed to Railway No. 8)
Cambrian Railways Co.	('Injurious to their rights and interests')
Charles Edwards of Dolseran Hall, Dolgelley	(Opposed to Railway No. 1)
G. W. Duff Assheton-Smith Owner of estates at Bettws Garmon etc.	('Railway will seriously injure the amenities. No public necessity for same')

Baroness Willoughby De Eresby	(Opposition included that of the 'gauge being inconvenient')
London & North Western Railway	(In connection with their promoted Bettws & Festiniog Railway, the land would be required for their own use)
Lord Penrhyn	('Inconvenience of gauge. Injury to his Glan Conway Estate')

The petition from Lord Penrhyn was accompanied by an account from his solicitors for £50!

The promoters were 'quarry owners, landed proprietors and other gentlemen interested in the district concerned . . . the scheme had been suggested by the success of the Festiniog Railway'.

Of the eight railway developments proposed, applications were made only for Railways Nos. 1, 6 and 7, the first to incorporate the scheme for Railway No. 4. Powers were granted by an Act 35/6 Vic. Cap. 175 of 6 August 1872 and this divided the venture into two Undertakings:

1. General Undertaking. Railway No. 1 (22 m. 6 fur. 4 ch.) from a junction with the Croesor & Port Madoc Railway and ending in a field called Cae Isa at Graig-glan-conway, Bettws-y-coed.
2. Moel Tryfan Undertaking. Railway No. 6 (5 m. 9 ch.) from Dinas to a farm called Vron Heulog (Top of Incline, Bryngwyn).
   Railway No. 7 (7 m. 1 fur. 8 ch.) from Tryfan Junction with Railway No. 6, ending in a field called Cae Mawr on Fridd Isa farm, parish of Beddgelert.

On the assumption that the Bettws & Festiniog Railway became law under the L.N.W.R. Additional Powers Bill in the 1872 Session (this was to be the narrow gauge extension of the Conway Valley line) and authority was given to proceed, then there was to be a junction with the Bettws & Festiniog Railway south of Bettws which would enable the General Undertaking's line to enter Bettws over Bettws & Festiniog metals. The station would be a joint one, with part of it given over to the use of the North Wales Narrow Gauge and Bettws & Festiniog Railways, the L.N.W.R. providing a third rail in their standard gauge where this was necessary. It appears that staffing would be carried out by the L.N.W.R., with N.W.N.G. running powers from the junction to the station.

The influence of local landowners was over-riding, not only in matters of the flesh, either. Under the threat of a £5 fine for every contravention, the Gwydr Estate was empowered to fine the

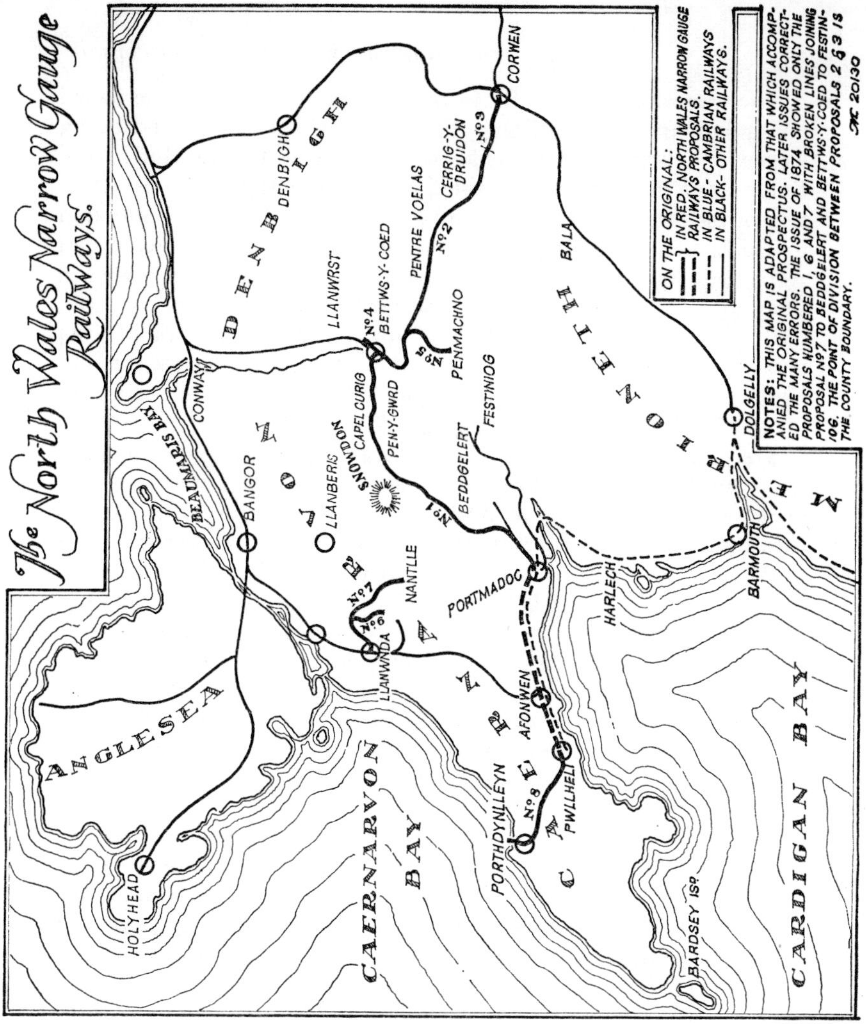

N.W.N.G. should it pick up or set down passengers within five miles of the famous Waterloo Bridge, Bettws-y-coed, between the hours of 5 a.m. and 10 p.m. on Sundays!

Under the Act the Portmadoc, Croesor & Beddgelert Tram Railway Co.'s line (still in practice the Croesor Tramway as completed in 1864) was to be relaid suitably for locomotive traffic by and at the expense of the N.W.N.G., between Portmadoc wharves and the junction with the south end of Railway No. 1. This work was not to be carried out until half Railway No. 1 was complete and land for the remainder obtained; the Tram Railway Co. would be given twelve month's notice of intention to commence. (Later, when powers to abandon the General Undertaking were sought and secured, the old tram line was left undisturbed for many years to come.)

The way was now clear for work to begin. A Prospectus was issued on 23 January 1873 outlining the Company's proposals, and on 23 December 1872 a contract had been given to H. U. McKie, co-Engineer of the Company, assisted by George Lea, for the construction of the line for a sum of £56,150. It was the Directors' intention to tackle the Moel Tryfan Undertaking first, regarding which an Agreement had been entered into also on 23 December 1872 between them and one of their number, the ubiquitous H. B. Roberts, who was prepared to lease the railway for 21 years from completion, according to the contracted finishing date. This Agreement was modified at a meeting on 23 April 1873 and Parliamentary authority for it was given by Act 36/7 Vic. Cap. 72 of 16 June 1873.

The terms were that the period of leasing should now commence from the date of the Board of Trade Certificate authorising the opening. The rent to be paid was a complex sum involving Debenture Rent, Administration Rent, Fixed Rent etc. and was set down in detail in the Schedule to the Act. It was calculated on the yearly interest @ 6% of the Debenture Stock of the Company—the amount of administration costs, a rent on the borrowed capital *for the time being*—allowances being made for occasions when the net profits did not exceed the combined Debenture and Administration Rents. It is remarkable that, under the financial clauses alone of this Agreement, Roberts should have so allowed himself to be tied down; his confidence in the amount of business the railway would bring is surprising.

The lessee also agreed to spend £10,000 (covenanted to be paid to him by the Company) on locomotives and rolling stock for working the line and 'turning to the utmost profit, the demised premises'. He was to consult the Company's Engineer before providing same, and was to keep them in full repair 'so that they shall always be of the full value of £10,000 or upwards, and sufficient for the development of traffic' (!)

This last section is quite extraordinary. Whilst we currently live in an age of inflation and rising values, machinery to be used in such circumstances as this was hardly likely to hold its value. Again, the frame of mind in which Roberts agreed to this is beyond understanding.

The next portion of the Agreement shows how adroitly, while keeping himself in the background, Robert Fairlie had imposed himself on C. E. Spooner; and how strongly the influence of Festiniog Railway experience lay on the promoters. Fairlie's financial benefit was in the publicity the opportunity afforded him rather than the Royalties: how much it cost him to influence can only be hinted at.

The lessee '. . . shall at all times (unless otherwise agreed) have all the locomotives (except the Shunting Engines) in use upon the demised premises constructed and maintained according to the principle known as "Fairlie's Patents" and shall pay the royalty of £300 per engine payable in respect of the same principle' (Section 12).

At the expiration of the lease, locomotives and stock 'to the full value of £10,000 to be given up and if exceeding the value "The Company to have option to acquire".' Roberts was not to assign his powers without the consent of the Company who would give him £10,000 within four weeks for the purchase of the stock.

McKie started work in the spring of 1873 and the first half-yearly meeting (reported in 'The Times' on 10 March) said it was hoped he would complete both lines within the twelvemonth. As time went by, it was apparent that McKie's progress was not that of a man who would finish his assignment within the hoped-for period. Payments to him began to falter and relations with Spooner were far from easy. This situation arose when McKie took up the contract and, ceasing to be co-Engineer from that time, found himself with Charles E. Spooner as Engineer remaining. Spooner's inspection of the work became irregular and as McKie was paid on results, his remuneration fell behind. As payments fell behind, McKie's interest flagged and his work became slower. The contracted completion date was 24 November 1874 and it soon became clear to the Board that this date would not be met. Worse still, Roberts, whose co-Director McKie was on the Croesor Tramway venture, began to have doubts too, and mindful of the problems of McKie, called a special meeting in August 1874 and threatened to repudiate the lease. The Company, not surprisingly alarmed by this, took legal advice but were recommended not to enforce the matter; the Company was in no position to stand firmly as it was short of cash and as McKie was unlikely to finish the contract to time, Roberts might enjoy a great deal of sympathy if the matter was taken into the Courts. By 12 November 1874 all work had practically ceased. McKie had overshot his time. The Company was behind in payment.

McKie claimed that his work had not been properly assessed by the Engineer and he was consistently underpaid; the matter went to arbitration before Mr Brunlees and a long battle ensued, no work being done again until April 1875. The arbitrator visited the site and discovered that the contractor should have received '£43,056 for work done to the value of £41,303, including £1,500 for rails not delivered'. Having found for McKie, he awarded him £440 costs to be paid out of the Company's retention reserves, the Company to pay the cost of Chancery proceedings and an award of £3,253 and

£300. When the Board met in Caernarvon on 24 May 1875 it reported, 'The Directors had been led to expect a different result from the reference, but they could only come to the conclusion that the Company's Engineer had not given the contractor credit for as much as had been executed, and they learned to their great surprise that the requirements of the contract for periodical measurements being regularly taken by the Engineer in the presence of the contractor, had not been complied with . . .'*

The Directors then announced that work would be hastened and could be completed in three or four months if 'vigorously prosecuted'; the contractor had been paid the award and there was no reason for further delay. They would use their endeavours to have the line opened as quickly as possible. Extra costs would certainly be involved. The Engineer reported that he thought £19,000 would be needed to open the line and it was added that local quarry owners wanted the railway extended so that they might use it (who 'they' were is not stated).

The end of the McKie affair was not yet however, and on 23 September 1874 the Board again reported that McKie was 'making far less progress than he should have done but that recently he had increased the number of men on the job'. They thought it unwise to make any change but gave the contractor notice to proceed 'with greater vigour generally and to direct his efforts to Railway No. 6

* In the case of the N.W.N.G. Railways Company v. M'Kie (papers filed 9 June 1874) Charles E. Spooner maintained that certain materials had been paid for by the Railway Company, such as rails. This was to be the form of 'advance' to M'Kie but M'Kie refused to accept this form of payment and pressed for £570 in cash for work already done. M'Kie had already received £40,000 in cash.

M'Kie had depot sites at Llanwnda and Bettws Garmon, together with an advance store at Nant Mill. As the Company would not pay him, he refused to take rails off the Company, inferring that this would suggest he was prepared to accept them instead of money. In consequence though rails were on hand, M'Kie would not bring them to the laying site and all work stopped.

On 1 June 1874 M'Kie began to remove materials lying at the three sites, including the rails. The Railway Company sent in a squad of men to prevent him but only succeeded for a day or so. The following materials were removed:

On 4 June 5 tons of dog spikes. These left Llanwnda and were shipped to the Isle of Man for use on the railway then building. The previous day 241 rails had left the lineside at this spot, and on the same day 174 rails were loaded away. The following day another 175 left similarly (this would have laid 2,360 yards of railway line).

On 6 June materials were moved from Nant Mill and placed in a field near M'Kie's residence, where they were under his surveillance. M'Kie informed the Company he intended to continue removal of the materials.

so that traffic may be brought upon the line from quarries on that branch'.

If there were evident problems out on the line, there were equal but not-so-obvious problems within the Board Room. Half yearly meetings were poorly attended; the consistently adverse reports probably demoralised shareholders. Throughout the early period Sir Llewellyn Turner (he had been knighted for services to Caernarvon and district, had seen the Harbour improved and been a Mayor of the Town) held the Chair. Livingston Thompson was an early casualty along with H. B. Roberts, but thereafter there was some continuity through the troublesome period, the Chairman frequently having to ask for volunteers to the Board from the floor of the scantily attended meetings. (A list of Directors quoted for specimen years, is given at the end of this section.) J. H. Oliver of Brondanw, Caernarvon, served, Sir Richard William Mostyn Lewis Bulkeley (Bart)—an original promoter—came on in later 1873 and was succeeded by his son in October 1875 after the father died. There were Messrs. C. Pearson, T. Bolland, A. Fitzgibbon and C. Celyn, some of them serving as being local shareholders of varying influence but all of whom were losing money on the venture! None had other railway interests or board experience. At the end of this troublesome start, Henry Watts was still Secretary but Spooner ultimately resigned in favour of his son, young Edwin Spooner.

The method of financing of the Company's rolling stock at this time is not completely clear. From the first set of Receiver's accounts it would appear that when Roberts faded from the scene as threatened, the matter of financing the stock purchased during his time was carried out in two ways. The first way may have been the continuance of an arrangement between Roberts and the builders which was suitably transferred to become an arrangement between the Railway Company and the builders; suffice to say that the coaches supplied by Ashbury Co. Ltd. and the brake-composites by Brown Marshall & Co. (sic) together with wagons supplied by either or both of these concerns were being paid for in instalments to the builders. The other way was of more consequence to the Company, for it tied itself to a financier who ultimately took office as Receiver and Chairman and who stood in the way of development until his death in 1912. This man was James C. Russell, of whom more anon.

From the brief surviving accounts it appears that Russell was the owner of the Fairlie locomotives *Snowdon Ranger* and *Moel Tryfan*, and the engine immediately mentioned, *Beddgelert* from Hunslet. Nor was this all. He also financed coaches 6, 7 and 8 and coal wagons 9–12 inclusive.

All were itemised when, as it will shortly be mentioned, Russell made an Agreement between The Moel Tryfan Rolling Stock Co. Ltd. and himself, dated 7 December 1878. In this it was detailed that the aforementioned rolling stock was each fitted with a plate stating that Russell was the owner, save for *Beddgelert* which presumably had not yet been so treated. The dates of Russell's Agreement with the Railways Company as to hire of the stock from him, were 18 November 1876, and 27 April and 18 October 1878.

On 3 December 1878 The Moel Tryfan Rolling Stock Co. Ltd. was incorporated to 'purchase or otherwise acquire the locomotives, engines, carriages, waggons, trucks and rolling stock now in use by the N.W.N.G. Railways Co.' The Capital was £10,000 and the subscribers were :

Chaloner W. Chute,	Lincolns Inn,	Barrister
A. C. Humphreys Owen,	Garthmyl, Montgomery	
J. C. Russell,	86 Queens Gate, S.W.	
Alex Mortimer,	Paper Buildings, Temple	
Ernest E. Lake,	Hampstead,	Solicitor
W. L. Wiggett Chute,	Basingstoke	
Robert E. Tidswell,	Lincolns Inn,	Barrister

The Agreements already made between Russell and the Railways Company were to be continued and the first directors were Chaloner W. Chute, Ernest E. Lake, and J. C. Russell; and of these Chute was already a director of the Railway, Russell was shortly to be appointed Receiver and Lake was to become a director, nearly thirty years later! On 7 December Russell made an Agreement with the Rolling Stock Company to sell such stock as he hired to the Railway (and listed above), for a sum of £3,630, partly in ordinary and partly in preference shares of the Stock Company, a balance of £630 in cash to be paid within 14 days. The vendor might take shares instead of cash if he wished.

Russell also agreed to assign a debt of £882 10s. 7d. which had been obtained by him against the Railways Company. This case had been heard in the Exchequer Division on 18 November 1878 when Russell took the Company to Court for non-payment of hire charges on the rolling stock. He obtained the above sum and costs. The judgement was recovered on a contract entered into by the Railway Company on 18 November 1876—(the date of the first Agreement between Russell and the Railway).

By indenture of 7 December 1878 Russell assigned the debt to the Stock Company and advised the Railway accordingly. The Railway however, was still in no position to pay, and accordingly the Rolling Stock Co. lodged a petition in the Chancery Division against the Railway (the Stock Company having the advantage of considerable legal weight on its Board!) on 9 December 1878. The outcome was obvious and it was recommended that the Railway Company's Secretary should be appointed Receiver but, in the event, Russell was decreed to be a fit and proper person to fill this role.

Thus Russell became the virtual dictator of the Railway Company and though it has been convenient to record the 'Russell Saga' in one section, it should be stressed that he was not the first Receiver to be appointed. The previous occasion came about in this way.

A firm of Financiers, Grant & Co., had advanced money to the Railway and took them to Court for non-repayment. They successfully had a Receiver appointed in the person of Samuel Lowell Price. The matter was an involved one and concerned action by the Trustees for the Debenture Holders against the Railway for not placing part of the Moel Tryfan capital. The Railway fought the decision and was successful in the Court of Appeal on 7 May 1878. Price's 'reign' from 5 December 1877 to 7 May 1878 was terminated. (ref: *The Times*, 11 May 1878.)

The Stock Company was paid £1,947 in 1878 and £922 in 1879, but the Railways Company, showing deficits for the years 1878, 1879, 1880 and 1881 of £101, £1,893, £592 and £74 was finding it even more difficult to carry on. Ultimately the Stock Company was to be owed about £7,000 and the problem of repaying this was not resolved until 1880.

A return must now be made to the Board Room, for it was here that most development was taking place. The half yearly meeting of 2 March 1876 reported that McKie had continued to delay and had placed matters before Mr. Brunlees for further arbitration. The Board had ultimately decided there was nothing for it but that McKie should have the works taken from him and he had been instructed to surrender all works, materials and plant by 7 February last. The Board was then negotiating with another contractor.

In the matter of shortage of funds, the outstanding item of the General Undertaking (on which no work had been done), was the subject of an Act 39/40 Vic. Cap. 125 of 13 July 1876. This empowered the Company to abandon the whole venture and nothing more was heard of it until resurrected by the North Wales Power & Traction Co. Ltd., who obtained a Light Railway Order in November 1903 for a line between Beddgelert and Bettws-y-coed ('The Bettws Application' as it was known) but for which powers lapsed on 3 August 1907 without any work being done. The powers for the work were then transferred to the Portmadoc, Beddgelert & South Snowdon Railway who could afford to do little about it either!

The next meeting on 17 August 1876 announced that a Mr. J. Boys had been appointed contractor to complete the Moel Tryfan Undertaking; he had already made considerable progress. Heavy losses had been incurred due to the line's incomplete state and the disputes between the contractor and the engineer. Mr. Brunlees had made a further award to McKie of £7,417 'and they had got rid of him' (McKie). There was still the matter of the lease to Roberts, who had made it clear in August 1874 he would be free of obligation if the line was incomplete by the contracted date. The Company had been unable to further the matter and never did.

The meeting empowered the Board to issue as much of the newly authorised £40,000 Share capital, as they thought fit. It was agreed that 3,000 6% Preference Shares of £10 be issued to rank next after the £22,000 mortgages and before the Ordinary Shares amounting to £66,000. £16,000 was needed immediately to meet debts and to complete the railway authorised by Parliament and the balance would be used for rolling stock and extra expenses when the line was complete. The Board was trying to arrange for some debts to be paid in shares, but if existing shareholders did not come forward and subscribe to the new issue, the Company would collapse. Several quarry-owners on the line had promised to subscribe and use the line when ready for traffic. The Directors again repeated their confidence in the future of the railway.

A circular to shareholders dated 4 September 1876 read:

> 'Mr. Beaver Roberts, the lessee of the Line under the Act of 1873, attended the recent meeting and stated that he considered the lease no longer binding; the Directors are advised to the contrary, but it is open to doubt whether the Company's interests would not be best served by making some arrangement with Mr. Roberts for the cancellation of the lease. That gentleman stated that if the lease were given up he would, until the line yielded a gross revenue of £10,000 a year, pay double rates on all slates carried from his quarry.' *

The Board were to consider this and report back to shareholders; it was two years since Roberts had made his feelings known, both sides had taken legal advice. It concluded with:

* The Receiver's accounts for the period December 1877 to May 1878 show Roberts have been by far the biggest user of the railway. The traffic from his quarry was worth, for instance, three times the value of either the 'Moel Tryfan Crown' or Alexandra Quarries.

'If this appeal is not promptly responded to, the Board will have no alternative but to resign the management, and the Mortgagees and other Creditors be left to take what is available to meet their claims.'

Administrative matters have now taken affairs up to the autumn of 1876 and it is now desirable to return to the railway to see how Boys the new contractor was getting on. He was making good progress and by May 1877 had reached Quellyn road bridge with the main line, enabling goods traffic to begin working publicly to that point within the third week of the month. The branch from Tryfan Junction to the top of the incline at Bryngwyn was also ready and open for goods and minerals services.

On 26 June 1877 the Secretary Joseph Oldham advised the Board of Trade that the line would be 'ready in about a fortnight'; plans were sent on 19 July and on the following day the Secretary says 'will be sufficiently completed for the safe conveyance of passengers by 23 July'. Second thoughts now prevailed and on 31 July he writes to the Board, 'it is found we are not in a position for working the passenger traffic on some parts of our line with perfect safety in all respects. Postpone inspection.'

Major F. A. Marindin made his first inspection on 31 July 1877* and found certain bridges and cuttings too narrow; he looked in again on 20 August but the widening had not been finished. It was not done until the year-end but on 28 January 1878 he passed the line for passenger traffic as far as the temporary station at Quellyn, and the Bryngwyn branch. Some off-the-record arrangement must have been made on 20 August previously, as both these lines had advertised a passenger service since the 15th of that month!

It has been emphasised that in many respects the Railway was a modernised version of the Festiniog line but without the physical limitations of that railway. This influence was felt in another way; certainly at the beginning, all slate trains were worked Down by gravity and the Inspector was careful to point out that they must carry the staff 'and be considered in the same light as an engine in

* There had been an informal visit on 23 July 1877. Major Marindin had then reported that the new line commenced half a mile north of the L.N.W.R.'s existing station at Llanwnda on the Caernarvonshire Railway. At the new junction the L.N.W.R. had built an exchange platform and sidings and up until then, the N.W.N.G. Railways called their station Llanwnda too; as the L.N.W.R. of that station was to remain open, the N.W.N.G. agreed to change their name to Dinas. Additional land for doubling the narrow gauge had not been purchased.

steam'. Presumably the decline in slate traffic obliged the Company to change to Mixed Train working.

The next section to be ready took the railway to Snowdon Ranger and the Major inspected this on 22 May 1878. This was 7 furlongs further than the temporary terminus which had by then 'been removed'. On the new section was a six chain curve and upward gradient of 1 in 79. The gauge was given as 1 ft. 11¼ in. The terminus had a run-round 'beyond it' and only Home and Distant signals were erected; as yet there was no nameboard and a waiting room with convenience for ladies had to be built. Approval to run a passenger service on the One Engine in Steam principle was given.

There were a number of features about the railway which the Inspector did not like, though on the whole he thought 'the works had been well carried out'. In some places the carriages cleared the cutting wall by only 2 ft. instead of 2 ft. 4 in. allowed; in most over-bridges and some rock cuttings the carriage doors would not fully open (shades of the Talyllyn Railway!) and it was necessary to slew the rails and cut away projecting rock or masonry.

Some of the ironwork on bridges had been in place so long that it already required re-painting; likewise some masonry required re-pointing. On bridges the rails had been fastened to longitudinal sleepers by spikes; these had to be altered to fang bolts. There were no nameboards or clocks on display as yet at stations; some signal boxes had clocks, but they were not all fitted up.

The new carriage stock was intended to carry four persons per side. The Major thought they were too narrow for that number and decreed that only three per side was sufficient!

The Distant Signal at Llanwnda was not visible from the cabin and some trees should be lopped to clear the view; similarly at Moel Tryfan Junction the top of a high hedge had to be taken off and some additional locking put into the frame.

The Major disliked the layout at Bryngwyn, where he insisted that the points at the foot of the incline should be weighted to keep them open for the sidings and form an additional protection for the passenger line.

Anticipating the day when more than one train would be worked and block working be introduced, the line would have to be fitted up with telegraph, block instruments, passenger loops and run-away points, with second platforms 'and proper shelter at Moel Tryfan, Rhostryfan and Bryngwyn which are on steep inclines'. The logic of the last statement is a little vague! Can one assume that at first these three stations had no buildings?

The matter of adequate clearances in cuttings had clearly been anticipated, for Oldham had written to Marindin in August 1877 with a truly Festiniog-like proposal! 'As alterations to bridges will take some time, may we run trains with bars fitted to the carriage windows and lock the doors on leaving stations?' To which Marindin replies 'altho' bars on carriage windows are objectionable, they are better than bashed heads'. The bars were to be removed when bridges were safe. Oldham contended on 3 January 1878 that this had been done.

Opening dates may be summarised thus:

Main line from Dinas	to Quellyn (temp.)	21 May 1877
Junction: Goods:	to Snowdon Ranger	1 June 1878
	to S. Snowdon (Rhydd-ddu)	14 May 1881
Passengers:	to Quellyn (temp.)	15 August 1877
	to Snowdon Ranger	1 June 1878
	to S. Snowdon (Rhydd-ddu)	14 May 1881
Branch line from Tryfan		
Junction: Goods:	to Drumhead	21 May 1877
Passengers:	to Bryngwyn	15 August 1877

Though taking the narrative beyond the date so far described, it is convenient to take matters out on the line to a conclusion; the last section was opened following inspection on 5 May 1881, a length of 2 m. 11 ch. with a formation width of 10 ft. Sidings at the terminus were centred at 6 ft. and station limits were: Snowdon Ranger (5 m. 18 ch.) 31 chains; Rhydd-ddu (7 m. 16 ch.) 24 chains; distances in brackets from Tryfan Junction.

There was a junction with a quarry system at Glanrafon and the upgrade varied between 1 in 74 and 1 in 332; the sharpest curve was 3½ chains radius. The major work in the section, and throughout the line in fact, was the Glanrafon Viaduct. Marindin found this to be 'exceedingly strong . . . under test'. He did not pass the line, as there was no buffer stop at Rhydd-ddu, the buildings there were incomplete, and there was no staff-key for the points there nor at Glanrafon, nor any interlocking with the signals. There was no Rhydd-ddu nameboard and the fencing was not finished; the yard was also incomplete. 'An undertaking must be given to work the line by One Engine in Steam and a Train Staff be provided with a key for Glanrafon Sidings, which have no signals.'

In this Report there is just one reference to the progress of work under McKie before he was dismissed—about the only one available; culverting and some preparatory earthwork had been done on this section as early as 1874 and the Inspector found them 'quite adequate'. It would seem therefore that McKie had not at first concentrated his efforts at the Dinas end of the line but must have prepared drainage at least throughout the length of the main line.

It appears that at first only temporary fences were installed between Glanrafon and Rhydd-ddu; the existing stone walls were completed after the line opened. The station at Rhydd-ddu was only temporary too; both walls and station proper were finished for mid-May 1881. On 13 May the Inspector had written to the Secretary of the Railway Department '. . . It is of great importance to this line to open tomorrow and I would recommend that upon the receipt of the undertaking as to the working which the Engineer will bring this afternoon, sanction for the opening should be given . . .' In this case the Inspector was asking for endorsement of his approval without making a further inspection at that juncture. A speed of 10 m.p.h. was to be the limit for Glanrafon Viaduct until the next visit. Temporary sanction to open was then given.

On 14 September 1881 Marindin was back again, his main concern being guard rails on the Glanrafon Viaduct which he found had not yet been installed; in no uncertain terms he recommended that 'final sanction for opening should be with-held'. The engineer had fixed inside instead of outside guard rails to the viaduct: he was told to alter them.

So at last the whole main line was open: Quellyn (road), convenient for the contractor but little else, had gone. Snowdon Ranger to South Snowdon, a sinuous stretch, was complete. The spelling of Quellyn seems to have presented its problems in various ways; there was an extreme Welsh version of Cwellyn and English Guides of the period used Quellyn. Ward Lock's Guide of 1903 called the station 'Quellyn Lake Station Hotel' and the same Guide showed the terminus plainly as Snowdon. Caught between the local Welsh names and common usage by visitors who were deterred by pronunciation, the Company made several efforts to please all parties by altering the names from time to time; they could not satisfy the Welsh by using English titles and the passengers on whom the Company relied were not attracted by the Welsh ones; one hundred years later in a more overall sense, the matter is not yet resolved!

It is now necessary to return to 1879 to examine the problems lying behind the ultimate completion of the railway.

A finish to the Moel Tryfan Undertaking there may have been, but it did not bring much hope to the Board Room. In reporting a loss for the half year ending 30 June 1879 the Directors complained there was 'presently a depression in the slate trade and the line is not working at a profit. The deficiency is mainly due to the line possessing no rolling stock of its own as the whole of it is hired' (this is the first mention of the matter in such a Report, it must be added). 'A Receiver has now been appointed on behalf of the owners of the rolling stock whose rentals are largely in arrears.'

The background of this greater problem was not of the Company's doing, as a slate slump was being felt throughout North Wales; it was going to be another three years before losses were eliminated. The continual drain on financial reserves had made its mark; just when the line might have come into profitable operation, the slate slump hit it. To judge from the returns, it was not so much the mineral tonnage which dropped but in the previous year over 47,000 3rd Class passengers had been carried, the bulk being quarrymen and workmen; in 1879 this fell by almost half and it was 1893 before such a figure was recorded again. Second Class passengers dropped to almost a quarter and never reached the same figure again. So the Company went into Receivership, in which it stayed for the remainder of its days.

As regards the Receiver appointed by the High Court on 13 December 1878 the information was not made public until the next June meeting.* Not surprisingly, Russell was made Chairman but Sir Llewellyn Turner remained on the Board. He and Fitzgibbon were the sole survivors of the Old Guard. Chaloner W. Chute and Richard Seymour Guiness both of London, filled the vacancies. Guiness was a Director of the Banbury & Cheltenham Direct Railway.

No actual date is available but Edwin Spooner had resigned his post before the end of 1877 following the opening to the temporary station at Quellyn. He later became the first General Manager of the Federated Malay States Railway. James Cleminson M.I.C.E. of 7 Westminster Chambers, London, S.W. was appointed Engineer in 1878. More usefully for the Company, R. H. Livesey, who had been made Traffic Superintendent in April 1877 at the age of 24, was appointed Manager and Secretary in November 1879 when, at the same time, the Company's offices were moved from London to Dinas Junction.

James Cleminson's reign lasted six years and as from 1 January 1884, Livesey took up the additional duties of Engineer and Locomotive Superintendent, taking on responsibility at the same time for permanent way and all rolling stock matters. Livesey, from 1879 to August 1890, *was* the N.W.N.G. and the Company's position, though not of the status of a financial goldmine, was at least stabilized and traffic increased. He left North Wales for Donegal's Finn Valley

* Later Receivers were Gowrie Colquhoun Aitchison, A.M.I.C.E., F.C.I.S., of South Collingham, Newark (from 15 January 1912) and Henry Joseph Jack of Dolgarrog, (from 9 April 1921).

Railway, later becoming Manager of the 3 ft. gauge Co. Donegal system, on which he left a profound mark, retiring in 1923.

When Livesey moved to Ireland, S. Tanner became Engineer, to be followed shortly by James W. Szlumper. During the Company's evolvement period of the early 1900s, G. C. Aitchison took up the fourfold role which Livesey had latterly held. Aitchison will also be seen as an executive of the North Wales Power & Traction Company, and the Portmadoc, Beddgelert & South Snowdon Railway, but this is to anticipate!

The shareholders met in Manchester on 15 April 1880 and agreed to raise £50,000* by Debentures 'to rid the railway of debt and to continue the line to its original terminus'. This special meeting was to obtain the assent of the shareholders to a Scheme of Arrangement filed in Chancery between the Company and its creditors. The Scheme was approved by the Court without opposition in early July.

In March 1881 the Board was able to report that 'the profit of £263 made in 1880 has been applied towards payment of hire of rolling stock, and the claims of the rolling stock company, which would amount in the whole to about £7,000, have been settled, and the rolling stock acquired for the Company by the issue of £2,650 in 'A' Debentures @ 4% and £3,350 @ 4½%, involving an annual charge of £257'.†

From a commercial-tactics viewpoint, it should be noted that Russell, Chairman and Receiver, became a mortgagee of the Croesor & Port Madoc Railway in 1882 and this gave him effective control of that railway.

At last on 3 July 1882, the Company was able to tell the Board of Trade that the outside guard rails had been fixed to the Dingle Viaduct (i.e. Glanrafon). Presumably the speed limit was then eased to conform with the rest of the line.

* Viz: £6,000 'A' Debentures in payment for Rolling Stock.
£30,000 'B' Debentures in payment of existing Debentures and completion of line.
£14,000 'C' Debentures for satisfying outstanding liabilities and the general purposes of the Company.

† The Rolling Stock Co. had had seventeen shareholders registered on 31 March 1879. Russell held five times as many shares as any one of the others. By 9 August 1884 Russell was one of seven shareholders and still the largest by eleven times of any one other shareholder. By then three of them only held one qualifying share; in March 1883 the shares were redeemed. On 31 July 1889 the Company filed a return showing final redemption of shares and stated 'The Company ceased to carry on business in June 1889, the cause was that the objects namely, the supply of rolling stock to a small railway company paid for by instalments over a series of years, was fulfilled.' The Company was dissolved on 27 April 1894.

After this shockingly shaky start, the Company was fortunate to enter a period when the slate trade—if not as intense as it had been earlier in the century—was to enjoy a reasonable period of busy-ness. However, the geographical shortcomings of the Moel Tryfan Undertaking were obvious to all; the collection of slate from quarries which the line served was reasonably well catered for, but the drawbacks of having a terminus within three miles of a port and yet, where slate was due for shipment, having to trans-ship it into the L.N.W.R. at Dinas Junction, only for it to be put aboard a boat at Caernarvon within hours, were patently evident. By some means, the narrow gauge must be extended northwards to give it independent access to Caernarvon harbour. Powers were sought to carry out this extension, and obtained by Act 48/9 Vic. Cap. 134 of 31 July 1885. At the same time it was intended to abandon the incline at the head of the Bryngwyn branch and substitute it by another more evenly graded route which would be suitable for passenger traffic. None of this work could be carried out under the aegis of the Moel Tryfan Undertaking, as a Receiver was in being for that Undertaking and no further capital might be raised for it. Separate capital would therefore be necessary.

In the event, authority was obtained for the following :

Railway No. 1 (3 m. 1 ch.) from a junction with the existing railway near Dinas Junction, terminating on the south shore of Caernarvon Harbour near the Rowing Club's Boathouse.

Railway No. 2 (1 m. 5 fur. 4 ch.) from a junction with the branch near Bryngwyn station and ending alongside the Bwlch-y-llyn–Carmel road 95 yds. west of its junction with the Rhostryfan–Cilgwyn Common road. An end-on junction with this Railway was the commencement of :

Railway No. 3 (3 fur. 3 ch.) which ended in the existing Drumhead at the summit of the Bryngwyn Incline.

The whole concept was to be a separate undertaking and distinct from the Moel Tryfan Undertaking, and to be known as the 'Caernarvon & Bryngwyn Extensions'. Separate capital was £28,000 in Ordinary shares or stocks in amounts of not less than £10. Borrowing powers were £9,300 and this was conditional in part upon Railway No. 1 being open to traffic. None was ever issued. Such stocks or etc. were to be offered to those who had already invested in the Moel Tryfan Undertaking, at par. Complicating the financing even further, Section 22 of the Act permitted the Company, following agreement at an Extraordinary General Meeting, to allow the Moel

Tryfan Undertaking to absorb Railways No. 2 and 3, for which purpose the accounts of these two lines were to be kept separate from the separate accounts of the remainder of the separate undertaking! Three years were permitted for the compulsory purchase of land and five for the completion of the work. Section 28 is of formidable length, protecting the L.N.W.R. (successors to the Caernarvonshire Railway and Nantlle Railway), especially at the point where Railway No. 1 would have passed under it. At Caernarvon Harbour, authority was given to build a bridge over the River Seiont and to purchase the Caernarvon ferry.

The Act was more complicated because at the summit of the Bryngwyn Incline, Crown Lands were involved, and it was intended to annex about 4 acres while building the new railway in order to abandon the existing incline. It may be added that certain quarries which sent goods and minerals down the incline were Her Majesty's property also, leased to sundry operators. It was intended that the Company should lease the required land from the Crown for 998 years from 10 October 1885 at a yearly rental of £5 on the basis of a draft lease signed by J. C. Russell on the Company's behalf. Over such lines as were laid over Crown Land, the rate of carriages was not to exceed that charged by the N.W.N.G. over the existing Incline.

No immediate attempt was made by the Company to raise the further capital which the Act authorised. Owing to serious illness the Chairman was unable to prosecute matters. Some evidence suggests that opinions were mixed regarding the advantages of the scheme and, it seems certain that it was prepared in anticipation of improvements in the slate trade—an industry which worked on a 'Jam Tomorrow' basis for over a century. Now and again, jam appeared, but not in the late 1880's. So it was that the time for completion was approaching and nothing had been done about the powers on hand. The fall in passenger traffic 'was fully accounted for by the fact that the terminus of the railway was not in the town of Caernarvon but 2½ miles from it and owing to the great delay in having to wait for trains on the main line they were not able to compete fully with the cars' (2 October 1886). By Act 53/4 Vic. Cap. 70 4 July 1890 an extension of time was obtained to 30 July 1892. Also the 'A' Debentures were redeemable, and substitution was sought for them. Lastly, as a result of the Railway Returns (Continuous Brakes) Act: 41/2 Vic. Cap. 20 of 1878 it was now illegal to operate passenger trains on any railway not exempt without continuous brakes and further capital was required to fit such brakes to existing stock and also purchase additional vehicles for working the Moel Tryfan Undertaking.

The Company was ultimately compelled to comply with both this and the Regulation of Railways Act 52/3 Vic. Cap. 57 of 1889 when the Board of Trade made an Order on the Company dated 30 December 1890. This instructed them to: (1) fit interlocking on points and signals and introduce the Block System within eighteen months and (2) fit continuous brakes on stock used by passenger trains within three years of the Order. One unbraked vehicle might be attached to the rear of braked trains. Proportions of braked/unbraked vehicles in mixed trains were laid down, the train not to exceed 25 vehicles and 25 m.p.h. and to stop at all stations. Two slate wagons were to count as one, and two goods wagons as one if not exceeding 2 tons when loaded.

The 1890 Act repealed certain 1885 sections regarding the separated accounts concerning Railways Nos. 2 and 3, and authorised the issue of £10,000 in new 'A' Debenture Stock, enabling the Company to redeem the current issue which, it may be recalled, were issued to repay the lessee of the original rolling stock. Thus £10,000 new 'A' stocks would redeem £6,000 old 'A' redeemable stocks and the balance of the capital was to be used to pay for the costs of the Act, fitting continuous brakes, providing new rolling stock, installing telephone or telegraphic communication. Other improvements specifically mentioned were '. . . turntables, additional buildings, shed, sidings, signals etc.'.

In 1892 after a season 'of unfavourable weather', a decision was taken to cease catering for 2nd Class passengers at the year end and with the funds now available new stock was bought. An Observation Carriage was obtained from Metropolitan in 1891, together with three bogie coaches from the same maker; in 1894 Ashbury's supplied five new bogie coaches and some new goods stock arrived. Later, two new engines were delivered and a further guards-composite coach was bought. The buying spree for rolling stock then ended, it being spread over eighteen years from the time of the 1890 Act. Commencing in Spring 1892 and completed early in 1894 Westinghouse brake was fitted to all existing bogie carriage stock, and the locomotives. The layout at Dinas Junction was enlarged, some signalling and communications' improvements carried out and in general, the railway was much uplifted from its then primitive state.

Of Railways Nos. 1, 2 and 3 nothing more was to be heard until after the First War. Nor did the turntables materialise; the practice of slewing the engines round from time to time, upon greased steel plates aided by jacks and ropes, persisted until Welsh Highland days when the Boston Lodge turntable became accessible.

Under the Railways Rates & Charges No. 6 (Festiniog Railway &

Etc.) Order of 1892, special provisions were laid down for the N.W.N.G.R. Company.

1. Slate traffic carried in the railway's own wagons on its main line to be charged at ½d. per ton mile.
2. Slate traffic carried in the railway's own wagons on the Bryngwyn branch (5¼ m.) was to be charged as for 6¼ miles which would cover the use of railway wagons by the quarry owners on the lines radiating from the 'Drumhead', all use of inclines and where N.W.N.G. services were provided over quarry owners' inclines and sidings.
3. Where slate traffic was carried in quarry owners' wagons (there were about thirty private owner quarry wagons before 1900) between Glanrafon and Dinas (8¼ m.) the Company would charge as for 9¼ miles but this would cover charges for using any of the Company's sidings at Dinas and the working of those sidings.
4. Where traffic (other than slate and other minerals) was carried in owner's wagons the rate was to be:

Bryngwyn–Drumhead–Dinas Junction	3d. per ton mile
Glanrafon Siding–Dinas Junction	4d. per ton mile

(The latter suggests that private owners' wagons originated in the Moel Tryfan quarries complex, and at Glanrafon Quarry only.)

As regards returning empty wagons into quarry sidings and the shunting of the sidings, the N.W.N.G. was not entitled to charge over and above the rates of sections 2 and 3.

An interesting addenda was to the effect that if quarry owners could load goods to or from Caernarvon without the necessity for loading or reloading at Dinas, then suitable equipment for this purpose must be provided at cost by the Railway Company for the use by quarry owners. Perhaps some sort of 'container' which would transfer rail–road–rail was under consideration?

It was probably too much to expect that other parties would not enter the field at a period when interest in 'light railways' (the actual Light Railway Act had not then been passed) was at its height. In 1889 a proposed Beddgelert & Rhydd-ddu Railway (Engineers Charles Minns and John S. Lawrence) was intended to link South Snowdon on the N.W.N.G. and the Croesor line on much the same course as other lines of earlier date had intended, save that south of the end-on connection with the N.W.N.G., the road would have been crossed and the new railway remained on the west side of the valley all the way south as far as and beyond the Aberglaslyn Pass where tunnels would have been avoided by circumventing the bluffs on the

Pass instead of cutting through them. Plans were deposited (Caernarvon R. O. 97) but no development took place.

More threatening to N.W.N.G. plans was the Portmadoc, Beddgelert & Rhydd-ddu Railway which intended to apply for Parliamentary powers in the 1892 Session for:

Railway No. 1 (4 m. 2 fur. 5 ch.) from a junction with the Portmadoc, Croesor & Beddgelert Tram Railway Co. (the Croesor tramway) 4 fur. 8 ch. from the west side of its Llanfrothen road level crossing, to Beddgelert close to and south-west of the Goat Hotel.

Railway No. 2 (4 m. 3 fur. 8 ch.) A link between this line at Beddgelert and the N.W.N.G. at Rhydd-ddu.

Notices of intent appeared in the *Cambrian News* during November 1891, from which it was hoped to establish links with the Festiniog, N.W.N.G. and P.C. & B.T.R. Companies and to enjoy running powers over a rebuilt Croesor tramway between the point of junction and Portmadoc. The promoters were William Hunt Scott and Joseph Wellington Burrows, neither of whom had any other local railway interests. The gauge was to be 1 ft. 11½ in. with powers to increase to standard gauge. (Caernarvon R. O. 100.)

Though nothing developed once again, the basic scheme was revived after the passing of the Light Railways Act of 1896, when a draft Light Railway Order to go before the Light Railway Commissioners in November 1897 was prepared for a Portmadoc, Beddgelert & Rhydd-ddu Light Railway. (Caernarvon R. O. 111.) Promoters were James W. Wyatt of Gwynant, Robert Isaac, Richard Davies and William Jones (local landowners etc.), and two Railways were proposed:

Railway No. 1 (6 m. 6 fur. 3 ch.) from the Gorseddau Railway's then disused site immediately east of the Cambrian Railway's road crossing at Portmadoc station, thence along the side of the Beddgelert Siding Cambrian interchange siding and running roughly parallel to the Croesor tramway, worked northwards along the Glaslyn's east bank and south of Beddgelert, crossed to the west side of the river and tunnelled part way through the Pass of Aberglaslyn. North of here and into Beddgelert was almost the same route as previously intended by other promoters.

Railway No. 2 (4 m. 5 fur. 52 ch.) was largely on the site of the Beddgelert & Rhydd-ddu Railway of 1889. All lines were to be 1 ft. 11½ in. gauge.

These plans were brought to an advanced stage and though the Draft Order makes no reference to, or use of, the Croesor Tramway course there must have been second thoughts for an Estimate of Costs omitting the Croesor and dated 8 November 1897 has been amended under date May 1898 and gives 'Length of Croesor Tramway 3 miles 1 furlong' and later provides for new railway and refurbishing of the Croesor line as respectively, £864 per mile and £688 per mile—indicating the major renewal of the tramway which would be necessary to bring it up to passenger standards. There were to be stations at Beddgelert and Portmadoc only. The tunnel would have been 280 yards long.

An interesting sidelight on the revised figures of the Estimate relating to Railway No. 2 was the £340 allowed for Crossing Gatekeepers' Houses and Signals in the 1897 Draft, is now deleted.

In the context of narrow gauge railway work now being carried out in North Wales, it is fitting to add the estimated costs of building a new line in 1898—including bridges, stations etc. New work was originally to cost £23,870 for 11 m. 3 fur. of railway and included all works. By May 1898, allowing for reduction in expenses but including rebuilding of Croesor, the figure was £24,720. Thomas Roberts & Son of Portmadoc were the Engineers and the maximum grade would have been 1 in 41.

Having reached this advanced stage of promotion, why was nothing further heard of this last scheme? The answer lies in an inability to carry out the necessary preliminaries before the N.W.N.G. Company, alarmed by the course of events, took matters into its own hands. The projected Portmadoc, Beddgelert & Rhydd-ddu Railway was still a paper-bound intention in May 1898 but the North Wales Narrow Gauge, for all its earlier failings, was very much an existing railway and in the same year it gave notice of applying for a Light Railway Order to extend its line to Beddgelert; the application went before the Light Railway Commissioners in November 1898 and provisional agreement was given, subject to a local enquiry. This astute move on the part of the N.W.N.G., diverted its outside threats.

A more subtle obstacle to various schemes for railways between Portmadoc and Beddgelert at this time was undoubtedly Russell himself. The Light Railway Commissioners themselves admitted, in a Report to the Board of Trade in 1900 regarding efforts of 1897 and 1898 . . . 'these schemes were rejected by the Commissioners owing to the legal difficulties of acquiring the Croesor Railway, a disused mineral line'(!) Clearly, the Commissioners were misinformed, as the Croesor was very much a going concern and, whether they felt the situation was too complex to tackle, or they were astute enough to appreciate how matters stood, they evaded the issue. There were in fact no real legal difficulties; at this time control of both N.W.N.G. Railways and the Croesor could be said to be in the hands of the same man though why he was disinterested is not clear. Did he feel that once he linked with other railways, control would pass from him?

The North Wales Narrow Gauge Railways 'Beddgelert Light Railway Extension Order' was obtained on 3 November 1900 with James W. and William W. Szlumper as Engineers (they were currently engaged on the Vale of Rheidol Railway promotion) for a line 4 m. 6 fur. 3 ch. long to the rear of the Goat Hotel, Beddgelert, a maximum grade of 1 in 41 with five years for building. It was intended to work the line by steam and for the scheme to be separate from the Moel Tryfan Undertaking.

Suitable and separate financing arrangements were proposed. The total cost would be £11,996. In the event, work done under this Order was carried out by the Portmadoc, Beddgelert & South Snowdon Railway and no longer concerned the N.W.N.G. Company. An Agreement to this effect between the two concerns was dated 26 August 1904.

Under the Beddgelert Extension Order a time of three years was permitted for completion, a period which was exceeded before the powers of the Order were taken over by the Portmadoc, Beddgelert & South Snowdon Railway. A maximum speed of 18 m.p.h. on the level or of 15 m.p.h. on grades exceeding 1 in 50 and an axle loading of 8 tons was allowed. The separate capital would be £13,800 called 'The Extension Capital', with borrowing powers dependent on the amount of subscribed capital at any time. Rails were to weigh no less than 41½ lb. per yard and curves of less than 3 chains were to be checkrailed and tied. Coachscrews and bearing plates were to be used in the track in addition to dog spikes.

In view of the Light Railway nature of the work, it is curious that provision for semaphore signalling was made. It was not carried out, but the relevant order reads: 'At places where trains pass one another there shall be a home signal in each direction . . . near the entrance points. If (it) cannot be seen from a distance of quarter of a mile, a distant signal must be erected . . .' Signals were to be interlocked with points and each other. Shelters and conveniences were not obligatory at stations.

A curious footnote to the Returns for 1902 states under 'Season and Period Tickets': 'Includes a receipt of £158 from a Quarry Company for settlement of a previous year's quarrymen's tickets.'

From this entry might be inferred that the quarrymen travelled 'free' at the cost of their employer, or more likely, the quarry deducted the cost of a block booking from their wages. It is also possible the booking was made by a 'Quarrymen's Club' for whom the quarry acted in this matter.

The Company now found itself in a somewhat untidy state in terms of 'status'. It was a fully fledged railway with a proposed appendage as a Light Railway and with aspirations—scarcely disguised—of becoming an electric railway drawing power from its own generating stations and working its trains by overhead conductors. So no surprise was occasioned when on 6 June 1905 an Order was obtained to work the existing line as a Light Railway and operate with electric traction. The P.B. & S.S.R. was given powers to lease the N.W.N.G. at any suitable time and work the two systems as a joint concern.

The spectacle of an overhead narrow gauge electric railway, with trains passing effortlessly over the steep gradients and sharp curves and driven by power obtained in the district from an abundant water supply is perhaps best known in Switzerland, where today there are many miles of mountain railway exactly as conceived for Caernarvonshire at the turn of the century. Even in 1972, a part of such a project in the county remains viable; but neither the N.W.N.G. nor the P.B. & S.S.R. was destined to provide it in 1905. In fact, the N.W.N.G. was already at its prime, and though a final locomotive and carriage was added to the stock, no further improvements to the line took place, nor did further behind-the-scenes empire-building affect the Company. The slate trade continued to decline in importance, whilst passenger traffic was suspended on the branch on 31 December 1913 and on the main line to all regular services on 31 October 1916.

Evidence of a run-down in conditions may lie behind a rumour which was circulating of which a notice in *The Times* for 20 April 1910 might have been significant. This suggested that the L.N.W.R. was to take over the Railways Company 'between Dinas and Beddgelert'. (A similar story that the L.N.W.R. would take over the Cambrian was rife about 1900.)

With the coming of the First War passenger returns dwindled and the railway fell on particularly hard times, as most of the quarries closed completely (never to re-open in many cases) and only a few worked with reduced output. The main line to Rhyddu-ddu was especially hit and proved quite uneconomic with its long arm and dwindling return. It was a sorry decline, and the whole railway gradually fell into that state which the Festiniog line experienced during the Second War. The passenger stock was pushed into a siding and the best of it went under such cover as Dinas Junction could provide; most of it deteriorated rapidly through lack of paint. Damaged slate wagons filled the yards as there was no work for them and no men to repair them even if required. The locomotive stock contrived to keep going, with *Russell* doing the brunt of the work. The newest engine was sold, and the signalling equipment, with a railway worked 'One Engine in Steam', decayed and fell out of use. The sleepers rotted and the rails hogged; nature began to reclaim the track bed.

An 'epilogue' to a railway which began with high hopes and extensive aspirations, which for many years had been not only a doubtful investment but a constant source of problems to its operators, came in the form of an ex-Royal Engineer's Report compiled by Major G. C. Spring in 1921. By then, all traffic was confined to the Bryngwyn branch and slate quarries, save for a small amount of coal working. The two engines were in good order, *Moel Tryfan* had been rebuilt in 1903 and retubed in 1912. It would haul four composite coaches up the steepest gradient; *Russell*, the other engine, would haul nine coaches, each holding 50 passengers. The coaches, however, were not in use and having received a minimum of paint, were extensively deteriorated. There were eleven composites, two brake-composites and a four-wheeled brake van. All were fitted with Westinghouse brake.

The various pattern of slate wagon numbered ninety. Additionally there were twelve open wagons of 2 tons capacity, thirteen coal wagons, fourteen bolsters and twenty bolster runners (flats).

The two-wire telegraph used on posts throughout the system, was out of order. The telephone, Dinas to Snowdon with a tapping at Waenfawr, was working. The block instruments provided throughout, were taken out save those at Tryfan Junction and Waenfawr which were passing places and where they were *in situ*.

Trains ran on the Bryngwyn branch four days a week and when required, ran up to Snowdon also with coal 'and smalls'. Only two men were employed to maintain the whole track which was in a poor state; new sleepers and tie bars had recently been put in on the branch; more were needed and Bryngwyn station 'needs immediate attention'. The main line was unsafe for passengers, requiring 300 new sleepers per mile; all curves needed packing, but from 8½ miles to Snowdon, the track was in good order. Timber on bridges and signal cabins had rotted away.

Distant, Home and Starter signals existed but were dilapidated and useless. All the machinery had gone from the Running Shed and repairs put out to contract. 'There was no place of any importance for passengers on the line.'

The track was 41 lb. U.F.F. steel rail in 30 ft. lengths, carried on 11 sleepers. Owing to spikes being loose, the rails had worked downgrade and together with the sharp curves, some station yards gave constant trouble; Bryngwyn for instance, was now unfit to take locomotives.

The Bryngwyn incline to the Amalgamated Quarries was $\frac{3}{4}$ m. long and 1 in 10 grade; it was worked by the Railway staff and connected with Alexandra, Moel Tryfan, Braich and Cilgwyn Quarries at the top; Vron was about to re-open. The incline rope was weak and only 3 slate wagons could descend at a time. In consequence, it took four hours to handle a 20-wagon train. (Spring preferred abandonment of the incline and as the country was suitable, a new line incorporating reversing necks. He also recommended an approach to the Pen-yr-orsedd Quarries to suggest they might divert their traffic to Drumhead instead of consigning it via the horse-worked Nantlle Railway.)

The existing signalling was extremely lavish; Tryfan Box had 10 signals and a 20 lever frame. The Report confirms that the last Aberglaslyn tunnel on the railway then building, had yet to be pierced; no viaducts were built, but 41 lb. rails were laid for a mile south of South Snowdon and had recently been used for 'timber logging', but were now out of use.

As a result of an intensive period of rehabilitation to bring the main line up to passenger standards, passenger services were resumed from 31 July 1922 using the Festiniog's *Palmerston* which had been on hire to the contractors and was conveniently available. Passenger services on the branch, though intended, did not materialise.

In 1922, Evan R. Davies, a new N.W.N.G. director, wrote to S. E. Tyrwhitt the newly-appointed Manager of the Festiniog and the new Welsh Highland Railway—into which the North Wales Narrow Gauge Railways was absorbed as from 1 January 1922. Advice was given that all matters of finance would now pass to Dolgarrog, the Welsh Highland headquarters. It was anticipated that the L.N.W.R. would begin its summer service on 10 July 1922 and Tyrwhitt was instructed to see that the Rhydd-ddu line would be ready for opening on that day. D. O. Jones had tendered a draft for a restored passenger service on the N.W.N.G. which could be worked with little addition to the then skeleton staff. (D. O. Jones was the factotum at Dinas Junction.) So almost unnoticed, the N.W.N.G. ceased its independent life.

The Route Described

The railway began at a junction at Llanwnda with the Carnarvonshire Railway* (as it was locally still known) a standard gauge line

* The statutory title and spelling.

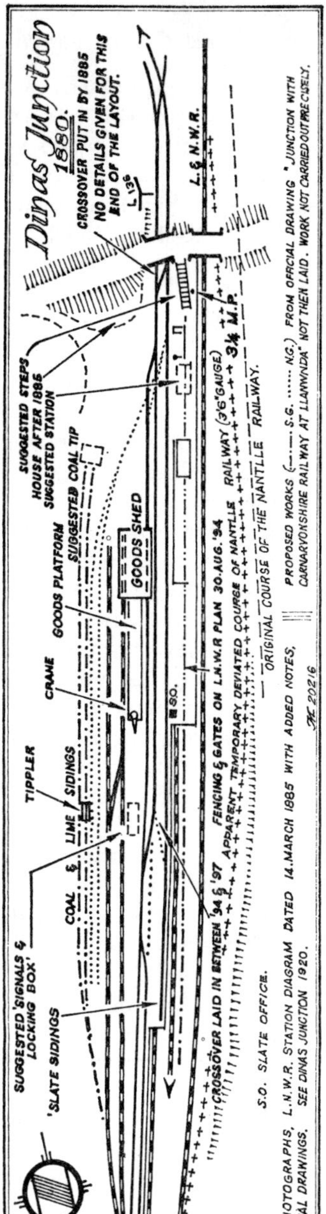
Dinas Junction 1880.
CROSSOVER PUT IN BY 1885
NO DETAILS GIVEN FOR THIS END OF THE LAYOUT.
L.136
L. & N.W.R.
SUGGESTED STEPS
HOUSE AFTER 1885
SUGGESTED STATION
SUGGESTED COAL TIP
GOODS SHED
SUGGESTED GOODS PLATFORM
CRANE
TIPPLER
COAL & LIME SIDINGS
SUGGESTED 'SIGNALS & LOCKING BOX'
'SLATE SIDINGS
FENCING & GATES ON L.N.W.R PLAN 30.AUG.'94
APPARENT TEMPORARY DEVIATED COURSE OF NANTLLE RAILWAY (3'6" GAUGE)
3¼ M.P.
CROSSOVER LAID IN BETWEEN '94 & '97
ORIGINAL COURSE OF THE NANTLLE RAILWAY.
S.O.
S.O. SLATE OFFICE.
PROPOSED WORKS (——S.G. ······N.G.) FROM OFFICIAL DRAWING 'JUNCTION WITH CARNARVONSHIRE RAILWAY AT LLANWNDA' NOT THEN LAID. WORK NOT CARRIED OUT PRECISELY.
BASED ON OLD PHOTOGRAPHS, L.N.W.R. STATION DIAGRAM DATED 14.MARCH 1885 WITH ADDED NOTES, AND VARIOUS OFFICIAL DRAWINGS. SEE DINAS JUNCTION 1920.
JIC 20216

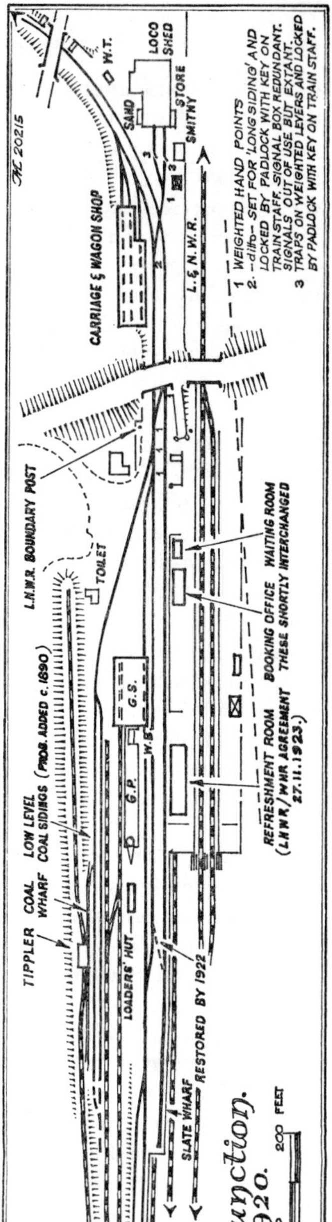
Dinas Junction 1920.
JIC 20215
W.T.
LOCO SHED
SAND
STORE
SMITHY
CARRIAGE & WAGON SHOP
L. & N.W.R.
1 WEIGHTED HAND POINTS
2 -ditto- SET FOR 'LONG SIDING' AND LOCKED BY PADLOCK WITH KEY ON TRAIN STAFF. SIGNAL BOX REDUNDANT. SIGNALS OUT OF USE BUT EXTANT.
3 TRAPS ON WEIGHTED LEVERS AND LOCKED BY PADLOCK WITH KEY ON TRAIN STAFF.
L.N.W.R. BOUNDARY POST
TOILET
BOOKING OFFICE
WAITING ROOM
THESE SHORTLY INTERCHANGED
G.S.
W.S.
G.P.
REFRESHMENT ROOM
(LNWR/WHR AGREEMENT 27.11.1923.)
TIPPLER
COAL WHARF
LOW LEVEL COAL SIDINGS (PROB. ADDED c.1890)
LOADERS' HUT
RESTORED BY 1922
SLATE WHARF
TIMBER WHARF
0 100 200 FEET
CRO REF 249.

which had commenced at a temporary station south of Caernarvon at Pant, had absorbed the old Nantlle Railway (opened in 1828, gauge 3 ft. 6 in.) and extended for 18¾ miles southward across the neck of the Lleyn Peninsula to a junction with the Cambrian Railways (Coast Section) at Afon Wen. The Carnarvonshire Railway was in practice part of the London & North Western Railway which had opened to Caernarvon (a separate station at the north end of the town) in July 1852 and had had aspirations of reaching Portmadoc as one point where the slate industry might be tapped.

At Llanwnda the Nantlle Tramway (or Railway) ran roughly parallel but to the west of the main Caernarvon–Pwllheli road, and the absorption of this horse-worked narrow gauge line permitted the Caernarvonshire Railway to use limited portions of its course between Caernarvon and Pen-y-groes for its new standard gauge line. The evidence of old photographs suggests that the new owners built their standard gauge track leaving not only most of the Nantlle Railway in use but re-siting some (including the section at Llanwnda) alongside its own new line, probably for contracting purposes. An early scene at Dinas Junction—the name for the station where interchange with the North Wales Narrow Gauge was made shows narrow gauge track apparently of 3 ft. 6 in. gauge running alongside and west of the standard gauge through the station (where later the L.N.W.R. were to provide a passing loop and Up platform). L.N.W.R. passenger trains began to call at Dinas from September 1877.

The N.W.N.G. occupied a narrow site between the L.N.W.R. and the main road on the east side of the standard gauge. There was an interchange platform between standard and narrow gauges, the former being of traditional height and the N.W.N.G. at rail level, but having in common with all N.W.N.G. stations, slab curbs to define the passenger area. The northern end of this platform was occupied by a similar two-level wharf for interchange of slate (later also of timber). The central portion contained a stone station building for N.W.N.G. purposes, the L.N.W.R. not having a building of its own at the time. East of this was a large stone goods shed containing tracks in both gauges divided by an exchange platform; at its north end was a goods platform with a crane at its extremity and later, a weighbridge for narrow gauge was added.

A feature of the site was a road crossing of the station premises at the south end. The N.W.N.G. bridge was in its standard brick and stone design, and the L.N.W.R. had its own overbridge alongside, the two being connected by an earthen embankment carrying the road. An early drawing (undated) headed 'Proposed Station and Transhipment for the North Wales Narrow Gauge Junction with the Caernarvonshire Railway at Llanwnda' undoubtedly comes from Spooner's office at Portmadoc though it is not marked in any way. Additional sidings in both gauges are provided on the drawing, but these do not appear to have been built at the outset, clearly due to shortage of funds. Lime and coal sidings on the east side (with high level L.N.W.R. tracks discharging into low level N.W.N.G. wagons) together with a tippler, did not materialise until further capital was available for such improvements under the N.W.N.G. Act of 1890.

South of the road overbridges, where in later years carriage and wagon shops, loco shed and workshops etc. were to be found, no detail is given and the tracks simply converge. Nor is signalling shown, and only the position of the starting signal is known for certain.

The Company was obliged to 'make do' with this limited arrangement until additional funds came to hand and extended facilities were provided:

1. Additional sidings were laid east of the goods shed for coal and lime traffic. The L.N.W.R. provided a single high level siding with tippler there, held up on a retaining wall. The double line and end tipper for the standard gauge, envisaged by Spooner, did not materialise.
2. The latterday facilities south of the road overbridge were erected. There was a three road carriage and wagon store shed and repair shop in corrugated iron with a long siding giving access. A feature of this in latter days was the string of broken wagons on it which, because of diminishing traffic, never had need to enter the works for repair.

Across on the west side of the curve was a double road engine shed built in timber with store and sand oven alongside in stone. (An original and smaller loco shed on this site is likely to have been a stone-built affair.) Here too, stood an iron water tank on a stone plinth, a feature which must have existed from the beginning. There was a small stone smithy beside the shed which, though not specifically provided, doubled up as a workshop. A wooden signal box on stone base completed the buildings; the box was at first to be placed north of the goods platform on the other side of the bridge so presumably at this period no intention of works and sheds on the south side was anticipated. Detail alterations and periods of disuse and refurbishing of certain pointwork throughout the life of the N.W.N.G. according to the times when no passenger trains were running at all, are evident in the trackage which it was necessary to retain or revive on the wharves.

It will be noted too that on the standard gauge side, an Up loop and platform were laid in the early 1880s and the signal box which had been some way north of the station near the sidings' throat, was placed on the Up platform before 1885 where it was also more convenient for handling the single line staff etc.

On the Down platform, the principal building remained the stone

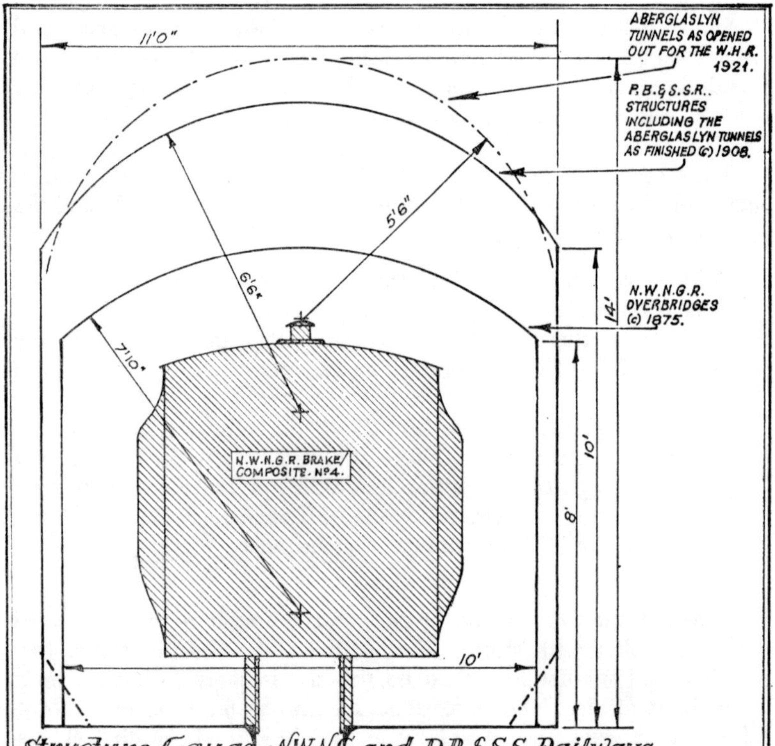

Structure Gauge—N.W.N.G and P.B.&S.S. Railways.

station of the N.W.N.G., but after the First War the Snowdon Mountain Tramroad and Hotel Co. operated a Refreshment Room at the north end—a large wooden affair on stone foundations—and a small wooden Booking Office was added south of the stone station.

Standard gauge facilities remained throughout the period of the narrow gauge's existence.

On leaving Dinas Junction the railway curved left through a right angle turn, entering a cutting to pass under the Caernarvon–Pwllheli road by means of the customary pattern of N.W.N.G. overbridge built in stone with brick lining to the arch—usually of four courses in either red or yellow. On the outer side of the curve, in front of the bridge, was the advance starting signal to cover movements made from the loco and carriage yard when using the main line as a headshunt.

Once under the roadbridge past the Home signal, after $\frac{1}{4}$ m. the track emerged from the cutting and after threading a narrow wooded belt ran along the left bank of the Gorfai stream for about $\frac{1}{8}$ m. before crossing it by a 12 ft. span girder bridge and passing under a secondary road (200 ft. above sea level). The surrounding land is low lying and tends to be marshy; the climb began from Dinas at 1 in 136 but the real collar-work had yet to begin.* A straight run of about $\frac{1}{4}$ m. brought the line to Bod-aden where another secondary road was crossed and the first milepost passed. In the next $\frac{3}{8}$ m. the stream was crossed twice more and the main road to Rhostryfan came in alongside on the left. The ground each side remains flat and somewhat uninteresting, besides being boggy and wet. The road on the left mounted over the railway by a bridge rebuilt in concrete in 1933 during road widening. The railway turned north-west here and followed a virtually straight course until the second milepost. The height is now 300 ft. as Wernlas-ddu is passed and climbing from here begins in earnest. There was a long pull up of 1 in 47 mainly on low embankment and through an ever-increasingly pleasant countryside. The course used the tip of the foothills of the mountain bloc, keeping it out of the wet lands below but still avoiding heavy earthworks and confining the gradient to a steady climb. The line was bounded by substantial stone walls, 12 yd. between each, and gated in wood where necessary. Much use of slab and worn flat-bottomed rails was made for gate posts; of the latter, perhaps most were taken from the N.W.N.G. when substantial relaying was done by the W.H.R. in the early 1920s. Some are marked 'Leeds Forge 1904' and 'Darlington Steel Co. Ltd.'; they are about 40 lb. weight and if in fact were taken from the N.W.N.G., were in very poor condition when renewed. This length of line must have been delightful in railway days; the land slopes upwards to the south in pasture and woodland, whilst to the north are water-meadows with grazing Welsh Blacks dotted over them. Farms tend to be large, by local standards.

Now came a slow right-hand curve and from a nominal 1 in 47 the gradient stiffened as the foothills' slopes steepened. The long low

* Gradients are quoted where known but the figures are insufficient to produce an accurate Gradient Profile. The profile which survives as part of the Deposited Plans is of passing interest only as it was not followed.

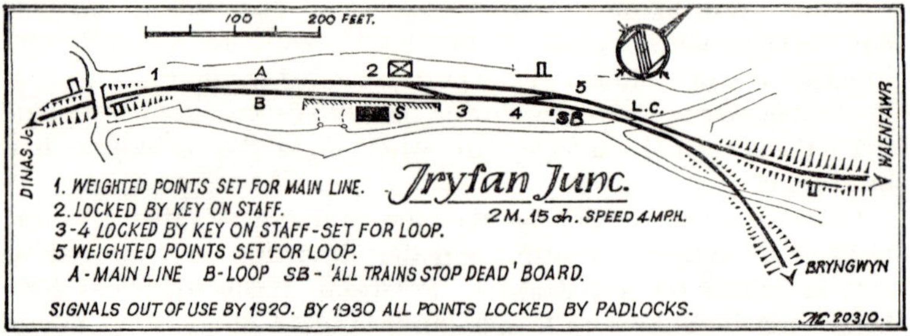

embankment ceased, there was a short length of open ground and after a short length of 1 in 37, a cutting and road overbridge. Immediately beyond extended a brief embankment and by means of a stone overbridge, the adjacent stream was crossed for the last time (2 m.). Almost at once there is another road overbridge—all within a length of about 75 yd. Beyond the second one and a slight reverse curve, the railway entered Tryfan Junction station (originally named Moel Tryfan Junction).

Tryfan Junction (2 m. 15 ch.) (372 ft.) must have been something of a disappointment to the stranger, but on the other hand, totally in keeping with that isolated meeting place of railways perhaps more commonly met with in Ireland than in Wales. Apart from the small stone and brick station building, with its generous nameboard below the eaves, giving the title in full, it was one of the remotest of places. Even today, a small road passes along the rear but it only serves two farms. In yesteryear, it would have been quieter still. It must be presumed that occasionally some folk changed from a Dinas-bound train for a Bryngwyn-bound one, but that would be about the whole of it. Originally the signalling was luxurious, with a Down Home signal before the first overbridge previously mentioned, and six other signals to keep it company. At the east end the Bryngwyn branch came in at a fearsome $3\frac{3}{4}$ chain curve which lay at the foot of a long 1 in 39 fall, so occasionally there may have been some exciting moments. Whether this had anything to do with the branch not having a Home signal but only a stop board is not known (!) but branch trains were required to make a dead stand at the incline foot in any case. However, the Junction was one of those places where one is bound to conclude that operating methods were evolved which suited the place and whereon management seldom gazed. There was one long passing loop which contained a facing crossover and from the south side of which the junction was made to Bryngwyn. This simple layout allowed great flexibility of movements—if ever they were required. There was no siding and no goods facilities. Opposite the station was a wooden signal box on stone base and the passenger platform, as at other stations, was simply a neat 6 in. edging of slab to retain a gravel stand. From a full passenger station, Tryfan Junction was reduced to Halt status in 1934, before the Welsh Highland lost its passenger services.

Resuming its course north-eastwards from the Junction, the line continued to rise at 1 in 690 and began to curve slowly in a more easterly direction. First there was a low embankment and a farm road came alongside on the left. This road then passed over the line which fell into a cutting below it. Now east of the bridge, there followed a considerable embankment pierced by a fine example of the Company's stone underbridges which carried the line over the road to Gwredog-isaf, a large farm now derelict. This place is of special interest as early 25-inch Plans show it to have had a railway system in the barnyard. Today there is no sign of railway connections save for inventive use of ex-Nantlle Railway fish-bellied rails to support the roofs of some outbuildings . . . indeed, such is the extensive use of these rails (presumably available when the Caernarvon–Pen-y-groes section was superseded by the standard gauge) that they may be found in remote localities all over the area serving as fencing posts or etc. A later generation of well-meaning investigators may well conclude that this was the form of rail used exclusively in this part of the county!

Eastwards of here the countryside becomes more wooded and the gradient steepened then eased as the line entered the south side of the Afon Gwyrfai valley, now meandering some way below to the left. After a short cutting the railway was carried on a shelf on the valley-side, with the river steeply down below (3 m.). This steep slope takes on a partially escarpment-like quality for a short distance below Tanyrallt, and the railway was forced to wind its way along to keep contact with the valley side. Now enveloped in woodland, it was a charming section of the train journey as the river gradually came up alongside.

The climb which was such a feature up to, and for quarter of a mile beyond Tryfan Junction, had reached a plateau thereafter; after a short fall at 1 in 200 the line into Waenfawr was level.

Another detail noticeable during the threading of the 'shelf section' was that four foot boundary walling topped by two wires had ceased and when fencing was resumed a mile or so west of Waenfawr, it was of the seven-wire and four foot wood-post variety which was retained almost for the whole of the remainder of the main line. Presumably stone walls were built where loose boulders from river deposits were

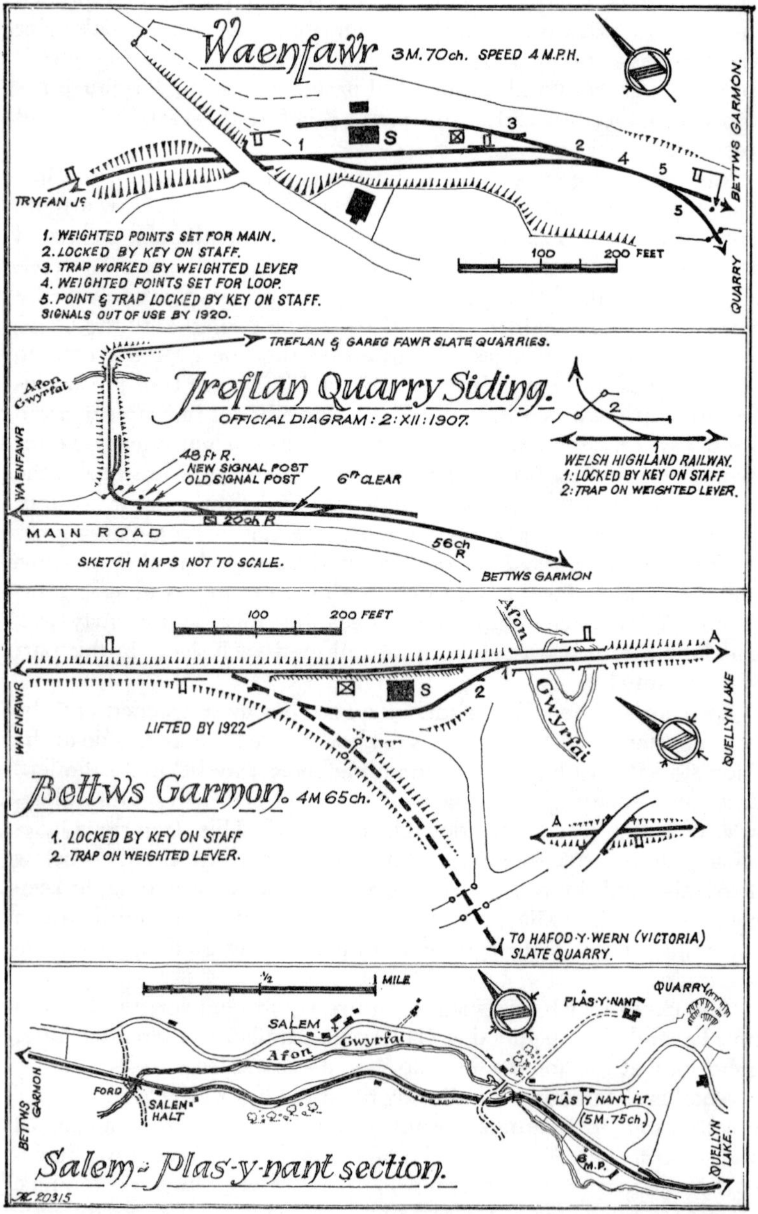
Waenfawr 3M.70ch. SPEED 4 M.P.H.
TRYFAN Jc
BETTWS GARMON.
QUARRY
100 200 FEET
1. WEIGHTED POINTS SET FOR MAIN.
2. LOCKED BY KEY ON STAFF.
3. TRAP WORKED BY WEIGHTED LEVER
4. WEIGHTED POINTS SET FOR LOOP.
5. POINT & TRAP LOCKED BY KEY ON STAFF.
SIGNALS OUT OF USE BY 1920.
TREFLAN & GAREG FAWR SLATE QUARRIES.
Afon Gwyrfai
Treflan Quarry Siding.
OFFICIAL DIAGRAM: 2: XII: 1907.
WAENFAWR
48 ft R.
NEW SIGNAL POST
OLD SIGNAL POST
6ft CLEAR
20ch R
MAIN ROAD
56ch R
SKETCH MAPS NOT TO SCALE.
BETTWS GARMON
WELSH HIGHLAND RAILWAY.
1: LOCKED BY KEY ON STAFF
2: TRAP ON WEIGHTED LEVER.
100 200 FEET
Afon Gwyrfai
WAENFAWR
QUELLYN LAKE
LIFTED BY 1922
Bettws Garmon. 4M 65ch.
1. LOCKED BY KEY ON STAFF
2. TRAP ON WEIGHTED LEVER.
TO HAFOD-Y-WERN (VICTORIA) SLATE QUARRY.
½ MILE
SALEM
Afon Gwyrfai
PLAS-Y-NANT
QUARRY
BETTWS GARMON
FORD
SALEM HALT
PLAS Y NANT HT.
(5M.75ch.)
6 M.P.
QUELLYN LAKE.
Salem - Plas-y-nant section.
JIC 20315

available on the lower stretches of the line. They resume again between Snowdon Ranger and Rhydd-ddu in Festiniog pattern with wire fence on top.

Before Waenfawr is reached the 400 ft. contour was crossed and there came a most intimate length where the river, now alongside and occasionally broken by rapids and islands, is enhanced by hillocks and large trees. Waenfawr itself, on the hillside to the north which is now a noticeable feature from the line, tumbles down in scattered fashion to meet river and railway. On this length of line some curious track spikes were found—they were of standard N.W.N.G. dome-head pattern but no less than 8 in. long. On this section the railway was heading almost due east but as Waenfawr Down Home signal was passed, it curved right and south-easterly, entered a short cutting and emerged from under a stone overbridge carrying the Caernarvon–Beddgelert road to enter Waenfawr station (3 m. 70 ch.). After the delightful mile or so preceding Waenfawr, this was something of an anticlimax. The countryside has changed and for some distance the railway was to run along the flood plain of the Gwyrfai, the foothills tending to hang back for a time as the valley widened out ready for an even more dramatic narrowing higher up.

After 1895 this had become the largest station between Dinas and South Snowdon. Up to that time it was neither a staff nor block station but then a loop siding—similar to that at Bettws Garmon was put in. Whilst it had catch points at each end it was not signalled. The points each end were locked by Annett's Key from the signal box. One ground lever at the south end was actually in a corner of the box, and the Dinas end alongside the turnout. Only one set of points could be worked at a time as there was only one key, which interlocked with the signals.

Col. R. A. Yorke reported on 28 November 1895 that if facing point locks were added the loop might be used for goods traffic but as the intention was to use it for all traffic the following must be done now it is both a block and staff station :

1. Signal the station as a proper passing place.
2. All trains to use left-hand side of loop.
3. Home signals capable of being lowered only for proper line.
4. Removal of catch points.
5. Starting signals at each loop to be installed.
6. Facing point locks fitted.

Until this had been done, subject to fitting facing point locks, the loop could be passed for goods traffic only.

Mr. Russell met Major Marindin and Col. Yorke and it was agreed that starting signals would not be required. The other work was carried out using Saxby & Farmer materials and the layout came into use on 21 July 1896. Trains could use it as a passing place (though most timetables did not require it) which could not be said of all stations, even though others boasted loops. There was the usual stone building, a signal box and one siding (with small goods shed) facing South Snowdon. After the demise of the box's locking frame, the point hand levers were weighted for left-hand running through the loop which was 250 ft. clear at 8 ft. centres. The traps in the siding were locked by the staff key. A quarry branch, south of the station, was opened to a nearby granite quarry in Welsh Highland days.

The climb from Waenfawr was a slighter one of 1 in 150, with the main road alongside on the right hand. The fencing which survives along the rail route in this section is worth a second glance—few railway museums have such a fine collection of various rail sections.

The fourth mile post was passed just south of Waenfawr; the line was now sandwiched between river and roadway, a rather boggy place. The next feature is to the left where a junction (facing South Snowdon) with a tramway to the Treflan and Gareg-fawr Slate Quarries was made. These quarries were open when the railway was built.

Though there may have been an earlier non-railway connection, it seems that the junction here was not made until 1901–2. It was the ironstone mine and not the slate quarry which wanted the link, but it could not obtain any more suitable land from Rev. Parry (the landowner) and the junction was the best that could be made in the circumstances. In the event a connection in the form of a stabling loop was made, the points being worked by Annett's Key attached to the staff. There were two signals (one at each end of the layout) and a small ground frame for each end. The work was inspected on 7 May 1902 and the Inspector's final recommendations carried out in the July. The two slate quarries, in practice, made far more use of the siding than did the ironstone mine adjacent to them.

Treflan ceased regular working in 1883 and Gareg-fawr closed in April 1885. The former was working again in the early 1920s as the Treflan Slate & Granite Co. Ltd. and in 1928 as the Welsh Standard Slate & Granite Quarries Ltd. of Liverpool. By then, work had ceased. The tramway itself passed through a gate, made for the far bank of the river by means of a very sharp curve from the N.W.N.G., a low embankment, a stone-piered span river bridge, yet another sharp curve, and a long low embankment made of quarry spoil to divide into two branches at the foot of the inclines. The tramway was probably laid in bridge rail, and was about half a mile long.

Returning to the main line, a feature of the course here was the width of the land purchased for the railway. It must have been cheap, for a double-tracked standard gauge railway could be made along it with room to spare. (Height 414 ft.).

Bettws Garmon (4 m. 65 ch.) is now reached. Several variations in spelling have been used and the N.W.N.G. did not always spell in accordance with local custom! To keep the track clear of low-lying floodland, the route was now raised on a five foot embankment. The adjacent road swings away from the line which, quite straight for a distance, entered the station which, like others, was really outside the hamlet of its namesake. The usual stone building and signal box were on the right, and a siding in the form of a loop passed round the rear of both. It had been installed in the Spring of 1902 and the points at each end were controlled by local ground frames each with locking lever released by a key on the Waenfawr–Rhydd-ddu staff. Major Druitt would not pass the installation until facing point locks were fitted. Off this siding a branch line, just over half a mile long, took a tramway to the Hafod-y-wern Slate Quarries, a working which provided the railway, in its time, with considerable traffice. This quarry, latterly one in the Moel Tryfan Crown group, was disused when the railway opened, but started work again as Wilson & Co. in the mid 1880s and on a moderate scale of output. The road was crossed on the level and here the rails were of grooved street-tram variety. Before the line closed, north-end loop points and quarry branch had been taken out.

Still rising, the railway crossed the Gwyrfai on leaving Bettws by one of its 'standard' bridges. This was a bowplate steel (originally wrought iron) structure of 48 ft. on stone piers. Immediately following it was a stone and slab spillway beneath the line, to carry flood water away. A field's length away, the line passed under the main road, which was carried above it by a curious bridge having cast-iron joists and some unusual brackets to hold up its span walls. The line was now in the centre of the narrowing valley, following a shallow cutting between farmlands until it was obliged to cross the river again by means of a second 'standard' bridge with adjacent spillway. Shortly before this and on the left, there was originally a branch with loop and sidings to the Gareg-fawr Ironstone & Copper Mines, a series of remarkable 'rabbit holes' which climb ladder-like up the mountainside to the east, and which have enjoyed a chequered career since before 1850 and have used both rail and wire ropeway haulage.

The branch crossed the main road—road users in this age must have been quite familiar with quarry tramway crossings along this route!—to reach a loading platform at the hill foot. What appear to be tramway inclines are not necessarily so. The branch was lifted during 1922 reconstruction and loop etc. removed.

Gareg-fawr iron mines were worked by Hickman Ltd. and in 1911 employed over thirty men below ground. Work was abandoned in October 1913. No records are available for the nearby Silurian iron mine, but the Ystrad mine hard at hand was worked by Bettws Garmon Iron Ore & Smelting Co. Ltd. up to 1916 and in 1919 by Silurian Iron Ore Co. Ltd. It shut down on 13 September 1919. Some inclines were described as abandoned as early as 1885.

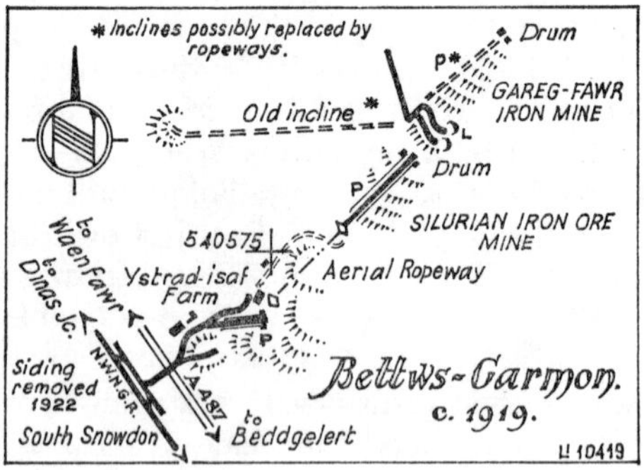

This branch line junction faced Dinas and was at the fifth milepost.

The main line now reached a lovely section of the valley. The steep mountainsides close in upon the river and force water, road and railway closer together. The railway wound its way around the slopes on the west side, the road passing through the hamlet of Salem on the east. Opposite a wooden footbridge over the river, a Halt was provided (not opened until 21 July 1922!). There was a rough 'platform' and wooden hut (5 m. 40 ch.). Climbing now at 1 in 122 this steepened to 1 in 84 at 5 m. 53 ch. and then came some more picturesque curves, the rugged hillsides now closing in more closely and forcing the railway on to a shelf which, to carry it above the river below, was now supported by a lengthy and fine piece of stone walling. On the right-hand side, a short siding trailed in which served the Railway's ballast pit known as Salem Quarry. This was controlled like Treflan Siding, by a small 2-lever ground frame. Rock and boulder rise up steeply above the railway's course. At the head of this defile (a most suitable place for an ambush, be it added!) the railway passed under a road bridge and made a reverse 3.12 ch. radius curve beside the river and Falls at Nant Mill (or Plas-y-nant). This was the sharpest bend on the main line. The old mill is now a memory but the water supplies now form part of a reservoir; railway travellers were the most fortunate for the train was carried in a continuous curve above the water, supported by stone walling five feet above it. Next, the course reversed its curve, passed round a rocky eminence and immediately this intimate setting became lost. The defile ended with the line crossing the river for the last time (using the standard 48 ft. bridge plus a stone spillway) and entered the flood-plain again. Here the mountains recede and ahead extends a magnificent view of mountain and lake with Snowdon to the left and the crags of Craig Cwm Bychan overhanging Llyn Cwellyn to the right. Over this section the climb eased from 1 in 400 to 1 in 551.

Just south of the river bridge was Plas-y-nant Halt, a semi-official stop before 1924 when in July it appeared in the Time-table (5 m. 75 ch.; 486 ft.) served by a gate in the road wall and a pathway on the river bank. There was no other facility other than the 17 yards 'platform' and just beyond was the sixth milepost.

There followed a short straight length down towards the lake, on embankment. There must have been subsidence here for the embankment suddenly becomes very narrow and sunken, and has been built up in milled quarry waste, to judge by the saw-cuts in the spoil. At the south end of this earthwork traces of a 40 yds. siding are visible on the left. This served the nearby Plas-y-nant and Brynmanllyn Slate Quarries, the latter very small. Both had closed before the turn of the century and though an actual tramway connection to the former is possible physically (including the inevitable level crossing of the road) there is no tangible evidence of it today. No records survive for Brynmanllyn, but Plas-y-nant was hard at work with 28 men in 1883. The slump hit suddenly: one man survived in 1885 and work stopped the next year.

Shortly after this siding, the railway quit the river bank, swung east with a short cutting in rising ground, and then passed under the main road again by means of the usual stone overbridge, this time arranged on the skew. There is a wide and considerable—though shallow—cutting on the south side where the temporary terminus was sited. On the north edge is a slab built wall, the remains of a top level roadway for offshooting materials from carts, and a good deal of milled slate and slab of cruder shapes and sizes. If this could tell its story we should be much wiser. Some of this material was obviously loaded here and the best of what there was has long been 'acquired' for local building purposes! Probably much of the residue has provided the railway and other users of filling with the necessary material over a great number of years. There is space for a run-round loop and at least two sidings (6 m. 45 ch.).*

Perhaps with the satisfaction of having completed the last stone bridge on the main line, the stone mason had permitted himself to carve 'W.E.W.' on a corner stone of the Quellyn road bridge.

Ahead there comes this new and mountainous scene. The somewhat melancholy lake is below to the right, a fine sweep of Mynydd Mawr behind it. For part of the day in summer and most of the day in winter, its western shore never receives any sunlight. To the left of the track, slopes pile on one another until the summit of Snowdon itself is reached and from suitable viewpoints, the mountain train may be seen climbing the final stages to the summit station. On the N.W.N.G., the grade steepened to 1 in 67, then 1 in 96, 79 and 94 along a superb run above the lakeside. There was not much civil engineering work here, the contours being kindly and allowing the course to meander slightly along the lower flank of Foel Gron. Numerous mountain streamlets are crossed by stone arches; these are dry for some seasons. Milepost 7 was passed and then came what was to become Snowdon Ranger station. At first it was named Quellyn Lake, but soon it was changed to that of the Hotel hard by which caried the name 'Snowdon Ranger'. Today this building is a Youth Hostel.†

The station (7 m. 35 ch.) had a siding with backshunt, a stone building (the only survivor and now a bungalow) with signal box alongside, and across the track, a water tank on a stone plinth. It was close by

* Despite the obviously ample space for a temporary station here, by the time of the Board of Trade inspection the layout was specifically described as having 'only 2 signals and no points'. If sidings or loop were put in here temporarily either before then, or later, they were not there at the time of inspection. This leaves the unanswered question; how did Marindin pass the layout if there was no means of running the engine round the train—surely he would not have permitted the engine to propel it?

† From the road in the Quellyn Lake area a sledgeway was built about 1810 to carry copper ore to Caernarvon on sledges for shipping to South Wales. These sledges carried 6 cwt. apiece and were drawn by two horses. In the main the workings were on the west side of the Snowdon bloc and the sledgeway extended from the Beddgelert road to the Upper Mine at Bwlch Glas, thence there was a footpath to the mine in Cwm Glaslyn. The proprietors also built a horse path (for pack animals) from Gorpwsfa—beyond Llanberis—to Bwlch Glas. The name Cwellyn is (Quellyn) assumed to be from Cae uwch y Llyn (The Field above the Lake) and a large residence nearby was owned by the Quellyn family who took their name from the place. It had been demolished by 1813. (Cambrian Traveller's Guide; 2 Edit. Geo. Nicholson 1813.)

the road. The next feature was a natural interception in the path of the railway, the Afon Treweunydd gorge over which a wrought iron bridge of 93 ft. 6 in. and 8 ft. span on stone piers had to be thrown at a height of 50 ft. above the ravine. The building of this was a subject of some delay in the already protracted construction of the line. The eighth milepost was at its south side.

The comfortable contour site now became more difficult to follow. But firstly after a cutting came a shelf-situation supported on a high stone wall. Here was the triangular junction to the Glanrafon Slate Quarries (8 m. 10 ch.; the northern side of the triangle was later lifted) the largest quarry on the main line. During its lifetime it had owned four locomotives but was closed down during the First War; this was almost the final nail in the coffin, for shortly afterwards, regular working over the South Snowdon section ceased, save for timber trains as required. The quarry had opened as the Glanrafon

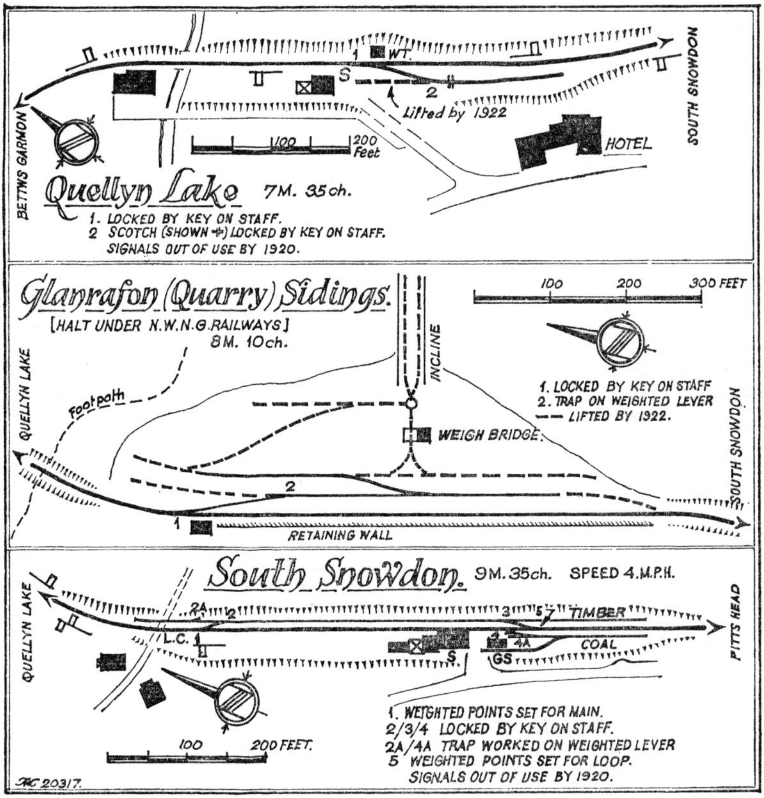

Slate Quarry Co. before the railway came. Together with Alexandra, it was the largest working quarry served by the railway. It survived the slump of the 1880s, employing about 190 in 1887. The quarry stands above the line, connected to it by incline and having a considerable trackage within its workings, including a quarter mile tunnel. The loop on the main was a stopping place for quarrymen's traffic.

For the last part of the journey the line, climbing at 1 in 47, was obliged to twist and turn its way through rugged terrain which was quite unhelpful to the engineer. For the passenger however, there was a feast of views either side of the train including an 'end-on' scene of Quellyn lake as the carriage wound its way round a final curve. Hereabouts the superelevation on curves was highly distinctive. On this length at 8 m. 52 ch. there was a 50 yd. interchange siding for the Rhos-clogwyn Slate Quarry. This connected to an incline which was closed before 1890; the connecting point was taken out but the siding survived and was reconnected again for the Snowdon Slate Co. in September 1903. The points were worked from a Ground Frame unlocked by a key on the staff. Major Druitt (16 September 1903) insisted that the engine be at the lower end of the train for all shunting here, in view of the gradient. However, there was a second period of activity in the 1920s and 1930s and output was taken down to the line by wire ropeway for which a new 20 yd. siding was put in at 8 m. 66 ch. Inside the curve which follows was the ninth milepost and after a reverse, the terminus was reached at 9 m. 35 ch., over the last ¾ m. the grade rose at 1 in 191, 100, 146, 430, (Level), 224, 1100 and 200 before levelling at the station!

Rhydd-ddu (Black Ford) can be a bleak spot even in summer. The village is very small and at 600 ft. it is the summit of the pass between Caernarvon and Beddgelert. However, it was the first point south of Llyn Quellyn where the line could re-tap the main road* and thus secure a measure of pasenger traffic. Local traffic would be very small, and would perhaps have included a few quarrymen, and it was also hoped to link up with the Llyn-y-gader Slate Quarry to the south-west across Llyn-y-gader which had its own tramway to the roadside at a point near the old woollen factory but which started to build a causeway and low viaduct across the marshland and river in the direction of Rhydd-ddu station. This connection was never completed, and a few drunken slab pillars stand as mute memorials to the unfinished bridge work.

* The Caernarvon–Pont Aberglaslyn road was reconstructed by public subscription in 1802 and levelled 'so that a horse could trot or gallop all the way'.

C. C. Green collection

Dinas c. 1892 with all three N.W.N.G. engines and almost all carriage stock. Note 'the three small four-wheelers' carriages, Beddgelert *running chimney first, the three Gloucester vehicles and an unidentified ridge-roofed covered wagon, right. Westinghouse brakes are visible, but points are worked from hand levers and there is no semaphore signalling.*

British Rail

General view of Dinas looking north 1911 with signalman about to hand staff to driver of 'Cauliflower' engine on Afon Wen train. Narrow gauge yard to right; the stone building is the N.W.N.G. accommodation, the wooden the L.N.W.R.

National Library

A train at South Snowdon from an original highly coloured postcard and showing a most unlikely-looking driver and fireman on the engine, and the rest of the family posed on the platform. The recipient of the card was young enough to add his own version of the smoke.

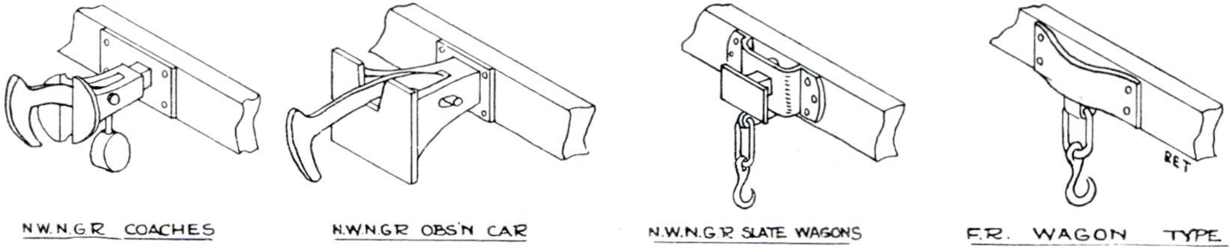

Locomotive Publishing Co.

Rhydd-ddu before the First World War; Moel Tryfan *(with corrugated-iron Refreshment Room behind) with train of Brown Marshalls' Guard's composite, 'Corridor' composite, Gloucester six-wheeler and 'Workman's' coaches.*

W. A. Camwell collection

North end of narrow gauge portion, Dinas Junction c. 1909; the passenger 'platform' is the left-hand line.

L. & G.R.P.

North end of the Dinas Junction trans-shipment platform, 1920.

Dunn Collection

Summer evening at Dinas Junction before 1885; Beddgelert *on N.W.N.G. Train right, and Webb 2-4-2T on Afon Wen train left.*

Dunn Collection

Welsh Highland train with Moel Tryfan, *posed with L.M.S. Up train headed by Webb 'Cauliflower' goods engine at Dinas 1925.*

K. A. C. R. Nunn

Dinas train at Rhydd-ddu in 1909 with Moel Tryfan *and Pickering and Metro-*

F. Frith & Co.

Re-furbished N.W.N.G. main line, looking north from Rhydd-ddu towards Glanrafon. Quellyn Lake in distance. 1931.

Llyn-y-gader quarry tramway, South Snowdon, still partly intact 1968, looking towards Rhydd-ddu.

J. I. C. Boyd

Locomotive Publishing Co.

Beddgelert, *now turned to run bunker-first from Dinas, outside the shed c. 1905. The shorter chimney probably dates from repairs by the builders in 1894.*

Locomotive Publishing Co.

Russell *and* Gowrie *(then very new) outside the signal box Dinas Junction,* Russell *still with boiler sandpot. c. 1909.* Gowrie *not yet fitted with nameplates.*

G. Perkins

Gowrie *at Dinas in 1909.*

L. & G. R. P.

Tryfan Junction looking east towards the junction, 1924. Train en route for Dinas Junction with Palmerston *and F.R. stock.*

K. A. C. R. Nunn

Southbound mixed train at Waenfawr 1926, with Moel Tryfan, *Festiniog bogie coach, dual-fitted ex-quarrymens' coach no. 4, and Festiniog and N.W.N.G. open wagons. Festiniog van in siding at right.*

R. W. Kidner

The derelict Bryngwyn passenger station in 1934, with incline to quarries ascending left.

Locomotive Publishing Co.

Snowdon Ranger *outside Dinas engine sheds in the early part of the century. Leading sand boxes are now fitted above the footplating, but extra sand is carried in a tub in front of the smokebox.*

Locomotive Publishing Co

Moel Tryfan *at Dinas passenger platform, showing brake reservoir, sand boxes on foot-plate and other detail differences. c. 1905.*

L. & G.R.P.

Moel Tryfan *and mixed train after restoration of passenger services. Rhydd-ddu (now Snowdon). August 1922.*

K. A. C. R. Nunn

Gowrie *on Dinas train at Rhydd-ddu with headlamp on wrong end. c. 1909.*

J. I. C. Boyd collection

Gloucester Wagon-built Cleminson six-wheeler. Second and Third Class was divided by the Guard's brake compartment.

J. I. C. Boyd collection

Tourist Observation Carriage at Dinas when first delivered. The drawings of this

Pickering's catalogue illustration of N.W.N.G. No. 4.

J. I. C. Boyd collection

J. I. C. Boyd collection

Official photograph of a most untypical slate wagon, one of a limited purchase. Makers unknown.

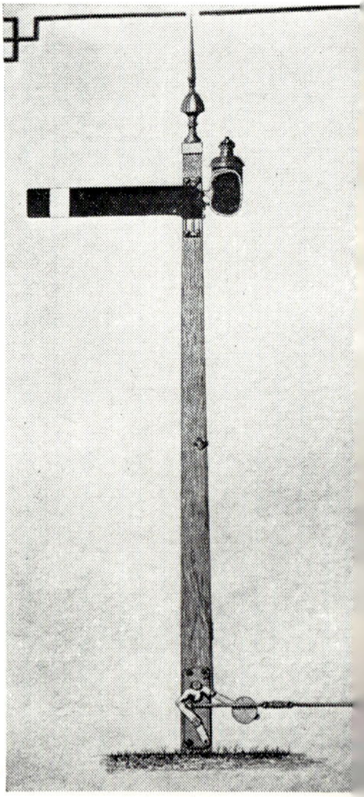

From the maker's catalog

McKenzie & Holland's sing spectacle semaphore as suppli to the N.W.N.G. Railways

W. A. Camwell collection

Ashbury 'Summer' coach No. 13 and 'Workmans' coach in Dinas carriage siding. c. 1909.

The year 1885 saw the start of a quarry here, owned by the North Wales Quarrymen's Union. It changed hands almost at once and closed down. In 1922 it was owned by Gader Lake Green & Rustic Slate Quarries Ltd. and was worked occasionally for a time.

Rhydd-ddu was more in fact a bridgehead, perhaps in the eyes of the promoters a springboard from which Beddgelert and other goals beyond might yet be reached. As it was, road services by horse bus were provided in the summer and the timetable helpfully stated connections. Mail and goods vehicles also ran.

As time went by, Snowdon station—as it came to be known—asumed more importance for its timber traffic than anything else. Parry's timber yard grew enormously on the east side of the station during the First War, when the unfinished section of the P.B. & S.S.R. beyond stretched into the Forestry Commission's woodlands around, using an ex-Glanrafon Quarry locomotive.

The layout was simple, with a 300 ft. long run round loop at 8 ft. 6 in. centres, station buildings in stone, a wooden refreshment room : part of the station building served as a signal box. One siding served a corrugated iron goods shed but did not enter it. There were Home and Distant signals and a Starter. A Bench Mark at the station rear read 627 ft.

In terms of the usual terminal station, Snowdon, like Tryfan Junction, was an anti-climax to the traveller and a delight to the connoisseur of the remote rail ending. Bog, bracken and rock—reminiscent of Donegal—surrounded it on all sides. Mist and rain enveloped it in winter, snow lay for long periods, blizzards funnelled up either side to blanket it. At least the road ran alongside and the place might be left reasonably easily, even if the train service was not running! Until 1896 it enjoyed the distinction of being the nearest railhead to the summit of Snowdon.

Looking back over the route of the main line, it was remarkable for its many changes of character. The first section of two miles was through farmland of increasing interest, then followed a wooded valley of peculiar beauty and not typically Welsh character, to Waenfawr. Here came complete contrast where the run up the flat valley floor ended with the defile at Plas-y-nant and yet another widening took place. From here to Glanrafon the course followed the side of a clean glacial slope, with fine views of lake and mountain. Lastly there ensued a rough mountainous section so commonly found in the Highlands of Scotland or the wilds of north-west Ireland. Tourists got full value for their money!

The station nameboards followed L.N.W.R. pattern using cast-iron lettering on a wooden board : these were fitted under the eaves of the buildings instead of the more conventional method of mounting on posts on the platform. In a reply to a Board of Trade circular the Secretary stated on 2 February 1895 that three years ago station names 'were fixed up with 10 in. deep cast-iron letters . . . which catch the eye very well there being no advertisements near either of these nameboards'. (It is assumed that for 'either' he meant 'any'.)

The four 'standard' 48 ft. river bridges were built in wrought iron but rebuilt in steel plate after 1895 (ref : B.O.T. Circular).

The Bryngwyn Branch

If the main line had many faces, the branch added an extra one. From it one of the most typical faces of Caernarvonshire might be seen, perhaps not that of the country best remembered by the visitor, but the more natural ones of stone cottages, stone walls, sheep farms and low uplands stretching down towards the Menai Straits. The branch gave something which the main line failed to do—a view to the north-west of coast, sea and Anglesey, with Caernarvon Castle for good measure. The Guide books of 1900 recommended a journey on the branch for its scenery '. . . you leave the main line at Tryfan Junction and should sit on the right-hand side, from which you will have an extensive view of Anglesey . . . Yr Eifl (The Rivals) and neighbouring chain form a prominent . . . object. Moel Tryfan is interesting to the geologist on account of its cap of marine deposit containing shells, which shows it must have once been submerged.' It must have been a dour slog for the train. Starting from rest at the Junction, the track rounded a 180 degree curve of 3¾ chains and the train would have to start up a long pound at 1 in 39 (the official figure, but certainly there were some steeper pitches). First came a cutting on the curve which when straightened, set the railway going in exactly a parallel and opposite direction to the main line, just one field's width away. The cutting ended with a stone road overbridge (408 ft.) followed by an embankment over that same stream which follows the main line down to Dinas. A long uphill but straight climb, easing to 1 in 48 took the line into Rhostryfan station, a scattered community of cottages littering the hillside, and apparently without a centre. By now the railway, still with sufficient local stone to fence its boundary with stone walls, was able to struggle up the face of the hillside without much earthwork. Up the slope to the left may be seen the ancient site of a prehistoric village and the nearby Gaerwen Camp. This part of the county is well blessed with ancient monuments such as these.

The station (0 m. 70 ch. from the Junction : 482 ft.) was a simple affair, built out on filling from the hillside and consisting of the stone

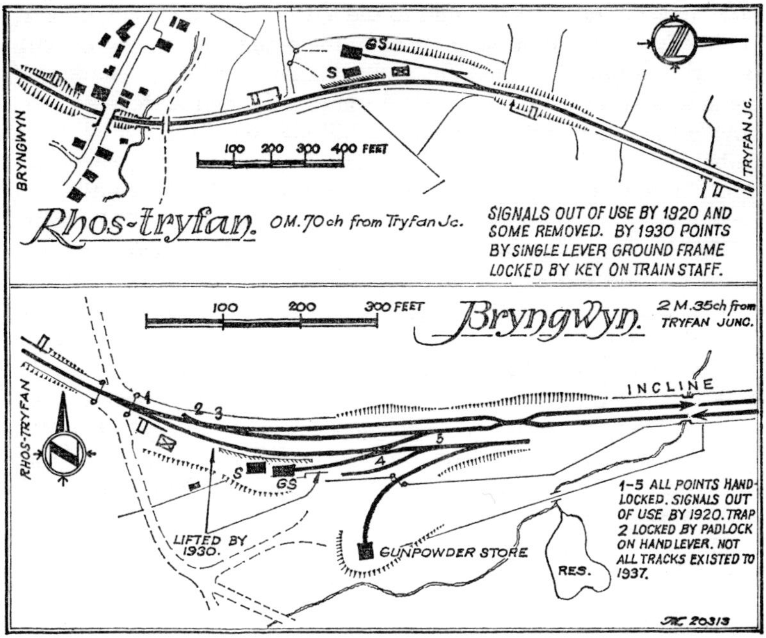

station building, and signal box. There was one siding with a goods shed at the end, which faced the junction. Latterly the only signal was the Home arm for descending trains; perhaps speed was always slow enough to prevent accidents to trains coming up the bank—certainly the other three signals had disappeared.

From the station, a cutting was entered, a stream crossed on a stone arch and the main road through the village passed over the line which then set off across moorland terrain of open uplands, giving pleasant views over sheep country. Earthworks were slight but curves frequent to allow the track to use the contours.

Shortly after the second milepost the Bryngwyn road was crossed on the level, an awkward site for both rail and road users. Here the builders of the line were obviously faced with Hobson's Choice; they could either have crossed the road on the level (as they did) or spent a good deal of money (of which they were short) in building a bridge. The former course resulted in a horrifying gradient immediately beyond the road crossing which, ignoring the official figure, is clearly nearer 1 in 30 than the 1 in 39 usually quoted. Coming at the end of a long pull it must have tried the fireman's art if they were hauling a long train of slate empties. The track went straight up the side of a large hillock and curved round to the left through a cutting on a $3\frac{3}{4}$ chain curve, all without any easing of the grade. On leaving the cutting, the railway flattened out and yet another of those changes of scene took place as the line passed round another 180 degree curve, now out and above the surrounding hillside and riding round on an embankment. Ahead stretched a wide open expanse of upper moorland; more walls, bracken, gorse and on the sky line, the outlines of grey tips of slate rubbish—the objective slate quarries almost in sight!

The curve now swung the other way and over an easy grade of about 1 in 200, passed round Bryngwyn Farm, came up alongside the road and crossed it for a second time. The gates were set on the skew. Immediately over the road was Bryngwyn station (2 m. 35 ch. from the Junction : 650 ft.) and if visitors had by now become used to the N.W.N.G.R., they would not be surprised in feeling they had not really arrived anywhere. Like Snowdon station, it happened to be the place where passenger trains stopped, but for real business the railway always looked beyond to the point known as The Drumhead, at the top of an ensuing incline.

The station with its runround loop lay entirely to the south of the line. It was a curious layout with the signal box beside the crossing gates, a storage loop for slate wagons and a passenger loop south of it. This cunningly allowed passenger trains an element of safety if runaway wagons came down the incline, and allowed freight working clear of the passenger platform. There was a goods shed alongside the station and set apart to the south, a gunpowder shed.

Rising reasonably easily for a slate line, the Incline in double track rose from 650 ft. to 895 ft. over half a mile. The land it crossed is still rough and untended, intersected by stream and by-road; the course simply went straight up the face of the hill, passed under the Fron road near the summit and after a cutting beyond, reached the drumhouse at the top. Unlike other similar situations, the Railway owned this mineral extension right up to the winding drum, and private tramways did not begin beforehand. A curious mystery in the working of the incline was the existence of one road which crossed it on the level in the middle of the slope; perhaps a flagman was on duty here and if traffic wished to cross, they allowed the wire haulage rope to slacken on to the road surface.

Beyond Drumhead lay a network of private tramways; an odd fact of the railway at this point is that whilst Dinas is only about two miles distant, the railway has covered over four miles to reach here.

Quarry Tramway Feeders (Quoted gradients are estimated).

According to an account of the 1840s (Lewis: Topographical Dictionary of Wales, 4th Edit.), most of the quarries in the Moel Tryfan area had opened in the 1840–50 period. These were among those about to be considered. An older group of quarries, connected to the Nantlle Railway, was to be found to the south.

At the Drumhead the line forked into three branches, the most southerly also dividing into what was known as the 'New Line' built in the early 1920s to connect with the Fron and Cilgwyn systems near Fron village. Of the three lines fanning out from the summit, each had a storage loop at its end which might also be used by locomotives running round the wagons.

The most northerly line took a sinuous course to the Alexandra Quarry and was 1½ miles long. Between Drumhead and the Quarry it climbed over 350 ft. Setting off in a northerly direction through a cutting it began climbing at approximately 1 in 50, steepening to 1 in 30 through a further cutting. Sleepers were spaced at yard intervals, but on the sharp right-hand curve below the Hermon Congregational Chapel, this was reduced to 2 ft. Rails were of 25 lb./yd. flat-bottom type. Below the chapel, shelf and cutting were to swing the line through a semicircle south-west; there followed an extremely steep section, almost straight, rising at about 1 in 20 and at its end, a formidable 1¾ chain curve, steeply superelevated and carried on a 30 ft. embankment, swung the track anti-clockwise through another semicircle below the rubbish tips from the Quarry far above. The course now took a long slow climbing semicircle round the summit of Moel Tryfan, climbing in the early stages at approximately 1 in 40 but easing at the most northerly section of the bend where the track could follow the contours. On the way up the west face of the mountain, a more recently opened section of the quarry (isolated from its parent) is found. The track ran between slab walls; there was an overbridge and sidings. An amount of Nantlle fishbelly rail was utilised in the workings, and some of its tracks were laid in chaired T-bulb rail (as Croesor).

Beyond the junction for this quarry was a passing loop. Now up on the flanks of Tryfan superb views are available where the line ran round the hilltop; this is undoubtedly one of the finest vantage points in all North Wales, with the mountains of Lleyn stretching away to the south-west, Anglesey and Holyhead Mountain to the west, and ahead a sweep which embraces the valley along which, out of sight and below the hill flank, drove the main line of the N.W.N.G.

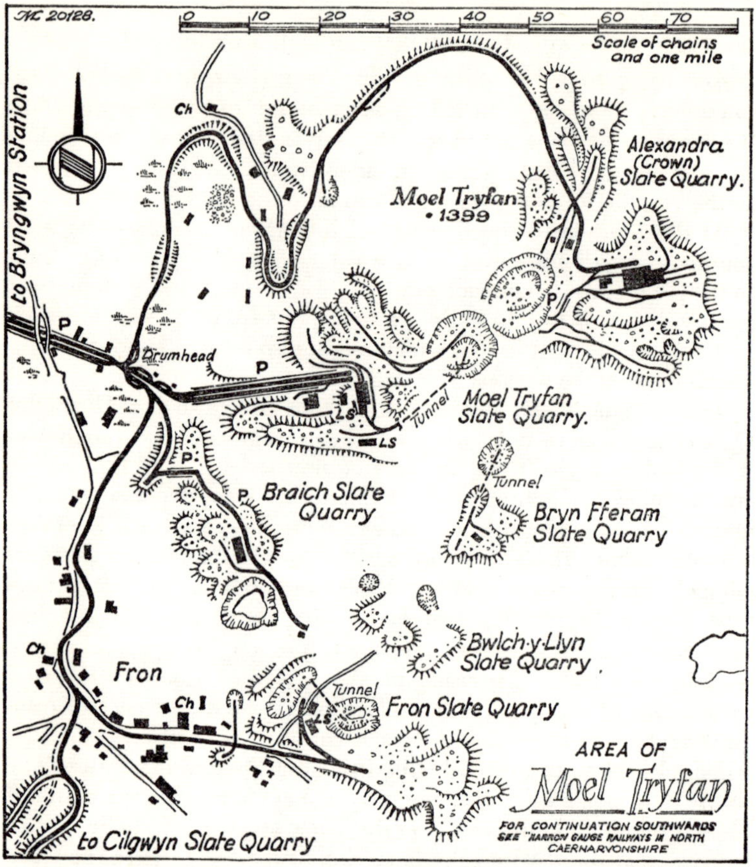

on its way to Waenfawr. Rounding east and disappearing from view behind the hill on which the tramway ran, was the whole Snowdonia bloc—a viewpoint from which few visitors must have seen it.

Ultimately the line reached the quarry, the largest and most profitable of any served by the N.W.N.G. and employing almost 200 in the 1880s. Until 22 April 1918 it was known as the Alexandra Slate Co. Ltd., or locally Cors-y-briniau Quarry and changed its name on reopening after the 1914–18 war. It closed again in June 1929 and on 1 April 1934 was included in quarries owned by the Amalgamated Slate Association Ltd. (which had gone into liquidation on 9 January 1931) in the name of Caernarvonshire Crown Slate Quarries Co. Ltd., formed 1 April 1932. Work began again in July 1934 but by 1939 it had closed and much equipment had been taken away. By September 1963 the rubbish was being taken away by lorry as filling. There is a tunnel connection with the Moel Tryfan Quarry adjacent, where the tramway was working up to 1966. (All these quarries have a tendency to sporadic working under varying titles, making them exceedingly difficult to discuss locally.) The first owners of this quarry were Spooner & Sons and details of the locomotives in use will be included in the Appendix to Volume 2.

The Alexandra Tramway was a microcosm of Welsh narrow gauge practice; a practical demonstration of Spooner doctrine and an engaging little example of what could be done in an inhospitable terrain. The site is still worth seeing on this score, if only to appreciate how overseas systems like the Darjeeling–Himalayan line developed along this basis.

Returning to the Drumhead: there was a tramway which went off along an E.S.E. direction and being on the level for only 10 chains, included two storage loops on this short stretch. It then curved almost westward and went up the west slope of Moel Tryfan on a double line incline. This lifted the track to 1,250 ft. and achieved almost the same level as the Alexandra line but in a much shorter distance and by different means. Quarry owners were mixed in their opinions as to whether Inclined Planes or more conventional tramways were most suitable. The Plane was expensive to construct, needed more men to operate, and when requiring repair was more delaying than a tramway. Here within a mile of each other, two tramway-accesses of varying type worked to the same end.

The quarry had been worked by C. Pearson until 1875, by a further operator up to 1 November 1879, and was known as the Moel Tryfan Slate & Slab Quarry Co. Ltd. until 22 April 1918. In the 1880s, nearly 100 men were employed; it was then the third largest quarry in the neighbourhood. Like Alexandra, it was closed during 1914–18. It was part of the Amalgamated and later, the Crown companies (see previously) and pre-Second War, opened and closed much as Alexandra. It was closed for about two years from 17 September 1958 and in September 1966 lorries took over. A tractor was observed working the line through the tunnel earlier that year; this tunnel had always connected the quarry with the slate mill, and latterly the quarry workings of Moel Tryfan and Alexandra had broken into each other. Material from this combined site was taken to the Moel Tryfan mills by rail.

The third and most southerly line from Drumhead ran south for 20 chains to a reversing neck, and included one storage loop at the Drum. The neck held only two or three wagons and there were two short inclines upwards from here, divided by a brief length of level tramway. The tramway for this quarry has, owing to the time since its abandonment and the marshy nature of the ground between Drumhead and incline foot, almost disappeared. Its principal interest lies in the fact that whilst Alexandra was owned from the first by the Spooner family, the Braich Quarry, the destination of this tramway, was owned by Hugh Beaver Roberts, the builder of the Croesor tramway. He sold it in 1881 at the time when his connection with the Croesor had terminated in October that year. It became the Braich Slate Quarry until 1887, Braich & Coedmadoc Slate Co. to 1891, John Robinson to c. 1897, Thomas Robinson to 15 May 1904 and Talysarn Slate Quarry Co. Ltd. to 2 November 1908. Thereafter it was the New Braich Slate Quarries Ltd., who went into liquidation on 10 October 1915. Work at the quarry had ceased in 1911. In size it was the second largest in the district, employing 125 men about the time the N.W.N.G. was opened.

The fourth and final branch from Drumhead was not built in its entirety until after the First War. It diverged from the Braich line 7 chains from the Drumhead and fell away downhill slightly, curving south and westerly to run between either slate walls or fences —the only tramway so protected in these parts. It ran on to the east side of the Fron road and proceeded southwards along the roadside. To keep the gradient as reasonable as possible, the track crossed over to the west of the road and almost immediately came back again, beginning a climb of approximately 1 to 25 and leaving the roadside for its own cutting a little distance east of the road. This diversion maintained the gradient and this short length was bounded by slab walling. Passing along the side of the main street in the village of Fron it now regained the roadside, crossed over, swung back again, used the east side down past the Post Office and then turned round the corner. Almost immediately opposite the Post Office there was a junction and a new connection crossed the junction of roads at this point and running due south, crossed open ground to effect a junction with the Cilgwyn 'Horseshoe'—an unusual loop of tramway entirely carried on embankment and a prominent local feature. This line was laid in and the connection to the Fron tramway made after 22 April 1918 when the Amalgamated Slate Association Ltd. began working Alexandra, Moel Tryfan and Cilgwyn Quarries.

Meanwhile, back at the Post Office, the original Fron branch crossed over to the south side of the road (now little but an unfenced rough track) and quarter of a mile further on, made a backshunt conection with the slate mill of the Fron Quarry. This working consisted of two open quarries connected by a small-bore tunnel. Connection with ground level and the mill was by an incline up and out of the workings. Fron Quarry opened at an unknown date but had closed by 1881. Some time after this a connection was laid in to the Drumhead. It was first named Vron & Old Braich Slate Quarries Co. Ltd. to 24 July 1902 (ex Vron Slate Co.—John Robinson) becoming Vron Welsh Slate Quarries Ltd. (Thomas and John Robinson were also associated with Talysarn quarrying, Nantlle.)

A similar working situation was to be found a little distance to the north of Fron Quarry, at the Bryn-fferam (or Brynefferam) Quarry, where two pits connected by a tunnel are to be seen. This quarry had no rail connection with the Drumhead but is of interest in that it was owned by the chairman of the Railways' Company, Sir Ll. Turner. In 1887 it only employed two!

Although these tramways were not strictly N.W.N.G. owned or worked, they were provided and owned by persons of influence on that railway. The Bryngwyn branch may be seen as the trunk of a tree, with roots spreading out to tap the rich slate deposits of Moel Tryfan. There was nothing quite like this arrangement elsewhere on the Welsh narrow gauge, and the spectacle of locomotives bringing trains to the Drumhead would be fascinating indeed . . . especially as some were designed by Spooner & Co. for this particular purpose.

Locomotives

Name	*Type*	*Builder*	*No.*	*Date*	*Withdrawn*
Moel Tryfan	0-6-4T	Vulcan Foundry Ltd.	738	1875	1937 Scrap 1954
Snowdon Ranger	0-6-4T	Vulcan Foundry Ltd.	739	1875	1917
Beddgelert	0-6-4T	Hunslet Engine Co. Ltd.	206	1878	1906
Gowrie	0-6-4T	Hunslet Engine Co. Ltd.	979	1908	Sold 1915 period

The Company did not number its locomotives. All were driven from the right-hand side of the footplate.

Moel Tryfan was taken into Festiniog Railway stock in June 1923 and numbered 11.

(The locomotive *Russell* which ran on the N.W.N.G. Railways line was not built for that Company and will be found under Portmadoc, Beddgelert & South Snowdon Railway.)

Moel Tryfan and Snowdon Ranger

Under Section 12 of the Agreement regarding a lease of the Railway, the lessee was committed to supplying engines of the Fairlie type. This resulted in two identical engines coming from the Vulcan Foundry in 1875. Coming as they did just a year before a similar but four-coupled engine from the same makers for the Festiniog Railway, the same parentage is obvious. The designer was nominally George Percival Spooner, a son of Charles Easton;* they had a six-coupled bogie under the boiler and a four-wheeled one under cab and bunker. Though not the first engines to be built on the Single Fairlie principle (as opposed to the Double Fairlie which in practice was two engine units mounted on bogies swivelling beneath a double-ended boiler having a divided firebox in the middle) the Single was more conventional though it retained the motorised bogie unit swivelling under the single boiler barrel. In both types, a full-length carrying frame was discarded and the boiler served as frame in the manner of a road engine.

The N.W.N.G. engines were the first 0–6–4 tank engines in the British Isles, being followed a few months later by a well-tank of this arrangement for the Great Southern & Western Railway of Ireland (5 ft. 3 in. gauge) and it would be hard to find two more differing conceptions of the same arrangement! The original drawings are signed 'C. E. Spooner per G. P. Spooner 12 January 1874' and stamped 'North Wales Narrow Gauge Railway. Engineer's Office, Portmadoc', and the maker's drawings are dated 10 October 1874—these are preserved in the City of Liverpool Museum. The leading frames carried outside cylinders, a six-coupled wheel arrangement with disc wheels and having inside bearings and valve gear. Steam entered the valve chest via a pendulum swung pipe pivoted immediately below the smoke box and, in order to reduce the movement of the flexible union as much as possible, the steam pipe was continued into a reception chamber behind and below the valve chest by means of a second flexible union. The exhaust pipe was similarly treated but owing to the smoke box being to the rear of the chimney centre-line, it was arranged to slope back into the smoke box. As usual on Fairlie designs, the front coupler was attached to the bogie frame. Stephenson valve gear was fitted. The main dimensions were :

* Other published drawings stated C. E. Spooner was the designer (e.g. in 'Engineering', 23 November 1877).

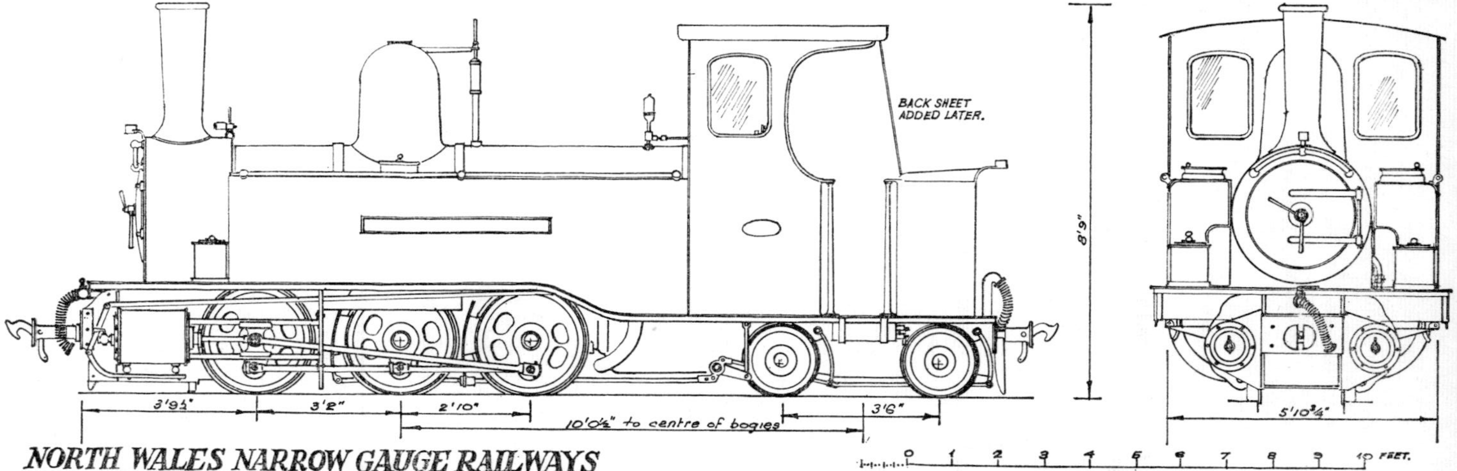

NORTH WALES NARROW GAUGE RAILWAYS

"SNOWDON RANGER" (WKS Nº 739) AND 'MOEL TRYFAN' (WKS Nº 738)   BUILT BY VULCAN FOUNDRY 1877 TO DESIGN OF G.P. SPOONER. REFS. "ENGINEERING NOV. 23rd 1877
DRAWING BASED ON MAKER'S DRAWING BUT DIFFERING IN DETAIL AS BUILT.

JMC 20505

Cylinders	8½ in. × 14 in.	Driving Wheels	2 ft. 6 in. dia.
Weight in working order	14 tons	Tractive Effort	3855 lb.
		Grate Area	5.9 sq. ft.
Heating Surface	366 sq. ft.	Tank Capacity	303 galls. (also given as 350)
Pressure	140 lb.		
Wheelbase:	Bogie: 6 ft.	Total:	14 ft. 11½ in.

The driving bogie pivoted under a cast-iron saddle on the underside of the boiler barrel and centrally above the middle axle. The cylinders drove on to the trailing driving wheels. Height to top of chimney was 8 ft. 9 in. and over the footplate was 6 ft. 7 in.; as on Festiniog designs the boiler was pitched low resulting in a neat design with tall boiler mountings and cab (backless and open to the elements), rounded tops to side tanks and to the corners of the footplating. The rear wheels were disc pattern also of 1 ft. 7 in. diameter; the bogie frame was inside and wheelbase 3 ft. 6 in. The boiler was 12 ft. long (8 ft. between tubeplates) and 2 ft. 0½ in. diameter without clothing . . . not large. There were 104 tubes of 1½ in. outside diameter. The Salter safety valve was mounted on the dome; the stovepipe chimney was typical of G. P. Spooner and used on his Spooner & Co. designs also.

Rear weatherboards (detachable) were fitted by the Company soon after delivery, a feature which the footplate staff clearly preferred for it persisted on the surviving engine until the end. When fitted, the Westinghouse brake reservoir was slung under the right-hand footplate under the cab and the compressor was carried inside the cab. When new, the domes were of polished brass but had been painted over by 1890. (Livery is given collectively later). Westinghouse brakes were fitted between 1890 and 1894.

The design was intended to handle 280 tons on the level, 140 tons on 1 in 100 and 75 tons on 1 in 50, figures which seem extremely optimistic! (The Festiniog Railway's first Double Fairlie of 1869 hauled 206 tons on 1 in 100.) Wiener in 'Articulated Locomotives' maintains that the Vulcan Single Fairlies—and the later Hunslet *Gowrie*—all with only a 4½ Ton axle loading, did in fact achieve these loadings over curves of 60 ft. radius (*yards* and not feet are more probable!).

In 1902 *Snowdon Ranger* went to Davies & Metcalfe, near Stockport, for a new boiler and heavy overhaul. Brass oval plates were fitted reading 'Davies & Metcalfe Ltd: Rebuilt 1903: Manchester'. It was previously considered that continuous brakes were fitted then, but if the Returns are to be believed, all stock had been fitted by 1894. In 1908 it was 'repaired by Hunslet' in Leeds.

In 1903 *Moel Tryfan* was treated similarly—it received new tubes in 1913.

In 1917 the frames of *Snowdon Ranger* were placed under *Moel Tryfan* and the latter was put into the best working order possible under wartime conditions by cannibalising the sister engine.

It is convenient to add that under Welsh Highland Railway auspices, *Moel Tryfan* went into the Festiniog Railway's Boston Lodge Works in 1923, when the cab and boiler mountings were cut down in height to enable it to work over the Festiniog line. Vacuum brake was substituted for the Westinghouse so as to make fittings standard on both railways. Between 1924 and 1936 the engine worked regularly between Dinas Junction and Blaenau Festiniog. Occasionally it was turned so as to run bunker first Up to Blaenau. *Moel Tryfan* was like the Festiniog's own Single Fairlie, a free steamer, a good and fast runner and well-liked by the enginemen. In 1937 the engine went into Boston Lodge for boiler and firebox repairs. The dismantled parts lay in various parts of the yard throughout the Second War, the boiler and driving bogie in the Engine Shed. In 1954, under the auspices of the 'New Order', the boiler etc. was towed across to the Harbour station and cut up for scrap. The trailing bogie survived.

Beddgelert

Though of the same wheel arrangement as the two previous engines (and curiously, an arrangement which the Company chose for every one of its own engines) *Beddgelert* was not of Fairlie type nor of Spooner design. A saddle tank with outside frames and cylinders and having outside bearings to the rear bogie together with a typical Hunslet full cab, the result was entirely different from her predecessors. And if these had been greyhound-like in their sleekness, then *Beddgelert* was a bulldog built for rough going, but none-the-less a good looking piece of machinery—as one would have expected from her makers. She is said to have been built for the Bryngwyn branch traffic, and though there is pictorial evidence of her working on the main line, this was a rare event as, unfortunately, were occasions when she featured in a photograph at all.

Her frames and wheelbase were rigid. Tradition has it that the boiler was inclined to offset the branch's gradient, but if the drawings (dated 5 August 1878) are to be believed, this was not so. The engine must have been slewed round on greased plates at some time, as early pictures show it running chimney first from Dinas and latterly, bunker first. The main dimensions were :

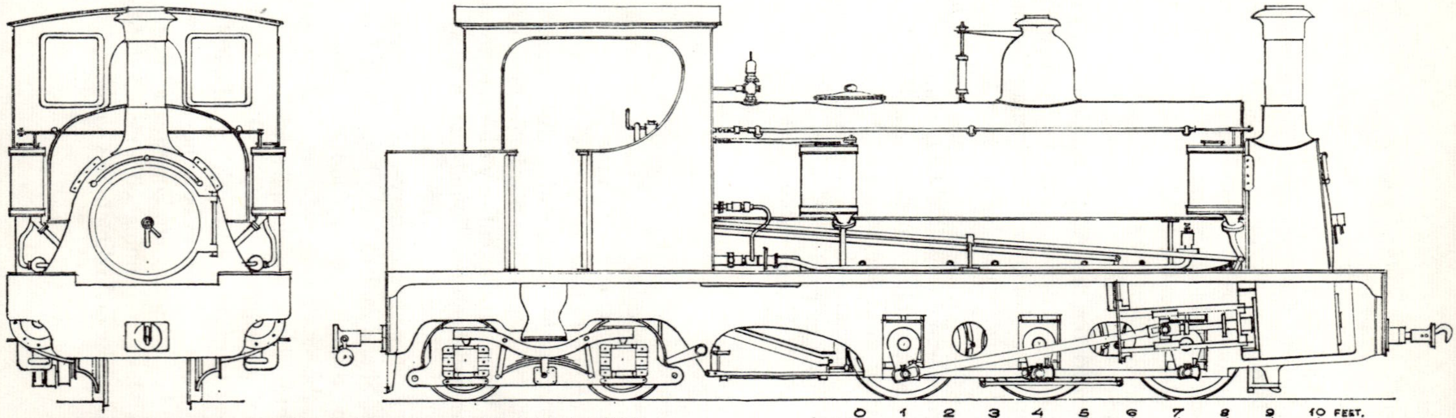

NORTH WALES NARROW GAUGE RAILWAYS.

HUNSLET 0-6-4 ST MAKER'S NUMBER 206 OF 1878. "BEDDGELERT".

Cylinders	10 in. × 16 in.	Driving Wheels	2 ft. 6 in. dia.
Weight in working order	17 tons	Tractive Effort	6400 lbs.
Heating Surface	416 sq. ft.	Grate Area	7½ sq. ft.
Pressure	160 lb.	Tank Capacity	450 galls.
Wheelbase total:	17 ft. 8 in.	Driving Bogie Wheelbase:	6 ft. 2 in.

The rail gauge on the drawings is shown as 1 ft. 11¾ in.

The rear bogie had a 3 ft. 6 in. wheelbase with 1 ft. 10 in. wheels.

The smokebox had a sloping front and was skirted out at the waist to meet the contour of the outside cylinders. With its built-up chimney the front end was quite in the Beyer Peacock tradition. The saddle tank did not extend over the smokebox but covered the firebox; the latter made full use of the ample width between the frames and the length between driving and bogie wheel flanges. The boiler was 9 ft. long in the barrel and 2 ft. 10½ in. diameter, pitched low into the frames. Chimney and cab were 8 ft. 11 in. from rail level but clearly a slightly lower chimney was fitted (or the sleeve shortened?) before the end. Perhaps this took place when the engine was 'altered by the makers' in 1894. One sandbox was placed for either direction of travel, two on each side of the tank.

The total length was 22 ft. 1⅝ in. and width over footplate was 6 ft. 3¾ in. Stephenson's Valve Gear was fitted behind the driving wheels. The engine is reputed to have been worn out in 1906 and scrapped that year. Another engine from Hunslet of quite different type replaced it; some doubts exist about its condition and suitability by 1906; it probably had its original boiler and perhaps a replacement firebox. These are likely to have been worn out. Tonnage of slate had declined in the new century and did in fact continue to do so; the peak of mineral traffic was reached and passed in 1897.

Gowrie

The last engine was purchased in 1908 in anticipation of the completion of the link between Rhydd-ddu and Portmadoc where a modern powerful engine would be needed to surmount the steep gradients north of Beddgelert and the several reverse curves on the same section. The basic design was that of the makers but Aitchison influenced it to the extent that the Single Fairlie arrangement was reverted to, perhaps some indication of its success in the Vulcan engines and its suitability to the Company's conditions. So far as is known, it was the last Single Fairlie to be built, and certainly so as regards these Islands. The maker's influence was complete in the

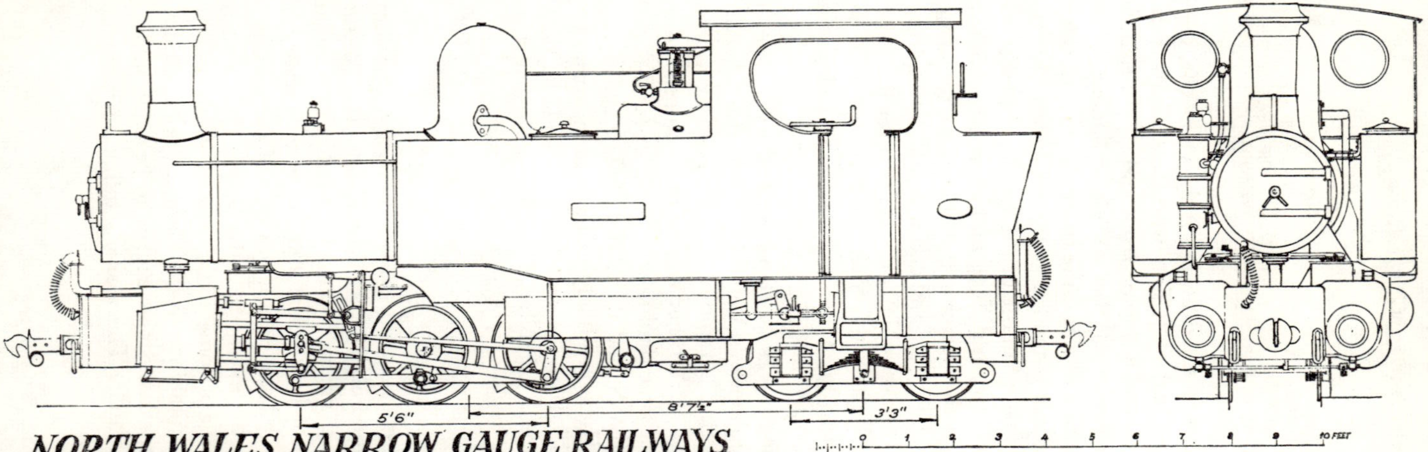

NORTH WALES NARROW GAUGE RAILWAYS.

HUNSLET 0-6-4T 979 OF 1908 "GOWRIE" AS SUPPLIED. BASED ON MAKERS RECORDS AND OFFICIAL PHOTOGRAPHS.

JMG 20515

standard components used for side tanks, cab, bunker, firebox etc.; the rear part of the engine was mounted on footplating in the usual way, but forward of the side tanks the boiler and smokebox extended without adornment or footplating. The engine was really an up-to-date version of the Spooner 1876 engines; there was an inside framed six-coupled bogie with outside cylinders though now the valve gear was Walshaert's outside. Many features such as cab, boiler mountings and firebox outlines were similar to *Russell.*

Delivery was made in September 1908 and for a time the engine ran without nameplates; ultimately it received the name *Gowrie* (Aitchison's Christian name) and together with *Russell*, the Hunslet-built engine which the P.B. & S.S.R. bought and which was Aitchison-influenced, it eventually meant that the Company operated two engines each named after its Receiver . . . though admittedly the same gentlemen also filled other positions with the Company!

The rear bogie had outside frames and the rear bunker sheet was flanged out to increase the capacity for coal. The saddle beneath the boiler which supported it on the driving bogie was pivoted slightly to the rear of the centre axle. The asbestos-covered main steam pipe was taken externally from the dome and led between boiler and side tank vertically down to a flexible coupling between the frames; from here it was carried forward horizontally to another flexible connection attached to the valve chest. The exhaust pipe showed nakedly beneath the smokebox. Sandboxes for forward running were on the bogie frames; for backward running in the top rear end of the side tanks. To allow for swivelling, they had rubber feed pipes. The brake equipment had the compressor on the right-hand side of the boiler barrel and the main air reservoir under the footplate; on the left-hand side under the footplate there was an auxiliary reservoir. Main dimensions were:

Cylinders	$9\frac{1}{2}$ in. × 14 in.	Driving Wheels	2 ft. 4 in. dia.
Weight in working order	$18\frac{1}{2}$ tons	Tractive Effort	5415 lb. at 75 per cent b.p.
Heating Surface	282 sq. ft.	Grate Area	5 sq. ft.
Pressure	160 lb.	Tank Capacity	400 galls.
Driving wheelbase	5 ft. 6 in.	Rear bogie wheelbase	3 ft. 3 in.

The boiler barrel was 8 ft. 10 in. long between tubeplates and 2 ft. 5 in. diameter; it was pitched 4 ft. $7\frac{1}{2}$ in. above the rails. The engine was 22 ft. 2 in. long over the beams, and 6 ft. 7 in. wide over footplating; from rail to chimney top was 8 ft. 6 in.

Tradition has it that the engine was not a success and after the 'wedding' of the two Vulcan engines in 1917, *Moel Tryfan* and *Russell* were adequate for the reduced service of the War period. By then there were no passenger trains and an opportunity was taken to sell the engine while prices were high.

The engine's movements when sold by 1918 (one source gives 1915) for Government use, are unknown. In 1919 she was in Wake's Geneva Yard, Darlington, bearing the number 1516 and still in possession of Westinghouse brake. In 1922 she was on contract work at an aerodrome site at Marske-by-Sea, Yorkshire, and was advertised for sale, along with other engines on this contract, by Messrs. Hughes, Bolckow & Co. Ltd. in 1928. This is the last trace.

Proposed Rack Locomotive

To appreciate the mood of optimism following the First War, and the expansive ideas of the promoters of the new Welsh Highland Railway (as it was shortly to become) we can but only give examples. Certainly the talk of increasing business in terms of a complete narrow gauge link between Dinas Junction and Portmadoc (now so near an accomplished fact) and the possibility of through running between Dinas and Blaenau Festiniog via Portmadoc, seems to have gone to the heads of the new 1922 Board.

Someone must have turned up a copy of Spooner's Grand Plan of 1875 (see Croesor Tramway section) among the papers which passed to Dolgarrog in the fusions of that time. Why had they not thought of it themselves? 'Let's have a Rack Railway to the summit of Snowdon!'

No English firm had ever built a rack engine for use in these Islands, but a letter dated 12 April 1922 on N.W.N.G. notepaper was received by Beyer Peacock & Co. Ltd. of Gorton, Manchester followed on 27 April by another on Aluminium Corporation notepaper. (It may have been that second thoughts prevailed at Dolgarrog; the Corporation was certainly more credit-worthy than the N.W.N.G.)

Beyer's noted the following from the letters: 'Can we let them know where they could buy a loco suitable for a 2 ft. gauge rack railway. To run part on rack and part on ordinary track. Either new or secondhand, want approx. price or could we give them a rough idea of the cost of making such an engine for hauling light passenger coaches'. Other details noted were: '2 ft. Gauge; Grade 1 in 6; Maximum load to be hauled 12 tons.'

Beyer duly sent sketch design No. 93574 for an outside cylinder 0–4–2 side tank with rack equipment; the drawing was dated 9 May

May 1922. The design was a modification of sketch No. 81294 for a similar engine prepared on 31 July 1912 for agents Sumner & Co. which never materialised into an order.

Beyer Peacock archives record nothing further following submission of design and quotation.

Contractor's Locomotives

It seems highly likely that both McKie and Boys would have used locomotives during the building of the railway. It is assumed that a spare England-built four-coupled tank-tender engine from the Festiniog Railway was hired for the purpose, for the Festiniog was certainly passing through a period when a small engine might have been available for the task. A Minute of that Railway dated 16 February 1876 reads 'To let Mr. Bray, the Contractor, hire a small engine for six months at £130'. It could be 'Bray' was a mistake for 'Boys'.

Passenger Stock

No official list of stock exists. In 1923 sixteen passenger vehicles survived, but as there had been no passenger services since 1916 and even before that date not all of the stock was required, six vehicles had been in store or out in the open for a number of years.

The only surviving record of stock is a photograph, found in a paper parcel in a wardrobe in Aberystwyth, and taken about 1895. With the help of Annual Returns, and a list of vehicles made by a member of the N.W.N.G. staff of such vehicles as he saw at Dinas in 1923, together with the photograph, a stock list has been prepared. It does not fit the Returns for 1893 when it must be presumed 12 vehicles were listed instead of 11; otherwise it is a possible base for further research.

In 1893 the Company took delivery of a vehicle numbered 8; an official picture of that time exists. It has been assumed that an earlier series of numbers had been used until then. From a Board of Trade Report of an accident on 24 February 1883 the existence of some small four-wheeled coaches is brought to light. A subsequent Manager's report to the Board states there were two of them; three are mentioned in a B.O.T. letter of November 1894 and they duly appear in the illustration referred to. As the Returns always appear to be short of three carriages, it could be these were ex-contractor's vehicles which the Company never included. These three probably carried numbers 3–4–5 and continued to do so despite the duplication of the numbers latterly, until withdrawn in late March 1897.

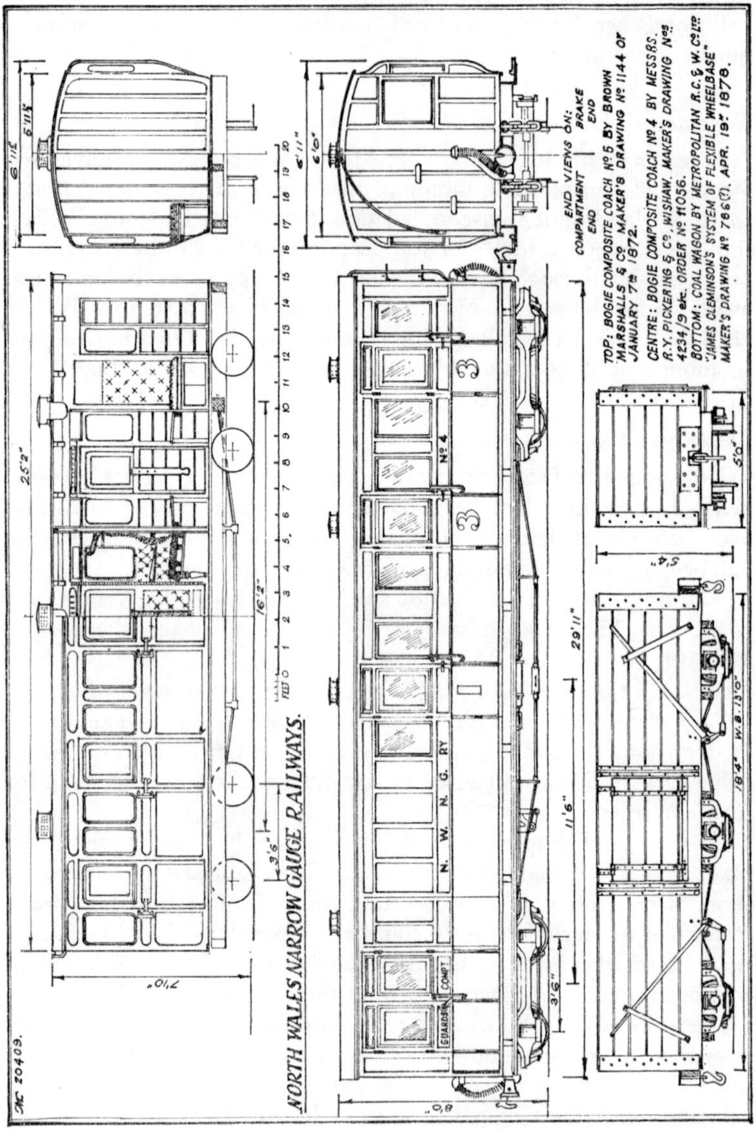
NORTH WALES NARROW GAUGE RAILWAYS.
JC 20409.
TOP: BOGIE COMPOSITE COACH No 5 BY BROWN MARSHALLS & Co. MAKER'S DRAWING No 1144 OF JANUARY 7th 1872.
CENTRE: BOGIE COMPOSITE COACH No 4 BY MESSRS. R.Y. PICKERING & Co, WISHAW. MAKER'S DRAWING Nos 4234/9 etc. ORDER No 11056.
BOTTOM: COAL WAGON BY METROPOLITAN R.C. & W. Co LTD "JAMES CLEMINSON'S SYSTEM OF FLEXIBLE WHEELBASE" MAKER'S DRAWING No 766(?). APR. 19th 1878.
END VIEWS ON: COMPARTMENT END BRAKE END
N. W. N. G. RY
No 4
GUARDS
COMPT
FEET 0 1 2 3 4 5 6 7 8 9 10 11 12 13 14 15 16 17 18 19 20
25'2"
16'2"
7'10"
3'6"
6'11½"
5'11½"
6'11"
6'0"
29'11"
11'6"
8'0"
5'0"
5'4"
18'4"
W.B. 13'0"

NWNG First Series	*NWNG Second Series*	*Wheels*	*Builder*	*Date to Stock*	*Content* (1923)	*Named* 1923	*W/dn*
1	(4)	Bogie	Brown Marshalls	1872	G/1/3/3 (scrapped)	—	1907
2	5	Bogie	Brown Marshalls	1872	G/1/3/3	—	by WHR
3	—	4 wheel	?Ashbury	?1872	3/3 (scrapped)	—	3/1897
4	—	4 wheel	?Ashbury	?1872	3/3 (scrapped)	—	3/1897
5	—	4 wheel	?Ashbury	?1872	3/3 (scrapped)	—	3/1897
6	?1	6 wheel	Gloucester	1877	2/G/3	—	1908
7	?2	6 wheel	Gloucester	1877	2/G/3	—	1908
8	?3	6 wheel	Gloucester	1877	3/3	—	1908
9	9	Bogie	?Metropolitan	1878	3 Saloon ex 1 Saloon	'Corridor'	by WHR
10	10	Bogie	?Metropolitan	1878	1/3 Saloon ex 3/3 Saloon	'Corridor'	by WHR
11	?16	Bogie	?Metropolitan	?1878	3 Saloon	'Workmans'*	by 1923
12	?6	Bogie	Metropolitan	1891	3 Saloon	'Workmans'*	by WHR
13	?7	Bogie	Metropolitan	1891	3 Saloon	'Workmans'*	by WHR
—	8	Bogie	Metropolitan	1893	3 Obs ex 1 Obs	'Tourist Carriage'	by WHR
—	?15	Bogie	Ashbury	1894	3 (7 compartment)	'Summer Coach'†	—
—	11	Bogie	Ashbury	1894	3 (7 compartment)	'Summer Coach'‡	by WHR
—	12	Bogie	Ashbury	1894	3 (7 compartment)	'Summer Coach'	by WHR
—	13	Bogie	Ashbury	1894	3 (7 compartment)	'Summer Coach'	by WHR
—	14	Bogie	Ashbury	1894	3 (7 compartment)	'Summer Coach'	by WHR
—	4	Bogie	Pickering	1907	G/1/3/3	— §	by WHR

* 'Workmans Coaches' was the Company's name; the staff called them 'Closed Coaches'.
† Not taken into stock by the employee listing carriages in 1923.
‡ Taken over as reparations and became Festiniog Railway stock 1936.
§ To replace the original No. 4 which was then withdrawn.

In the absorption of 1923, the combined Welsh Highland/Festiniog series numbering was prepared and with the exception of the two Guards/composites the carriages numbers allotted followed the Festiniog series viz:

4 became	8	11 became	23
5	9	12	24
?6	32	13	27
?7	34	14	28
8	29	?15	26
9	35	?16	(33)
10	36		

No. 16 was apparently withdrawn in 1923 but still existed; it was ascribed No. 33 but never carried it. Nos. 23 and 26 are still in existence on the Festiniog Railway. The remainder were disposed of from Dinas when the Welsh Highland ceased to run; details are given in due course.

The three six-wheelers, probably carrying numbers 1–2–3, had been withdrawn in 1908. All were sold or used as stores sheds by the Railway; if still on their wheels in 1923, they were not 'listed'.

Numbers 37–42 in the 1923 series were given to new coaches purchased outside the period under review, and this completed the numbering.

The coaches supplied up to 1878 were not fitted with continuous brake. It will be noted later that Westinghouse brake was fitted to all stock between 1892 and 1894, though the Chairman had complained about the six-wheelers. These, according to him, were only piped at first because their low bodies made them unsuitable for the brake cylinders. Despite protests as regards costs, the Company fully fitted them, possibly by putting cylinders above the floors. The three four-wheeled carriages remained only piped to the end.

The history of the surviving coaches under the Welsh Highland will be found in the appropriate Part and having examined the carriage stock at the end of the N.W.N.G. Company's life in order to clarify its earlier history, it is convenient to consider each variety of carriage in turn, and in date order.

Original Series Nos. 3, 4 and 5, Four-wheeled Coaches

Virtually nothing is known about these three carriages. From their small size and primitive accommodation, they were of vintage appearance by the time the first N.W.N.G. track was laid. They may have come secondhand and been the contractor's purchase as the

Company did not Return them though they came into possession of them ultimately and ran them among their own stock. They appear to have been 3rd Class and each had only two compartments. From their appearance, they resemble the early Festiniog coaches from Ashbury or the similar vehicles on the Festiniog & Blaenau Railway. There is no reason to suppose they had been built for either and not taken up; the design suggests Ashbury or Brown Marshalls was the builder and the style that they were built in the 1860s. The wheels are known to have been 1 ft. 6 in. diameter; the bodies are estimated at 10 ft. long, about 6 ft. 6 in. from rail to roof excluding lamp, and slightly less than 6 ft. wide. One large lamp did duty for both compartments and there was unlikely to have been a full division between them. The Board of Trade made the Company withdraw them in March 1897 because they had only been piped for brakes and the Company said it would be too expensive to fit them fully.

Nos. 1 and 2, Brake/Composite

These were supplied by Brown Marshalls & Co. in 1874 at a time when contruction was in its infancy and following the lease of the undertaking to H. B. Roberts in the previous year, and ordered by Charles Edwin Spooner before he resigned. They were a Guard's Brake/Composite carriage with one 1st and two 3rd Class compartments with look-out duckets for the guard and surmounted by three oil lamps, the central one serving the 1st Class compartment. The drawing was stamped 'North Wales Narrow Gauge Railway. Engineer's Office, Portmadoc' and the job was Brown Marshalls' Works No. 2040. The drawing date is 19 January 1872, signed 'C. E. Spooner'* and the vehicles were unmistakably sisters of the bodies then being supplied by the same Birmingham firm for the Festiniog Railway, Nos. 15 and 16 having been delivered a few weeks before the drawing in question was made, allowing Spooner to examine the workmanship and design very carefully. The drawing does not show running gear—this was usually the subject of a separate drawing—but possibly in this case (as with the Festiniog bodies) the bogies may have been supplied from Boston Lodge. The body was 25 ft. 2 in. long by 5 ft. 11½ in. wide (6 ft. 11½ in. over duckets) and rooftop to rail measured 7 ft. 10 ins. not including the height of the lamps. It was carried on 1 ft. 7⅛ in. diameter wheels mounted in 3 ft. 6 in. wheelbase bogies (Festiniog standards). The 3rd Class compartments were in bare wood with moulded seats. The 1st compartment was upholstered in blue broadcloth, padded doors and sides, coathooks, mirrors, and floral decorations on the interior panelling.

* i.e. Charles Edwin Spooner.

Coupling gear is not shown but the Festiniog G. P. Spooner type of central buffer-coupler was fitted for most of the coach's life (ref. 'Festiniog Railway', Vol. 1, pp. 167–70 for added details). One vehicle was replaced by a new similar one in 1907. The other existed in 1923 and was given a WHR/FR number.

Doubtless the Company would have benefitted from further elegant coaches of this type, but with Spooner's departure from the N.W.N.G. scene in 1876 or early 1877, James Cleminson was appointed Engineer, and so far as carriage design was concerned, the clock was turned back to the Dark Ages when three carriages to his 'Patent' were ordered in 1877.

Nos. 6, 7 and 8, Brake/Composite and Composite

These three remarkable coaches are something of a mystery. It could be that they appealed to the Company in its financially embarrassed situation because of their cheap and simple construction, which was in the manner of a vertically planked goods van with outside framing, the spartan interiors having a modicum of seat upholstery for 2nd Class and bare boarding for the 3rds. The classes and Guard's central compartment were separated by light partitioning without communicating doors and the seats arranged round the perimeters. Nos. 6 and 7 were 2nd and 3rd Class divided by the Guard's compartment with its lookout ducket. No. 8 was an all 3rd Class. The finish was simple varnished boarding and for the official photograph the makers suspended a board reading 'North Wales Narrow Gauge Ry' from the cant-rail. The class was printed in full above each door and on the solebar was the maker's plate and an oval plate reading 'James Cleminson's Patent Flexible Wheel Base'. The initials of the Company were in yellow above the right-hand windows and the number above the left hand. On top of each coach were some grotesque lamp cases which must have doubled up as ventilators; there were three on those with the Guard's compartment and two on the other. Coupling was by simple 'chopper' buffer-coupler, held down by counterweight. Being low-slung, there were no footboards and such was this deficiency that a step under each door was soon added. The extraordinary ventilators were also removed, for their clearance under bridges must have been minimal. There was a droplight in each door and the furthest window from each door (on either side of the partition) opened too.

The builders were the Gloucester Wagon Co. Ltd. to Orders 249/50. The weight/seating ratio may have attracted the Company; they carried 40 in a $4\frac{1}{4}$ ton vehicle whilst Nos. 1 and 2 carried 30 in a $5\frac{1}{2}$ ton one.

The flexible wheelbase consisted of mounting each pair of wheels on its own small sub-frame. The middle pair was allowed generous lateral movement and, connected to the sliding frame so formed, radius arms stretched to either side and were fastened to the sub-frames on which the end pairs of wheels were mounted. When the middle pair slid laterally, the end pairs (which were pivoted to the coach frame) were angled in such a way as to take up something of the radius of the curve and offset the conventional stiffness of a rigid six-wheeled vehicle passing over a curve. In point of fact, such a system was unnecesary on the N.W.N.G., which had no severe curves, but Cleminson's Patent was later used elsewhere in the British Isles, among the owners being the Southwold Railway (1878), Manx Northern (1878), and several Irish railways (1879–1887), all 3 ft. gauge.

Although Cleminson appears to have been the first to use this idea on rail vehicles, a similar scheme is described and illustrated in 'Mechanics' Magazine' 10 September 1825 for a six-wheeler road vehicle in which the central pair of wheels were rigid but the outer pairs swivelled and were connected together at their extremities by a pair of crossed chains 'upon a principle of leverage, from its counterpoise motion upon the centre wheels . . .' The inventor was Sir Sydney Smith. At the time of writing a number of the Manx Northern's Cleminson coaches still exist.

These carriages were 30 ft. long over body, 5 ft. 11 in. wide, 7 ft. 10 in. from rail to roof-top and the wheelbase was equally divided over 23 ft. The non-Guard's vehicles carried 42 passengers and weighed 4¼ Tons tare.

Nos. 9 and 10, 'Corridor Coaches'

The next pair of vehicles (taking them by date and not by number) are those about which least is known. They were the last two to be supplied in the leasing period and the date of entry into traffic has been deduced from the Annual Returns. They are known to be bogie vehicles of 'saloon' type having end doors and glazing all along each side. Possibly they were supplied by Metropolitan, but there is some doubt of this as no drawing survives for them.

The pair were known as 'Corridor Coaches' by the staff. There was a door in the partition between the two compartments into which the Composite saloon was divided; the all-3rd had none. It is thought the carriages may have been supplied for the use of quarrymen and others. Certainly in their latter-day form they had been refurbished at Dinas and were used as Composite and 3rd Class coaches. The term 'Corridor' did not imply there was any passenger connection with the adjacent vehicle in the train, nor that they were side corridor.

General dimensions of the carriages are estimated to be: Length 29 ft. over body, width 5 ft. 11 in. over body, height 7 ft. 9 in. from rail to roof centre-line, bogie wheelbase 3 ft. 6 in. at 23 ft. bogie centres, and mounted on 1 ft. 10 in. diameter wheels. There was no visible solebar as the vertically planked sides masked them. The roof had two large lampcases and louvred ventilators ran below the cant-rail. By 1914 No. 10 was fitted up with a smaller 1st Class Saloon at one end, the revelant door having '1' on it on a white ground. The lettering 'N.W.N.G.R.', flanked slightly lower on each end with '10', appeared on the upper waist and, in the centre, the Company's arms were mounted on a panel. The coaches were very smart and nicely proportioned. Westinghouse brakes had been fitted. There were steps under each door individually.

These two vehicles survived to become 35 and 36 in WHR/FR books, the latter being rebuilt into a Buffet Car in its latter days.

Nos. 11, 12 and 13, 'Workman's Cars'

The curious title of these carriages comes from the heading given to Metropolitan's drawing of 1 June 1891, 'Workman's Car'. From the Returns it appears one was built as early as 1878 and two added in 1891–2. In outward appearance they resembled the rebuilt 9 and 10, except there was only one central ventilator and the body dimensions were reduced to length 26 ft. 0 in., width 5 ft. 5½ in., height 7 ft. 8 in. rail to roof centre line, bogie wheelbase 3 ft. 6 in., bogie pin centres 18 ft. 6 in., wheel diameter 1 ft. 10 in.

There is one unsolved mystery concerning this collection of three vehicles; although the 1923 rough list conveniently groups them as 'Closed coaches' and the Annual Returns' dates coincide with the Metropolitan drawing of 1891 for a 'Workman's Car', they were not all built to the 1891 drawing. Unfortunately the only illustration which shows the type reasonably well is of a train at South Snowdon whereon—reading from the engine—is shown No. 5, No. 10, a Gloucester 6-wheeler and a vehicle which conforms to the 'Workman's Car' drawing in *proportions*, but is clearly far from being the same height as the drawing's 7 ft. 8 in. Careful checking of the picture suggests the height to have been 7 ft. or fractionally over. Perhaps this was the 'odd' 1878 vehicle? The two 'Closed coaches' which survived to go to Boston Lodge and be cut down in height ended their lives so similar in height to the distant coach of the illustration referred to, that we are left without proof of the exact position.

Westinghouse brakes were fitted as supplied and all windows were

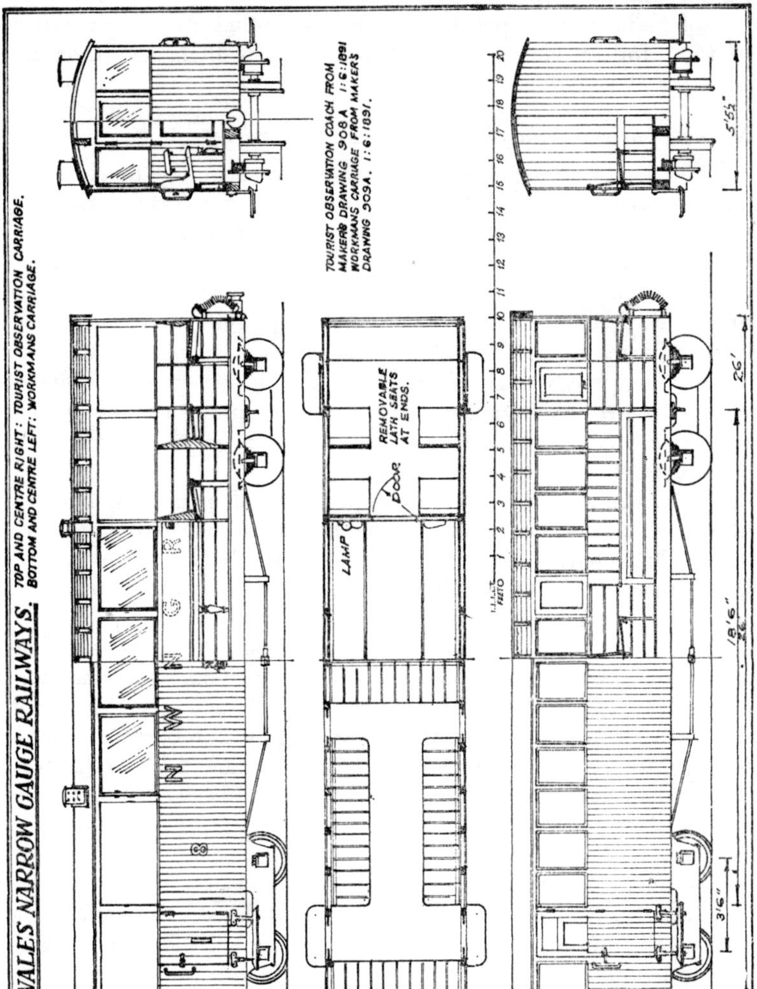
NORTH WALES NARROW GAUGE RAILWAYS.
TOP AND CENTRE RIGHT: TOURIST OBSERVATION CARRIAGE.
BOTTOM AND CENTRE LEFT: WORKMANS CARRIAGE.
TOURIST OBSERVATION COACH FROM MAKERS DRAWING 908 A 1:6:1891
WORKMANS CARRIAGE FROM MAKERS DRAWING 909A. 1:6:1891.
REMOVABLE LATH SEATS AT ENDS.
DOOR
LAMP
FEET 0 1 2 3 4 5 6 7 8 9 10 11 12 13 14 15 16 17 18 19 20
8'8"
7'8"
18'6"
26'
3'6"
5'5½"

glazed. The staff knew them as the 'Closed Coaches'. Being lower than previous stock, the windows merged at the top with the cant-rails, giving them the appearance of long garden sheds. The seating was of plain wooden perimeter type and though all three survived to 1923, former No. 11 was out of service by then and never ran again.

No. 8, 'Tourist Carriage' (second series numbering)

This coach was one of the first attempts to encourage tourist travel on any narrow gauge railway in Britain; it went further than any previous design in recognising the attractions of open balconies and yet having somewhere to retire when the weather turned unfavourable. This lesson seems to have been very slow in making its mark upon railway carriage designers though shipbuilders had been practising it for many years!

The Company's staff looked upon it with special favour and it received more maintenance than the rest of the stock! By 1922 it had been given a coat of vermilion paint and with 'N.W.N.G.R.' flanked by '8' each end and the crest on a plaque below, it looked very smart indeed. The body had open end balconies with a central all-glazed saloon, curtained, upholstered and carpeted. It was an all-1st Class vehicle and, along with 9 and 10, the first to be supplied new with continuous brake. Each door had an individual step and the sides were of matchboarding. Automatic central couplers with safety chains were fitted, lighting and those various small appointments which place a vehicle in a class of its own. Mr. Gladstone, then well over eighty, travelled in it on the way to a holiday at Nant Gwynant, so we read in 'Doctor in the Whips' Room', the autobiography of Sir Henry Morris-Jones. Thereafter it was nicknamed the 'Gladstone Car'. When new, it was painted with cream upper works and white roof, with the customary red waist; the lettering etc. was in gold-shaded vermilion.

The builders were The Metropolitan Railway Carriage & Wagon Co. Ltd. of Birmingham and the drawing is dated 1 June 1891; the original intention was clearly for a spartan 3rd Class coach with four individual lath seats plus a full-width seat in each balcony, and the interior had side seats in street-tram style having contoured and perforated seat and backs in wood. The balcony seats were to be removable and four Colza lamps were to be fitted, one in each corner of the compartment, up against the partition which had a perforated zinc panel inserted in it behind the lamp. The body was 26 ft. long over headstocks by 5 ft. $5\frac{1}{2}$ in. over sides; it was carried on plate-sided bogies having 3 ft. 6 in. wheelbase and 1 ft. 10 in. wheels. The

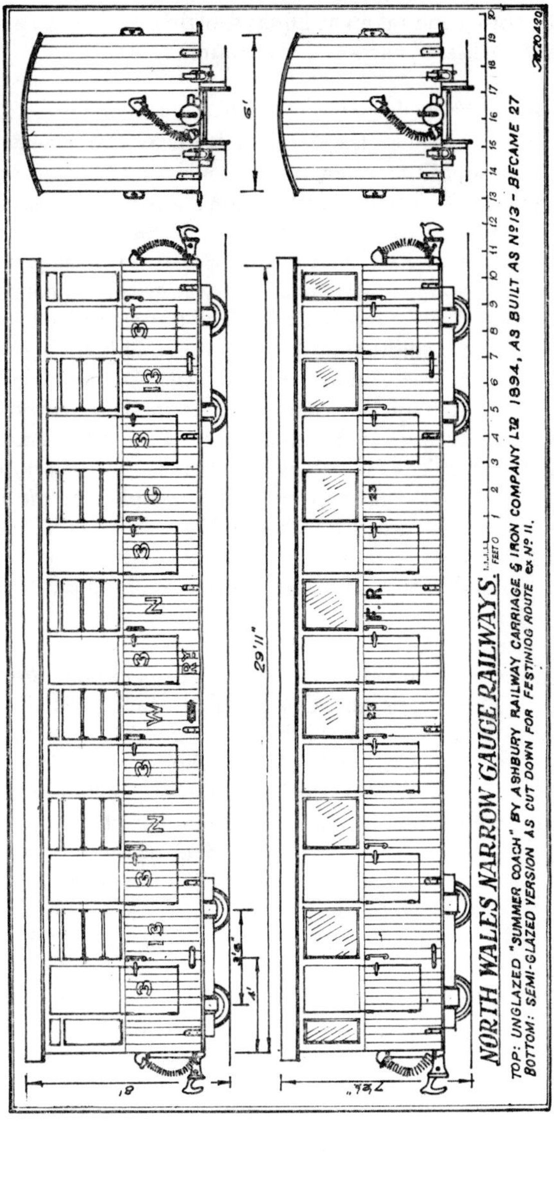
NORTH WALES NARROW GAUGE RAILWAYS.
TOP: UNGLAZED "SUMMER COACH" BY ASHBURY RAILWAY CARRIAGE & IRON COMPANY LTD 1894, AS BUILT AS No 13 - BECAME 27
BOTTOM: SEMI-GLAZED VERSION AS CUT DOWN FOR FESTINIOG ROUTE ex No 11.
29'11"
6'
FEET

drawing shows a customary plain and sprung buffer at each end, strengthened by a supporting framework to take lateral shocks; these and other features did not appear in the finished vehicle which had its official photograph taken at Dinas shortly after delivery, complete with upholstered seats, carpets and curtaining.

Nos. 11–15?, 'Summer Coaches'

The Company went to the Ashbury Railway Carriage & Iron Co. Ltd. of Belle Vue, Manchester, for five tourist carriages in 1894. Each carried the plate 'Ashbury Co. Ltd. 1894'. The N.W.N.G. number 15 for the last is subject to confirmation, but three vehicles (11, 12 and 15?) were semi-glazed whilst 13 and 14 had no glazing. Otherwise the bodies were quite similar, having seven 3rd Class compartments and being open throughout inside. All of them survived until 1923, though the last one, allotted and given No. 26 in combined numbers' series, does not feature on the list of N.W.N.G. vehicles lying at Dinas in 1923. It may be conjectured that at an early stage the N.W.N.G. vehicles were given stencilled numbers for the combined series, but this carriage, which was definitely out of service at the time, had either been taken away or the compiler of the list heard of its fate so did not record it! The body was sold, complete and on its wheels, to a purchaser at Groeslon and was ultimately recovered in October 1958 and brought back to Portmadoc by road. (In this way it escaped destruction, and one wonders how many instances there have been of carriages being sold by one owner, leapfrogging ownership by an incomer and then being brought back and restored by a later owner. The Corris and Glyn Valley coaches on the Talyllyn Railway do not quite qualify for this distinction.)

The carriages came new with Westinghouse brake, class numbering on doors and 'N.W.N.G.' flanked by the vehicle number on the side in the same colours as No. 8. The number of characters on the waist was seventeen, there being at the foot of the fourth door 'Ry'. The non-glazed bodies had stable doors like the semi-glazed variety, but where the other bodies had glass 13 and 14 were given window bars. Norwegian couplers and side chains, lighting and ventilators were fitted.

The principal dimensions of these vehicles were: Length over body 29 ft. 11 in. Width over body 6 ft. 0 in. Bogie wheelbase 3 ft. 6 in. Wheels 1 ft. 8 in. diameter. Height of body centreline from rail 7 ft. 5 in.

No. 4, Guard's Brake/Composite

This vehicle was bought to replace the original vehicle of similar type, No. 5 of 1874. It was the last to be supplied and, giving more space for luggage than No. 5, it was arranged as a Guard/1st/3rd/3rd coach finished in red with gilt lining etc. a truly attractive vehicle. The makers, R. Y. Pickering & Co. Ltd. of Wishaw, built the body to their standard design for 60 cm. gauge and it was offered in their catalogue, including the French-language version. The drawing is dated 5 April 1907. The 1st Class was fully upholstered, the 3rds having lath seats. The guard's end had duckets and end windows, the other having steps and handrail for access to the roof oil lamps. 1st Class seating was 2 ft. 4½ in. wide, the 3rds 'making do' on 1 ft. 11 in.; leg space between seats was 2 ft. in both cases and the floor of the 1st was covered in 'linoleum and rugs' the 3rds being plain Red Deal. The body was 29 ft. 11 in. over headstocks, 6 ft. wide (and 6 ft. 11 in. over duckets) 8 ft. in centreline from rail, and the 3 ft. 6 in. wheelbase bogies with their 1 ft. 8 in. wheels were at 23 ft. centres. The bogie side frames were of Great Northern Railway type outline with boxes and springs behind the frames.

The Company's initials appeared on the waist band, together with the number. Each door bore the Class figure. The carriage survived into the combined series stock.

So much for the Railways' carriage stock, all of which had Colza oil lighting by 1909 but which was said by the Festiniog staff to be 'very poor'. The last nine vehicles built i.e. those introduced from 1891, which had Westinghouse brake from the start, were not only a most useful selection of stock primarily intended for holiday traffi, but were a handsome collection as well. Of the North Wales narrow gauge lines, the Company had no competitor at the turn of the century in the recent acquisitions of carriages it had made. The Festiniog by comparison made a poor showing and it was not until the last year or two of the century that other lines like the Lynton & Barnstaple, the Welshpool & Llanfair and the Rheidol followed a trend which the N.W.N.G. had begun a decade earlier.

GOODS STOCK

One fact may be stated about N.W.N.G. goods stock with positive certainty—very little is known about it! Small companies like this one did not keep records, and as nothing is available for the original purchases and building of stock, only the Annual Returns showing totals of wagons survive. A summary of this reads: 1877, 114; 1878–

90, 120;* 1891–2, 147; 1893–6, varying at about 135; 1897–1907, varying at about 145. About 1910 there was a severe reduction, probably due to scrapping of many redundant slate wagons for which there was no further use, and the remaining years (the First War Returns were not made) were 1910, 118; 1911, 117; 1913, 92. After the War, more informative Returns were made :

	Open Merchandise & Mineral Wagons	*Rail/Timber Wagons*	*Misc.*	*Service*
1913	98	—	29*	4
1919	107	34	1	—
1920	107	39	—	—
1921	82 open + 13 other = 95†	18	—	—

* Presumably some of this total were converted into rail or timber bolsters which swelled the total for 1919; forestry traffic was at its height during the First War.
† It is likely that 82 were wooden or iron-frame slate wagons, and the 13 coal wagons, vans, etc.

There would not appear to be a block system of numbering wagons, and some of the larger, later wagons and vans came at the beginning of the numbering system, suggesting the oft-used method of trying to create order from chaos when a new batch of stock was obtained, by being given the early series numbers. Slate and other wagon numbers (such as are known) do not appear to duplicate, suggesting that only one series was in use.

Slate Wagons (Steel frame type)

Three versions of this wagon have been traced. Basically they were of the design in use far and wide over the county, but in detail they were entirely different from those used by other companies. The framing was of bar and angle, the top member being angle. The 2 ton wagons (specimen numbers 120 and 127) were commonest, and had a rectangular plate buffing pad at each end with hook and chain coupling. Some had brakes with shoes and handle on one side only; handles were fitted in various positions and were shaped in S, J or straight varieties. Wheel bearings were unlike other Welsh lines. Some were lanky plain pedestals, others had a somewhat sophisticated axle-box cover on a bevelled face with grease-box lid occasionally fitted

* House of Commons Sessional papers for this year disclose 105 wagons fitted with hook and link couplers, 15 wagons with hooks worked by eccentric and ball weight (i.e. Norwegian type couplings) making 120 in all. Presumable stock which might be attached to passenger trains had the semi-automatic coupling (self-acting). Standard height of coupling above rail was 1 ft. 8 in. Two shunters were employed; there was 15 in. between wagons. Regarding a question on use of shunter's poles, the reply given was 'They are able to do this without going either between or under them'.

at the top of the pedestal, and another version was sprung with small W irons to hold a box whose body and spring were behind the W iron. Bearings were swopped about. Probably dimensions were 5 ft. 6 in. long × 3 ft. 6 in. wide. The 3 ton wagons were similar to the two ton, but wider. They were distinguished by having curved buffing plates at each end and most had spring boxes in W irons. Probable dimensions were 6 ft. long × 4 ft. 6 in. wide. Specimen numbers 46 and 52

The above types had wooden floors and their top rails varied in height with each other depending on bearings in use and wear and tear. A suggested rail-top side dimension is 3 ft.

The final variety of steel frame wagon was quite the most sophisticated design to be seen in Wales; the 'Railway Magazine' of 1917, p. 38 illustrated the builder's official photograph of one, with a most untypical 'foreign' background and on temporary rail. Of 3 tons capacity, a chassis with axleboxes supporting coil springs and with central sprung buffers, a handbrake working on all wheels and having the axlebox horns suitably 'tied' with a frame connecting solebar and boxes, these wagons were much in advance of anything else to be seen on such humble duty. One source suggests the builders were Kerr Stuart & Co. Ltd., of Stoke on Trent, but this cannot be confirmed and the number purchased is not known. There cannot have been many of them but their chassis appear (stripped of their bodies) in the demolition train where they were used as rail bolsters. They may have dated from the capital available with the Act of 1890.

Slate Wagons (Two plank wooden type) (also used as general purpose wagons, coal, manure, etc.)

It may be that these are older than the framed wagons just described. Possibly too, they were built at the Festiniog Railway's Boston Lodge Works as they were very similar to their own construction.

The smallest type held 2 tons of slate, and was of fixed two-plank type with rectangular buffing plates each end. Some had brakes, and levers (also wheel bearings) enjoyed the same wide variety as did the framed wagons. Two vertical members of square section timber were bolted from frame to top on each side. Dimensions appear to be similar to the frame wagons of this capacity, but their height was lower.

The next size held about 2½ tons and though similar to the above, had higher sides and levelled up with the 2 and 3 ton frame wagons. Probably due to damage in the quarries, many of the vertical side frame timbers were replaced with T section steel strip.

The largest wooden slate wagons were of dimension similar to the 3 ton frame wagons i.e. were wider in the body but otherwise built in the same way as the smaller wooden wagons. Specimen numbers 50, 56 and 70.

Side Tip Wagons

There were about half a dozen three-plank wooden bodied side tippers. The bodies overhung the underframes from which they tipped on one side only. They were larger than any of the slate wagons and probably held 4 tons of stone. Specimen number 123.

Coal Wagons

It is possible these too were the fruits of the finance available under the 1890 Act and certainly they were kept in good condition to judge by illustrations of the First War period. Perhaps they were not so abused. There were at least thirteen of them and in general style they resembled the large wooden mineral wagons on the Festiniog and probably came from the same drawing board and perhaps, Boston Lodge. They were usually used for coal, but in the First War, for pit props also. There was a lift-up door of 4 planks in the five-plank side on the one side; the other side was masked by the brake lever. the doors were arranged on the west side. Large curved metal buffing plates were fitted, some wagons having additional side chains as well as the central link and hooks which, unlike any other concern's link and hook varieties, had two links plus hook.

This arrangement had its dangers as a disengaged hook would trail along between the rails and tend to hook up point blades 'en passant'. Specimen numbers 3, 9, 10 and 12. All these wagons had heavy duty axleboxes in W irons and coil springs. These fittings were similar to those fitted by the Festiniog Railway to their Quarrymen's Coaches. Suggested dimensions: 10 ft. × 5 ft. wide × 5 ft. 6 in. from rail. Average capacity was 4.31 tons.

Covered Vans

There were at least two covered vans carrying numbers 2 and 4, and they were based on the 5 ton Coal Wagons. There were double opening doors on one side only, the brake handle being on the east side. No. 4 had wider doors arranged with the opening in the form of an arched curve; quite unusual. Buffing and couplers, and running gear was the same as the Coal Wagons. The Official Returns ignored them under the heading 'Covered Wagons'!

Cleminson 6-wheeled Patent Wheelbase Open Wagons

No illustrations survive showing this wagon(s) but a drawing was prepared and presumably at least one wagon went into service. It may be compared with the Cleminson 6-wheeled Open which the Festiniog used for coal traffic from 1878.

4-Wheeled Goods Brake Vans

One was Westinghouse fitted and survived to receive a W.H.R. number. It had outside framing, two windows in each end and was of 'Road Van' type, completely enclosed. The van portion had a single sliding door each side and at one end there were full-height solid outward-opening doors (one per side) for personal access. It was mounted on sprung axleboxes and approximately 11 ft. long by 5 ft. wide. It carried 'No. 2'. There was certainly a second van distinguished by having no roof ventilator nor Westinghouse brake.

Private Owner Wagons

The slate quarries ran about 30 open wagons over N.WN.G. metals. They are believed to be of wooden frame and wood plank varieties and appear in pictures before the turn of the century.

Goods Stock—general

Wheelbases were generally (except for the large coal wagons and covered vans) as for Festiniog stock, with 3 ft. on the 2 Ton slate wagons and 6 ft. on the coal wagons and closed vans. All wheels were 1 ft. 6 in. diameter.

Timber Bolster Wagons

Prior to the First War the Company began timber traffic over the uncompleted portion of the P.B. & S.S.R. There were two varieties of bolster wagon, one in iron and the other of wood. The latter had curved buffing plates like the coal wagons and pedestal bearings of considerable height, unlike any others. The solebars were cut away to allow the grease-box lids to be lifted. Dimensions were approximately as for the 2 Ton slate wagons where relevant. Most had a brake fitted and average capacity was two tons. There were thirty-nine of them in 1920 reduced to eighteen in 1921.

Flat Wagons

These were used as runners between bolsters for long timber, and were braked, having tall plain pedestal bearings of singular design.

Goods Stock in 1922

Spring's Report summarises the survivors as:

1	4-wh. Brake Van (fitted continuous brake)*
90	Slate Wagons (various)
12	2-Ton Open Wagons
13	4½-Ton Coal Wagons
14	Bolster Wagons
20	Bolster Runner Wagons

These figures differ slightly from the Official Returns.

Permanent Way

An accident report of 1883 verifies the construction of the main line track of the period. The gauge was 1 ft. 11¼ in. (on a later accident report this becomes 1 ft. 11½ in.) with flat-bottomed rails in 24 ft. lengths weighing 35 lbs. per yard. Fang-bolts and dog-spikes were used alternately on the sleepers which were of half round section, in larch, measuring 4 ft. 6 in. long, 9 in. × 4½ in. in section laid at 2 ft. 5¼ in. centres except at joints where they were 2 ft. Fish-plates had four bolts. Ballast was of gravel mixed with shale or cinders to a depth of 7 in.

Another report of the same period refers to 'iron rails' and says that 35, 38½ and 40 lb. sections in 24 ft. lengths were in use. At joints there were two fang-bolts to hold the rail, and intermediately single spiking. This account also refers to half round *and* rectangular section sleepers in use at the same time. Clearly, there was some variation in the materials used along the line. Starting in January 1884, 41¼ lb. Indian Metre Gauge standard rail of steel in 30 ft. lengths, spiked with four dogs per fastening took the place of iron rails. At first, three miles were so treated and this was ultimately extended to the whole line. The balance of steel rails was purchased in the latter half of 1886 when it was reported that 2,000 replacement sleepers had been laid too. At this time the increase in working expenses was almost entirely due to relaying. In the 1922 reconditioning of the line, the Indian rail was replaced by 40 lb. B.S.S. rails, 33 ft. long. Smaller sleepers only 4 ft. long and a shallower depth of ballast were among the economies practised in the 1922 relaying.

The formation level width was 10 ft.

An account in 'Railway Press' of 21 June 1889 refers to the numerous sharp curves of 3½ to 4 chains radius on gradients of 1 in

* There were certainly two.

36 to 1 in 48 and the continual problem caused thereby of the tendency of rails to spread on the 'excessively sharp curves' and cause derailments. (The Company enjoyed plenty of these.) In 1886 Livesey designed iron ties which were fitted, three to each rail length, to hold the gauge on the sharpest curves. These proved very successful and were later extended to almost every curve on the line. So poorly had the track stood up to traffic on curves that in the early days plate-layers were constantly respiking the rails until the sleepers quickly became useless. Livesey introduced barbed dog spikes which, together with ties, reduced maintenance and derailments considerably.

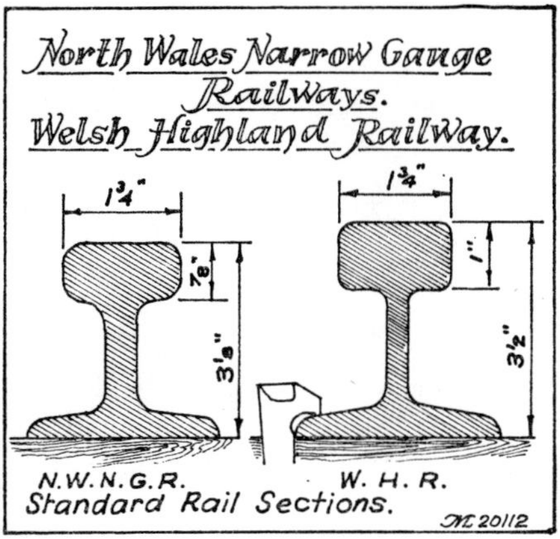

By 1921 only two men were employed on the whole railway to tend the track. Some new sleepers had been put in on the branch and tie bars inserted. Bryngwyn station was unsafe for a locomotive. All curves needed packing, joints had broken and sagged. From a point north of Glanrafon and into Rhydd-ddu the main line was good. Otherwise it was 'unsafe for passengers'.

SIGNALLING

The main line and branch was of single line and no land was obtained for doubling it. The Official Returns of Single Line read :

1877	9 m. 0 ch.	—Dinas—Bryngwyn 4 m. 50 ch.: Tryfan Junc.—Quellyn 4 m. 30 ch.
1878	9 m. 70 ch.	—Dinas—Bryngwyn 4 m. 50 ch.: Tryfan Junc.—Snowdon Ranger 5 m. 20 ch.
1880 on.	11 m. 70 ch.	—Dinas—Bryngwyn 4 m. 50 ch.: Tryfan Junc.—Rhydd-ddu 7 m. 20 ch.

Goods/Mineral Traffic only:

1892	1 m. 8 ch.	Incline & Above
1893 on	0 m. 44 ch.	Incline only

It will be seen that on the latter Returns, a change of emphasis prevailed, the tramways above the Bryngwyn Drumhead not being N.W.N.G. property!

There were signal boxes at the following stations, and at those marked * it was ultimately possible for the engine to run round a train (from which it must not be assumed that the Board of Trade viewed the loop as a suitable passing place for passenger working): Dinas Junction*, Tryfan Junction*, Waenfawr*, Bettws Garmon*, Snowdon Ranger, Rhydd-ddu*, Rhostryfan, Bryngwyn*. Of course at first there were no instruments of any kind, the railway being worked on the One Engine in Steam method. At opening the equipment was:

Llanwnda	12 levers	3 spare included
Moel Tryfan	20	1
Rhostryfan	8	2
Bryngwyn	8	3
Waenfawr	8	2
Bettws-y-Garmon	12	4
Quellyn	2	–

These are the original spellings; probably Quellyn was just a ground frame for the temporary layout. After 1895 track alterations, Waenfawr had 7 levers and 1 spare. By 1921 the timber work on the signal boxes had 'quite rotted'.

Frames and semaphore signals were supplied by McKenzie & Holland of Worcester; block instruments (not an original installation) came from the Railway Signal Company of Liverpool. (Ref: Light Railway Investigation Committee Report 1921).

Distant, Home and Starting signals were installed, there were no Starters at Waenfawr, but only those at Dinas, Tryfan, Bettws Garmon, Snowdon Ranger and Rhydd-ddu remained intact (though out of use and derelict) by 1922. Previously all stations were signalled. The signals were of the single spectacle type showing a white light for clear and having a blue spectacle back light.

There was a telephone link between Dinas, Tryfan and Rhydd-ddu, with tappings at Waenfawr and all intermediate quarry sidings. The block instruments were connected by 2-wire circuits on overhead poles, some of which were cast-iron tubes. The block instruments were at Dinas, Tryfan Junction, Waenfawr and Rhydd-ddu, also at Bryngwyn on the branch. All these had been taken out before 1920 save Tryfan Junction and Waenfawr, and both these were out of order.

From the time of opening until at least 1888 both main line and branch were worked on the One Engine in Steam principle or when required, by using the only available staff for a section and sending a train(s) ahead on a ticket. Only the engine carrying the staff would be able to enter any sidings as the key was attached to the staff. The Company returned this method of working over the 2 m. 35 ch. Tryfan Junction–Bryngwyn branch for the whole period of its history. The returns show that on the main line, Wise's Patent Train Staff & Ticket system and Absolute Block working was introduced over the 9 m. 35 ch. main line in 1892; presumably in the period 1888–1892 there was a mixture of working while Wise's system was being installed.

The Interlocking Returns of 1888 gave nine sidings and one cross-

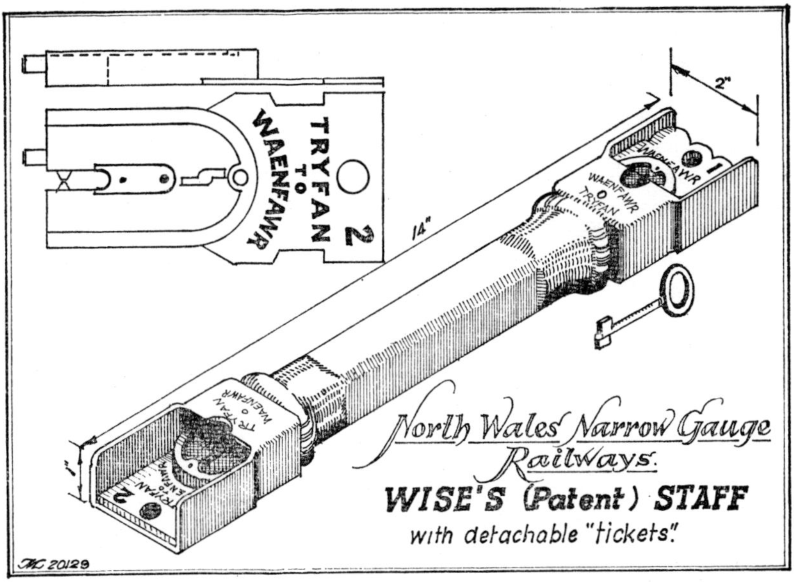

over, and five sidings in main and branch respectively where interlocking was fitted. There were ten main line and five branch locations where point and signal locking was concentrated, i.e. signal boxes or ground frames.

Wise's Staff is not commonly found; there are samples of it in the Armagh Museum (ex-Clogher Valley Railway), the Science Museum (that used by McKenzie & Holland who were agents for it) as a sample from India, and the Narrow Gauge Railway Museum, Towyn, has an original N.W.N.G. example. The staff is metal and has pockets attached at each end into which metal tabs are slipped.

Berkeley D. Wise was Engineer to the Belfast & Co. Down Railway having been previously on the Belfast & Northern Counties line. His aim in designing the staff was to eliminate the use of card or paper tickets in connection with ordinary staff working; these were vulnerable and had to be collected and returned to higher authority. Wise's system used metal tabs as tickets; engraved on each was the section for which the ticket was intended and the direction of travel, i.e. A–B or B–A. A ticket from one end would not fit the pocket at the other. At the issuing station the Station Master had a key to unlock the staff; he did so in front of the train driver who saw the staff and was given a ticket from it. At the end of the appropriate section the ticket would be given up; the Station Master there, on receipt of the staff itself which followed on the last working, would be able to slip the one or more tickets into the appropriate end of the staff; he would not of course, have a key for the end into which he replaced the tickets, but only for the other end which released tickets for the return journey. The staff was customarily used with its full complement of tickets for the contrary journey, locked in the one end of it; this was an added safeguard as not only would a ticket from the other end not fit, but the end having its full complement of tickets, there would be no vacancy to enable anyone to try and force in a ticket.

Users of the System, which lasted well into the time of the Electric Token, included the Clogher Valley as mentioned, Great Eastern and parts of the (English) Great Northern Railways, The Belfast & County Down, and the Seacombe, Hoylake & Deeside Railway. Most of these installed it in the 1880s and McKenzie & Holland illustrated it in their catalogue.

Crest and Garter

The Company used two 'devices'. There was a proper Coat of Arms 8 in. × 8¾ in. having a Red Dragon against a white decorated background. Beneath, on an elaborated scroll, read 'North Wales Narrow Gauge Railways Company'.

There was also a Garter Device. This was the same as that used by the Festiniog Railway and may have been introduced by Spooner, for instance, before a Coat of Arms proper was sanctioned. The Garter was 6 in. diameter and read 'North Wales Narrow Gauge Railways' and was surmounted by a Red Dragon. The garter could encircle a vehicle number, but an illustration of it in use on any vehicle has not come to notice. The Crest on the other hand, was used on engines and carriages but probably not all coaches received it. The Ashbury delivery of the 1894 period did not have it, but it is thought that the 6-wheelers apart, coaches up to that time were given it when new. On the carriages, it was customarily mounted on its own panel.

Livery

Locomotives

The main colour was difficult to define because in weathering it changed its tone. It began as a red-brown which some sources say was like that of the North British Railway, and others as Midland Railway red. The latter is the likely starting shade, and being unstable, it would become more brown with weathering and rubbing down. The lining was black, edged each side with a thin yellow line. Hall cranks on outside framed engines, and buffer beams were vermilion, as was the ground of all brass name etc. plates. Frames, smokebox and cab roofs were black. The Company's initials were not carried. *Beddgelert* carried the Coat of Arms on the cab panel.

Coaches

The six-wheelers were teak with black ironwork and white roofs. Lettering etc. was in gilt with black shading, under the eaves.

Bogie coaches were Midland Railway red lettered and lined in gold but by the early 1900s the lining had begun to disappear. Roofs were grey latterly, white originally.

When delivered, the bogie coaches from Ashbury had light brown upper panels and were chocolate below the waist in a style similar to that used by the Lancashire & Yorkshire Railway. Roofs were originally white; lettering etc. was gilt and each door had the Class number on it together with 'N.W.N.G. Ry.' and the vehicle number . . . all of which somewhat cluttered up the waist panels!

The Observation Carriage No. 8 was similarly treated and for good measure had the Company's Arms on a plaque mounted on the side.

By the end of the First War some carriages were grey without marking of any kind save for the number in small figures in a bottom corner of the side.

Goods Stock

Slate wagons were Midland red but became grey with black running gear. Vans may have been Midland Railway red originally but were grey latterly. On some open planked wagons, the top plank would read (for example) 'N.W.N.G. 58' in white, but this gave way to stencil characters on soles or elsewhere. No additional marking was given; tare weight or loaded weight was not shown. The large open coal wagons were always smartly turned out, the number being in a large white stencil on the top right-hand plank or in the centre of the side.

Extremely little is known about wagon colours and clearly no basic method of painting, numbering etc. was used. Paint was simply a medium to preserve the vehicle and identify it by a number.

Time Tables

February 1878 Week-days only 1st & 3rd Class General Manager & Secretary: J. Oldham

DOWN	Gov.		A	B		A
Dinas	7.20	9.58	12.30	3.03	5.03	7.43
Tryfan Junction	7.30	10.08	12.40	3.13	5.13	7.53
Rhostryfan	7.40	10.13	12.45	3.18	5.18	7.58
Bryngwyn	7.55	10.22	12.55	3.27	5.27	8.05
Waenfawr	7.45	10.17	12.50	3.23	5.23	8.03
Bettws Garmon	7.55	10.22	12.55	3.28	5.28	8.08
Quellyn*	8.05	10.32	1.10	3.40	5.40	8.20

UP			A	B	Gov.	A
Quellyn	8.20	11.40	1.30	4.20	6.15	8.20
Bettws Garmon	8.33	11.53	1.43	4.33	6.28	8.33
Waenfawr	8.40	12.00	1.50	4.40	6.35	8.40
Bryngwyn	8.30	11.50	1.40	4.30	6.25	8.30
Rhostryfan	8.40	12.00	1.50	4.40	6.35	8.40
Tryfan Junction	8.50	12.10	2.00	4.50	6.45	8.50
Dinas	8.58	12.18	2.08	5.00	6.55	9.00

A Saturdays only B Saturdays excepted Gov = Parliamentary (* Temporary station)

August 1892 Secretary: S. Ta

DOWN	Gov.		SO				SO	SO
Dinas	6.00	7.45	9.40	12.47	3.12	5.00	7.00	8.25
Tryfan Junction	6.09	7.55	9.50	12.56	3.21	5.10	7.09	8.35
Rhostryfan	—	8.04	9.58	1.05x	3.30	5.18	7.15	8.43
Bryngwyn	—	8.14	10.06	1.15x	3.40	5.28	7.24	8.53
Waenfawr	6.18		10.00	1.05	3.30	5.20		8.45
Bettws Garmon	6.23		10.05	1.10	3.35	5.25		8.50
Snowdon Ranger	6.36		10.18	1.23	3.47	5.38		—
Rhydd-ddu*	6.50		10.31	1.36	4.00	5.55		—
Beddgelert (coach)	—		11.15	2.15	4.30	6.30		—

UP	SE	SO	Gov.					SO
Beddgelert (coach)	—		9.40	12.50	3.10		6.10	—
Rhydd-ddu (train)	7.20	8.20	10.35	1.45	4.05		7.05	—
Snowdon Ranger	7.34	8.33	10.48	1.49	4.17		7.18	—
Bettws Garmon	7.47	8.46	11.01	2.12	4.29		7.31	8.55
Waenfawr	7.53	8.51	11.06	2.17	4.34		7.36	9.00
Bryngwyn		8.35	10.50	2.00x	4.17	5.35		8.55
Rhostryfan		8.43	11.00	2.10x	4.27	5.45		9.04
Tryfan Junction	8.03	9.00	11.15	2.27	4.42	5.52	7.45	9.11
Dinas	8.13	9.10	11.24	2.37	4.51	6.00	7.55	9.20

Gov = Parliamentary SO Saturdays only SE Saturdays excepted x = Saturdays only * '2½ miles from the summit of Snowdon'

June 1909 Snowdon & Beddgelert District—N.W.N.G.—Secretary & Manager G. C. Aitchison

DOWN	A		SO		SO	SO
Dinas	6.51	9.55	12.48	3.10	5.25	7.00
Tryfan Junction	7.00	10.03	12.56	3.18	5.34	7.09
Tryfan Junction		10.08	12.58	3.20	5.36	7.10
Rhostryfan		10.15	1.04	3.25	5.42	7.15
Bryngwyn		10.25	1.14	3.35	5.52	7.25
Tryfan Junction	7.00	10.04	12.57	3.19		7.11
Waenfawr	7.09	10.17	1.05	3.29		7.19
Bettws Garmon	7.13	10.25	1.10	3.25		7.24
Quellyn Lake	7.26	10.38	1.23	3.48		7.37
Snowdon*	7.38	10.50	1.35	4.00		7.50
Beddgelert (coach)	—	11.15	2.10	5.40		—

UP	A		SO	SO	SE		SO	SO	SO
Beddgelert (coach)	—	10.00	12.30	—	—	4.00			
Snowdon (train)	7.45	11.05	1.40			5.30			7.55
Quellyn Lake	7.58	11.17	1.50			5.43			Sig.
Bettws Garmon	8.10	11.31	2.00			5.54			Sig.
Waenfawr	8.15	11.40	2.04			5.58			8.25
Tryfan Junction	8.25	11.47	2.14			6.05			8.32
Bryngwyn	—	11.30	2.00	4.28	5.34	—	6.00	7.27	—
Rhostryfan	—	11.40	2.10	4.38	5.44	—	6.10	7.35	—
Tryfan Junction	—	11.45	2.15	4.44	5.49	—	6.15	7.40	—
Tryfan Junction	8.26	11.48	2.16	4.45	5.50	6.05	6.16	7.40	8.32
Dinas	8.35	11.58	2.25	4.54	6.00	6.13	6.26	7.50	8.40

A 1st Class & Gov. SO Saturdays only SE Saturdays excepted * 'About 3 miles to the summit of Snowdon'
Sig. Stops to set down on notice being given to Guard.

March 1916 Weekdays only G. C. Aitchison

DOWN		
Dinas	9.35	3.20
Tryfan Junction	Sig.	—
Tryfan Junction	—	—
Rhostryfan	—	—
Bryngwyn	—	—
Tryfan Junction	Sig.	—
Waenfawr	9.55	3.40
Bettws Garmon	Sig.	Sig.
Quellyn Lake	Sig.	Sig.
Snowdon	10.35	4.10
Beddgelert (coach)	11.20	4.50

UP		
Beddgelert (coach)	10.00	3.20
Snowdon (train)	10.45	4.15
Quellyn Lake	Sig.	Sig.
Bettws Garmon	Sig.	Sig.
Waenfawr	11.25	4.40
Tryfan Junction	Sig.	—
Bryngwyn	—	—
Rhostryfan	—	—
Tryfan Junction	—	—
Tryfan Junction	Sig.	—
Dinas	12.05	5.10

(Footnotes as for June 1909.)

Notes on Timetables

The Company never ran trains on Sundays.

The nature of the surviving documents makes it impossible to be precise in comment on timetables, and these notes are observations only. No copies of Working Timetables, Rule Book or Minutes are available.

February 1878

1. The Railway had only just opened; the branch was complete and probably provided the bulk of all traffic—certainly the bulk of slate traffic.
2. The Timetable would require two engines in steam. The Company only possessed two at this time, *Beddgelert* not being delivered until the end of 1878. There was thus no margin for engine failures.
3. The service was probably based on through trains between Dinas and Bryngwyn with a branch service (so to speak) on the unfinished main line from Tryfan Junction to Quellyn. Presumably the engine on the latter service would fill in its duties on materials' etc. trains for the contractor. It is likely that during the course of the day the engines on the two duties were swopped over, for instance, the 5.00 p.m. arrival at Dinas Mondays–Fridays with the 5.03 p.m. departure on all weekdays would not allow the same engine time to run round, coal and take water.
4. Working over the steep gradient between Tryfan Junction and Bryngwyn the following times were allowed between the three stations involved for Down (uphill) trains :

Tryfan Junction to Rhostryfan	10 mins.	5	5	5	5	5
Rhostryfan to Bryngwyn	15 mins.	9	10	9	9	7

The first train was the morning Government or workman's train which would have the heaviest loading. The third train was Saturdays only and would carry a greater passenger load that day. The last train, at a not-very-late hour of evening, presumably carried little traffic between Rhostryfan and Bryngwyn—as might be expected !

On the Up (downhill) run ten minutes were allowed for each of the two sections of the branch journey between the three stations. All trains were timed the same. This would allow opportunity for braking of slate wagons when required.

5. The timetable shows passenger workings only. It is believed that other-than-passenger workings were run as required and not pro-

vided for in the working timetable. Most advertised trains ran with wagons at the rear of the passenger portion. The accounts show that Saturday passenger takings were five to six times those of Monday to Friday inclusive.

August 1892

1. This table could be worked by using one engine on the main line and one on the branch. On Saturday evenings the last working Bryngwyn–Dinas which made connection with the last train Tryfan Junction to Dinas, would either have to combine and form one train with two engines at Tryfan, or run the branch set back to Dinas as empty stock.
2. The Saturday evening train to Bettws Garmon only and back is a feature of this period. Presumably lack of population beyond did not warrant extending this service. There must have been a suitable layout for running round the engine at Bettws but there is no record of it before Spring 1902 when the latterday loop was put in. Perhaps the coaches were pushed into a siding and hand-shunted behind the engine again, i.e. pushed!
3. Some of the turnround times at Rhydd-ddu were quite short but probably time could be made up on the downhill return run if late starts from there were involved.

June 1909

1. This table could be worked with one engine on the main line and another for the branch. The main line engine could work the same set of carriages to and fro throughout the day except that on Saturdays, after arrival at Dinas at 6.13 p.m. of the 5.30 p.m. from Snowdon, the engine and train would have to work back empty stock as far as Tryfan Junction to make connection with the 7.00 p.m. Dinas–Bryngwyn train (also Saturdays only) to extend this Saturday service to Snowdon.

   By the above arrangement, the Bryngwyn branch engine would make all its journeys on a revenue-earning basis.
2. The ample Up Dinas–Bryngwyn service on Saturdays is notable though it ceases at an early hour; the last trip of the day on the branch is notable for the two minutes allowed to hook on and off the train and run round at Bryngwyn. This train was then allowed only eight minutes to Rhostryfan, the fastest of the day. Doubtless it seldom failed to keep time, as last workings-of-the-day and a homeward run enjoy a beneficial effect!
3. Branch times vary from 5 to 7 minutes for the climb from Try-

fan Junction to Rhostryfan, and 10 minutes was allowed thereafter. With the exception of the working just mentioned, Up trains were also given 10 minutes for the return journey and 5 or 6 minutes from Rhostryfan to Tryfan Junction.

4. The fastest main line run was the Up working at 5.30 p.m. from Snowdon which was allowed 43 minutes for the 9½ miles.

March 1916

1. This was the nadir of the passenger service. The branch train had gone and nothing was provided for passengers (at least as an advertised service) in place of the ample schedules of seven years previously. It now took an hour to work from Dinas to Snowdon and an hour and twenty minutes to return—presumably to allow time to pick up slate wagons bound for Dinas.
2. The table could be worked entirely with one engine; between 12.05 p.m. and 3.20 p.m. there was opportunity to make a freight working up to Bryngwyn and back when required.
3. On the main line, Tryfan Junction, Bettws Garmon and Quellyn Lake had been reduced to 'Halt' category.

The passenger service finished entirely at the end of this year.

A Report of 1921–2 implies that there was fair traffic on the Bryngwyn branch (freight only) and the track was in good order. Tryfan Junction–Snowdon was used only about once a week and very unprofitably, mainly for timber off the incomplete P.B. & S.S.R. This somewhat contradicts Spring's Report of 1921 which quotes Bryngwyn workings on four days a week (etc.) and implies that little of the track was in good order. Latterly both surviving engines were said to be in 'good order' and *Moel Tryfan* would haul four coaches and *Russell* nine on the Bryngwyn branch.

Incidents and Accidents

From the number of reported accidents, the Company had one of the worst records with a predilection to derailments. Whether this was due to an honest streak which would not hide the slightest reportable incident, or whether only the worst was notified, cannot be said. What is clear is that whether during the time of the hire of rolling stock, the early Company stock or the later bogie stock, trains were prone to leave the rails and there having been plenty of opportunity to put the running gear of stock into good order, we can only assume there was insufficient manpower, available finance or materials to keep the track in fair order. A sample of reported items may be sufficient to illustrate this.

1878		One collision between passenger trains
		One passenger train derailment
		One passenger injured
		One Railway Servant killed by falling from engine on moving train
24 February 1883		(See separate account of collision)
1892		One non-classified accident—carriage blown off rails at Bettws Garmon
1894	January–March	One passenger train derailment
1896	January–March	One goods train derailment
1899	June–December	One goods train derailment
1901	June–September	Two passenger train derailments
	September–December	One Railway Servant killed (Cause classed as 'Miscellaneous')
1902	June–September	Three passenger train derailments
1903	March–June	One passenger train derailment
		One Railway Servant injured
	September–December	One passenger train derailment
1906	January–March	One goods train derailment
		One passenger train derailment
31 July 1906		(See separate account of collision)
	September–December	Collision between passenger and goods trains; one passenger injured
1907	January–March	One goods train derailment
	March–June	One Railway Servant injured whilst shunting
	June–September	One passenger train derailment
		One goods train derailment
	September–December	One coupling failure

Over a span of twenty years on what had been a newly-built railway, this list makes impressive reading. The two most interesting occasions deserve separate mention.

On 24 February 1883 the 8.25 p.m. left Rhydd-ddu for Dinas in darkness and in good order. The Single Fairlie engine ran, bunker leading, followed by Gloucester brake composite six-wheeler coach and two small third class four-wheelers. They duly stopped at Snowdon Ranger and shortly after re-starting, the two four-wheelers at the rear left the rails, coming to a stand 960 yards west of the station. Parted from the derailed coaches, the engine and coach sped on for another 580 yards and it was Quellyn Bridge before the Guard sensed they were alone. He managed to signal the driver to stop and ordered him to set back along the line to find the missing carriages. The driver lost no time in doing so and contact between the Gloucester and the four-wheelers was so violent that the former was considerably damaged and the latter thrown off down the lineside on their sides. The only passenger was in the Gloucester and no one was injured.

At 11.30 p.m. Guard Morris knocked up R. H. Livesey at his Caernarvon home and told him that some of the 8.25 from Rhydd-ddu lay battered down the bank near Snowdon Ranger. Livesey went at once to Dinas Junction where he found Driver Jones asleep on the engine. He was drunk but the fireman was sober. The Guard too had been drinking, but was not so drunk as the driver. The engine being in steam, Livesey drove out to Ranger. He found the derailed coaches lying one side of the line. The fireman had admitted they (the three trainmen) had been drinking at the Snowdon Ranger Hotel and were running fast to make up time. The Guard had not made up the train correctly; the brake vehicle should have been at the rear. The derailed vehicles had run for 420 yards along the ballast.

William Roberts the ganger arrived on the scene at 2 p.m. Sunday. He found the track there true to gauge and the materials quite sound. Thomas Morris the Guard had been a fireman on the L.N.W.R. at Crewe but came to the N.W.N.G. when it opened. They had arrived at Snowdon Ranger at 8.37 p.m., a minute early, and left at 8.50 p.m. he thought. He maintained he was with the stationmaster from Rhydd-ddu all the time, 'who had come down with the train' ... 'doing the accounts and changing the date in the press ready for Monday' ... 'I did not go to the Hotel. I did not have anything to drink ... I noticed the carriages were missing at Quellyn Bridge and we set back at not more than 4 miles an hour ... I went into Caernarvon for Mr. Livesey and had two glasses or beer before going to him. I did not know that the driver and fireman had been to the hotel at Snowdon Ranger. I spoke to the driver at Quellyn Bridge; I was too frightened to notice what state he was in ... I know I should have gone back with my handlamp to look for the missing coaches instead of setting back ...'

John Williams, Fireman, had been cleaner and fireman almost since the line opened. He said they all went into the hotel for a glass of beer and were there about five minutes. 'I don't think any of us had more than two glasses' ... 'the stationmaster from Rhydd-ddu never does come down on that train on Saturday night' ... 'put my brake on a little harder than usual that night as I must admit we were running a little faster than usual'.

The inspector concluded that the two light carriages must have been jerked off the track by a sudden application of the break (sic) when the train was running at a high rate of speed to make up time lost at Snowdon Ranger, the Guard having disobeyed the rule about having the heavy brake carriage at the rear of the train. The second collision was caused by the carelessness of the driver and disregard of the rules shown by the guard; had the coupling merely broken and the coaches following the train downgrade at a high rate of speed, the collision would have been greatly magnified. The disregard for the truth on the part of the guard and the gross mismanagement of the train by all three servants was something about which it was hard to imagine anything more unsatisfactory . . . so Major Marindin summed up. He recommended that a better class of employee be engaged and though there was insufficient work for a stationmaster at Snowdon Ranger, had a man been there in that capacity, the accident would probably not have happened. He thought the conduct of the landlord at the hotel deserved the attention of the county's licensing authorities '. . . to have allowed the driver to get so drunk upon his premises that he was a serious risk to the public'. The driver was discharged from employment.

A less colourful accident occurred on 31 July 1906 when the 10.00 a.m. excursion train from Dinas to Rhydd-ddu hit a vagrant coal truck which had become detached from the 9.47 a.m. mixed train from Tryfan Junction which was running ahead. The coal truck ran back and impaled itself on the engine of the excursion near Nant Mill overbridge. This train was headed by a Single Fairlie engine. Due to the train running over a section where a speed restriction was always in force and the coal wagon having slowed on a more level grade, the impact was not too great. Engine buffer and coupling was broken and the cylinder covers cracked; headstock plate was bent, steam-chest covers cracked and rear beam and trailing buffer coupling bent. The rear engine bogie left the rails. The coal wagon survived with a broken end and coach No. 9, behind the engine had its end smashed in and some glass broken.

Driver Beaumont came on duty at 7.45 a.m. to work until 5.30 p.m. He took the excursion, giving the staff to Hughes, Waenfawr Stationmaster who gave him the Waenfawr to Snowdon staff without making any remark. After two minutes they set off and as he was slackening speed for the restriction, he got a 15 yards view of the oncoming wagon due to the curve and the bridge. He closed regulator and applied brakes before the impact.

Hughes had been at Waenfawr since the line opened. He was offered the mixed train from Tryfan at 9.57. He accepted it at once and received 'Train entering section' for it at once. Snowdon accepted it at 10.3 and it left Waenfawr at that time. Snowdon did not give him 'Train out of section' for it. He accepted the excursion at 10.19 a.m. and got 'Train entering section' at the same time. He offered it to Snowdon who accepted it at 10.25, at which time it left Waenfawr. He said that on that day, and the day previously, he did not receive 'Out of section' for the mixed train from Snowdon but worked to the timetable. On the latter day, at 10.37 a.m. he got a message from Idwal Owen, Snowdon stationmaster, saying, 'Not one of the trains arrived here yet' but could do nothing.

Owen had spent all his 17 years at Snowdon. He accepted the

mixed at 10.03 a.m. and got section for it at the same time. He was offered the excursion at 10.25 a.m. and accepted it, although the mixed train had not arrived. 'We never give "Train arrived" signal, as under our regulations this need not be sent unless special instructions are given for so doing.' The mixed train arrived a little after 11.00 a.m.

The inspector maintained that the collision was due to failure to carry out the ordinary rules for signalling by block telegraph. Owen should not have accepted the excursion when the mixed had not arrived. Worse, the mixed, on finding the wagon was missing short of Snowdon, had set back down-grade to find it! He had at least instructed the passengers to alight first. Apparently the centre buffer-coupler of the wagon had jerked undone and it was recommended that additional chains be fitted.

Personnel

(Extracted from Official Returns as available)

31 March 1884

General Manager, secretary.

Superintendent's Dept.: 8 station masters (also act as signalmen), 2 guards, 1 porter/messenger.

Goods Dept.: 1 inspector, 5 porter/messengers.

Loco Dept.: 2 mechanics, 2 drivers, 2 firemen, 2 labourers.

Engineers Dept: 1 ganger, 4 platelayers

1 December 1898

General Manager, secretary, 1 clerk.

4 station masters, 2 guards, 1 porter (boy), 2 labourers, 8 sheeter/loaders, 4 mechanics + 1 boy, 2 drivers, 2 firemen, 1 cleaner, 6 permanent way.

1911

Secretary, manager, 2 clerks.

7 station masters &/or clerks, 5 porter/ticket collectors, 1 traffic supt., 1 fitter, 3 Locomotive Dept. men, 5 footplate men, (permanent way not stated).

July 1886	Drivers and firemen working 12 hour day, occasionally 14 hour; 2 Station masters occasionally working 14 hours day; 'Examiner' did not work 12 hour day.	
1905	3 Passenger guards & brakesmen	(same the following July)
	5 Drivers & firemen	(6 the following July)
	1 Guard/1 driver/1 fireman work 6.20 a.m. to 8.30 p.m. with two hour rest at mid-day.	
Spring 1922	20 men employed; they were all paid by daily rate.	

			Weekly Gross £	s.	d.
D. O. Jones	Traffic superintendent		4	5	0
M. O. Jones	Booking clerk		1	10	9
M. Williams	at Snowdon station		1	2	6
T. Morris	General duties		not quoted		
T. R. Thomas	Foreman		3	16	0
Caradoc Jones, Thomas Ore, W. Ll. Jones, R. J. Roberts, J. Williams, W. G. Jones	Slate loaders	each	2	7	3
D. Lloyd Hughes	at Bryngwyn		2	9	4
W. H. Williams, John Williams	Drivers	each	2	10	1
A. E. Bailey	Fitter		3	3	9
Jeff Limerick	Ganger		2	11	8
S. Williams	Platelayer		2	5	9
D. Daniels	Carpenter		2	12	6
R. Williams	Blacksmith		2	12	6
W. Ll. Thomas	Striker			19	6

The gross fortnightly wage bill was £89 12*s.* 2*d.* and it was currently proposed to reduce wages by 15 per cent to enforce economies.

Relations with the Board of Trade

Having set down most of the available information concerning the Company, its financial problems, its physical difficulties regarding the finding of traffic, the working of trains and its instructions from higher authority to do certain work, it is possible to see more clearly the day-to-day worries of the Company.

The Board of Trade must have found the Company a grievous trial! This stemmed in part from lack of experience on the part of the railway staff and stubbornness on the part of the Railway Board; both of these stemmed from shortage of money. For instance, the constant succession of accidents, large and small, was religiously reported to the Board and from their records it is clear that in true Civil Service manner, each case was examined from the roots upwards, the ground being covered again and again to ascertain whether the Railway Company was working according to the previous instructions of the Board. The fact that these enquiries had probably been investigated a mere week or two previously by the Board made no difference—each case was opened without reference to earlier decisions and the facts quantified on the Report Forms . . . a policy of full employment at the Board.

The Railway was ever quoting that the Board had given it authority to run all trains as mixed trains save for one train in each direction per day. In 1890 it maintained that this authority was still in force and all trains were mixed. The Chairman of the Railway complained that they could not adhere to the Board's instruction of 30 December 1890 (refitting of continuous brakes, block signalling etc.) having insufficient time and money for the work. He asserted that working

One Engine in Steam should be sufficient to meet the Board's requirements, and that in any case, in his view, the instructions of 30 December 1890 did not apply to the Bryngwyn branch! There was no telephone or telegraph along the line and the Company's passenger tickets did not adhere to regulations by showing the fare on the face. The Chairman made his point and won the day; the Board allowed him another three years to carry out the work. General Hutchinson of the Board complained to the Railway, regarding One Engine in Steam working, that 'there was a somewhat lax observance of the regulations'.

The correspondence at first stated the Company's coaches weighed 4½ tons, later corrected to 6½ tons and added that at the time, there were no separate brake vans—an important point when later accidents were investigated.

By early 1891 the Company said that four large passenger vehicles contained a Guard's compartment and had brakes. (By 'large' they meant either bogie or six-wheel stock, and not the four-wheelers: Author.) A train usually consisted of one passenger vehicle and wagons, the passenger vehicle contained the brake and was used as a brake van and marshalled at the rear of the train. The Board of Trade 'saw red' at this and reminded the Company that if the coach was fitted with continuous brake it must be marshalled next to the engine or else the brake would be ineffective. In reply the Company said that if this were done, the vehicle would not be available as a brake van for a mixed train. This was typical of correspondence passing between the two parties and emphasises the gulf between them—deliberately dug by the Chairman no doubt, who was no fool. From time to time the Chairman wrote to emphasise the Company's poverty, that it could not afford brake vans, and of the 'unnecessary restrictions'.

The correspondence also shows that before the large coal wagons were built in the 1890s, the small mineral wagons were used for it and ran into the various slate quarries to serve the boilers of stationary winding engines etc.

The Board of Trade wanted more facts and were told (November 1890):

1. The grade was 1 in 47 between Dinas Junction and Tryfan Junction. After that 'there were comparatively easy grades' to the original terminal at Quellyn. The line then rose at 1 in 76 to Snowdon Ranger and to Glanrafon Siding at 1 in 79–290 there being 3½ chain curves between there and Rhydd-ddu. On the branch the grade was 1 in 41 to Rhostryfan, then 1 in 41 and 1 in

35 to Bryngwyn. (These figures do not exactly accord with the limited selection available from other sources.)

2. The six-wheeled stock was piped for brakes but could not be fitted with brake gear (presumably because the floors were too low). Two of these coaches had Guard's brake compartments; the third had not. The Chairman wanted 'to run these piped coaches in trains of fitted coaches, if permitted . . . without great expense the six-wheelers could not be fitted with continuous brake and could not be altered to bogie (the Board had made this suggestion) as the cost would be half that of building new stock.'

This last observation is dated 1 July 1892.

By 5 November 1894 the Company, through their Secretary, S. Tanner, reported that *all* stock now had continuous brakes 'except the three small four-wheeled coaches fitted with blow-through pipes'. It was hoped to fit brakes on them this year, if it could be afforded.

That same year the main line was fitted out with Wise's Staff and Tyer's One Wire Block Telegraphing System. A sealed Undertaking was given to the Board of Trade to the effect that the branch would be worked by One Engine in Steam or Two Engines Coupled Together which would carry the staff (29 November 1894).

Further details of composition of trains were available in 1896; one coach was used on the branch and two on the main line. This was sufficient except on Saturdays. Between Dinas and Tryfan Junction, passenger and goods trains now usually ran separately. The Company appeared to be unable to keep from under the Board of Trade's feet; the goods train derailment (listed earlier but without details) which occurred on 14 February 1896 was typical. The 4.50 p.m. Down from Bryngwyn had proceeded only 800 yards from that station when a wagon came off the track and brought five others off the line with it. The cause was a loose wheel on an axle—a common enough happening. This derailment happened at probably the nastiest section of the whole railway, being on the very steepest part of the branch involving a sharp curve and a road crossing on the level. The Board of Trade got its teeth into the case. After evasive replies by the Company, the Secretary at last admitted that the coach with the brake was at the rear of the train, and the whole weary investigation began again! The Chairman said that it was not necessary for the Company to marshall the passenger portion next to the engine 'the usual load on the branch was three or four passengers anyway, not more'. The train had consisted of *Beddgelert* leading chimney first, seven loaded slate wagons, a bogie brake composite carriage and four empty coal wagons at the rear, an assemblage which might be calculated to make the coolest Inspector at the Board hot under the collar. The Board advised the Company of its obligations in the most direct language. They also took up the matter of continuous brakes again and in April of the same year the Company reported that thirteen bogie or six-wheeled coaches had the brake but that the three small four-wheelers had not. From this may be deduced that the Cleminson carriages had had to be fitted (perhaps by mounting the brake cylinders Festiniog-fashion inside the coaches, on the floor). Under further pressure, Russell told the Board of Trade that he would rebuild or withdraw the four-wheelers by the end of 1897 and the Board wrote back that this was not good enough. The outcome was that it was agreed they be withdrawn from service on 31 March 1897 and there was instead 'a new large coach (fitted) in place thereof'. (The latter must have been a paper transfer only, or pure fiction to suit the case. No new coach was actually purchased in 1897).

Reference has been made to tip wagons and that the Company owned side tippers. There must also have been a number of privately-owned side tip wagons for iron-ore traffic because on 9 August 1902 such a wagon left the track and overturned, pulling two other wagons off the line with it. This was between Tryfan Junction and Waenfawr. Once again the Company was in dire trouble with the Board of Trade. The train's composition was now the first question the Board asked; once more it was a mixed train with the brake coach in the rear! This time it was Aitchison who was in trouble; he pleaded that he had only been appointed in 1898 and had been given nothing to guide him, 'matters being in a very mixed condition' and no instructions about train working. Instructions from the Official Receiver were verbal and vague, he hinted.

In December 1904 the B.O.T. wanted to know more about explosives carried on the line. It was carried in metallic cylinders in quarry owners' wagons and passed off the N.W.N.G. onto their branches. The Board wanted vans to be used instead of open wagons, but were told these were unsuited to the Bryngwyn Incline, where the winding drum at the summit would have fouled their roofs. Though the Company was adamant that this traffic was small, the Board imposed a limit of five wagons to be dealt with at a time if containing explosives—which was probably more than generous or likely to be the case. There were no Gunpowder Vans; all powder was loaded at Dinas Junction.

At this same period—the turn of the century—there was correspondence with the Board of Trade regarding the Company's proposals to extend to Beddgelert. The Board wanted an explanation of the choice of route and the cause of delays to the scheme. It was revealed that the route had been surveyed for electric traction (a feature which has been mentioned earlier in respect of the sharp curves and steep gradients at first proposed) and that one reason why the Company would have to seek an Extension of Time was that the main landowner involved was still away at the Boer War and had been unable to finalise matters with them.

Among the papers at the Public Record Office is a batch of material dealing with the proposed electrification of the N.W.N.G. and Portmadoc Beddgelert & South Snowdon Railway; this is dated 20 March 1905 from Messrs. W. A. and H. W. Harper, Consulting Engineers and for a 600 volts 3-phase system, two phases from overhead wires 27½ inches apart and 16 ft. 10 in. above the rails. The third phase was to come from the running rails. Steel sleepers were to be installed in tunnels and there were to be ten substations betwen Portmadoc and Caernarvon. The electric locomotives would have had an output of 90 B.H.P.

The N.W.N.G. Railways Company—a concluding note

The history of this railway has up to now, been neglected almost completely. This presentation is the result of working through every known source in the knowledge that many of the basic documents of the Company itself have not come to light; the section alone would have been worthy of a publication in its own right for without doubt, the Company was the most complex undertaking of any of the narrow gauge railways in the Kingdom. Whilst possibly the Festiniog Railway (because of its great age) holds a pioneering place in Welsh lines, the Narrow Gauge Railways Company has no equals when it comes to sheer qualities of survival against all odds.

Where else could be found a Company whose start was marred by the failure of a Director to lease the line as he was bound? Whose contractor began to ship the Company's materials overseas instead of laying them himself? Which was saddled by an extraordinary agreement to work with Fairlie engines? Which threw one Receiver off its back only to be saddled by another within weeks? Whose constant embarrassment was shortage of capital? Whose constant burden was a Chairman/Receiver who held all the aces but refused to play them? Whose rolling stock was hired from one who assigned his recognised credit from the Company, to a new company in which he himself was the largest shareholder and through which he became Receiver of the Railway? Whose traffic began to fall away almost from the time of opening, due to the end of the slate boom? Which held on to what it had, operating in similarly neglected conditions as

Directors (Quorum = Two)

	ORIGINAL	*1873*	*5/1875*	*3/1876*	*6/1879*	*1880*	*1891*	*1893*	*1900*	*1906*	*1911*	*1914*	*1919*	*1920*	*1922*
Sir Ll. Turner	X	X	X	X	X	X		X	X						
Livingston Thompson	X														
H. B. Roberts[10]	X														
Jas. H. Oliver	X	X	X	X											
T. Bolland		X	X												
C. Pearson[9]		X	X	X											
Sir R. W. M. L. Bulkeley (Senr)[1]		X	X												
Sir R. W. M. L. Bulkeley (Junr)				X											
C. Celyn		X													
Abr. Fitzgibbon		X	X	X	X	X									
C. Davidson			X	X											
— Hill				X											
Chaloner W. Chute[2]				X	X	X	X								
J. C. Russell[3]					X	X	X	X	X	X	X				
R. S. Guiness					X										
John Menzies						X									
Hugh Pugh						X									
Chas. Davison[4]							X	X	X	X					
Ernest E. Lake[5]										X	X	X			
Sir Jas. W. Slzumper[6]										X	X				
G. C. Aitchison[7]												X	X	X	
G. W. Fosbery												X	X	X	
Sir J. H. Stewart[8 11]															X
Henry J. Jack[8 11]															X
Evan R. Davies[11]															X
J. W. Cassells[8]															X
	4	7	7	8	5	6	3	3	3	4	3	3	2	2	4

1. Replaced by his son at death in June 1875. Prominent Anglesey etc. landowner.
2. Barrister and quarry owner.
3. Receiver N.W.N.G.R. Co.; Director, Barking Gas Co.; ex Moel Tryfan Rolling Stock Co. Ltd.
4. Firebrick manufr.; ship owner Connah's Quay; Director, Hawarden & Dist. W. W., Halkyn District Mines Drainage Co. etc.
5. Solicitor; later Chairman N.W.N.G.R. Co. (following Russell).
6. ex Director Vale of Rheidol; Civil Engineer to N.W.N.G. and V. of R.
7. Receiver N.W.N.G. also Secretary & Engineer; also connected P.B. & S.S., N.W.P. & T. Co. Ltd.
8. Director, Aluminium Corporation Ltd., Dolgarrog.
9. Owner of Moel Tryfan Slate Quarry until 1875.*
10. Owner of Braich Slate Quarry until 1881.
11. Became the new Board of Festiniog Railway, June 1921.

In the period 1919–1920, two Directors only (Aitchison and Fosbery). Both o. South Collingham, Newark on Trent; the former of Smith Woolley & Co., Land Agents, Civil Engineers etc. of South Collingham.

* Same family also owned: Coed Madoc Slate Co. Ltd., Nantlle (John Pearson until 1887; C. E. Pearson to 9/10/1896).

did the Talyllyn, until absorbed by an even more starry-eyed undertaking which far from bringing success, brought the end—which was sooner or later inevitable.

Needless to say, the loss carried forward from year to year, the fact that no dividends were ever paid on the ordinary shares and that vast monies were poured out and lost, is not peculiar to the North Wales Narrow Gauge. But against all the other odds, the Company stood out; it was certainly one of the few outstanding railways of any gauge which, until now has not received the attention which it certainly merits. One may feel for those who risked their capital and lost but what must it have been like to work every day for a railway whose accident record was astounding and yet every time fresh capital was raised, re-appeared in a bonanza of new equipment and now and again, a fresh engine, only to continue once more on the long path of declining fortunes?

Right from the start it was a compromise . . . only two parts of an eight-part dream achieved. On the purely physical side it may be commented that there were no tunnels, heavy earthworks or embankments despite a mountain location; there were no level crossings over public roads nor turntables. Even the sharpest curves had no check rails. But the worst feature was not so clearly perceived; the Railway had no money, and never made any. Or not enough!

	m.	ch.	*Original Name*	*Open Goods*	*Open Passenger*	*Closed Goods**	*Closed Passenger†*	*Changes in Title*
	0	0	Dinas	21/5/1877	15/8/1877	19/6/1937	29/9/1936	6/1891–9/1938 Dinas Junction
	2	15	Tryfan Junction	21/5/1877	15/8/1877	29/9/1936	29/9/1936	
	3	70	Waenfawr	21/5/1877	15/8/1877	19/6/1937	29/9/1936	
	4	65	Bettws Garmon	21/5/1877	15/8/1877	19/6/1937	29/9/1936	
	5	40	Salem Halt	—	31/7/1922[2]	—	29/9/1936	
	5	75[7]	Plas-y-Nant Halt	—	[4]	—	29/9/1936	
	7	35	Snowdon Ranger	1/6/1878	1/6/1878	19/6/1937	29/9/1936	By 7/1922 Quellyn Lake
	8	10	Glanrafon Halt	prob from c. 1878	[3]	19/6/1937	31/10/1916[1]	
	9	35	Rhydd-ddu[5]	14/5/1881	14/5/1881	19/6/1937	29/9/1936	By 4/1895 Snowdon; 7/1922 South Snowdon: 10/1922 Snowdon; 10/1923 South Snowdon.
Mileage from	0	70	Rhostryfan	21/5/1877	15/8/1877	19/6/1937	31/12/1913[6]	
Tryfan Junc.	2	35	Bryngwyn	21/5/1877	15/8/1877	19/6/1937	31/12/1913[6]	

* Date of last Goods Train.

† Tryfan Junction–Rhydd-ddu closed to passengers also between 31/10/1916 and 31/7/1922.

1 Not re-opened by Welsh Highland Railway.

2 Not strictly a N.W.N.G. Rlys. Halt, but may have been unofficially used before 31/7/1922. Regularised at this date.

3 Unofficial Halt for quarrymen and etc. probably from time of line opening.

4 No precise date available; thought to have been an unofficial stop before 7/1924 when regularised. Did not always appear in timetable.

5 Usual footnote '2½ miles from the summit of Snowdon' but mileage given as 3 miles (or) at various times; later '1½ hours for ascent and 1 hour for descent of Snowdon'.

6 Bryngwyn branch. It was intended to restore the passenger service in 1924 but this was never done.

7 Between 21/5/1877 and 1/6/1878 there was a temporary terminus at 'Quellan (Station for Beddgelert)', open for goods and passenger services at dates of preceding section of railway (6 m. 45 ch. from Dinas).

ANNUAL RETURNS

		1877	*1878*	*1879*	*1880*	*1881*	*1882*	*1883*	*1884*	*1885*	*1886*	*1887*	*1888*	*1889*	*1890*	*1891*
Cost hire r/stock		26	211	1947	922	—	—	—	—	—	—	—	—	—	—	—
Maintenance Works and Way		27	231	131	178	374	512	629	634	475	768	1150	932	978	1010	836
Loco Power		417	728	605	720	713	802	753	694	758	806	822	705	797	757	743
C and W maint. and repair		45	186	193	357	650	355	446	482	582	312	370	318	250	163	136
Traffic Expenses		543	880	618	664	719	715	769	783	903	858	851	866	794	729	759
Legal Expenses					29	50	20	20	25	18	—	23	—	15	45	232
Profit/Loss on Wkg.		4	(101)	(1893)	(592)	(74)	168	211	355	367	450	466	470	450	427	279
Merchandise	Tons	304	809	509	611	698	1054	647	720	594	670	1118	1053	973	739	726
Minerals	Tons	5418	9736	8707	10,809	13,306	13,847	15,598	16,573	17,544	18,803	21,752	17,957	17,763	17,179	15,677
Class	1st	359	598	540	531	462	496	433	409	431	362	282	325	385	400	331
	2nd	—	1712	435	848	953	1204	1073	1076	1012	1139	719	810	877	911	554
	3rd	18,518	47,294	26,905	31,859	30,042	29,074	29,210	32,266	32,577	33,114	33,944	34,501	37,752	36,362	27,606
* Season tickets													193	190	214	198
Pass. train miles		9388	Mixed from 1878													
Goods train miles		953														
Mixed train miles		10,341	27,118	23,479	27,953	28,341	31,405	28,621	31,456	31,703	31,102	30,912	30,685	30,697	30,466	30,573
Locos (own, not hire)		2	3	3	3	3	3	3	3	3	3	3	3	3	3	3
Carriages Total		5	8	8	8	8	8	8	8	8	8	8	8	8	8	10
Wagons Merchandise		114	120	120	120	120	120	120	120	120	120	120	120	120	120	147
Other Wagons																
Other Vehicles																

* Mainly Quarrymen's Seasons paid for by the quarry in certain cases.

		1892	*1893*	*1894*	*1895*	*1896*	*1897*	*1898*	*1899*	*1900*	*1901*	*1902*	*1903*	*1904*	*1905*	*1906*
Cost hire r/stock		—	—	—	—	—	—	—	—	—	—	—	—	—	—	—
Maintenance Works and Way		952	1024	841	1011	1370	1275	668	602	481	447	380	388	390	555	409
Loco Power		829	1050	1367	1435	843	949	1096	969	1006	1023	1079	763	814	840	875
C & W maint. and repair		263	369	337	444	636	479	359	390	428	342	596	353	268	428	307
Traffic expenses		710	827	944	895	926	955	952	913	891	891	853	911	862	883	862
Legal Expenses		20	26	26	32	30	14	—	10	12	14	26	15	29	14	17
Profit/Loss on Wkg.		348	502	455	502	704	615	971	899	586	563	570	419	700	483	532
Merchandise	Tons	842	756	1087	1352	1241	1363	1448	1328	1169	1168	1160	1060	1873	1754	885
Minerals	Tons	6112	17,055	17,093	18,210	21,626	23,057	23,020	21,791	20,519	20,436	25,234	20,238	17,950	180,30	18,126
Class	1st	473	643	642	699	726	716	659	494	572	585	660	491	582	805	489
	2nd	515	415	—	—	—	—	—	—	—	—	—	—	—	—	—
	3rd	38,550	54,162	51,305	55,072	52,069	49,709	45,626	53,688	35,878	37,917	37,891	37,233	42,853	51,451	48,713
* Season tickets		220	328	351	331	362	312	309	13,575	4949	806	7	15	9	8	8
Pass. train miles																
Goods train miles																
Mixed train miles		30,747	31,645	33,206	32,637	32,631	30,228	30,636	32,714	31,363	29,314	28,631	27,569	28,011	31,632	28,798
Locos (own, not hire)		3	3	3	3	3	3	3	3	3	3	3	3	3	3	3
Carriages																
Total		10	12	16†	16	16	16	16	16	16	16	16	16	16	16	16
Wagons Merchandise		147	134	137	137	145	147	148	148	148	147	147	147	147	147	147
Other Wagons																
Other Vehicles												1	1	1	1	1

		1907	*1908*	*1909*	*1910*	*1911*	*1912*	*1913*	*1919*	*1920*	*1921*	
Cost hire r/stock		—	—	—	—	—	—	—	—	—	—	No Returns
Maint. Works and Way		432	350	391	413	353	299	333	—	—	—	
Loco Power		972	1022	884	842	925	687	735	—	—	—	
C & W maint. and repair		353	339	372	293	286	87	225	—	—	—	
Traffic Expenses		912	894	853	782	800	678	675	—	—	—	
Legal Expenses		14	15	67	27	24	43	27	—	—	—	
Profit/Loss on Wkg.		535	466	177	(10)	(165)	220	(205)	(62)	(246)	(1208)‡	
Merchandise	Tons	799	532	553	535	797	827	1784	4203	2550	185	Tons General Merchandise
								4353	—	—	—	Coal
Minerals	Tons	18,235	17,724	18,523	16,915	14,364	14,422	7017	7297	7588	7320	Other Minerals
Class	1st	497	347	343	245	285	174	226	Closed to Passengers			
	2nd	—	—	—	—	—	—	—				
	3rd	44,141	41,394	43,632	40,549	40,351	23,419	23,399				
* Season tickets		24	25	3	1	1	1	2				
Pass. train miles												
Goods train miles									Goods	Goods	Goods	
Mixed train miles		30,072	31,565	31,907	27,423	27,471	18,516	18,800	7987	7054	5330	
Locos (own, not hire)		3	1	4	4	4	4	3	2	2	2	
Carriages				8	8	8	8	8	8	8	8	Carriages of uniform class
				5	5	5	5	5	5	5	5	Carriages of composite class
Total		16	16	13	13	13	13	13	13	13	13	
Wagons Merchandise		143	143	118	117	117	92	98	107	107	95	= 82 Opens + 13 Mineral Merchandise and Mineral wagons (slate, etc.)
Other Wagons		4	4	4	4	4	12	—	34	39	18	Rail and Timber trucks
Other Vehicles		1	1	1	1	1	1	29	1	—	—	Miscellaneous Wagons
								4	—	—	—	Service Vehicles

* Mainly Quarrymen's Seasons paid for by the quarry in certain cases.
† 13 fitted continuous brake and 'three exceptionally small coaches' (these are piped only).
‡ Debit carried forward 1921 £58,919.

PORTMADOC BEDDGELERT & SOUTH SNOWDON RAILWAY

(*Gauge* 1 ft. 11½ in.)

Incorporated by Act: 1 Edward VII chap. 262 of 17 August 1901 (following Agreement of 18 March 1901 with Portmadoc, Croesor & Beddgelert Tram Railway Co. for sale to new undertaking and dissolution of P.C. & B.T.R. Co.).

Act: 4 Edward VII Ed. Cap. 194 of 15 August 1904. Arrangements with N.W.N.G. Railways and extensions in Caernarvon district.

The above two Acts to be treated as one in future.

Agreement: of 26 August 1904 with N.W.N.G. Railways. Powers of the N.W.N.G. Railways Order.
of 3 November 1900 (extension to Beddgelert) to pass to P.B. & S.S.R. by means of:

Light Railway Order: of 24 October 1906. Powers to build lapsed 24 October 1909.

Light Railway Order: of 8 July 1908. Extensions to Caernarvon.

Light Railway Order: of 27 July 1908. P.B. & S.S.R. becomes Light Railway (application of November 1904 for Light Railway was unsuccesful).

Opened: Partially constructed section built between 1906 and 1910 unofficially in use before 1911 for timber etc. purposes. Total length partially constructed at this time, 4 m. 60 ch.
Never officially opened, nor extended in operational length.

Closed: Acquired by Welsh Highland Railway (Light Railway) Co. 1 January 1922 as part of new system.

Registered Office: Llanberis (1914). 4 Broad Street Place, London, E.C.3 and Clark Street, Dolgarrog (1919)—offices of N. Wales Power & Electric Traction Co.

Length: 12 m. 45 ch. authorised. 4 m. 60 ch. built.

Capital: See text, p. 00.

The Official Returns of 1919 (last available) state that '4 m. 60 ch. is finished and being worked by horse traction: construction is at present in abeyance'.

Under the terms of the 17 August 1901 P.B. & S.S. Act, it is convenient to deal with the position of the Portmadoc, Croesor & Beddgelert Tram Railway Co. first, as being the only portion of the scheme where some tangible evidence of railway (strictly, tramway) existed. The 18 March 1901 agreement between three parties, namely, the P.C. & B.T.R. Co., H. W. A. Littledale (who had succeeded to the £8,000 mortgage) and Messrs. George Edward Heyl Dia and William John Glover (together) provided for the sale of the undertaking to the P.B. & S.S.R. for £10,000. Russell was not included in the arrangements as he was to be paid off. It was said that 'there had never been any passenger traffic over the railways of the Croesor Co. and the present condition and state of repair thereof are not such as to justify or allow the conveyance of passengers thereon and it is expedient that the said railway should be repaired and improved as by this Act provided'. Under sections 6, 7, and 8, the Croesor undertaking was acquired, dissolved and transferred in that order!

Working agreements between the P.B. & S.S. and N.W.N.G. Railways Co., Cambrian, Festiniog and Snowdon Mountain Tramroad Co. were envisaged.

The agreement for the purchase of the Portmadoc, Croesor & Beddgelert Tram Railway Co. was to be completed within twelve months of the Act, and this being done, the Company would be dissolved. A Receiver was appointed to wind up its affairs—currently he was John Edward Jones. As to working over the Cambrian crossing, the Cambrian was to have control of this . . . an important factor in later years.

The new Company was also given powers as a supplier of electrical power, a feature which was later to link the later Welsh Highland Railway with some curious bed-fellows. This involved the building of dams and generating stations, and power to negotiate with local authorities for the supply of electric power.

George Edward Heyl Dia, William John Glover and Samuel Oppenheim were the first-named subscribers and two railways were to be built:

Railway No. 1. 5 fur. 1 ch. long from the existing Portmadoc, Croesor & Beddgelert Tram Railway Co. at Penymount to a point on the bed of the old Gorseddau Railway 87 ft. to the east of the frontage of the Queen's Hotel, Portmadoc.

Railway No. 2. 7 m. 1 fur. 4 ch. 15 yd. long commencing with junction of Portmadoc, Croesor & Beddgelert Tram Railway Co. at a point 3 m. 4 fur. from its commencement to terminate in a field at Bwlch Mwyalchen farm on the north bank of the Glaslyn river at the point of the Llyn Gwynant outlet.

The gauge was 1 ft. 11½ in. with powers to increase to standard gauge. Powers for three years were obtained to purchase lands etc., and seven years for the completion of the line. As regards the one proposed tunnel in the Aberglaslyn Pass, this was to be restricted in length and no tipping of rubbish was to be allowed in the Pass or on the Glaslyn banks, though permission might be given for additional tunnels and tipping availability. Festiniog merchandise rates were to apply. If a junction was made with that Railway, a signal box, points etc., would be provided at the expense of the promoters.

Separate regulations applied to the electrical side of the business, and accounts were to be kept apart.

As to the Portmadoc, Croesor & Beddgelert Tram Railway Co.'s powers to build an extension to Borth-y-gest (never exercised), the plans did in fact propose an electrified single line with three chain passing loops extending from Black Rock Sands, near Criccieth, extending westwards through Morfa Bychan, round Borth Bay and, following the proposed extension of the Portmadoc & Croesor Railway (Act 1865) would have tunnelled through the headland to make end-on junction with the original Croesor Tramway. The line would have used the existing Croesor Tramway to the junction where a new line to Beddgelert via Aberglaslyn would have branched off. Then following almost exactly the abandoned route of the North Wales Narrow Gauge Railways General Undertaking (see p. 000) it would, however, have reached Llyn Gwynant by keeping south of Llyn Dinas to its terminal on the east shore of Llyn Gwynant. There was to be an overhead power line thence to Nant Gwynant Generating Station.

Like the Portmadoc, Beddgelert & Rhydd-ddu scheme of 1898, a branch from north of the Beddgelert Siding (Railway No. 1) to terminate on the course of the old Gorseddau Railway, was empowered.

The Engineers were Messrs. Bennett & Ward Thomas, and A. M. Fowler. Though it would have been advantageous to apply for a Light Railway Order, the inclusion of electrical works, for which an Act of Parliament was required, ruled this out.

The Festiniog Railway, fearful for the intrusion of the new line on the preserve at Portmadoc, were given little or no time to consider the proposition in full. To protect their interests, they lodged an objection which resulted in the clauses provided to protect them. This was fortunate, for the Festiniog was in no position to pay further expense at this time; even the Directors' salary cheques for the month of February 1901 had been sent out with the request that they be not presented for payment until the month end and so avoid over-drawing on the bank!

The electrical work in connection with the Act was, over a period of time and with additional time permitted, carried out. Nothing was done about the railway, but the scheme has been presented in some detail because almost every aspect of it was part of the foundation for a later scheme. We may envisage the railway, if built, as similar in conception to the Manx Electric Railway.

On 15 August 1904 (the same date as another Act affecting the Portmadoc, Beddgelert & South Snowdon Railway, about to be described) the North Wales Electric Power Act was passed. This transferred the authority to build Power Stations, dams, etc., from the railway to a new body, and left the railway company entirely as a transport undertaking.

To give additional time for the completion of the above work, the Company obtained another Act (15 August 1904) with Harper Bros., Consultants, and Sir Douglas Fox & Partners as Engineers. Three new lines were to be built; all in the County of Caernarvon. A Bristol contractor was said to be at work in 1904.

Railway No. 1. 2 m. 3 fur. 9 ch. long, from a junction with the North Wales Narrow Gauge Railways 70 yards south of the Dinas Junction station Goods Shed to terminate on the west bank of the Afon Seiont (the river in Caernarvon town) approximately opposite the town Gas Works—which lay on the east bank of the river.

Railway No. 2. 3 fur. 5½ ch. long being an extension from the terminus of Railway No. 1, involving a crossing of the river and terminating on the quays northeast of the river Seiont.

A 'Railway No. 3' is shown in the Plans but not covered by the Act, which would have continued along the west bank of the Seiont to a point opposite the east bank terminal.

The really interesting feature of this Act was the clear intention of the promoters. For the first time it might be seen that to all intents and purposes, the North Wales Narrow Gauge Railways and the Portmadoc, Beddgelert & South Snowdon Railway were soon to merge if not into one undertaking, certainly under one management. How otherwise did the Portmadoc, Beddgelert & South Snowdon Railway (which after all at this stage was a horse tramway between Portmadoc and Croesor) intend to reach Caernarvon? At this time one might only conjecture, for the North Wales Narrow Gauge Railways held the key to the section between Beddgelert and South Snowdon and there were no plans at all for a railway to cross the Glaslyn and link the Portmadoc, Beddgelert & South Snowdon Railway with the North Wales Narrow Gauge Railways' Beddgelert Extension. The route between South Snowdon and Dinas Junction was the N.W.N.G. Railways' main line and clearly that Company was now willing to permit the Portmadoc, Beddgelert & South Snowdon to extend on its behalf into Caernarvon itself. This was a desirable and positive goal, for its present terminus at Dinas Junction involved interchange of passengers and freight—not to mention being at the behest of the London & North Western Railway—and was seen to be but a temporary and embarrassing arrangement for which a speedy remedy was sought.

Railway No. 1 made much use of the abandoned course of the former Nantlle Railway which, upon becoming part of the Caernarvonshire Railway had gone into the Euston Empire. Parts of its sinuous course were abandoned when an improved site was found. Even the old tunnel at Coed Helen would be put to use. There was a nominal junction between this line and Railway No. 2 in the woodlands on the steep west bank of the river; here Railway No. 2 branched off eastwards to cross the river on the same site of a bridge as had been used by the Nantlle Railway but which had by then been demolished. Railway No. 3 (shown on the Plans but not empowered in the Act) would have continued for about 3 furlongs along the west bank. Once across the river, Railway No. 2 would have passed the Gas Work's entrance, run up alongside the L.N.W.R.'s branch down on to the quays and passed to a terminus beneath the Castle walls.

Five years were allowed for the completion of the work and a considerable portion of the Act was given over to clauses protecting the L.N.W.R.'s line between Caernarvon and Dinas Junction—as would be expected! Section 24 permits the Portmadoc, Beddgelert & South Snowdon and North Wales Narrow Gauge companies to enter into fully integral working agreements respecting the proposed and all existing lines. Although no work was done under this Act, it laid the foundations for closer relationships between the two companies, first to be revealed in the North Wales Narrow Gauge Railways Light Railway Order of 6 June 1905.

Following an Agreement between the North Wales Narrow Gauge Railways and the Portmadoc, Beddgelert & South Snowdon Railway dated 26 August 1904—and so rapidly following on the Act just discussed—the powers given to the North Wales Narrow Gauge Railways Company under a Light Railway Order of 3 November 1900 were given to the Portmadoc, Beddgelert & South Snowdon Railway. This Agreement was ratified by a Light Railway Order dated 24 October 1906 which allowed three years for completion of the work specified. The project in question was the extension of the North Wales Narrow Gauge Railways' line from its unsatisfactory terminus at Rhydd-ddu southwards to Beddgelert, where junction could be made with the new railway intended to be built northwards off the old Croesor Tramway from Portmadoc. This was known as the 'Beddgelert Extension'.

It is convenient to mention this extension here as well as under the title of the North Wales Narrow Gauge Railways; in the period between November 1900 and October 1906 owing to shortage of funds, very little had been done on the extension by the North Wales Company. In view of the many schemes for railways in the area about which *nothing* was ever done, it is surprising to record that at least a minimal amount of work took place. This was mainly immediately north of Beddgelert and to the Portmadoc, Beddgelert & South Snowdon Engineers (Sir Douglas Fox & Partners) was clearly of unsuitable grade and curve, as the October 1906 Order permitted the Portmadoc, Beddgelert & South Snowdon Railway to abandon certain unfinished work of the North Wales Narrow Gauge Railways. More of tactical importance was authority to make a new line from the Goat Hotel, Beddgelert (extending from the N.W.N.G. Extension 6 furlongs 1 chain) to pass behind the south-west corner of the Hotel, pass south of Gelert's Grave and make end-on junction with the Portmadoc, Beddgelert & South Snowdon's Railway of its Act of 17 August 1901, on the east bank of the River Glaslyn and 350 yards south of Sygyn Terrace, Beddgelert. The Order gave full working agreement with the North Wales Narrow Gauge Railways and gave Caernarvonshire County Council the right to advance capital.

No work had been done on the P.B. & S.S.R.'s line of 17 August 1901, but nevertheless the work done under the aforementioned Order was almost entirely based on Beddgelert, which became one centre for activities. To the north the line was re-surveyed and a number of sharp curves on stiff gradients were eased to provide a better start for northbound trains from Beddgelert (under the later Welsh Highland Order, the same length of line was abandoned almost completely in favour of a longer and more sinuous course involving heavier earthworks but easing curves and grade still more.) To the south, the cutting and tunnel behind the Goat Hotel was completed, and a stone overbridge crossing the Beddgelert-Portmadoc road was made. In the field between this bridge and the Glaslyn, the abutments for an occupation bridge beneath the line, and stone culverting to take the Glaslyn's flood water away, were built. Some of this work has recently been removed but it had remained unfinished and unused for over sixty years.

Some interesting documents on this subject survive.* These refer, *inter alia*, to the Light Railway Commissioners' Enquiry at Beddgelert on 3 February 1904 re the Extension (or 'Beddgelert Light Railway' as they refer to it). From this it is clear that though Mr. W. A. Harper was dubbed 'Engineer' to the scheme, he continued to rely on Randall Casson (solicitor of Breese, Jones & Casson, Portmadoc) to

* C.C.R.O.: Box 12: Breese, Jones & Casson Collection.

act for him. Harper and Fox both agreed the proposed course under the P.B. & S.S. Act of 17 August 1901 was impossible and some work on the site, working far into the night, produced detail alterations in time for the February 1904 Enquiry. The Lord Lieutenant of the County (Greaves) was involved and the National Trust was concerned for conservation of the Aberglaslyn Pass. The new idea was for a line '200 yd. from the Goat Hotel, Beddgelert, round a corner and out of sight of the hotel windows' which would forestall the proprietor's early opposition to the new railway. (This idea paved the way for the October 1906 Order just mentioned.) So little idea had some correspondents involved—who should have known better—that they imagined the junction between a line from Beddgelert and a line up to Llyn Gwynant would meet (on paper at least) inside the Aberglaslyn Tunnel.

A contractor's railway was laid from the road overbridge south of Beddgelert (just described) to a point on the formation at Tyn-y-coed. Some formation had been completed between there and Rhydd-ddu when powers lapsed (under the P.B. & S.S. Order of 1906) on 24 October 1909.

The contractor's track was the T rail and chair used on the Croesor and elsewhere. A clue as to the source might be found in the abandonment and lifting of the Gorseddau line during the 1890s, which would explain the availability of such material, possibly from a local scrap dealer. Certainly there were flooded sections of abandoned course with this track in them still to be seen during the 1960s.

All the foregoing was done under the auspices of the 1906 Order, which, to give it its full title, was known as The Portmadoc, Beddgelert & South Snowdon Railway (Beddgelert Light Railway Extension) Order, 1906. From the Order itself it may be learned that North Wales Narrow Gauge Railways powers to build the Extension had lapsed on 3 August 1903; three years were now permitted to complete the intended new programme.

The Railway No. 1 of the North Wales Narrow Gauge Railways 'Beddgelert Light Railway Extension' Order of 1900, i.e. that part lying between its terminal and the junction with Railway No. 1, was to be abandoned.

The bridge south of Beddgelert was to be of stone and the surrounding embankments etc. were to be planted out with trees, shrubs etc. All this was duly done. An interesting clause was that no station was to be built within a mile of the Goat Hotel except for one which would have been near the junction with the proposed Llyn Dinas line on the *east* bank of the Glaslyn, where there might be 'a platform for passenger traffic only'. Objections from the hotel must have been completely overcome when the Welsh Highland scheme was prepared, for the Beddgelert station was only a little distance from the hotel yard!

The gauge was to be the usual 1 ft. 11½ in. and steam or electric power was permitted.

Work under the Order tended to be carried out in a desultory fashion and during this somewhat spasmodic progress, some more statutory progress was accomplished in the shape of two more Orders during 1908, neither of which was destined to make any visible difference to the actual construction or to be seen in the field!

It remains to look briefly at the Orders just mentioned. The second was dated 27 July 1908, and gave authority to work the Portmadoc, Beddgelert & South Snowdon Railway schemes of its Acts of 1901 and 1904 as Light Railways; (it was only the second Order of that year, a matter of nineteen days, and as it concerns the immediately previous Orders, it may be taken out of date order). The real purpose was to—once more—give authority to the P.B. & S.S.R. to construct new railways which had earlier been granted to other undertakings within the same parentage. In this case the North Wales Power & Traction Co. Ltd. had in November 1903 applied for and obtained a Light Railway Order to build the Railways Nos. 1 & 2 about to be described.* They would have made junction with the empowered P.B. & S.S.R.'s new railways near Beddgelert and underline the extraordinary attractions of a narrow gauge line between Beddgelert and Bettws-y-coed. Such a line had first been planned by the North Wales Narrow Gauge Railways but had never materialised, even though it was part of something much longer. Now, thirty-six years later, a 'Bettws Application' (as it was called) still held its magnetism. The North Wales Power & Traction Co. Ltd.'s powers had lapsed on 3 August 1907 and by this Order, the Portmadoc, Beddgelert & South Snowdon Railway took over. Though never built, the railway is well worth description.

Railway No. 1 (7 m. 2 fur. 75 ch.) from an end-on junction with the terminus of the 1901 line, along the south-east shore of Llyn Gwynant in a northerly direction parallel to and on the west side of the Beddgelert road.

The line would have tunnelled under this road near the Pen-y-gwryd Hotel, and then swung north-east, running south of the same road to enter Capel Curig from the north-west.

* Management, Secretariat and Registered Office was identical with that of the Portmadoc, Beddgelert & South Snowdon Railway Company.

Railway No. 2 (5 m. 6 fur. 5.95 ch.) from an end-on junction with Railway No. 1 and by tunnel under land behind the Royal Hotel, Capel Curig, the property of Lord Penrhyn (the tunnel not to exceed 350 yd. length). Thence over the Nant-y-gwryd river, south-east then north-east parallel to the Beddgelert road. Then crossing the same road and the Llugwy River to enter Bettws from the north-west and north of the same road.

Five years were given for completion, and an interesting feature in view of environmental awareness in the present day, is the new protection given to the National Trust (which appears for the first time) in that overhead structures etc. in the Aberglaslyn Pass should be of such colour as the Lord Lieutenant might direct, and that all insulators must be 'of a brown colour'. All walls etc. were to have broken tops and be planted out where possible, as must be crevices etc. in retaining walls. Lord Penrhyn's property around Capel Curig was similarly guarded and he had the right to have a station provided for this hotel there on its east side, and to have a private path between the two premises. The Earl of Ancaster too (owner of the Gwydr Estate) was to have a Goods Station built for him 1 m. 4 fur. from the commencement of Railway No. 2 and he too, had the right to plant trees, saplings etc. along with Lord Penrhyn. J. W. Wyatt's land alongside Llyn Gwynant was protected by having the line laid as near as possible to the public road; all boathouses destroyed had to be replaced. In short, public awareness of amenity values were extensively covered by the Order and showed very advanced thinking. The Swallow Falls, Miners' Bridge, banks of the Llugwy, position of stations not already mentioned, the design and construction of bridges, the penalties for erecting buildings of any kind between certain points on the line, the erection of rustic screen walls to hide trains passing from the eyes of those 'standing on the southern bank of the River Llugwy were among the ordinary and extraordinary details . . . in fact, the Company were to be considerably restricted by the Order's conditions which alone might have been sufficient to deter the promoters! As if this was not enough, there was a financial penalty clause for failure to complete by date and for every day thereafter. Harper Bros. were again the Engineers.

Finally, the Order of 8 July 1908 (Light Railway Extension at Caernarvon) began by giving power to abandon Railway No. 2 of the 15 August 1904 Act regarding a railway in Caernarvon (crossing the Seiont and ending on the east quay) and of course, not built.

Instead, two lines were to be constructed viz:

Railway No. 1 (3 fur. 4 ch.) from a junction with the proposed line between Dinas and Caernarvon (authorised by the 1904 Act) at a point 2 m. 58 ch. north of Dinas, thence north and west along St. Helen's Road, Caernarvon, to end 103 yds. north of the Harbour Office on the east quayside.

Railway No. 2 (6 ch.) from an end-on junction with Railway No. 1, thence west and ending at a point 42 ft. north-east of the Slate Quay at Aber Ferry, Caernarvon harbour.

Three years were permitted for completion. As the line would have been virtually a street tramway along St. Helen's Road and the Quays, a speed limit of 8 m.p.h. was imposed. Another curious imposition was that the Company must 'dig up and remove the pig market of the Corporation . . . and at their own expense . . . relay the same in such other part of the Borough. . . .' Eight pounds a year were to be charged for upkeep of St. Helen's Road.

The L.N.W.R.'s harbour lines would have to be crossed on the level and De Winton's works (the firm was by then in liquidation) would have had to have temporary road access made to them during the line's construction.

No work was done under the Order and the powers lapsed. With the coming of the First War, the only working line in the district which had bearing on these schemes—the North Wales Narrow Gauge line—was hard hit; there was but little passenger traffic, the tourist traffic was greatly reduced, and the system was whittled down eventually to being a slate carrier of much diminished tonnages. Ultimately, under the provisional title of 'The Portmadoc, Beddgelert & South Snowdon Railway (Light Railway) and The North Wales Narrow Gauge Railways (Light Railways) Revival and Transfer of Powers Order', an application was made to the Light Railway Commissioners in 1914, but consideration had to be postponed. A Public Enquiry was held by the Commissioners in the County Hall, Caernarvon on 18 October 1921. This event led to the marriage of the North Wales Narrow Gauge Railways to the Portmadoc, Beddgelert & South Snowdon Railway and the ultimate birth of their sole offspring, the Welsh Highland Railway. However, to return to the pre-war years: the capital status of the undertaking changed continuously as a result of Orders giving powers previously owned by other companies. It is no small wonder that, bemused by their position, the Company wrote to the Commissioners on 26 May 1909 for clarification. They stated that share capital and borrowing powers given by the Acts of 1901 and 1904, and the Order of 1906, were amended by the Order of 1908. This resulted in a share capital of £100,000 with borrowing powers for the same amount for a railway between Portmadoc and Rhydd-ddu via Beddgelert and including a line between Dinas and Caernarvon. For the authorised railway between Beddgelert and Bettws-y-coed additional amounts were sanctioned: viz.: Capital £90,000 and borrowing powers £30,000.

From the Commissioners' reply it was clear that to remedy their financial embarrassment, the Company was considering an application for a Treasury Grant, for which they were told they would have to enter into a contract for the completion and working of their lines with an existing railway. The Commissioners felt that in view of the impoverished state of the North Wales Narrow Gauge Railways, the Treasury would hardly accept that Company to be 'an existing railway', and a free grant would not necessarily guarantee that the North Wales Narrow Gauge Railways could complete the unfinished portions of the authorised Portmadoc, Beddgelert & South Snowdon Railway. Rather, the Commissioners felt, it would be preferable to make arrangements with the Cambrian or L.N.W.R. companies! It might too be acceptable if arrangements were made with the North Wales Power & Traction Co. Ltd., who would take up share capital under a different section of the Light Railways Act. Under the Act of 1901 and the Order of 1906, local councils were permitted to advance money to a total of £32,000. Additionally, under the Order of 1908 the Caernarvon County Council was permitted to advance a further £10,000, but under a resolution of that Council this second advance was allocated to the proposed line from Beddgelert to Bettws-y-coed! As the Portmadoc, Beddgelert & South Snowdon Railway was only interested in completing its partially constructed Portmadoc–Rhydd-ddu section, this was not the sort of reply to give them much-needed encouragement; worse, the final paragraph of the Commissioners' reply reminded them that five months hence, on 24 October 1909, the period for completion of the Beddgelert–Rhydd-ddu section would expire.

This skirmishing around by the Company, and the enquiries it was making for assistance from various sources, did not reveal what had been happening in the background. To find out why work finally faltered and stopped, and how the remains of the construction work and the unused powers of the various companies interwoven in the affray were put to further use, the confidential documents of an Investigation Committee which kept the idea alive, must be consulted. The facts were not made public at the time. The summary is presented in the simplest way:

1. The Portmadoc, Beddgelert & South Snowdon Railway was financed by the North Wales Power & Traction Co. The Power

Co. were the only shareholders in the Railway Co. Preliminary enquiries to the Manager of the P.B. & S.S. in November 1907 by Johnathan Davies (of Davies Bros., slate merchants, Pormadoc, and destined to become the Chairman of the Investigation Committee) revealed that 'the P.B. & S.S. was trying to complete the line but the position of the money market . . . is a serious obstacle'.

2. The P.B. & S.S. was a front; the Power Co. did in fact obtain its Acts, its Powers, made all its purchases and completed construction. All Railway expenses were met by the Power Co. until such time as the Board of Trade passed the Railway for traffic, when the Power Co. would receive payment in shares. A list of Power Co. expenses was tendered up to 18 February 1909.
3. By early 1909 the Power Co. was unable to finance the Railway Co. any further. In the private opinion of Aitchison (Manager of the P.B. & S.S.) the Power Co. had used its assets wastefully, and it was no wonder there was a shortage of money.
4. The Power Co. was now looking round for means of financing the completion of the P.B. & S.S. without having to raise the money itself. It would however co-operate with others who might find the capital to finish the work.
5. Only the basic fact of inability to finance completion was then made known publicly by the Power Co. Detail was unknown, even to Aitchison. In consequence several local authorities (among them the Caernarvon Harbour Trustees, the Caernarvon County Council, and other local bodies) had formed a Special Committee to investigate the matter. This Committee ultimately entitled itself the 'Portmadoc Beddgelert & Caernarvon Light Railway Committee' (or Joint or Investigation Committee) being made up of various representatives of interested parties.
6. The first meeting was in Portmadoc during February 1909, the unfinished work being known as the 'Beddgelert Railway'. The meeting was followed by a conference on 25 February 'to consider the affairs of the Beddgelert Railway'. By now, 'the Railway' was understood by all to mean not only the P.B. & S.S. link between Beddgelert and the Croesor tramway, but Beddgelert to Rhydd-ddu and further, a line from Dinas Junction to Caernarvon.
7. The physical position of the P.B. & S.S. in the February was given by Aitchison :

> Between Croesor Junction and the south end of the Aberglaslyn tunnel all work, fencing and drainage had been done.

> No rails or ballast had been laid. No bridges were in, but the latter had been delivered and were lying at Portmadoc. The south end of the long tunnel was finished. The north half required completion. From the north tunnel end to the east bank bridge abutment opposite Beddgelert the formation was complete. The other abutment was ready and the bridge also lay at Portmadoc. The link from there to Beddgelert station was done 'except for a big bank which will pass across the meadow, the material for which will have to come from a point between Beddgelert and Rhydd-ddu'. The line could be opened 'at little cost as far as Nantmor'.

A lot of materials lay on the site; a small amount had been disposed of.

8. Aitchison stressed, for the information of the Committee, that there was no connection between the P.B. & S.S. and N.W.N.G. concerns, save that agreement was there for the N.W.N.G. to work the P.B. & S.S. lines when open, with N.W.N.G. stock etc.
9. Aitchison's position was tenuous. He was acting for the N.W.N.G., P.B. & S.S. and Power Companies as Manager and Engineer. The Power Co. had asked him to negotiate a means to complete the P.B. & S.S. Aitchison's involvement had reached a stage where he was at odds with his employers, he was likely to lose his position with the P.B. & S.S. as they were cutting down on expenses, and he might have to take the Power Co. to court on certain matters. Therefore if he attended the Committee by invitation, it would be in a private capacity as a Civil Engineer only.

There followed years of slow and painful negotiation to see what might be done. The local authorities were each hesitant to commit themselves and waited to see who would take initiative. Each had an axe to grind, and it was not the same axe. Authorities interested in keeping full employment in slate quarries in the Croesor Valley, for instance, were not especially worried about the link to Beddgelert; the P.B. & S.S. had bought land in anticipation of opening the extension from Dinas to Caernarvon, but powers had lapsed—The Harbour Trustees were anxious to see this scheme revived and the land bought at the harbour-side put to use. This would not interest the ratepayers in Croesor. Davies' job as Chairman was unenviable.

By 1911 the preparations were as complete as they could be. It seemed impossible to find dates when all the local representatives could meet together and neither Portmadoc nor Caernarvon suited some as a venue. Prominent industrialists and landowners already had their hands full. However, in January 1912, a Joint Committee meeting made some progress. Noel Humphreys was by then the 'Secretary pro tem' of the P.B. & S.S. and attended as the representative of that Railway and the Power Co. He had no connection with the N.W.N.G. He stated his principals were ready to sell their interests for cash and emphasised that Aitchison's earlier recommendation that they be sold for shares in a new concern was no longer acceptable. In order to qualify for a Treasury Loan under the Light Railway Act, they had got the L.N.W.R. to agree to construct, finish and work the line so long as it did not have to finance it. Consultations with Frank Ree, the L.N.W.R. General Manager, had dragged on owing to his ill health, hence delay in calling a meeting. The P.B. & S.S. offered for sale :

1. Land at Caernarvon Harbour.
2. The Croesor Railway (cost £10,000) which had been 'relaid and remetalled and was now being worked by horse traffic'.
3. The work done on the line and fencing.
4. The unused Orders for a line Beddgelert–Rhydd-ddu and Portmadoc–Beddgelert still in force (as they would be until 1913, but the extension to Caernarvon's powers had lapsed).

At the meeting it was suggested that the G.W.R. should take over both Festiniog and North Wales Narrow Gauge lines and complete the link. The first step, however, was for the Committee to open negotiations with J. C. Russell who, as Receiver of the North Wales Narrow Gauge, was virtually the only person who might decree one way or another. Meanwhile Humphreys added that rails and bridge materials on site in 1908 had subsequently been disposed of.

The stumbling block now proved to be Russell, who would not come to terms. This impasse was cleared by his death in late 1911, but the news that Aitchison would become Receiver from 15 January 1912 was not available to the meeting of that month and Humphreys had to add from Old Bank Buildings, Chester that :

1. He could confirm the L.N.W.R. would construct and work the line as a Light Railway.
2. Russell's recent death afforded an opportunity . . . for a complete scheme for completion of the Light Railways.
3. Mr. Lake, the N.W.N.G. Railway's Chairman, was willing to bring his Company into the scheme. He was just waiting for Aitchison to come back from holiday. (August 1912.)

4. Success depended on all local authorities being prepared to come in and finance the venture (as they were permitted to do under the Light Railway Act). Finance depended on them.
5. He suggested their title should now be the 'Caernarvon–Portmadoc Light Railway Investigation Committee'.

He was able to add that the N.W.N.G. line was operating at a profit 'and earning sufficient to pay the Debenture Interest', and that the P.B. & S.S. was operating at a profit as between Portmadoc and Croesor. He and Aitchison were ready to attend the Committee on invitation.

Breese & George were made solicitors to the Committee. They were later to be closely involved in local railway matters.*

Davies, the Chairman, continued his investigations. For some reason the proposal of the L.N.W.R. was not entirely acceptable to the Committee. Davies approached the Cambrian to see if they would work and construct—and find one third of the Capital too if asked—but Williamson their Manager could get no real satisfaction from his Board, and before January 1915, when correspondence ceased, Davies had had to tell him they were now negotiating with Euston again. It was clear that the Cambrian's position north of Afon Wen was the old stumbling block; they certainly refused to work a narrow gauge link between Dinas and Caernarvon in a territory which seemed quite hostile! Instead, Davies hammered away at Euston and to overcome the problem of trans-shipment at Dinas, he suggested a mixed gauge railway into Caernarvon and an extension on narrow gauge on to the quays there. By now (October 1914) estimators for the work had decided to leave out the Caernarvon Extension altogether.

At this stage the Joint Committee recommended that the promoters of the scheme should be the Caernarvon County Council and it be proposed by individuals without using the title of the Council. The Light Railway Commissioners considered a draft Order in November 1914 for the 'Transfer & Revival of Powers' of both P.B. & S.S. and N.W.N.G. concerns.

By now it seemed the Cambrian was on the point of answering proposals; the L.N.W.R. was apparently hooked but not landed. In the outcome a firm decision was made by neither, for both were becoming too heavily involved in wartime matters to consider the pro-

* Formerly Lloyd George & George of Pwllheli. Name changed to Breese & George summer 1914 (William George: sole partner). Later Evan R. Davies and William George. (Evan R. Davies was later to be prominent with the Festiniog Railway).

positions from the Joint Committee for the time being. The Committee decided it must summarise its findings by a Report and then shelve the matter until the war's end. It was rejuvenated as the 'Portmadoc Beddgelert & Rhyddu Light Railway'* and met at the County Offices, Caernarvon on 24 September 1921 to prepare for a Light Railway Commissioners' Local Enquiry at the same venue on 18 Offices, Caernarvon, on 24 September 1921 to prepare for a Light land Railway was formed.

Summary of Joint Committee Report (undated but c. January 1915)

P.B. & S.S.R. Expenses to date:	Purchase of Croesor Railway	£11,518
	Land at Cost	6,150
	Cost of construction	73,000
	Legal & Engineering expenses	12,000
		£102,668

N.W.N.G. 'This line worked at a disadvantage from the start. It depends on the L.N.W.R. at Dinas for passenger traffic and all goods traffic has to be trans-shipped. The terminus at Rhyddu is disadvantageously placed . . ..' (Various efforts to link it with Portmadoc since 1901 are recited.)

All local industry has lacked efficient railway service especially mines and quarries where the effect of war has been to put many on short time and close other workings. Present cost per ton of coal or etc. to such workings averages 3s. 2d. to 15s. from Portmadoc or Caernarvon and would be reduced by three quarters if carried by rail. (A list of local quarries and mines from the Report is appended.)

The owners of the two Railways were prepared to sell the same for £30,000 or £10,000 in cash and £30,000 in shares if any company could be formed to acquire them.

Estimated cost of the work is:	
To completion of undertaking	£50,000
Land	1,500
Repair of N.W.N.G.	5,000
Legal & Engineering expenses	3,500
or £4,000 per mile.†	£60,000

The purchase price would be divisible as $\frac{2}{3}$ to N.W.N.G. and $\frac{1}{3}$ to P.B. & S.S.

The Report goes on to describe sources of capital and suggested amounts; these include the Development Commission, Treasury, Local Authorities. It concludes that the L.N.W.R. is ready to work the line, on terms to be arranged.

* And practically any other permutation of names did duty at this time!

† On the basis of a 12-mile line the cost was likely to be nearer £5,000 per mile.

Quarries & Mines in district served by Croesor, P.B. & S.S. and N.W.N.G. lines in 1915, together with Parish and number of employees, from the Joint Committe Report.

Parish	*Undertaking*	*Employees*
Llandwrog	Alexandra	250
	Moel Tryfan	250
	Braich	80
	Vron	100
	Bryn fferam	60
Beddgelert	Cwmllan	100
	Gerynt	60
	Cwmcloch	20
	Goat	5
	Meillionien	10
	Cwmcath	10
	Dinas Ddu	20
	Castell	15
	Llyn Llagi	6
	Lliwedd (Lead & Copper)	65
	Lliwedd bach (Lead & Copper)	26
	Braich yr Oen (Lead & Copper)	24
	Hafod y Porth (Lead & Copper)	5
	Gwynant Lake (Lead & Copper)	6
	Perthi (Manganese)	?
	Sygun & Mynydd Mawr (Lead & Copper)	55
Llanfrothen	Croesor	300
	Rhosydd	250
	Pant Mawr	140
	Tan Rhiw, Nantmor (ochre)	8
	Brynfelin (copper)	60
	Bryndu (copper)	4
Llanfrothen	Croesor bach or Cynicht	25
	Aberglaslyn (copper)	12
	Park	55
	Brondanw	6
	Fron Boeth	50
	Hafodty	30
Bettws Garmon & Rhydd-ddu	Ystrad (iron)	30
	Hickman's (iron)	80
	Garn & Cwm Trysgwl (copper)	10
	Glanrafon	400
	Victoria	120
	Dreflan	35
	Garreg Fawr	30
	Plas-y-nant	40
	Snowdon	50
	Castell Cidwm	25
	West Snowdon	80
	Ffridd	20
	Gader Wyallt	45
	Llyn Gader	20
	Bwlch-y-ddeillior	35
	Princess	30
	Prince of Wales	100
	Quellyn	25

(*All names used are spelt as in the Report and may not agree with the text*)
Unless otherwise stated, slate or slab is obtained.
(Some listed concerns had long been out of business.)

The Route described

Sufficient work was done on the civil engineering of the railway to enable a description of the railway as finally abandoned (unfinished) to be given. Briefly, work was accomplished from South Snowdon to a point just above the Welsh Highland's Hafod Ruffydd Halt, and on further short isolated sections a few chains to the south, and then became minimal or non-existent southward to Tyn-y-coed. South of here and right into Beddgelert, earthworks were almost finished, and an abandoned stub earthwork remains south of Beddgelert. Further on, on the east bank of the Glaslyn, embankment, earthworks, tunnels and bridges were completed through the Aberglaslyn Pass, Nantmor and up to a point half a mile south of Nantmor Halt site, where the earthworks reached floodplain level. The formation was done between here and the intended bridge over the Afon Dylif but from the east bank of this river, embankment was complete with track as far as a junction with the Croesor Tramway, a length of 45 chains. It also appears that the Croesor tramway between Llanfrothen road crossing and the Cambrian crossing Portmadoc, was re-sleepered in 4-ft. 6-in. ×9-in. ×4½-in. sleepers carrying Indian metre gauge standard 41¼-lb. flat bottomed rails. As much of the abandoned work can still be seen, and is worthy of study, detail will now be given.

The contractors, Messrs. Bruce Peebles of Edinburgh, started work at South Snowdon, Beddgelert and the junction with the Croesor Tramway. Southwards from South Snowdon work proceeded fairly rapidly and easily along a slightly undulating course involving gradients of 1 in 80–95 but maintaining a gradual climb all the way until with a slight curve to the west and by building up the Beddgelert road to avoid a railway cutting of size, the track passed under the road by means of a segmental skew stone arch of 11 ft. span of rather larger loading gauge than those on the North Wales Narrow Gauge section to the north. (See structure diagram.) Immediately beyond the road bridge, stone abutments were built for a cattle overbridge of 18 ft. span, but this was never completed. The course then entered a somewhat turbarish area at the summit of the Pass, with mountain on either hand, and there was a shallow cutting to the summit. The situation here is remarkably similar in surroundings to the summit of the narrow gauge Ballymena, Cushendall & Red Bay Railway in Antrim, with its highest point in a cutting in bleak boggy moorland. At the summit (650 ft.) the Portmadoc, Beddgelert & South Snowdon works were 1 m. 10 ch. from South Snowdon. This locality is known as Pitt's Head, a nickname taken from a mass of boulders standing near the road overbridge, one of which was said to resemble the profile of that statesman.

On the foregoing section, Harper's Section Drawings* for what is headed 'N.W.N.G. Rly. Beddgelert Extension' involve intended gradients of Level, up 80, down 95, Level, up 81, Level (ending with Pitt's Head bridge), up 50, Level (Summit). As the works were never fined-down, these precise figures may not have been achieved, but on

* Significantly, the originals are signed 'G. C. Aitchison' and dated 8 April 1904 at Llanberis. Due to delays, Harper's copies therefrom are over-stamped 12 September 1907.

the summit section where no rock-work was involved, the finished formation was completed.

South from the summit, the line dropped at 1 in 50, 66 and (at 1 m. 9 ch. from Snowdon) began a long fall at 1 in 40, immediately below a level crossing of the road leading to Gader Slate Quarry, which would take it to 1 m. 68 ch. where the downgrade would have eased to 1 in 41. From the level crossing, a considerable cutting, followed by a long embankment on a high clockwise horse-shoe curve, was to be built. The cutting was never fully deepened, but the ensuing embankments were almost finished.

This summit length was one of the few places on the whole (ultimate) new railway where there was no sound foundation for the track. Even the Portmadoc, Beddgelert & South Snowdon work mentioned here, had sunk and lost stability by the time of refurbishment by the Welsh Highland Railway. Hundreds of tons of stone were tipped in by Fox & Partners to improve the trackbed, but enginemen always took the length at reduced speed to counteract the roll of the engine. The Welsh Highland's 'Baldwin' was in particular, a rough performer here.

By taking the line westward round the horse-shoe, the formation was able to follow the hill contours and so avoid a steep drop down the valley of the Afon Colwyn into Beddgelert. So as the railway swung away from its intended destination, road and river veered away to its left hand and fell steeply down the valley. In a fashion almost without parallel since the Festiniog Railway was built in the 1830s, the Portmadoc, Beddgelert & South Snowdon course presented a traditional narrow gauge route, of a type which had become a feature of overseas railways, but for which British terrain never seemed to call in great measure.

After a short run south-westward along this embankment, another curve took the line north-west briefly and then, by a complete half circle, it passed anti-clockwise through a cutting and then over an embankment to cross the Afon Cwm-ddu, a tributary of the Colwyn. It was intended here to place a girder bridge and, on its further side, to reduce the gradient slightly to 1 in 41 as previously mentioned. However, the contractors never tipped in sufficient fill to complete the embankments up to the bridge abutments, and a temporary bridge involving a steep inclination each side, was utilised until, in the early 1920s, the Welsh Highland contractors completed the work and used a comparatively small ferro-concrete culvert to take the river through the embankment.

At this point, the northern section of P.B. & S.S. work came to a halt. It was sufficiently far advanced for Parry, the timber contractor with his mill at South Snowdon station, to use a locomotive and gain admittance to the forestry at this point. Immediately south of the unfinished Cwm-ddu bridge, a loop was installed and, a few yards south of here, the metals laid by the contractor ended in a shallow cutting. It has not been possible to determine how much of the foregoing was laid with permanent way; it would seem that most if not all of it received 'Leeds Forge 1904' 41¼ lb./yard flat bottomed rails and again, most if not all the ballasting was done. There is also evidence that T-bulb rails were used, possibly firstly as contractor's line and additionally as temporary forestry tracks, a use for the uncompleted work to which the First War gave birth, and which the promoters could not have anticipated! *

Beyond here, desultory earthworks were carried out. Most of the embankment (now running almost due south) to the Hafod-ruffydd road crossing was finished, as was the low short embankment beyond. This was exactly 2 m. from South Snowdon. A shallow cutting beside Hafod-ruffydd house was begun and 30 chains further on, there was to be a magnificent double horseshoe curve through Coed Mawr, bringing the railway alongside the Afon Colwyn again. Part of the southern extremity of earthwork (an embankment beside the Afon Meillionen) was finished, but work ceased abruptly on this at a point where today a modern forestry road comes up beside the abandoned formation. To visit the spot today does not even entail leaving the seat of the car! Nothing at all was attempted on the remainder of the horseshoe, where the later contractor met with much heavy work. There was the beginning of a bridge over the Afon Meillionen and a small isolated cutting built opposite Beudy Tan-y-llwyn-isaf, but nothing again until at 3 m. 43 ch. the work which had come northwards from Beddgelert was met. Here again, the ultimate purpose proved to be a horse-worked forestry line which though temporary, found its way onto large scale Plans. On Harper's sections, the intention was to increase the fall following the double horseshoe, and below Afon Meillionen bridge, to drop at 1 in 37 from 3 m. 50 ch.

The forestry line was taken straight off the contractor's railway just beyond what became a cutting behind Tyn-y-Coed (house). Here it had been intended to carry the small Afon Glochig stream over the line on an aqueduct, but for temporary purposes it was bridged south of the house and a steep line carried away up and northwestwards

* According to C. R. Clinker, local information suggested that earth and track work was being done in winter/spring 1912–13. Perhaps this was only on the length worked by Parry, to put the section into some sort of runnable condition?

into Parc Tyn-y-Coed forest. This timber line curved west and west-south-west and ended just below the sheepfold south of Beudy Ysgubor. There is virtually nothing to be seen on the site today, save for the most primitive and light earthworks near the top. The line was 27 chains long from the main route and very steep indeed. Horse power and gravity were sufficient for its needs.

South of Tyn-y-Coed the P.B. & S.S.R. is on a very different course to that adopted by the Welsh Highland. For the first few yards, the P.B. & S.S. earthworks have been destroyed by Welsh Highland building. Then, below and to the east of the W.H.R. formation, there opens up a quite remarkable rock cutting of ever-increasing depth and curve, resulting finally in a left-hand horseshoe in part rock cutting and then embankment immediately north of Cwm-cloch-isaf. The works are remarkably preserved and even in their overgrown and waterlogged state remain a monument to the strength of purpose and confirmed optimism of the P.B. & S.S. promoters. When it is also-considered that from the point behind Tyn-y-Coed where the civil engineering work re-commenced (3 m. 43 ch. from South Snowdon) the gradient was to be an unbroken 1 in 28 to within a few yards of Beddgelert station, the confidence of the builders was remarkable.

Emerging on to open ground beside Cwm-cloch-isaf, the contractor's track in T-bulb rail with chairs and sleepers, lay intact but under water until very recently. Some chairs were rudely fashioned in wood at this point.

Curving now west and then south, the embankment falls to merge with the later Welsh Highland cutting which comes in on its right hand and then, by embankment used also by the W.H.R., into Beddgelert. There is an interesting place where the P.B. & S.S. crossed an occupation road by overbridge, the W.H.R. by level crossing. Beyond, a stone P.B. & S.S. road overbridge was completed in concrete by the W.H.R. and shortly afterwards, there is a fine P.B. & S.S. stone bridge crossing the Afon Cwm-cloch.

The site of Beddgelert station was cleared. The grade eased to 1 in 42 on entering, but the site was level. Of the work north from here to Tyn-y-Coed, most embankment was complete, but the cuttings in rock were not all fully opened out and some not finally deepened. They were sufficient for the timber trains, however. Falling at 1 in 29, the track entered a rock cutting south of Beddgelert and at 3 m. 30 ch. there was a 132-ft. tunnel in bare rock from whence the course swung south-east and, emerging from the cutting crossed the Beddgelert–Portmadoc road by a stone bridge still in situ. The embankment continued for a few yards beyond and then petered out. Further on still, stand the isolated abutments for an underbridge to connect the lands divided by the new embankment. Unsupported by earth filling, they make a bizarre monument. Until recently there was also the stonework for a flood water culvert. Beyond this point, the Afon Glaslyn would have been crossed, but the records give no clue as to the form of bridge.

It is significant that the drawings for the route from here to the Croesor Tramway are headed 'Croesor, Beddgelert section' (no company being stated), dated 21 June 1904, and probably originated from Aitchison at Llanberis. Harper's copies are again dated 12 September 1907.

The 'Beddgelert Extension' survey only takes the Extension to the Glaslyn river bank just mentioned (but beyond its authorised terminal). These records, therefore, embody the link from the authorised junction on the east side of the Glaslyn with the 1901 proposals for a line up the Gwynant valley. One detail is worth mentioning. In view of the ultimate abandonment of the works south and east of Beddgelert station tunnel, and the new course to Bryn-y-felin adopted by the Welsh Highland, it is ironic that a short railway was in fact built by the P.B. & S.S. along this later-adopted course. It led along the west side of the Portmadoc road, at a point south of the Beddgelert tunnel mouth, for about five chains. Steeply inclined, it ended at the roadside and enabled equipment to be loaded there for building this isolated section which otherwise had no convenient link with a road.

To take up the next section of work, the Glaslyn had to be crossed. The point where the bridge was to be built is still visible, and from here, down through Aberglaslyn all civil engineering work was finished. It begins with rubble embankment on the riverside, and entering the canyon-like Pass of Aberglaslyn * with its river and rapids falling below on the right, takes up a shelf position on the craggy side of the gorge. Tunnels were required where shoulders of mountain stood in the way. The first is 132 ft. long and is followed almost immediately by a second of 99 ft. The third pierces the side of Craig-y-llan and is 957 ft. in length with a slight curve at the north end. All are unlined and no ornamentation has been attempted. The fall from the Glaslyn bridge was 1 in 105, 266, then level; then came a short 1 in 57 rise, then level, and through the tunnels, 1 in 114 and throughout the third, 1 in 40. At the south mouth it was intended to steepen the fall to 1 in 32, and the rubble embankment with a stone

* The name *Aber Glaslyn* (the confluence of the Blue Pool) was probably derived from copper deposits in the water. There were several mines in the vicinity.

overbridge carrying the road to the Cwm Bychan mine, was completed.* The tunnels just mentioned, however, were not fully opened out by the contractor. No record survives of P.B. & S.S. intention except that the bores were probably to be the same as their overbridge clearances. Certainly Fox & Partners survey for the Welsh Highland allowed for opening out the Aberglaslyn tunnels to their present dimensions. What does survive is an interesting letter from Harper's to the Festiniog Manager dated 18 July 1904:

13, St. Helens Place,
London, E.C.

Size of Tunnel. If it is not troubling you too much, we should be glad if you would let us know the height and width of the tunnels on the Festiniog line. Also the maximum height and width of your locomotives.

We are thinking of making the Aberglaslyn Tunnel 11 ft. 6 ins. high by 11 ft. wide. In case at any time your Rolling Stock should come on to our line, would it pass through our tunnel?

Yours faithfully,

Of course at this juncture, it was thought that *one* tunnel in the Pass would suffice (but three were part-finished on abandonment). The envisaged possibility of through running might be wishful thinking, careful forethought or sudden inspiration. There was no special link between the North Wales Narrow Gauge and Festiniog at this time.

The long tunnel was provided with three refuges at each side, mainly at its southernmost end. A fourth on the west side was to be found nearer the north end whilst the W.H.R. contractors added two more at equal distances along the east wall at the north end. Although the tunnel was opened out later to standard gauge dimensions, Welsh Highland rolling stock never really necessitated this lavish provision, and when Festiniog coaches came over the line, the recesses were even more of a luxury! Far-sighted though the large bores may have been, they added immensely to costs.† The long tunnel varied in width throughout, caused by differing rock; it was widest at the south end but in the middle increased momentarily to 12 ft. 9 in.‡

The civil engineering south of the long tunnel was heavy and not

* Transport at the mine was by a wire ropeway supplied by R. White & Sons, Widnes. Though derelict, part survives (1971).

† Welsh Highland Tunnels: Height 14 ft. (centre of arch), Width 11 ft.; English average: Height 13 ft. 6 in. (centre of arch), Width 9 ft. (1930 Official).

‡ A letter from Aitchison to Robert Casson of 30 November 1903 claimed that the line had to be in tunnel through the Aberglaslyn Pass for aesthetic reasons, but that this was impossible from the engineering standpoint.

finally completed by the P.B. & S.S.R. The tunnel had provided much material for the ensuing embankment over the Mine road and the bridge over the Afon Bychan, but this had not been brought to formation level when work stopped. Just beyond was a formidable cutting in rock which was not completely pierced either. It was not possible to run between the Aberglaslyn section of the work and the remainder further south for this reason.

As previously mentioned, south from the tunnel the intended grade was 1 in 32, but at the Nantmor road, reached at the end of the rock cutting, the grade was to ease to 1 in 70. Second thoughts about making a Halt on level track beside the road crossing prevailed, and a fresh section was drawn providing for this, but altering the fall from the tunnel mouth to 1 in 40 with a short level section for the Halt. When the Welsh Highland completed these works, the Halt had to do without its level, and the grade remained consistent at 1 in 40.

The P.B. & S.S.R. diverted the Nantmor road, and the Halt was to stand just south of a new road crossing on the level. From here the work had been finished, in part rubble embankment and less formidable cuttings to a point where the Llanfrothen road was to be crossed and for which it was diverted. The bridge was not begun. South again, (and below the Nantmor Halt site falling at 1 in 36 and 250) not only had the formation been brought up to the required standard, but the fences had been erected too. The fall was completed down to the Glaslyn flood plain by a long embankment of 1 in 67 ending at 6½ miles from South Snowdon, and then, by earthworks and fencing ready to receive the permanent way, a fall of 1 in 2,200 ended before the 7th milepost, so bringing the finished works on to the flood plain. Just beyond here was the Welsh Highland Halt at Hafod-y-llyn, not of course even considered at this time.

The P.B. & S.S. formation—mainly on level ground—to the point where the Afon Dylif was to be crossed (a grade of 118 up and 152 down was required to climb up and over the bridge which was not built)—and included in this finished length was a crossing of the Afon Nant-y-mor on which work was not started.

East of the site of the Dylif bridge, some old Croesor rails had been laid over what was to be level railway as far as the point of junction with the Croesor Tramway. Formation work on this length was almost complete.

With the cessation of powers in 1909, all construction ceased, but it would seem that on the scale of what had been achieved (probably over two years rather than the whole three-year term permitted by the Act) another twelve months—and sufficient funds—would have been ample to bring the line to operating condition.

Locomotive

Name	*Type*	*Builder*	*No.*	*Date*	*Withdrawn*
Russell	2–6–2T	Hunslet Engine Co. Ltd.	901	1906	Extant

Cylinders	10¾ in. × 15 in.*	Total Heat. Surface	381 sq. ft.
Driving wheels	2 ft. 4 in.	Fuel capacity	14½ cwt.
Pony wheels	1 ft. 6 in.	Tank capacity	440 galls.
Wheelbase	15 ft. 6 in.	Weight Working Order	20 tons
Pressure	160 lb. sq. in.	Tractive Effort at 75 per cent b.p.	7425 lb.

In the face of the fact that the railway was incomplete, it would seem reckless for the Company to order a locomotive—the only one in its own name—before the railway was nearly ready. The reason lay in the close liaison with the N.W.N.G.R., whose own engines were by then over thirty years old and were out-dated, if not unsuited to working a railway which would include some of the most remarkable gradients in the British Isles. The Directors therefore felt justified in ordering something for the Beddgelert Extension which could be relied upon to operate south of South Snowdon with a margin of power. The N.W.N.G. line already owned one engine by the Hunslet Engine Co. of Leeds, and to them went the order.

Hunslet had sent a specification on 31 January and G. C. Aitchison, A.M.I.C.E., F.C.I.S., Manager of the P.B. & S.S.R., placed the order on 13 February 1906, so there was little delay. Drawings were prepared between 20 March and 14 May and by 26 May the engine was already undergoing steam trials; it left Leeds for North Wales on 29 May.

The remarkably short time in which the engine was built has produced several theories, the most recent being that as the engine was urgently required, priority was given. This seems a most unlikely tale, unless it could be supported by some surcharge on cost; there seldom was a manufacturer whose customers did not want their goods as a matter of urgency! More probably—though there is no supporting evidence—by using certain standard parts and existing designs where available, expedition was possible. The new engine was larger than anything used before on the N.W.N.G. The design was based on a class of 2–6–2T engines built in 1898 for the Sierra Leone Government Railway. Details differed, and it was larger than the Sierra Leone class, though of a narrower gauge. It was carried on outside frames to the driving wheels, with inside frames to the pony trucks, whilst Walschaert's Valve Gear was employed, only for the third time by the makers.

There was a curious feature about the gauge as ordered. The P.B. & S.S.R. returned its official gauge as 1 ft. 11½ in. The N.W.N.G.

* Boston Lodge records (Festiniog Railway) of 1921 give 9½ in. × 14 in.

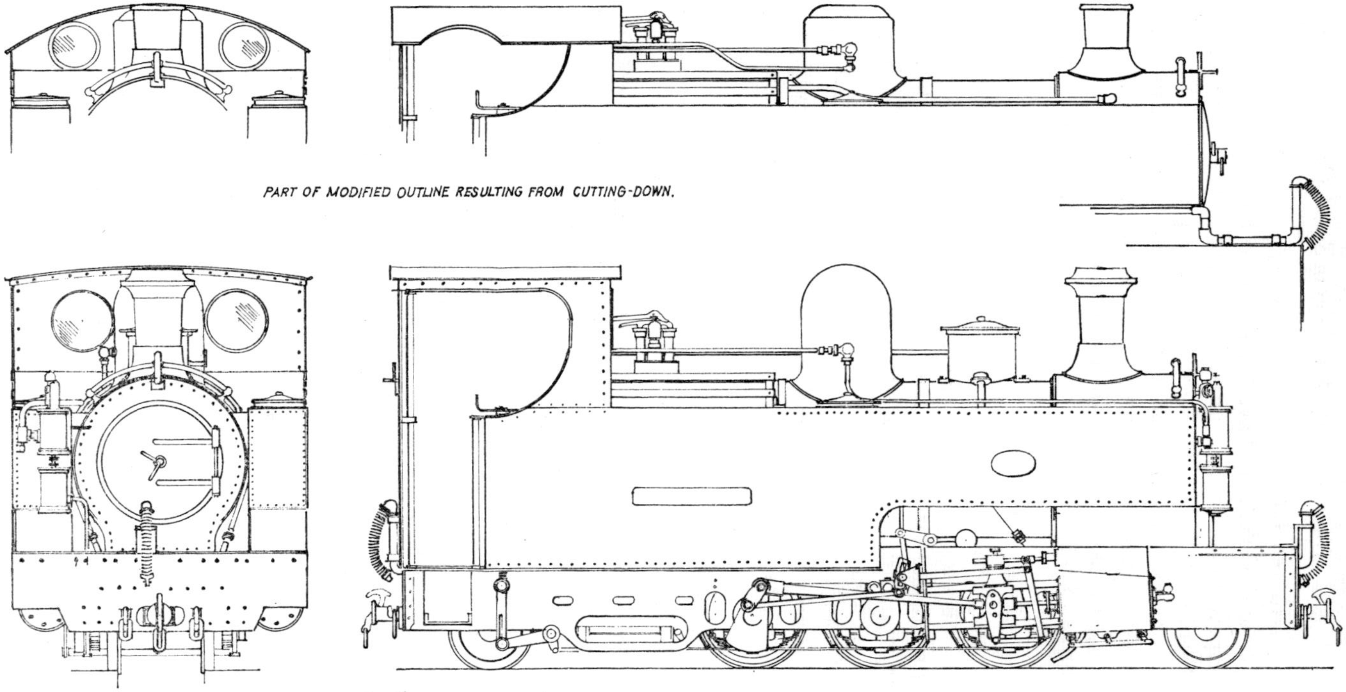

WELSH HIGHLAND RAILWAY (P.B.&S.S.R.)

"RUSSELL" BY HUNSLET, MAKER'S NUMBER 901 OF 1906 IN ORIGINAL FORM. MANY MODIFICATIONS WERE MADE OVER THE YEARS CULMINATING IN THE DRASTIC CUTTING-DOWN OF 1923-24. BASED ON MAKER'S DRAWINGS UNDER Nº 28900 DATED MAY 14 1906.

JMC 20510

Railway's returned 1 ft. $11\frac{1}{4}$ in., 1 ft. $11\frac{1}{2}$ in. and 2 ft.! Hunslet's records show the engine to have been ordered for 1 ft. $11\frac{1}{4}$ in. and in this respect it may be emphasised that so long as wheel tyres are of ample tread-width, and dimensions of flange profile and through flangeways at points etc. are standard, nominal changes in gauge can be tolerated. Apparently the original order was given for a gauge of 1 ft. $11\frac{7}{8}$ in.—a dimension which was among some *not* quoted in the Returns! However, it was amended before completion of the engine.

Among the items common to the Sierra Leone engines and *Russell* were the coupled wheels, reversing gear, springs, axleboxes and outside motion generally. A special design was made up for the frames and cylinders and the engine above, so that a number of drawings were necessary where departure from Sierra Leone standards was made. The boiler was larger and based on one supplied on an engine for Leeds Corporation Waterworks (0–6–2T No. 865 of 1905). The minimum radius curve for the N.W.N.G. was 198 feet radius (as against 120 feet for Sierra Leone) and it was not necessary to cut away the side frames to allow the pony trucks to swing; these had inside bearings.

Behind the outside main frames, compensating beams linked the coupled axle-boxes. There was a spark-arrester, Ramsbottom safety valves, sand reservoir in a dome fitting between chimney and steam dome* (later moved), Westinghouse Class F Pump on the leading end of the right-hand tank with a reservoir between the mainframes, centre buffer-couplers with side chains, bunker over and alongside the firebox top with access on the left hand through the cab weather-sheet and the side tanks ran the full length of the engine. The coupled wheelbase was 5 ft. 6 in. (the original overall wheelbase was reduced from 15 ft. 8 in. to keep it as short as possible).

Painting was in N.W.N.G. colours, the principal being a red-brown (some sources state brown—similar to North British Railway,† and others 'Midland Red') lined in black, the black having a thin yellow line each side of it. The Hall cranks and buffer beams were vermilion, as was the ground of the brass nameplate on the tank sides. There was no lettering or number.

* For forward direction only; the other reservoir was a saddle over the firebox.

† An Authority on North British Railway matters states that the locomotive livery was a most unstable colour. It was described as brown and also as Olive Green and shown either way by coloured views of the times. It depended largely on the lighting conditions in which it was seen, and the foreman painter of the Railway admitted they had no basic formula, so that often engines and tenders were paired in differing shades.

Of course, *Russell* never went into service on the actual P.B. & S.S.R., as even the track immediately south of South Snowdon was unready for use. She was delivered to Dinas Junction and took up duties as if just another member of the N.W.N.G.R. locomotive stock.

No other locos or rolling stock were ordered by the Company, whose expenditure by 1920 was £47,791, and visible assets on abandonment were an unfinished railway between South Snowdon and Croesor Junction, and a new locomotive at work only on an associate railway.

	Directors	*Other directorships include*
1911	Col. Henry PLATT, Llanfairfechan	Liverpool & N. Wales Steamship Co.
	Joseph BEECHING, Huyton	Lancs. United Tramways Co.
	Henry R. HOGG, Kensington	Canadian Electric Traction Co. N. Wales Power & Traction Co. Sunderland Dist. Elec. Tramways Co.
	E. Noel HUMPHREYS, Chester (Chartered Accountant)	East Halkyn Mining Co.
1919	Arthur Francis BOTT, Stevenage	Cleobury Mortimer & Ditton Priors Light Rly.† Aluminium Corp. Ltd.
	Joseph Walker CASSELLS, Orford	Aluminium Corp. Ltd.
	Capt. Samuel G. BIBBY, Sutton (Chartered Accountant)	N. Wales Power & Traction Co. (Deputy Chairman) Aluminium Corp. Ltd.
	* Henry Joseph JACK, Maenan Manor, Llanrwst	Aluminium Corp. Ltd. (Managing Director) N. Wales Power & Traction Co. (numerous other coys. in aluminium business)
	Kenneth McKenzie CLARK, Sudbourne	N. Wales Power & Traction Co. (Chairman) Aluminium Corp. Ltd.
* 1922	Board unchanged but JACK Managing Director. By 1925 his other directorships included :	Bauxite Refining Co. Ltd. (Managing Director) Gwalia Ltd. Gwynedd Trust Ltd. Snowdon Mountain Tramroad & Hotels Co. Unity Investment Trust Ltd. Welsh Highland Railway Festiniog Railway

† Seat on Board given to contractors, Bott & Stennett, who held shares under terms of construction contract.

(Up to 1901 see Portmadoc, Croesor & Beddgelert Tram Railway Co.)

	1902	1903	1904[5]	1905	1906[4]	1907	1908	1909	1910[6]	1911	1912	1913	1920	1921
Maintenance Works and Way	No Return	'No information returned'	83	64	78	69	60	63	62	72	51	56	N.R.	N.R.
Loco Power Cost			242	203	172	176	185	195	181	191	175	154	N.R.	N.R.
Repairs and Renewals														
Carr. and Wagons			10	10	11	10	10	9	15	—	—	3	N.R.	N.R.
Traffic Expenses			73	71	60	60	51	53	58	56	52	52	N.R.	N.R.
Profit/Loss on Working			81	(96)	(76)	(66)	16	107	151	204	183	86	(51)	(17)
Merchandise Tons			698[2]	311	308	Nil	259	530	314	359	230	*	*	*
Minerals Tons			9035[2]	8005	6553	7195	7299	7841	7290	7637	7112	*	*	*
Train miles (Goods)[1]			x	x	x	x	x	2772	2772	2772	2772	2772	1173	1311
Wagons for merchandise[3]			Nil	4	4	4	4	4	4	4	4	4	4	4

(1913–1921 wagons: Given as 1½ ton capacity (slate))

* *Tonnages for*	*1913*	*1919*	*1920*	*1921*
General Merchandise	244	906	161	256
Coal, Coke, etc.	467	282	315	282
Other Minerals (slate, etc.)	5820	N.R.	1510	1730
Livestock	N.R.	N.R.	5	6

Notes not shown by above

1901 Authorised Capital £270,000. Authorised Loan £60,000 + £15,000 from Local Authority.
1904 ,, ,, £294,000. ,, ,, £98,000.
1909 ,, ,, £318,000. ,, ,, £106,000—to 1921.
1904 Issued Shares £13,535.
1905 ,, ,, £50,000—to 1921.

Notes on Returns

x No mileage returned for these years 'cannot be given: haulage by horses only'. (sic)
1 Figures for 1909–1919 (no other figures for 1919 available) clearly fictitious—all same.
2 'Partly estimated'. (sic)
3 Predecessors' Returns showed nil return for all types of Rolling Stock. From 1913 the four were returned as 'Mineral' not 'Merchandise' (!)
4 'The Croesor Section (a horse tramroad) was the only section of the Coy.'s line open for traffic in 1906.' (This repeated each year thereafter).
5 'The Line is being constructed under an arrangement by the North Wales Power & Traction Coy. Ltd., that Coy. taking the shares and debentures on payment.'
6 'The actual construction was in abeyance at the end of the year 1910' (this repeated for ensuing years).

WELSH HIGHLAND RAILWAY (LIGHT RAILWAY) COMPANY

(*Gauge* 1 ft. 11½ in. nominal)

Incorporated by: Light Railway Order of 30 March 1922.
Amendment Order of 7 February 1923.
(Acquired North Wales Narrow Gauge Railways Company and Portmadoc Beddgelert & South Snowdon Railway Company as from 1 January 1922.)
Registered Office: Clark Street, Dolgarrog (1922). Later 56 Buckingham Gate, S.W.1. (thereafter the premises of the Receiver then acting).
Capital: £120,000 in £1 shares—£90,000 issued to cover purchase of above two railways, no cash passing. £120,000 in loans.
Debentures: £84,774 @ 5% issued. Interest only paid to 31 December 1923.
Opened: Goods—N.W.N.G. officially remained open.
W.H.R. new line 1 June 1923.
Passenger—N.W.N.G. section from 31 July 1922 (main line only).
W.H.R. new line 1 June 1923.
Length authorised (1923): 12 m. 17 ch. = existing N.W.N.G.
8 m. 57 ch. = new line W.H.R.
3 m. 40 ch. = Caernarvon extension (not built).
Total mileage returned after 1924: 26 m. 30 ch. (including sidings)*
Maximum Gradient: 1 in 40.
Minimum Curve: 3 ch.
Maximum Speed: 15 m.p.h.
Receiver appointed: 5 March 1927.
Closed: Passenger—by W.H.R. 31 December 1933; worked under F.R. lease from 9 July 1934–29 September 1934.
8 July 1935–28 September 1935.
6 July 1936–26 September 1936.
Goods—by W.H.R. 31 December 1933; worked under F.R. lease—last train ran 1 June 1937.†
Leased by Festiniog Railway between: 9 July 1934–31 December 1942.
Winding-up Order issued: 7 February 1944.

* Break-down of official mileages (1922).

Length	*First Track*	*Second Track*	*Sidings*	*Total (exc. sidings)*
Dinas–S. Snowdon	9m 20c	0m 22c	0m 51c	9m 42c
Port–Croesor Junction	3m 64c	0m 13c	0m 10c	3m 77c
Bryngwyn Branch	3m 0c	0m 45c	0m 12c	3m 45c
Croesor Branch	0m 65c	—	—	0m 65c
S. Snowdon–Croesor Junction	8m 57c	'under construction'		
Dinas–Caernarvon	3m 40c	'not yet commenced'		

Official mileage leased by Festiniog Railway—25m 42c (which together with Festiniog Railway 13m 62c = 39 miles 24 chains).

† Festiniog gave Railway Clearing House, L.M.S. and G.W. Railways 31 May 1937 as official date of cessation of goods services.

HISTORY

Earlier reference has been made to efforts which sought to bring the N.W.N.G. and P.B. & S.S. Railways together under a Revival of Powers, Light Railway Order. The promoters of this plan were working under many difficulties, none greater than that there were so many interested parties who had been in the fray, and others who, though in a spectator role at that time, had an interest in the matter—if only that they might be expected to make some financial contribution. Ultimately hopes of an early settlement were dashed by the onset of the First War, so that it was not until things were settling down and problems of employment and the post-war development of the slate quarrying industry were becoming urgent, that attention was again given to the matter. On 18 October 1921 the Light Railway Commissioners held a Public Enquiry in the County Hall, Caernarvon. For the first time, the North Wales Power Co. and the Festiniog Railway was represented, both of them in the person of Henry Joseph Jack.

The Festiniog Railway was finding that costs and labour charges had risen enormously since the war; many small lines which had been running at a loss about 1912, on being taken over by the Government during the War, enjoyed a financial honeymoon. Now free from Government control, losses were bigger than before. The Festiniog was in this condition.

The Caernarvon meeting had been prefaced by a meeting of the old-established Joint Committee of pre-war days, on 24 September. They had a spokesman at the Public Enquiry, who thought that the delay caused by war had been fortunate for the N. Wales Power & Electric Traction Co. (who owned both N.W.N.G. and P.B. & S.S.) as this concern now also had control of the Festiniog. With powerful interests in the Power Co. and also the Aluminium Corporation with headquarters at Dolgarrog, Jack was virtually dictator of the railway position in the area. The meeting was reminded that the N.W.N.G. never paid a dividend on its Ordinary Shares and was saddled with three classes of Debenture. The spokesman recommended that all lapsed powers be renewed under a new organisation to be termed the Welsh Highland Railway.

The new promoters, like others before them, were resolved that the town of Caernarvon should be their northerly goal, an achievement which the N.W.N.G. had never realised. A spokesman for the L.N.W.R. said his Company was ready to support the schemes, but would object to an extension into Caernarvon (somewhat naturally). His Company feared that a larger Company stood hidden in the

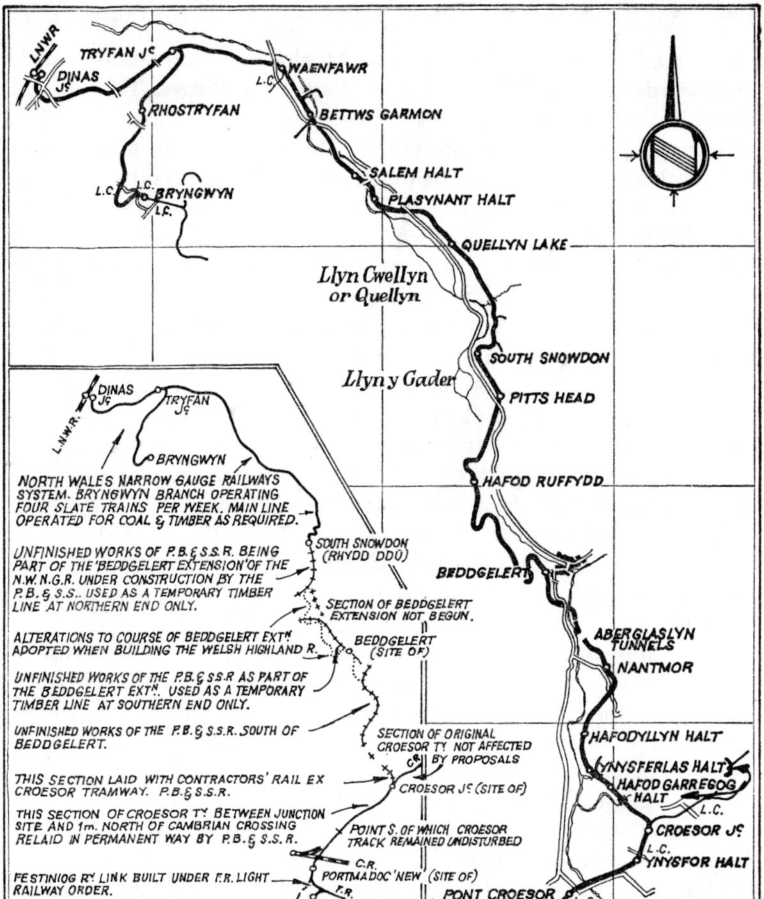
LNWR
TRYFAN Jc
DINAS Jc
WAENFAWR
L.C.
RHOSTRYFAN
BETTWS GARMON
SALEM HALT
L.C.
BRYNGWYN
PLASYNANT HALT
QUELLYN LAKE
Llyn Cwellyn or Quellyn
SOUTH SNOWDON
Llyn y Gader
PITTS HEAD
HAFOD RUFFYDD
BEDDGELERT
ABERGLASLYN TUNNELS
NANTMOR
HAFODYLLYN HALT
YNYSFERLAS HALT
HAFOD GARREGOG HALT
L.C.
CROESOR Jc
YNYSFOR HALT
PONT CROESOR
PORTREUDDYN
PORTMADOC
NEW 1933
NEW 1923
C.R.
HARBOUR (F.R.)
F.R.
DINAS Jc
TRYFAN Jc
L.N.W.R.
BRYNGWYN
NORTH WALES NARROW GAUGE RAILWAYS SYSTEM. BRYNGWYN BRANCH OPERATING FOUR SLATE TRAINS PER WEEK. MAIN LINE OPERATED FOR COAL & TIMBER AS REQUIRED.
SOUTH SNOWDON (RHYDD DDU)
UNFINISHED WORKS OF P.B.& S.S.R. BEING PART OF THE 'BEDDGELERT EXTENSION' OF THE N.W.N.G.R. UNDER CONSTRUCTION BY THE P.B. & S.S.. USED AS A TEMPORARY TIMBER LINE AT NORTHERN END ONLY.
SECTION OF BEDDGELERT EXTENSION NOT BEGUN.
ALTERATIONS TO COURSE OF BEDDGELERT EXTN. ADOPTED WHEN BUILDING THE WELSH HIGHLAND R.
BEDDGELERT (SITE OF)
UNFINISHED WORKS OF THE P.B.& S.S.R AS PART OF THE BEDDGELERT EXTN. USED AS A TEMPORARY TIMBER LINE AT SOUTHERN END ONLY.
UNFINISHED WORKS OF THE P.B.& S.S.R. SOUTH OF BEDDGELERT.
SECTION OF ORIGINAL CROESOR TY. NOT AFFECTED BY PROPOSALS
THIS SECTION LAID WITH CONTRACTORS' RAIL EX CROESOR TRAMWAY. P.B.& S.S.R.
CROESOR Jc (SITE OF)
THIS SECTION OF CROESOR TY. BETWEEN JUNCTION SITE AND 1m. NORTH OF CAMBRIAN CROSSING RELAID IN PERMANENT WAY BY P.B.& S.S.R.
POINT S. OF WHICH CROESOR TRACK REMAINED UNDISTURBED
C.R.
FESTINIOG RY. LINK BUILT UNDER F.R. LIGHT RAILWAY ORDER.
PORTMADOC 'NEW' (SITE OF)
F.R.
FORMER CROESOR TY. HARBOUR LINE LATER MADE REDUNDANT BY IMPROVEMENTS.
HARBOUR STN.
The Welsh Highland Railway.
and
state of railway construction c.1919.
0 1 2 3 4 5 6 7 MILES

wings ready to tap traffic from the Moel Tryfan area and send it southwards via Cambrian or Great Western Railways. They would then lose the traffic transhipped to them at Dinas Junction.

The spokesman for the promoters (Jack) was able to assure them that no large railway stood behind them; in fact he said with some satisfaction that 'they had been able to get the Festiniog Railway excluded from the Great Western group' (under the new Grouping of Railways Act). He confirmed that plans for a line from Beddgelert to Bettws-y-coed had been shelved and that only a through route from Portmadoc to Caernarvon via Dinas interested them. Construction of about 4 m. 60 ch. (the Croesor section) was considered 'complete' and the remainder of the new link 'nearly complete'. Some land had been acquired from Caernarvon Harbour Trustees but nothing had been done between Dinas and Caernarvon.

He continued by saying there would be no actual cash transaction at takeover, but that the new Company was ready to pay £10,000 in Debentures and £90,000 in Ordinary Shares for the two Companies together; he asked that the new Company be the Welsh Highland Railway Co. Ltd. For the moment at least, they would not electrify the line.

Jack's appearance was in a multiple capacity; he was Receiver to the N.W.N.G. and Chairman of the Festiniog; he was Managing Director of the Power Co. and a director of the P.B. & S.S. Under interrogation he admitted the Festiniog would make working agreements with the new Company, but thought that unified control of administration and stock would bring many economies. This would be centred on Dolgarrog. On the Festiniog, the slate traffic had dropped by 60% since 1913, but passenger traffic was up by 92%.

The Chairman of the Commissioners was blunt. He told Jack that many local people held him in suspicion. He was a member of the County Council and wielded far too much influence to suit everyone.

Mr. Freeman spoke for Sir Douglas Fox & Partners, the Engineers to the new railway. He said the L.N.W.R. did not give proper facilities for passengers to and from Caernarvon and buses took much of the traffic. The town and Harbour wanted the narrow gauge extended to them. This had no avail however, for when the Chairman announced a decision in favour of the scheme, he excluded the Caernarvon extension. He added that if powers had been sought to acquire land for this purpose, he would have considered it; the promoters were at liberty to seek such powers at a later stage if they wished. In the next year or two some effort was made to obtain a census of traffic between Dinas and Caernarvon by road, but the new enterprise was never financially strong enough to take on the matter.

On 30 March 1922 The Welsh Highland Railway (Light Railway) Company was formed—a somewhat cumbersome title. It acquired the N.W.N.G. and P.B. & S.S. systems, back-dated to 1 January 1922. £40,000 was given for the N. Wales Company and £50,000 for the Portmadoc, being some indication of the run-down value of the former's assets. The Government agreed to subscribe half the cost of (1) rebuilding the N.W.N.G. section, (2) refurbishing the Croesor section, (3) the cost of the unfinished intermediate link, providing the cost did not exceed £37,500. Other subscribers included the Ministry of Transport, Caernarvonshire County Council, Caernarvon Corporation and many other local authorities including Portmadoc. The supporting authorities were authorised to appoint one director each to the Company.

On the day the new Company came into being (30 March) the Ministry of Transport—successor in these matters to the Board of Trade—confirmed the Light Railway Order. Under a prior agreement between the M.O.T. and the promoters it was arranged that 'All unskilled labour required locally for the work of completing the said railway to be obtained from neighbouring centres to be designated by the Ministry of Labour.'

The capital was £120,000 in £1 shares with powers to borrow up to the same amount under conditions. Rates of carriage were not to exceed those currently in force on the Festiniog Railway. The Dinas to Caernarvon extension might be proceeded with under separate application, but the route would be amended somewhat more easterly than provided under the 1904 Act so as to protect Lady Armstrong-Jones's property.

Under a second prior agreement between Herbert Aubrey Crowe (representing the afore-mentioned Light Railway Committee and as the promoter of the Welsh Highland scheme) Jack as Receiver of the N.W.N.G., the P.B. & S.S., the N. Wales Power & Traction Co. Ltd. and Sir John Henderson Stewart—i.e. the parties involved as between the Welsh Highland promoters on the one hand, and the 'Dolgarrog parties' on the other—dated 1 February 1922, satisfactory financial settlement was given for the acquisition of the absorbed undertakings by the Welsh Highland. In the agreement the dates of the three consecutive Receivers of the N. Wales N.G.R. Company are given :

James Cholmeley Russell	appointed	13 December 1878
Gowrie Colquhoun Aitchison	„	15 January 1912
Henry Joseph Jack	„	8 April 1921

By this time the outstanding debt of the N.W.N.G. on Principal and Interest on the three classes of Debenture stocks exceeded £93,000, calculated to the end of 1921! Of this, Sir J. H. Stewart (see above) held more than three-quarters of the Debentures and was owed the accrued interest. At no time had the revenue of the Company been sufficient to pay the full interest on the Debentures, nor the debts and liabilities due to the holders of Lloyds Bonds or the unsecured creditors at the period of Russell's appointment as Receiver.

The same agreement also tells that the goods traffic (which had operated alone since 1 October 1916) had been insufficient in revenue earning to pay the interest on the 'A' Debentures since 31 December 1913, nor to meet its daily expenses. Since 1 January 1921 Sir John had made provision for £1,500 to 'enable the Receiver to carry on the Undertaking'. This had resulted in an agreement between Sir John and the Power Co. on 25 January 1922 whereby the Power Co.'s issued capital in the P.B. & S.S. (they were the owners of all the issued capital in it) was assigned to Sir John, in exchange for certain rights. Thus Sir John was enabled to agree the acquisition of the N. Wales Company, the P.B. & S.S. (through his acceptance of the Power Co.'s interest in that Company) and so, when £40,000 was paid for the N. Wales Company—no actual cash passing it should be recalled—Sir John was the main beneficiary.

As the prospect of operating the new railway by electricity seemed as remote as when first mooted, second thoughts prevailed on the course (as yet incomplete), which the P.B. & S.S. had built. To say it was steep was an understatement. Consequently, an Amendment Order was granted by the Ministry on 7 February 1923 which allowed portions of the unfinished line to be abandoned and the following to be built:

1. Railway No. 1. A Deviation railway (2 miles 1 furlong 7 chains) from a junction with the railway 3 chains south of Hafod-Ruffydd-Ganol, thence south-east and joining the railway again 6 chains north-east of Cwm-cloch-isaf. (This eliminated a section of railway just north of Beddgelert with a grade of 1 in 28 for almost three miles and supplanted it with a new line with a ruling grade of 1 in 40 and introduced return loops to lessen the inclination.)
2. Railway No. 2. A Deviation railway (4 furlongs 7 chains) from a junction with the railway where it leaves the 47 yard tunnel south of the Goat Hotel, Beddgelert, thence in a south-east direction and rejoining the railway on the east bank of the Glaslyn, 14 chains east of Bryn-y-felin. (This eliminated two road level crossings and replaced them with one road overbridge.)

Having seen the new railway company successfully launched, it is as well to retrace steps in both time and distance to see what had been taking place on the north end of the new system i.e. the former N.W.N.G. section. This end of the line had gone into a frightful state, details of which will be given in due course. Of course there were no passenger services, but by dint of overhauling the track and stock (let it be added at once, to the minimum standard and with the least expense) it was possible to re-open the Dinas Junction–Rhydd-ddu section to passenger trains again with a new timetable commencing 31 July 1922. The work entailed in bringing this about is given later. It was hoped to restore passenger services on the Bryngwyn branch by 1924, but this was never achieved.

Tenders had been received by the Company to carry out the whole work from Dinas to Portmadoc as follows:

Sir Robert McAlpine	£60,819
Laing & Son	57,637
Alban Richards & Co.	74,783
Macdonald Gibbs & Co.	81,611
Muirhead Macdonald	93,648

and the Board of Trade had recommended McAlpine as their rates for scheduled work were better and Laing's had had no experience of railway construction. The Board's interest was a very keen one, seeing that the construction was regarded as one form of mitigation for unemployment in the district, and they classed the scheme as Priority No. 1. The Board of Agriculture, on the other hand (who would be expected to give financial support on the grounds that the railway would help agriculture) classed it as Priority No. 3 (desirable at some future date). The Railway Commissioners, having inspected the N.W.N.G. section in 1922, said simply 'unsafe through bad repair for passengers and hardly fit for goods.' It would appear throughout this part of the proceedings that Jack was the main impetus for the scheme and by enlisting the support of the then Prime Minister's Personal Secretary, brought it to the notice of those in the corridors of power.

McAlpine worked from Dinas and Portmadoc and also had a depot at Beddgelert. They used both steam and i/c engines for contracting work, the Festiniog engine *Palmerston* being hired for the south end on several occasions and notably between 9 May 1923 and some days after the opening of the Rhydd-ddu to Portmadoc new section on 1 June 1923; on each occasion Festiniog men went with the engine, which between its visits to Aberystwyth for use on the Rheidol line, was certainly the most-travelled of the Festiniog stud. When used by McAlpine, it was stored in the open at Beddgelert Siding, there being no cover anywhere. (More detail of these locomotives is given in the locomotive section.)

A meeting held in the Town Hall, Portmadoc on 7 September 1922 under the auspices of the Ministry of Transport was primarily to discuss the Amendment Order which, for the sake of continuity, has already been mentioned. This meeting also heard other matters, the importance of which no doubt varied with the party who brought it to the attention of the meeting. The local authorities complained that the Welsh Highland Order stipulated that the railway should not be assessed for rates at a higher level than would the land have been had no railway been built upon it. There is no doubt that certain local authorities looked upon the railway as some form of goldmine on their doorstep. Rates were to be pegged for five years and protests were unanimous; Glaslyn R.D.C.'s loan would cost the ratepayers 4s. 5d. in the £ and they refused to forward the loan unless the rates could be reviewed within two years.

At the same meeting the Festiniog Railway (Jack again, of course) announced that it was applying to work as a Light Railway and for an Order; it intended to link with the W.H.R. in Portmadoc by means of a new direct line. From accounts of the meeting, its original purpose was somewhat submerged by the strong opposition of the local bodies. Evan R. Davies, for the Welsh Highland, put it to them that they would place too great a financial burden on the railway. Let them pay off the loans first; the local authorities could not have it both ways; the Festiniog Railway paid £1,630 annually in rates and was 12½ miles long; if rated likewise for its 21 miles, the new railway would be severely handicapped.

Economies were essential too, on the Festiniog; if the Light Railway Order was refused, curtailed services would result, and if it was granted, employees on the F.R. would be pruned and those affected would be given the first opportunity of working on the W.H.R. The Order would enable the Harbour station to be linked with the Croesor Tramway route direct instead of by a back-shunt; through trains between Blaenau Festiniog and Dinas Junction could begin at once; a new station for the joint use of both lines in Portmadoc would be commenced; the Britannia Bridge, Portmadoc, would be widened to enable the new link line to be built along one side of it. At present the double Fairlie engines were not permitted to work over the bridge; this restriction would end; and finally, Boston Lodge Works would be closed down and a new works built alongside the joint station.

The link between F.R. and W.H.R. was to pass over High Street off the Britannia Bridge, and so along the former Croesor site to the G.W.R. (ex-Cambrian) crossing. This length was to be built (and was built) under a Festiniog Light Railway Order and financed by them with Debentures for £11,500. Full details of the tedious bickering between the Portmadoc Council (who engaged an engineer to advise them), the contractors (McAlpines), the F.R. and the W.H.R. and which lasted over five years before the road crossing and the widening of the bridge was to everyone's satisfaction, not least the Railway Inspector's, are given in the briefest manner possible in 'Festiniog Railway' (Volume 2). It would seem that almost everyone had lost sight of the spirit of the project whereby all might pull together in common enterprise.

Reverting once again to matters out on the line, the most convenient way of describing the work which faced the contractors is to take the system from north to south and examine what had to be done.

In general terms, all the N. Wales track needed re-sleepering and to economise, 4 ft. instead of 4 ft. 6 in. sleepers were to be used. Ballast was renewed to shallow depth only, and only where required; a new ballast quarry be opened out four chains south of Salem Halt.

Dinas Junction Layout:* 2 loading wharf sidings; 2 coal yard sidings; 1 warehouse siding; 3 coal shed sidings; 2 engine shed sidings; 1 small stabling siding. A new diamond crossing to be laid in between Loco Shed and running line. New 1 in 8 turnouts to be fitted to crossover under road bridge. New water tank at loco shed. New rails in running line opposite water tank. Signalling to be removed.

Tryfan Junction Layout: no sidings. Loop line only. Signalling to be removed.

Waenfawr Layout: 1 coal yard siding. Spiked and disused points to be worked from lever with key on staff. Signals to go.

Treflan Quarry Junction Layout: 1 stabling siding. This was to be lifted.

Bettws Garmon Layout: 1 let-off siding to Hafod-y-wern Quarry. (This was also called Victoria Quarry.) The north end of the loop here was to be lifted. The quarry siding was to go—some of this work had been done by the N.W.N.G. Signals to go.

Gareg-fawr (not listed in the Second Schedule and possibly already removed before W.H.R. took over): there had been loop and storage sidings.

Salem Halt (not listed): installed officially; 'platform' added.

Plas-y-nant Halt: ditto.

Quarry Siding (not listed): siding etc. already removed?

Quellyn Lake Station Layout: 1 stabling siding. New water tank

* The items listed under 'Layout' are taken verbatim from the Second Schedule of the Inventory.

with hydraulic ram to be fitted.* Siding to be lifted but point retained to act as trap. Signals to go.

Glanrafon Quarry : Some simplification had already been done after closure of quarry. Layout : 1 stabling siding. It is believed that a loop was retained here by the W.H.R. at first.

Sidings between Glanrafon and Rhydd-ddu : No reference on Schedule. The northerly connection to the Quarry incline with siding, had already gone. A second siding on a different site to connect with this quarry's wire ropeway, was put in about 1925; it was south of the old connection.

Rhydd-ddu (now *South Snowdon*) Layout. 1 coal yard siding; 1 warehouse line siding.

On the foregoing section, all bridges to have decking renewed, and longitudinal timbers also.

Bryngwyn Branch: Rhostryfan Layout : 1 stabling siding for coal wagons. Signalling to go.

Bryngwyn Layout : 1 loopline; 1 stabling siding for quarry material; 1 line to warehouse; 1 coal yard stabling siding. Signalling to go.

Drumhead Layout : Small yard, with lines and 3 crossings. No work done for W.H.R.

The Schedule of work now passes on to the new line, and it is convenient to add to the layout descriptions, the position as regards work already done (if any) at this location.

In general terms, the line from South Snowdon to Beddgelert had had the formation completed alongside the road to Pitt's Head. A Halt at Pitt's Head was to be installed. The nearby road overbridge was complete, but the cattle overbridge just beyond had been abandoned, unfinished. Additional material was necessary at this summit level to stabilise the formation over the bog. From here the formation was complete southwards to Hafod Ruffydd, and the necessary underbridges had been built in ferro-concrete. The temporary P.B. & S.S. loop north of Hafod had to be lifted and a corrugated iron shelter put up at the Halt there, with 40 ft. stabling siding.

For 3,000 yards south of Rhydd-ddu P.B. & S.S. 41¼ lb. rail, 30 ft. long, was laid. This track needed reconditioning and re-ballasting. South of here, 40 lb. B.S.S. rails 33 ft. long were to be used. As laid, however, insufficient gaps were left for expansion and oak chocks had to be placed outside the rails on curves of under 4 chains radius.

Between Hafod Ruffydd and Tyn-y-coed most of the line was built. A few isolated sections had not been started. Southwards from Tyn-y-

* An illustration of 1910 shows two tanks here, side by side, suggesting there were times of water shortage.

coed to Cwm-cloch-isaf a new formation had to be made abandoning the old P.B. & S.S. works which ran nearly alongside. Beween a point east of Cwm-cloch-isaf and Beddgelert, the formation was finished and Beddgelert station formation was done. Here the layout was to be; 1 warehouse line; 1 coal yard siding; 1 outside pit, with line over. The loop was to be 320 ft. long and 8 ft. 6 in. between centres, but having been thus laid, the Inspector had it altered later. Under the Amendment Order of February 1923 the grade through the station was eased from 1 in 28 to 1 in 40. Originally it was hoped to build separate goods and loco sheds and a siding to stable a whole train. This was not done.

South of Beddgelert the 47 yard tunnel had to be opened out and completed. Under the Amendment Order, the formation south of here was abandoned and a new route must be built. A girder bridge was to be provided over the Glaslyn at Bryn-y-felin Farm. Formation and tunnels in the Glaslyn Pass required bringing up to completion; the long tunnel had not been fully driven at the north end; widening in it was required on one side and nine refuges had to be built. All these tunnels were unlined, being in granite. It was said with truth that a train could be taken through them with all doors wide open.

Provision was to be made for a Halt ('Aberglaslyn') 6 miles 10 chains south of Rhydd-ddu; this had no siding or waiting shelter. From thence the formation and cuttings required extensive digging as far as Nantmor Halt. Layout: 1 small 40 ft. stabling siding. The road was diverted here and a gateless crossing with cattle guards built. A corrugated iron shelter was to be provided and two ex-Festiniog four-wheeled carriage bodies (of the original type) were placed side by side for use as a goods warehouse.

Further down the line the formation had been graded down to river-plain level and the concrete bridge over the Llanfrothen road needed completion. Fencing between here and Croesor Junction was to be finished. Along this section there was Hafod-y-llyn Halt to build with a 40 ft. siding. Beyond, the river crossing at Nant-y-mor was made with a similar bridge to Bryn-y-felin and after a level formation over fields, Ynysferlas required a 40 ft. siding (this was before the name was changed to Hafod Garregog—a name previously used for a point where trains might stop at a hamlet between Hafod-y-llyn and Ynysferlas). Just beyond Ynysferlas a third girder bridge (again of the same pattern) was required over the Dylif, making three identical bridges in this section. For this one, approach embankments required finishing.

There was then but a short run on low embankment to reach a

junction with the Croesor line; this length was finished in most particulars and already had contractor's track on it.

Passing now on to the old Croesor tramway line, there was a simple junction with that tramway. The track between here and the Cambrian crossing at Portmadoc had already been relaid under the P.B. & S.S. in part; the new materials extended southwards to within a mile of the railways' crossing, but thence southward, was still the old Croesor track. The relaid length was in the P.B. & S.S. standard track, i.e. Indian Standard $41\frac{1}{4}$ lb. rails, 30 ft. long on 11 sleepers per length. Spring referred to it as 'a good steel rail' . . . 'on the partially constructed Beddgelert Railway' . . . he continued; 'the sleepers are in fair condition except where damaged by the horses' hooves. All points however, on the section, are still of the quarry type without switch blades'. The Croesor materials lifted from this length became distributed far and wide about the district, some being used by the P.B. & S.S. contractor's as described earlier, or on other railways. The subject of this type of track is a story in itself.*

The more elaborate loop etc. at Croesor Junction did not exist at this time, so the contractors passed south to Ynysfor Halt and pro-

* Close investigation of this form of track suggests it was widely used in North Wales before the time of flatbottomed or bridge rails. It was not exclusive to the Principality, but has been found in differing size at Llangollen (Horse Shoe Pass), Aberllefenni (Corris) and Arthog (Barmouth) as well as in Caernarvonshire. Probably the materials were made locally in each case.

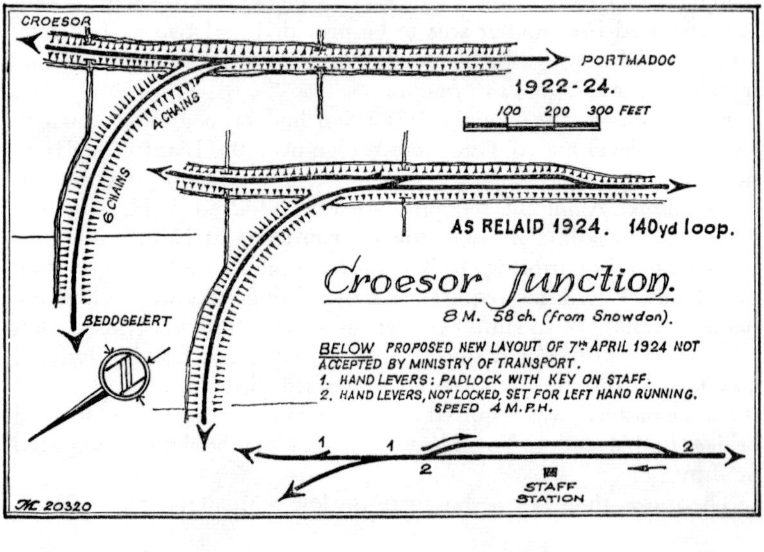

vided a corrugated iron shelter; the original Croesor tramway siding there was left, to be renewed with a 40 ft. one in Autumn 1924.

At Pont Croesor the existing wooden bridge was to be demolished and a steel one substituted. Another iron shelter was placed by the road crossing and the 100 ft. Croesor-period siding lengthened to 300 ft. A water tank, formed by mounting an iron tank on top of a wooden wagon chassis (this had Corris Railway-type oval and sprung buffers and an S-shaped brake handle and was probably off a N.W.N.G. goods wagon) mounted up on a sleeper tower, stood at the northwest end of the bridge and drew its water from the river. It was installed by the Welsh Highland and could be used by engines south of the Beddgelert tank which could not use the supply at the north end of the New station.

At Portreuddyn the loop was to be re-conditioned, though no use was now made of it and there was no stopping place. On this section the contractors would have to relay completely into Portmadoc, where just north of the Cambrian Crossing the Beddgelert Siding (known by the new owners as the Gelert Siding) required relaying and proper pointwork fitting out. The loop was 250 ft. long.

At the crossing itself the Cambrian had a 'hut' manned by a woman flag attendant. In 1923 the incoming Great Western, having achieved advantageous terms over the Welsh Highland regarding use of the crossing, installed a small signal box manned by a porter-signalman; this work was not carried out by McAlpine.

In due course, and not in the immediate conversion period, a new station was to be built south of the crossing, and the Croesor converted to W.H.R. standards to the point where it was about to cross High Street; here a completely new link with the F.R. was also McAlpine's responsibility, and reference has been made to it as coming under the F.R. application for a Light Railway Order. In the same area there were amendments to be made to the Flour Mill loop nearby, the Britannia Bridge reconstructed etc. All details of the finished work are given under 'the route described'.

McAlpine's job was a most extended one. The firm was soon in difficulty with labour. Over 400 men were employed on the project and in the spring of 1923, 393 were unskilled. McAlpine received a strong letter from the Ministry of Labour pointing out that only 250 of these had been recruited locally and they were in breach of their contract and causing local resentment. McAlpine's reply was to the effect that many of the local people were unsuited and unused to this type of heavy work; they had had to use some Irish labourers who had been with them on previous contracts. Though they had tried to avoid using 'tramp labour' they had been compelled by circumstances to do so.

It has already been mentioned that in fact, the Welsh Highland Railway was the controlling body in the new set-up, and that although Festiniog Railway headed notepaper was rubber-stamped beneath 'Operating also Welsh Highland Railway', the Dolgarrog

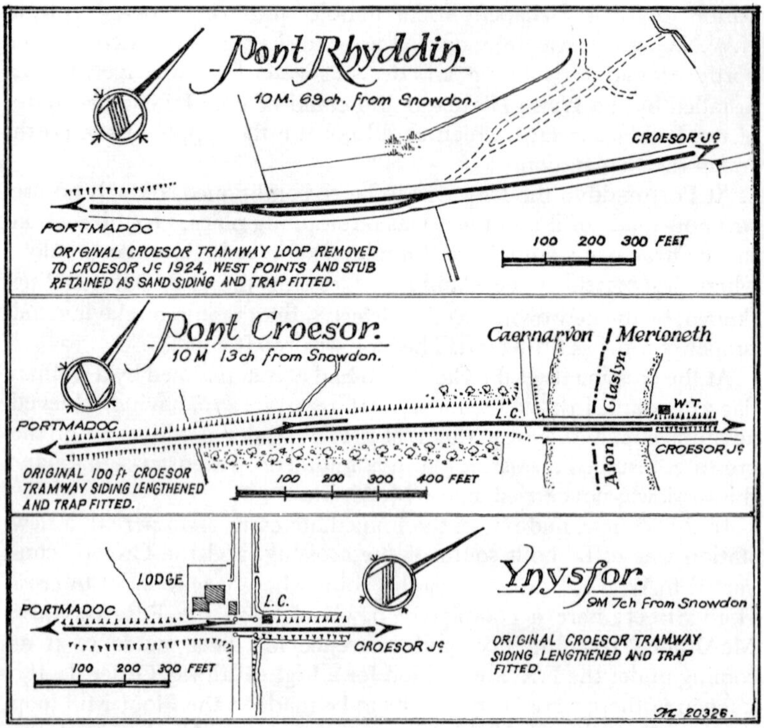

headquarters were strictly operating both and giving priority to the Highland, their special 'baby'. A great number of things were happening which meant items were passing from the Festiniog to the Highland, as was some labour. Almost all the administration was taken from the Festiniog office at Portmadoc and the former N.W.N.G. office on Dinas station. Both went up to Clark Street, Dolgarrog. As Dolgarrog was quite unfamiliar with both lines and had no experience of the operation of railways, the circulation of correspondence between Boston Lodge, Harbour office, Dinas office, Dolgarrog and soon, other persons involved in the running of the railways, was hopelessly inefficient and confusing. In practice, the situation meant that apart from D. O. Jones who remained at Dinas Junction office, the burden of administration and running of the new railway fell on Harbour office and Boston Lodge, respectively. The employees in these places rightly complained at the extra work with which they were saddled, but for which they were given nothing extra. This burden grew greater as time went on. Relations between Dolgarrog and the rest were greatly strained, very naturally. The Festiniog greatly resented the intrusion of W.H.R. affairs, and still more the passing of control of their railway from local gentry whom at least they knew, to a fresh possé of faceless industrialists who had no understanding of them. This unhappy relationship existed throughout the life of the Welsh Highland. It can be read between the lines of most correspondence and was plainly seen in exchanges between senior officials.

At this time, there was an attempt by the Welsh Highland board to acquire shares of Festiniog Railway members; certainly some of the larger holders were approached and a very low offer was made to them. It is known that the Huddart family were so approached and refused to part with their shares.

As McAlpine's converted the junction line from the Cambrian crossing down to High Street, and with the many vicissitudes already referred to made trailing junction with the Festiniog's Harbour station across the road opposite Britannia Terrace (Highland trains never actually entered the Harbour station), they were enabled in due course to remove the old direct Croesor line on to the wharves, which now had to be reached by a back-shunt over Britannia Bridge. This new section, in part strictly Festiniog Railway, was the 'Junction Railway contract' commenced on 14 March 1923, and though connecting trains began to run during the summer of 1923, by August the bridge was far from complete. This work was done under the Festiniog Railway Light Railway Order of 30 January 1923. which also gave powers to build the new joint station which would enable the Harbour station to be abandoned. The lines were :

1. Railway No. 1, of about 5 chains constructed on a widened and rebuilt Britannia Bridge (the old Sluice Bridge) and extending either side of that bridge 1–2 chains and making an end-on junction with the Festiniog Railway at the Harbour station.
2. Railway No. 2, from an end-on junction with Railway No. 1 near the west abutment of the bridge, thence across High Street and along Madoc Street and making an end-on junction with the Welsh Highland approximately due east of the south boundary of

the property at the corner of Madoc Street and Smith Street. Length *c.* 5 chains.

Despite the wordiness of the specification, this only carried the Festiniog to the point where it entered the housing property on the edge of the town centre. The speed limit was 15 m.p.h and powers given to work over the Highland Railway as far as the (now) G.W.R. crossing were given. A plan to divide the railway from the road over the bridge by means of a concrete wall was considered too dangerous.

The New Station—as it was to be known—would contain a Goods Shed with twice the capacity of the old Harbour shed, a shed to contain 13 Festiniog bogie carriages, with repair and paint shops. No provision was made for ex-N.W.N.G. stock, which would continue to be stabled at Dinas. The materials for station and shed were delivered to Boston Lodge and Beddgelert Siding and lay unused until January 1924 when they were disposed of. The correspondence which covers this imaginative scheme—which would have meant so much to the Festiniog of the present-day—shows that there was no clear local understanding of ownership of land, materials etc. as between W.H.R. and F.R. Dolgarrog wrote sharply to Portmadoc saying they were writing Festiniog matters on Welsh Highland notepaper and vice versa, and that their filing system was consequently chaotic. (One's close knowledge of Festiniog office matters would tend to suggest that this was done deliberately to confound headquarters!)

The New Station was never more than a corrugated iron building; the land bought was later leased off to a local butcher for grazing. There was a wooden hut like the one at Dinas, used for Refreshments; both belonged to the Snowdon Mountain Railway whose directors—need one add—were of course among the same persons who administered at Dolgarrog!

In the summer of 1923, the new railway was ready for a series of tests, some of which were done for the benefit of the Ministry's Inspector of Railways.

12 May 1923 : An inspection by the directors and contractors using *Palmerston* and 10 loaded slate wagons. Girder bridges tested. Personnel carried in the Oakeley family private carriage (open 'toastrack' stored in Boston Lodge).

15 May 1923 : Festiniog double Fairlie locomotive and three coaches from Portmadoc to Dinas. Those on train included Jack, Evan R. Davies (Directors), S. E. Tyrwhitt (General Manager of both F.R. and W.H.R.) A. McAlpine, Mr. Prendergast of Fox & Partners, the engineers.

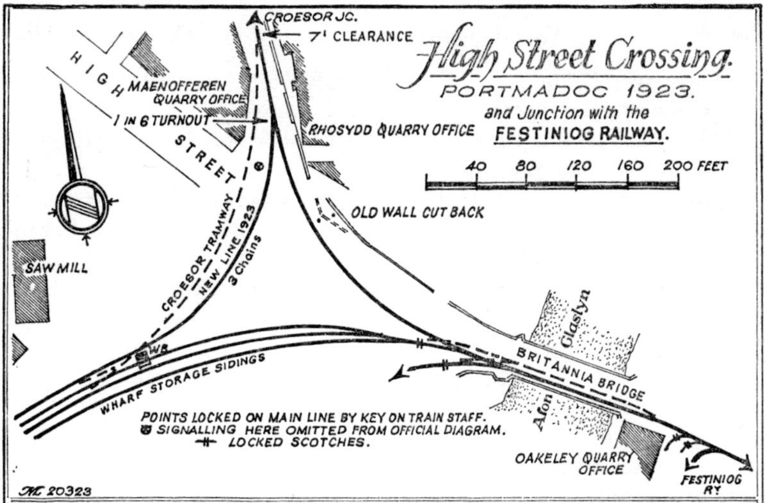
High Street Crossing.
PORTMADOC 1923.
and Junction with the
FESTINIOG RAILWAY.
CROESOR JC.
7' CLEARANCE
HIGH STREET
MAENOFFEREN QUARRY OFFICE
1 IN 6 TURNOUT
RHOSYDD QUARRY OFFICE
40 80 120 160 200 FEET
OLD WALL CUT BACK
SAW MILL
CROESOR TRAMWAY
NEW LINE 1923
3 Chains
Glaslyn
BRITANNIA BRIDGE
Afon
W.B.
WHARF STORAGE SIDINGS
POINTS LOCKED ON MAIN LINE BY KEY ON TRAIN STAFF.
SIGNALLING HERE OMITTED FROM OFFICIAL DIAGRAM.
LOCKED SCOTCHES.
OAKELEY QUARRY OFFICE
FESTINIOG RY
JIC 20323

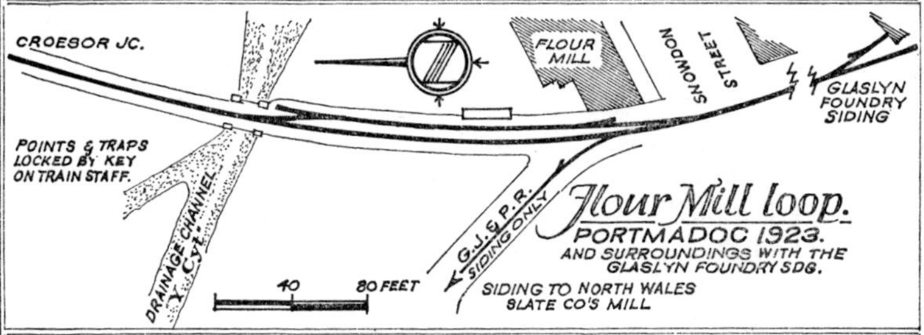
CROESOR JC.
FLOUR MILL
SNOWDON STREET
GLASLYN FOUNDRY SIDING
POINTS & TRAPS LOCKED BY KEY ON TRAIN STAFF.
G.J.&P.R. SIDING ONLY
Flour Mill loop.
PORTMADOC 1923.
AND SURROUNDINGS WITH THE GLASLYN FOUNDRY SDG.
DRAINAGE CHANNEL
Y Cyt
40 80 FEET
SIDING TO NORTH WALES SLATE CO'S MILL

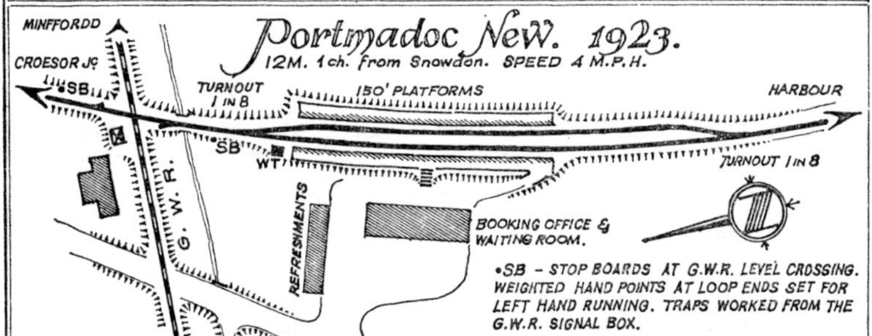
Portmadoc New. 1923.
12M. 1ch. from Snowdon. SPEED 4 M.P.H.
MINFFORDD
CROESOR Jc
SB
TURNOUT 1 IN 8
150' PLATFORMS
HARBOUR
SB
WT
TURNOUT 1 IN 8
G. W. R.
REFRESHMENTS
BOOKING OFFICE & WAITING ROOM.
•SB – STOP BOARDS AT G.W.R. LEVEL CROSSING. WEIGHTED HAND POINTS AT LOOP ENDS SET FOR LEFT HAND RUNNING. TRAPS WORKED FROM THE G.W.R. SIGNAL BOX.
40 80 120 160 FEET
PORTMADOC
NEW ACCESS FOOTPATH

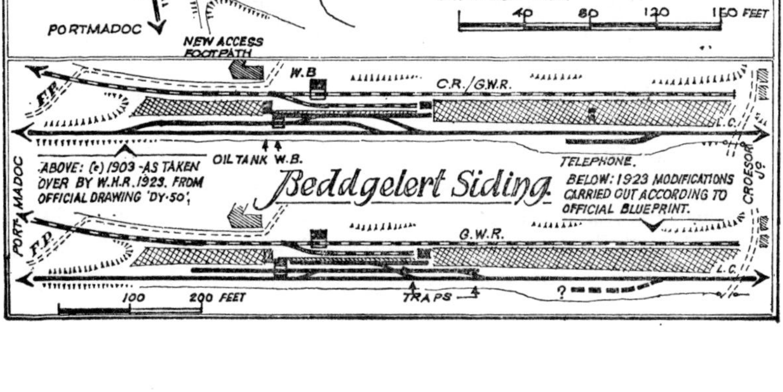
W.B
C.R./G.W.R.
F.P.
L.C.
OIL TANK W.B.
TELEPHONE.
ABOVE: (c) 1903 - AS TAKEN OVER BY W.H.R. 1923. FROM OFFICIAL DRAWING 'DY·50'.
Beddgelert Siding.
BELOW: 1923 MODIFICATIONS CARRIED OUT ACCORDING TO OFFICIAL BLUEPRINT.
PORTMADOC
CROESOR Jc
G.W.R.
F.P.
L.C.
100 200 FEET
TRAPS
?

19 May 1923: details not recorded. 'Gladstone' car substituted for Oakeley coach (perhaps the weather was wet!)

22 May 1923: thought to have been a mock-run for the Ministry inspection two days later.

24 May 1923: Ministry Inspection. There was a separate inspection at Waenfawr and a journey plus inspection between South Snowdon and Portmadoc.

The Inspector was carried from Bettws by car to Waenfawr at 8.30 a.m. to inspect the loop there. The inspection train was boarded at South Snowdon. This consisted of double Fairlie loco *Merddin Emrys*, passenger brake, 1/3 class composition, 'Gladstone Car' (then termed the W.H.R. Inspection Saloon), 'or if fine Oakeley Trolley'. The empty train had left Portmadoc New at 7.30 a.m. to arrive Snowdon 'not later than 9.30 a.m.' where shunting took place so that the Saloon or Trolley was at the rear of the train.

The double Fairlie *James Spooner* was also steamed, leaving Portmadoc light engine at 9 a.m. It was to be at Beddgelert ready to accompany the inspection train from Beddgelert to Portmadoc at about 10 a.m. It was to couple up to *Merddin Emrys* and run double-headed to Portmadoc.

As watering facilities appear not to have been ready at Beddgelert, or might be in short supply, water was to be available at Aberglaslyn from '8.15 a.m. until the Inspection Train has passed on downward journey'. The Beddgelert stationmaster H. D. Jones was instructed to be on duty from 8.30 a.m. until departure of the train, and 'as far as possible, keep the station clear of the public'. Miss Williams (the factotum) was to be on duty at South Snowdon from 9.15 a.m. D. O. Jones of Dinas, was to attend at Waenfawr until the party left. Stationmaster H. E. Jones was to be on duty for both Up and Down trains at Portmadoc New. R. Williams, the Festiniog's Locomotive Superintendent and G. L. Griffiths, were on the train, with Guard Lewis in charge of it.

Returning now to the previous year and to the Dinas end of the railway, an inspection of the N.W.N.G. section was carried out by Col. J. W. Pringle on 22 May 1922 though details of the train are not available. If the condition of *Moel Tryfan* was the same then as it was in the following November, then *Russell* must have been used. Pringle emphasised that at Tryfan Junction passenger trains in either direction used the platform and the loop was only used by goods—again, for either direction. A proportion of the old sleepers would soon need further replacement and not all the old signalling had been taken away. Siding connections at Waenfawr and Bettws Garmon, out of use, had had their point blades spiked and if they were to be retained, they should be fitted up properly with a weighted and locked point lever. At halts too, the 'platform area' should be marked out and gravel applied to define clearance points. On all handworked points, one key should be available instead of a number as then pertaining. The new water tank at Quellyn fouled the carriage door when open.

On the bridges with timber decks, a cat-walk was provided on one side only; both sides must be fitted out.

Pringle was also unhappy about instructions for workings between Dinas and Tryfan Junction; trains carrying tickets and running before the train with the staff, must be reported on arrival back to the starting station before another train was despatched from there. Subject to 5 m.p.h. restrictions through facing points and 15 m.p.h. on the main line, he recommended the opening to passenger traffic.

So much for the former N.W.N.G. section, now back on some sort of operational footing. At Dolgarrog, the Board of the Welsh Highland had throughout this period been casting anxious glances at the Festiniog; there were so many common factors to both lines that they were indivisible by now. The new Board of the Festiniog had taken office after that Company had suffered serious losses; economy of working was the goal and losses were somewhat less in 1922. The obtaining of the Light Railway Order would help them to economise still further. Both Festiniog and Welsh Highland realised that neither could look any longer to slate and goods traffic for their business. A circular to Festiniog shareholders dated 17 February 1923 said 'It is evident that the Company must look to the Holiday Traffic if its fortunes are to be more firmly established and improved. After fruitless efforts on many occasions over the last thirty years, the Welsh Highland Railway is about to be completed and opened . . . It is proposed to make working arrangements between this Company and the Welsh Highland so as to run through trains between Blaenau Festiniog and Dinas Junction . . .' The circular continues to explain that a link line and new station will be required in Portmadoc, and this should lead to economy and efficiency whilst one Managerial staff would fulfil the requirements of both concerns. £6,000 would be needed for the Junction Railway and land for it, the National Provincial Bank was prepared to continue its overdraft facilities and the Light Railway Order authorised the issue of £20,000 in Debenture Stock, of which they now proposed to issue £10,000. The shareholders were invited to attend an Extraordinary General Meeting to authorise the issue of that Stock.

The Festiniog Board (elected in June 1921) made Jack its Chairman on 16 July following, the other directors being Sir John Stewart (the subject of some explanation on a previous page) and Evan R. Davies. Of the long-standing Festiniog Board, Greaves had retired, Bowton, Robjent and Vaughan had been swept aside. The three directors of the June 1921 'coup', were as already noted, the then board of the N.W.N.G. Railways Company.

The key to the new organisation lay not at Dolgarrog however, but in the appointment of Col. Holman Fred Stephens M.I.C.E. of Tonbridge, Kent, as Civil Engineer and Locomotive Superintendent of both railways as from 1 April 1923. The Colonel was by then already a byword in the field of minor railways and fresh from activities with the Royal Engineers in the recent War, his mind was full of the possibilities of using ex-Military equipment. This appointment further complicated the administration for at a single stroke, the engineering side of all activities was moved to Kent, a factor from which neither of the railways ever recovered.

An issue which might have offered further economy was also considered at this time as an alternative to connecting the Welsh Highland with the Festiniog; this idea would have been unheard of had the Festiniog been on a sounder financial footing and it was only the granting of its Light Railway Order which altered the circumstances. The scheme was to have been to terminate the Welsh Highland north of the Cambrian rail crossing and build a new station at the Beddgelert Siding; this would have made exchange with the Cambrian and involved mixed gauge transfer sidings. Oddly, the Cambrian was not in favour of the idea; it could hardly have lost by it.

Local management of the Companies was centred on Portmadoc Harbour and S. E. Tyrwhitt at first filled Frederick Vaughan's long-held post when the latter retired on 5 April 1922. Tyrwhitt became Manager of the Festiniog in May of that year and was already Manager of the N.W.N.G., having taken Aitchison's place. As General Manager of both railways he was the first of a succession of Managers, a situation which impeded the launch of the enterprise, as the only link in personnel on the administration was Robert Evans, Chief Clerk to the Festiniog, who ultimately became (because he was the only person who knew anything about the total situation and the staff employed) the king-pin about which the organisation creaked. Tyrwhitt was followed by John May (a Stephens' appointment) and in 1924 E. H. R. Nicholls took over. Nicholls was a G.W.R. man and fully qualified. Stephens offered to retire to give Nicholls full rein, but the G.W.R. would not allow an employee—for such he still was—to act on another railway except as Consultant. Jack would not accept this; Stephens remained and Nicholls went.

The arrangements for the inspection train of 24 May 1923 have already been noted. The purpose of having two double Fairlie engines at the head of the train was to test the girder bridges for deflection. Lt.-Col. A. H. L. Mount's report of 29 May was a lengthy one:

1. Ballasting was insufficient in many places, especially on the outside of curves. 'Many curves are not in true level or alignment due to the track having been sprung out as the result of inaccurate or insufficient bending of the rails when laid.' There was a temporary watering point at the south of the Aberglaslyn tunnels (noted in connection with the special train). The curve here was especially bad in this respect.
2. The new line would be divided into two staff and ticket sections; South Snowdon–Beddgelert; Beddgelert–Portmadoc New. It might be necessary later to add an extra staff post at Portreuddyn 'where a loop already exists'. (This was never done, the section being divided at Croesor Junction instead.) At this loop the points must be spiked for the single line. Passenger trains, he understood, were not yet to work over the link line between the 'new and old (Festiniog) stations at Portmadoc'. However, he insisted there must be staff working between these places for goods trains working to and from the Beddgelert Siding. To control this, all trains working off the Festiniog to the New Station must stop at No. 6 points of the Harbour station and a Stop Board should be erected there. The various 'dock sidings connected with the main line at the old station must be fitted with stop blocks padlocked in position by a key on the staff'. (This instruction was of course nullified when re-signalling was done by the Festiniog.)
3. The Colonel threatened more severe locking arrangements if points were not suitably fastened in the normal position, and speed limits observed.
4. Much fencing still required to be done, especially along the former Croesor tramway section. The position was so bad that cattle were walking down the narrow gauge and straying on to the Great Western at the crossing.
5. En passant, the highest embankment was given as 30 ft. near m.p. 6 and the deepest cutting of 42 ft. near m.p. 4. The four tunnels are detailed (as already given earlier).
6. Of the concrete culvertings, not all were in good order 'due to slack workmanship in erection'.
7. Of the three girder bridges at 5¼, 7¾ and 8¼ miles, each of 75 ft. square span with through lattice 'N' type girders 8 ft. 6 in. deep

and open decks, he thought these were adequate for present needs, but in the floods of 19 September 1922 the water was at one time only 6 in. below the girders, and this would want watching.

The Bryn-y-felin bridge, tested with two Fairlie engines at 21 and 24 tons each deflected ·42 in. at 15 m.p.h. None of these bridges had been painted after erection 'for some reason' and 'they should be scraped, two coats paint applied, holes drilled in the bottom booms to drain moisture away and side decking applied to enable walkways to safeguard men on the bridge when trains pass by.'

8. The Pont Croesor bridge at m.p. 10 had 8 spans of 24 ft. clear each of rolled steel beams. Deflection at 15 m.p.h. was ·47 in.
9. There were 16 private crossings or footpaths; 'the gates to them should be fitted with stops to prevent them opening in on the railway'. This work was incomplete. (At this time there were no cattle guards save for the crossing at m.p. 1½ on which the Colonel remarked it was fitted with both gates and guards, which he did not understand.)
10. At Nantmor the public road crossing without gates but with cattle guards, should be passed at 5 m.p.h. 'and whistle boards need erecting.'
11. At the G.W.R. rail crossing there were 40 main line movements and 12 shunting movements per day. The recent horse-drawn movements by the Croesor tramway were about 12 a day.

He thought the crossing was made up in manganese steel; it was right-angled. The narrow gauge was built up in G.W.R. standard gauge materials up to a point where traps (single tongue) were fitted. On the north side this was inside the gate on the G.W.R. boundary and on the south side, outside the similar gate.* It was hoped that the gates might be dispensed with when the new railway's fencing was repaired.

The signal box was described together with full details of protective measures for safety. The Light Railway timetables would be drawn up in consultation with the G.W.R. to facilitate the working of the crossing. It was anticipated that there would be 14 daily movements on the narrow gauge with 16 on Saturdays. Of these about four would not be passenger trains.

The Colonel recommended placing both trap points outside

* At this time the Cambrian had protected itself with gates across the tramway contiguous with its boundary fencing, and the single-bladed traps. The former kept off cattle which strayed on to the tramway and then on to the Cambrian; the latter kept off wagons which were equally prone to stray.

the boundary and substituting the gates with long cattle guards. Illuminated Stop Boards should be placed outside the traps for night running. The G.W.R. signalman would be in full charge of the crossing and narrow gauge movements would only be made on a hand signal from him.

If this was unsatisfactory, it might be necessary to replace the gates and alter the G.W.R. signalling.

12. At South Snowdon the station floor was falling in. There was no lighting. Traps were needed at the north end of the loop. The stationmistress needed clear instructions about working the staff and ticket. On the loop line a platform area should be marked out and bounded. At the south end of the loop, the points should normally be set for the siding and unlocked for Up trains leaving the station. (From this it was clear that the Festiniog was describing Dinas-bound trains as Up and the Colonel using the same term for Portmadoc-bound trains!)

13. At Beddgelert the corrugated iron buildings were incomplete. (They were later to be blown away in a freak gale of 1927). Ballasting was unfinished and platform areas not marked off. There was no platform on the west side as the approach line was in deep cutting and such a platform was considered unsafe; with this in mind the Company proposed to halt Down trains at the south end of the loop but the Colonel considered this did not safeguard passengers who might not see one approaching. The distance between the loop lines was only 8 ft. 6 in. and 'pinching between trains might take place'. To make the tracks 13 ft. centre to centre, 'the loop should be slewed towards the station building for about 4 ft. 6 in.'

    He did not like the approach from the village, nor the water pipe carried above the line in the south cutting, to feed the Goat Hotel. Both needed attention.

14. The telephone was connected but the wires were carried through the tunnels on temporary posts foul of the loading gauge. The line could not be opened until this was corrected.

15. Halt buildings were still to be put up at Hafod Ruffydd, Ynysfor and Pont Croesor, and the necessary platform area marked off.

16. He understood that a halt was contemplated at Aberglaslyn. It would be a platform 100 ft. long built up in wood to rail level on concrete piers and channel iron. This was sited outside the long tunnel at m.p. $6\frac{1}{8}$. (The Author can find no evidence that it took this form and it seems to have been but an informal gravelled stopping area).

17. At Croesor Junction the point lever was not locked, nor was there a trap point on the tramway.
18. Flour Mill loop, Portmadoc: this required relaying and fitting with traps. It was only used by goods trains.
19. There was to be a 15 m.p.h. speed limit on the line except for: All curves taken by southbound trains between miles 2–3 and 4–5; southbound trains through Aberglaslyn tunnels; between Portmadoc New and Madoc Street. On the foregoing sections the speed should be limited to 10 m.p.h. Between Madoc Street and over Britannia Bridge, on facing points and over public road crossings speed should not exceed 5 m.p.h.
20. Apart from the instruction about trains stopping before leaving Portmadoc old station, compulsory stops must be made either side of the G.W.R crossing and either side of High Street, Portmadoc in either direction.

Subject to the completion of telephone links and several other urgent matters, he approved opening to passengers 'for a temporary period of six months' after which re-inspection of the line and the Festiniog (where signalling alterations were taking place) should be made, especially in regards the locking of points.

Colonel Mount's report seems to have taken the Ministry of Transport aback. They had never seen the like of it. In an internal exchange of Minutes it was noted '(this line) . . . Its condition does not appear to be very satisfactory but I doubt whether we can legally sanction the use of the line only temporarily for passenger traffic for six months; our position being we can only sanction or postpone opening'. There was some further exchange of views and ultimately the position was resolved thus: 'I think we should proceed on the lines proposed saying that in view of the terms of the Report we are unable to sanction the opening but, that if the Company on their own responsibility wish to initiate a service we will, subject to the terms of the Report and the particular conditions mentioned . . . take no steps to prevent them doing so. If however, the Company are not prepared to bind themselves to the full acceptance of these conditions this letter must be taken as formal notice that opening must be postponed for a month.'

It was now well into the summer season for 1923 and the Company could not really afford to dither; income was essential and in view of its remarks about the importance of the holiday traffic, it had no choice but to take responsibility upon itself and open a service. Taking the whole Welsh Highland system together, the opening dates to passenger traffic were:

Dinas Junction–South Snowdon (Rhydd-ddu)	31 July 1922
South Snowdon–Portmadoc New	1 June 1923
Portmadoc New–Portmadoc Harbour	8 June 1923

The Colonel's inspection of 24 May was extended into a second report dated 1 June. This in part concerns the Festiniog but must be mentioned here. The work concerned the Junction railway and the New station, Portmadoc. Here there was a loop and platforms 150 ft. long; the corrugated iron station building 40 ft. × 12 ft. was incomplete. A water tank was to be erected at the north end. There was no lighting. As regards the triangle of lines formed at the High Street crossing, the Croesor tramway track (the west side of the triangle) was lifted and relaid with a minimum of 135 ft. radius—it was to be lifted altogether a few years later.

There follows a long description of the manner of track laid in the road surface over the Britannia Bridge, and its timber decking between the rails, together with comments on durability, bad drainage etc. into which the report goes fully; 'it is clear however, that the works have not been carried out to the reasonable requirements of the Council'. The manner of point rodding and levers in the street at the top of the triangle of tracks, called for criticism too.

New station was passed for traffic, also Railways Nos. 1 and 2, but final approval would not be given until the Railway Company and the local authority settled their differences!

The problems involving the actual operation of trains and the expenditure of time and money on converting N. Wales Company's stock to vacuum brake plus the plan to work their locomotives over the Festiniog with attendant efforts to reduce their bulk to allow them to work through Moelwyn Tunnel, are described elsewhere. Due to the rising cost of labour efforts to economise by cutting down wages and the number of staff to a minimum—payment to railway employees in the neighbourhood was of course, far higher on the G.W.R. than on the adjacent narrow gauge systems—were well intended, but did not bite deeply enough. The fact was that the scheme was ill-timed, road competition was keen, and there was economic slackness throughout the country following the first boom of the war's aftermath. Jack's prediction that holiday traffic would now be the most important source of income was well off the mark, for the Welsh Highland's initial receipts for goods and passenger trains read thus:

Year	*1922*	*1923*	*1924*	*1925*	*1926*	*1927*
	£	£	£	£	£	£
Goods	3644	3422	3827	3929	3337	3479
Passenger	246	2517	2014	1139	616	686
and which resulted in a loss on Revenue Account of:						
	599	1573	2331	742	787	3304

the last figure being the worst in the whole history of the Welsh Highland and resulting in the appointment of a Receiver in March 1927. But this is to anticipate. The first shake-up came after the losses of 1922–3 and at the Annual General Meeting of 12 April 1924. It was a stormy occasion.

Jack was made the scapegoat for the disappointing outcome of the combined venture, though it is easy to look back and see why he had incorrectly forecast that better times would return for the slate industry. It is unlikely that anyone could have foreseen the keen rates for business charged by small local bus operators, who were not only cutting the railway rates, but putting each other out of business. Jack, with the disadvantage of being already suspect, saw only too well that his predictions had only served to worsen relationships, and very wisely he offered his resignation as Chairman; this took effect from 1 November 1924. Stephens appealed to the shareholders far more; he had railway experience and most of his undertakings lived side by side with financial embarrassment. Not surprisingly, he became the Man of the Hour, chosen because he alone of any of the administration knew this sort of situation only too well. But even Stephens could not control rising costs, revive the slate trade or bring back passengers—the declining passenger figures speak for themselves. Stephens was made a Director on 20 November 1924 and whilst still retaining his earlier posts, became Chairman and Managing Director on 1 January 1925. He continued in this multiple capacity until his death on 23 October 1931 (also given as 30 November).

Of Jack, the master-mind behind the consolidation of the scattered systems into one unit, and the man who wielded so much influence with the County Council and the supply of electricity, and of whom so much was hoped to alleviate the unemployment in the district, little more can be learned. Other researchers have failed to trace much more of him following the disaster of the evening of 2 November 1925. Before midnight on this day, the Eigiau Dam of the Aluminium Corporation collapsed. Water percolated under the dam, which remained intact in itself. This water poured into the Coedty Reservoir which was small, and could not hold it. It too collapsed and the Power Station and village of Dolgarrog, one mile below, was engulfed. Luckily most of the village was in the Assembly Hall for the weekly film show, and being on high ground and having its own power supply, continued there without being aware that sixteen of their fellows had lost their lives. It is said that 'Jack did not come out of the affair very well'.

The Times of 5 November (giving the disaster date as the 3rd) said the dam had been built in 1908, about the time when the P.B.

& S.S. schemes were given up for shortage of money. Jack, as Managing Director of the Company 'and its allied Companies' was interviewed with General R. F. Legge, who was the Treasury Director of the N. Wales Power & Traction Co. . . . the Government was said to be interested in the Power Co. 'to which the Aluminium Corporation stands as contractor for the supply of electricity'. The village population at the time was given as 1,000 and the Aluminium Works as being out of action, flooded, for several days.

The Minutes of the Company have not come to light, but from the Annual Returns some idea of losses for the early years can be gauged. Despite complaints about road competition, the passenger figures for the first three full years of operation were quite considerable :

1923	1924	1925
58,203	50,485	24,653

and one can only assume that in order to compete with road vehicles, the fares were made too low. It was locomotive operating costs in the years above which really reduced margins, plus considerable general charges and permanent way costs. The figures are given in a later section.

Anxiety was felt about the failure to pay interest on the Debentures —the first call on the Company. By 1927 these amounted to nearly £17,000 in unpaid interest and dividends generally. On 16 January 1925 the Treasury advised that it did not intend to appoint a Receiver, notwithstanding that no interest had been paid on its Debentures.

One of the causes of high operating costs was the somewhat luxurious passenger service provided by the railway at the beginning. For instance, a reasonable timetable operated throughout the period 1923–4 including the winter, and was continuing as only two trains throughout the winter of 1924–5 when Col. Stephens stepped in and on 15 December 1924 suspended it completely from then until next July. It ran until September, and a limited service ran again in the winter of 1925–6, but the scale of operations was never the same again. For instance, between September 1925 and June 1926, and from September 1926 to 1 June 1927, the winter train was one each way per day. After a somewhat 'thin' summer passenger timetable, during the winter of 1927–8 trains worked from each end; at the end of summer 1930, winter passenger workings ceased altogether. However, this is to anticipate; the object of outlining the timetable here being to show its decline in an effort to cut running costs.

Stephens's Railway Empire was based on Tonbridge, and his

method was to make flying visits to his railway outposts, inspect and deliver instructions, and then return to his eyrie. Such visits would be followed by some terse correspondence and reflections on his findings. Boston Lodge was now responsible for all but minor repairs to W.H.R. stock. Stephens held a poor opinion of all its employees and they had no respect for him. His military manner and bearing cut no ice with the Celts, who found it convenient to forget most of his instructions once he had gone. A Consulting Engineer was given local charge as Stephens' representatives from 1927, but the slow methodical methods of Boston Lodge tested Stephens's patience still; at his death, his assistant W. H. Austen, took over the duties of Engineer & Locomotive Superintendent.

It was inevitable that sooner or later, a creditor would have a Receiver put into the Company. This took place at last on 5 March 1927 when Caernarvonshire County Council petitioned, their debenture interest overdue being £2,000. The Petition, before Mr. Justice Eve, was successful, Mr. Eve remarking, 'The service was not a very regular one. After one had waited a considerable time one might be told there was no train and one would have to walk!' That was his experience. He was sorry the Company had fallen on evil days. Col. Stephens took on the additional role of Receiver and Manager. When Stephens died, R. T. Griffiths of 22 Castle Square, Caernarvon, became Receiver and Manager. This made administration a little easier for Robert Evans at the Harbour, who at last had a fellow countryman at a reasonable distance, with whom to liaise. Clearly, Griffiths had little experience of railway matters, so by now the feeble Highland line relied on the extra-Festiniog efforts of Evans at the Harbour office and Morris Jones the foreman of Boston Lodge. It was too much to expect. The Dolgarrog regime had ended abruptly when Jack resigned; the Col. Stephens's regime ended abruptly at his death (for his successor Austen, though a capable man, was not a person in the same mould); at last accountant Griffiths put local government back into the hands of the men on the job and so, within ten years, it could truthfully be said that the Festiniog was in practical terms, truly operating the Welsh Highland! How were the mighty fallen!

Strangely, for some reason, the Highland had never been a really unified railway. The old N.W.N.G. character and control resumed ex-Dinas Junction, and in fact it was extended down to Beddgelert as if that Company had always achieved this goal. On the other hand, the southern end of the system was more conveniently administered from Portmadoc, and so Beddgelert became a sort of frontier post, made clear when the method of operating passenger trains is examined. These often 'went into Purdah' on arrival there, lingering to coal and water and allow their passengers time to walk round and take tea. In many instances what appeared to be a through service on the timetables involved a change of train at Beddgelert; Festiniog England engines would bring a train of Festiniog stock from Portmadoc New to there, and return again. Ex-N.W.N.G. stock and engine, working out from Dinas, would also return there at night. The New station, Portmadoc, was always a 'Festiniog' station; it was never staffed by Highland men. Harbour station did all the work for this station and F.R. staff saw that all passengers and luggage were transferred from F.R. to W.H.R. trains. Of course most of the trains were manned by Festiniog crews and guard. The Harbour station was full of Highland stationery and the problems of charging the Highland with costs incurred by the Festiniog, together with liaising quickly with Griffiths, were only a little easier than before. Colonel Stephens had taken the accountancy of the Welsh Highland out of Robert Evans's hands. Evans wrote to Griffiths on the latter's appointment as Receiver, and explained how much more convenient it would be (under the operating methods just described) to have the books at the Harbour station. The reply came :

2 May 1932

'. . . I understand from the Auditor that you used to act as agent at the Portmadoc end of the Welsh Highland Railway at a weekly salary of 9s. 8d. I find out there is hardly any traffic now for the Welsh Highland Railway at your end, and while still anxious to retain your services, I am afraid that in the present financial circumstances of the Company, I cannot ask you to continue on your present salary. I shall therefore be glad if you will let me know what is the lowest figure at which you are prepared to act until things improve.

R. T. Griffith.'

It seems too, that about this period the Highland's own stock was suffering from want of maintenance and repair, so that they took the opportunity of borrowing Festiniog vehicles whenever circumstances allowed. This annoyed the Festiniog administration intensely, and threatening notes went to Dinas Junction. Up there they seemed to enjoy some sense of immunity, for apparently no one at the Portmadoc end had time to come over and see them personally. When the Welsh Highland closed down five years later, the Festiniog stock was still on their metals.

In an attempt further to reduce running expenses, the link between the two railways in Portmadoc was virtually closed at the start of the summer table for 1929 when Highland passenger trains ceased to cross over the G.W.R. metals and passengers were made to cross the line on foot, accompanied by a member of staff from the Harbour station sent for that purpose. At first a Festiniog train was standing at the New station to meet them, but latterly passengers had to find their own way through the 'backs' of the town to the other station. This was far from popular with them. By avoiding the use of the crossing, the W.H.R. was enabled to avoid payment to Paddington which had long been a bone of contention. For long enough the Festiniog–Welsh Highland had been trying to establish what they received in exchange for annual payments exceeding £150 a year. The G.W.R. 6-lever signal cabin had been quickly established as soon as that Company took over from the Cambrian; it all had to be paid for. Robert Evans made several 'visits' to the cabin and on one, for instance, found the clock for which the Western charged, was no longer in the cabin at all. Interviews and correspondence on the subject continued years after the Welsh Highland closed. At first, small loads were carried across the standard gauge in porters' barrows or wheelbarrows. Exchange traffic between the Beddgelert Siding and the wharves was taken in single wagons which were either loose-shunted over (the engine remaining on narrow gauge property!) or handled across by an employee. By 1929 the Highland goods train crossed but once a day, and when Croesor traffic ceased, traffic was simply 'as required', which was seldom. Traffic over the crossing resumed for the north-bound through Excursions off the Festiniog during 1935 and 1936.

At this time the Croesor 'trip' was, like the remainder of the southern end, a Festiniog responsibility . . . in fact, for most of the Highland's existence it had been convenient to work it from Boston Lodge as an extension of the work of the Bottom Shunter, i.e. the engine which shunted Portmadoc wharves. Latterly the tonnage from this source was about 70 tons a week over the crossing. This was carried mainly in the quarries' own or Festiniog wagons on hire; at first the run to Croesor was made daily, then thrice a week. The Croesor horse would leave wagons at the Llanfrothen road crossing or the Junction. At times when slate traffic was enjoying a boom, the Bottom Shunter would not be available and a special working from Boston Lodge was made either by tractor (it was a useful trial ground for the latest Stephens' gimmick in internal combustion) or steam engines sent specially for the purpose. The latter are said at times to have nosed their way to the foot of the Lower Parc Incline, over original Croesor rails! It may be added that in considering traffic over the railways' crossing, the Croesor traffic would at first have been sufficiently frequent to perhaps justify the usually careful protective measures of Paddington; together with the evidence of the train service initially instigated by the W.H.R. and the high hopes of increased traffic, the crossing would have been a most interesting place in the early 1920s. By the end of the decade however, narrow gauge traffic was but a trickle, and a review of the system was appropriate in the circumstances. It is amusing to note that when Colonel Mount returned to make a final inspection on 11 October 1926, he found both cattle guards and gates across the narrow gauge, the latter having been *re-erected*! Clearly, the Welsh Highland's fencing was not good enough.

During the latter 1920s, the Company made efforts to bring the signalling in line with the Ministry requirements. New semaphores at Harbour station did away with the need for a Stop Board on to the Junction line there. Many of the intermediate siding connections had had traps fitted to replace the scotches, and some scotches had been properly locked. Not all points were worked with weighted hand levers, and there was continued criticism of locking on these points. The Colonel added in 1926 that it was intended to continue these signalling improvements through on to the Dinas–South Snowdon section.

At Tryfan an alteration had been made whereby a branch train wishing to enter the Junction must wait for telephone permission from Dinas Junction before the guard of that train could unlock the loop points with the key on the Wise staff; to give greater effect to this, a pair of traps kept open was installed by the Stop Board at the foot of the branch's falling gradient. This move followed the decision not to restore passenger working to Bryngwyn. It was felt that with the existing track, a converging collision with a train from Waenfawr was possible. Final approval for Welsh Highland and Festiniog Light Railways for passenger working was then recommended—trains had been running on the Highland line since early June 1923 of course, and there had been a continuing service on the Festiniog.

Other track alterations had been taking place during the period under review. A new branch line was opened south of Waenfawr station to connect the railway with the Dudley Park Granite Quarry. This lay on the west side of the line, and there was an ungated crossing over the main road adjacent. Welsh Highland open wagons were run under a loading chute; the junction was made through a trapped connection. Colonel Mount inspected on 13 October 1926.

As was anticipated, the Beddgelert–Portmadoc New section proved too long and the Porteuddyn loop materials were moved to Croesor Junction in March 1924. This was inspected on the same day as the Waenfawr branch. It had facing points 142 yards apart. The place was unattended, the staff and tickets being kept in a cabin unlocked by a key on the staff, and connected to the telephone circuit. The loop line was then on the main line and the Croesor tramway made junction with the main; this was to be altered so that junction was made into the loop, as was already done at Tryfan Junction. This would enable the points to be secured by the Portmadoc New–Croesor Junction staff instead of the Croesor Junction–Beddgelert staff currently in use; the latter was inconvenient and if properly worked, involved unnecessary light engine mileage. Branch trains would then come to a stop at the trap points and permission be asked for to enter the loop, as at Tryfan. The arrangements were duly altered to the satisfaction of the Inspector.

As the financial position grew worse the Local Authorities became more concerned about their loans. They had noted that the Treasury did not intend to act as regards non-payment of interest on £35,774, but these were faceless men and through the Joint Committee they pressed their Members of Parliament and County Councillors to act before matters grew worse. It was suggested that the Board of Trade might persuade the L.M.S.R. and G.W.R. to take over the railway between them. Their representatives met Sir Cyril Hurcombe for the Board, but they confirmed the issue which had they put on the several overtures put to them previously . . . they would only be prepared to work it if their costs were covered by a guarantee from the Board. No guarantee was available.

With the end of the '20s and the early '30s came the slump which hit the whole country. Once more the Board of Trade was asked to enquire if more quarry owners could not be encouraged to send their products by W.H.R. The figures given by the quarries in reply showed that by using the railway their transport costs would be 3–4 times greater than using a lorry. The following resume of the local quarry position was categorised : (February 1931)

Alexandra, Moel Tryfan, Cilgwyn	Not working. Stocks going to Caernarvon Quay—traffic will end the following month.
Clogwyn-y-gwyn	Output goes to Dinas and Portmadoc by W.H.R.
Glanrafon, Gareg-fawr, Victoria	All closed
Parc & Croesor, Rhosydd	(Croesor Tramway) Not using tramway, what is despatched goes to Penmaenmawr (by road?)

Seeing no hope for the venture whose accumulated deficit was now of the order of £24,000, the Joint Committee met and decided to press the Debenture Holders to at least suspend the train service. For some reason no Returns had been made for 1932, but for 1931 the income from freight was but 1/5th of what it had been in 1930 and 1/7th of the 1929 figure. The 1931 passenger income was 1/8th of the 1927 total in terms of passengers originating on the Company's own system and only 1/6th of that originating elsewhere. There did not seem to be any point in carrying on as track, locomotive and traffic expenses ate up all the income from carriage, regardless of additional overheads. The exceptional expense under 'Law Charges' (normally around £50 per annum) of £1,395 in the year a Receiver was appointed, was yet another millstone. There was little for the Joint Committee to be optimistic about; Stephens (perhaps their only champion) was dead and his successors were willing but had little experience. The country was still in the doldrums, though the economy looked more promising. They had only recently been shown that the freight traffic, which brought in most of the revenue, had probably been lost for ever.

In November 1933 a meeting of the Joint Committee still clung to the hope that the Croesor quarries might bring back traffic to the old Croesor section at least, and it was agreed to modify the idea of closing the railway completely and leave that length *in situ*. This would benefit Portmadoc, which was keen not to dispose of anything which might bring business. Quick to sense the position, some local authorities suggested that Portmadoc might make itself responsible for that part of the line. A conference of representatives of local authorities met and obtained the agreement of the Debenture Holders to retain the Portmadoc end of the line. Deputations also went to the Festiniog, L.M.S. and G.W. Railways but neither of the London-based concerns would take over the Welsh Highland without the Board of Trade guarantee. On 31 December the Company suspended all services.

In June 1934, at the eleventh hour so far as summer services for the year were concerned, the Festiniog Board made an extraordinary announcement; it would take a 42-year lease of the Welsh Highland from 1 July. Negotiations had been prolonged and would have been completed earlier, but the decision lay before the Master of the Court. The decision seems to have been based on the improvement in the Festiniog's own traffic position, but in the event the reasonably better returns of 1934 did not re-occur, and during 1935 the cost of working both systems was disastrous. The actual rent was purely nominal of course, a mere 20s. per half year at first. The second year's rent of £100 3s. od. seemed extortionate against the losses occasioned in working, however. Employees were dismissed and a letter passing between staff regarding the accounts reads, '... one keeps thinking how much better off this Company (the Festiniog) would have been without the W.H. Railway. I am sorry to say that things on that railway are in a very bad condition ... the outlook as regards the goods traffic is as gloomy as ever, it is a great problem what can be done with it, but I suppose we will carry on and see what we can do next summer again....'

Every avenue of reducing overheads was explored. Festiniog officials met L.M.S. representatives at Euston on 5 April 1935 to revise the agreement between the North Wales Narrow Gauge Railways Co. and the L.N.W.R. dated 16 March 1877 and 9 June 1884 regarding expenses at Dinas Junction. The Festiniog made it clear that working the Highland line for the six months to 31 December 1934 (the first half-year of the lease) had incurred a loss of £200. The line required £600–£700 spending on the track and rolling stock. The goods and mineral traffic was virtually nil. The narrow gauge line was paying a proportion for signalling apparatus and wages at Dinas which was quite out of keeping with the business they were doing. Agreement was reached and this saved the W.H.R. £170 a year, back-dated to 1 January 1935. The signalling expenses were in fact, based on an allocation of 9½ levers to the W.H. Company whilst at the time under discussion, all signalling was virtually in respect of L.M.S. movements. The Chairman pointed out however, that the N.W.N.G. had been the Incomers under the Railway Clauses Act and were liable for the signalling. In the event the legal commitment of the W.H.R. was to continue to pay maintenance proportion on the levers and telegraph apparatus, but they would be relieved of the working costs of the box. If traffic reappeared, the matter would be re-opened.

In the Annual Report for 1936 the Festiniog Board announced they had decided not to re-open the Welsh Highland to passenger traffic that coming season. The 1936 services had in fact ended on 26 September . . . 'too difficult to run with advantage owing to its length' was their conclusion about the line. So negotiations were put in hand to surrender the lease, but this was not finalised until 3 November 1942.

The Welsh Highland Railway of the 1930s must have been a railway with the hand of death on it anyway. Goods trains seldom worked on the Tryfan Junction–Croesor Junction length, and passenger working lasted for about three months of each year. Even the Tryfan branch line decayed and if the replies of the quarries in 1931 were reliable, there could have been little traffic on the branch either. A similar situation was to come to the Festiniog itself in ten years later and the spectacle of nature reclaiming the track and right of way is well remembered. So it was that Welsh Highland latter-day services ran on a railway which gave every evidence of scraping and saving to stave off the inevitable. The loss to the Festiniog on working both lines in the period 1 January–1 May 1936 was £850, but the Festiniog did not publish individual Highland losses save for a cumulative figure of £600, said to cover the period 1 July 1934–31 December 1935.

There being no call for goods and mineral services, a train was sent to collect all the stabled wagons along the line. At the time there was a once-weekly freight train down the length of the line worked from Dinas, with a Dinas–Beddgelert working extra when required. Most of this was wagon-load stuff but there was some domestic coal. The quarry at Bettws Garmon opened for a short time during 1933 and there was a small panic at Dinas to repair a number of slate wagons; the business was short-lived, but serves to show that if the quarry branch had been abandoned and the connection removed, it was certainly re-instated hurriedly.

The quarries up at Moel Tryfan also re-opened on a small scale, but the L.M.S. had opened a new loading dock at Pen-y-groes and by 1933 the slates from this area were being taken by road for loading there. This was a big loss to the Welsh Highland, whose Brygwyn branch traffic in the late 1920s was the most important they had.

The train which as noted collected the remainder of wagons resulting from this sporadic freight service, ran on 19 June 1937. (There was also a locomotive at Boston Lodge which had to be collected; it was the Baldwin 4–6–0 tank which the Welsh Highland had acquired in 1923 and which had gone to the Lodge Works in late 1936 after working the passenger season.) The train consisted of *Russell* which brought Festiniog wagons back on to their parent line and returned with the Baldwin. Owing to the weight, and wet and greasy rails, the collection had ultimately to be made in two trips, and the stock was pushed into the sidings at Dinas.

Dinas represented a woebegone sight in the late 1930s. Some of the passenger stock was under cover in the carriage shed, but a long train mainly of Ashbury carriages, stood out partly beneath the road bridge on the main running line. In the engine shed *Russell* and the Baldwin were left to rot. The sidings outside the workshops were choked with broken wagons and the yard around the transfer sidings became a jungle of weeds in which overturned stock lay or dismembered in the weather. The running line was encroached by overhanging boscage, but the track remained reasonably free except in wet cuttings.

There were three lots of rolling stock which were acquired by the Festiniog under the terms of surrender of the lease, and in lieu of £186 owing for the supply of engines, coal and labour. These were:

1. One 0–6–4 Tank locomotive, *Moel Tryfan.*
2. One bogie carriage No. 23 (combined series numbering).
3. Three ex-W.D. bogie open wagons used for coal traffic.

Apart from the purely Festiniog part of the Junction line in Portmadoc, i.e. that short length at Britannia Bridge which was its own line, the permanent way materials beyond there into New station were also allotted to it. The F.R. said that the cost of lifting the track would be quite economic, but that they would sell it for scrap on site. In correspondence they admitted it was only the *Moel Tryfan* which interested them; this was dismantled in Boston Lodge and it would hardly have been feasible to re-assemble and return to Dinas!

Until the surrender of lease the Festiniog had its problems with the W.H.R., which was not over-seen in any way. Parts of Dinas yard were used for wartime coal storage. The Snowdon Mountain building there was used by Vanwil Oil Co. The composite goods warehouse was still being used by the L.M.S. In late 1939 the boys of Rockferry High School, Birkenhead (evacuated to Portmadoc County School) were said to have had a 'field day' with the layout and wagons on the Beddgelert Siding and to have run wagons through the boundary gate with the G.W.R. The allegation that it was English and not Welsh children who were responsible was probably perfectly valid—to the local children the sight of small wagons waiting just for them would long have ceased to be an attraction.

The L.M.S. made an offer for the Welsh Highland land at Dinas in 1941. They would lift the track and leave it on one side for recovery. The road bridge had been maintained by the standard gauge since 1877 for 15s. a year charge to the narrow (whose responsibility it was) and there would be a financial arrangement for the whole site which would include offsetting the money owed by the Highland to the L.M.S. The W.H.R. still owned the Station Master's house there and this might be excluded; the L.M.S. would remove and scrap their tracks on W.H.R. land. It was proposed to discharge D. O. Jones, the last member of W.H.R. staff, and fence off the L.M.S. property entirely. This was ultimately done and the W.H.R. site became premises of the County Council. Despite the fact that no narrow gauge trains ran, the responsibility of part-costs for signalling in the L.M.S. box remained a charge on the Festiniog until surrender of the lease.

Net receipts to the Festiniog of the Welsh Highland over the years 1938–43 inclusive (when no trains ran) were almost £400, 1942 bringing in £120 gross. Almost all of this came from rentals. Five guineas was owed to the W.H.R. under the leasing agreement, at the end of the leasing period. Of rents the War Department leased sections of the line based on Rhydd-ddu, Rhostryfan and Beddgelert and Dinas carriage shed was temporarily leased to the War Aricultural Executive Committee. There was also rent from the old station house at Snowdon Ranger which had been converted into a private dwelling house, long before the W.H.R. closed.

Messrs. Richard Williams & Co. of Portmadoc Slate Works, wrote to the Festiniog in August 1943 asking for services to their private siding which lay off the Welsh Highland. This was due to petrol rationing, as they had not used rail transport for some years. Robert Evans's reply not only pointed out that Festiniog lease of the W.H.R. had ended, but added a few hometruths for good measure! At one time Williams had paid the Festiniog 15s. a year for having slab taken there from Blaenau; theirs was the last operative siding off the W.H.R.—being actually off the Gorseddau's course.

The Ramblers' Association (Liverpool & District Federation) prepared an appeal dated November 1942 'Welsh Highland Railway Footpath Proposal' and sent deputations to all the local Councils asking that the track should be dedicated to the public for walking. They pointed out the success of converting the Leek & Manifold Valley narrow gauge line into a footpath and of failures and success in Jersey. It was the occupation of the War Department which blocked progress at the time as, when the railway was lifted, the Ramblers' Association had not realised that a length southwards from Pitt's Head was being used for gunnery practice by letting Festiniog slate wagons run down by gravity to be shot at by anti-tank guns, and the ex-Croesor section was not dismantled either.

The effective date of ending the Festiniog lease of the Welsh Highland was 31 December 1942. Cessation of arrangements with the L.M.S. at Dinas ended on 30 June 1943. Official date of closure to all traffic was 31 May 1937.

The Welsh Highland track was removed under a Requisition Order No. 205/Gen/163 issued under the Defence Regulations 1939 which authorised the British Iron & Steel Corporation (Scrap) Ltd. of Caxton House, Tothill St., S.W.1, to enter the land occupied by the railway and remove . . . 'all the articles specified . . .' This was dated 13 March 1941. The specification was :

1. Main line including loops and sidings except that portion about 3½ miles in length which is between Portmadoc and the Crossing which joins the Croesor Railway (1).
2. One engine, water column tank, all tools etc. in engine shed store and Smiths shop (2).
3. Slate wagons, coal trucks, other wagon and vans.
4. 50 pairs of wheels and axles.
5. One steam engine by the Hunslett Engine Co. of Leeds No. 901 dated 1906 and one steam engine by Baldwin of Philadelphia No. 45172 of 1917 (3).
6. Various scrap metal lying about the permanent way.

The above is given exactly as scheduled. (1) is a little vague geographically but in fact the length from Llanfrothen road crossing right into the Harbour station was left alone. This was all relaid in heavy FB rail. The Croesor tramway beyond Llanfrothen crossing was left; this was original track material. (2) The engine referred to was a stationary one to drive the workshop. (3) The 'Hunslett' engine was removed for further use and the Baldwin cut up in the yard outside the shed.

There was some consternation at Headquarters when the Order was received as item 2 was thought to refer to *Moel Tryan* 'now at Boston Lodge in a dismantled state which was to pass to us as one of the terms of surrender'. This was contained in a letter from the Chairman showing that neither directors nor anyone else responsible for the Welsh Highland, knew what it had, where it was, nor what exactly was to be scrapped! The point of relief for the Festiniog came with this Order; they recommended the W.H.R. Receiver (now Gregory Williams) to point out that his tenants could hardly be expected to operate a railway which had been taken up for scrap. This ruse was at last to meet with success. Up until then the Master of the Court had ruled that there was no statutory provision enabling the running of the railway to be discontinued.

On the other hand, there was joy in the Festiniog office . . . 'we are getting rid of the Welsh Highland Railway . . .' (12 November 1942) for on 4 November the Registered Office of the Festiniog at 56 Buckingham Gate, London, wrote, 'You will I am sure be glad to know that yesterday the Court made an Order giving leave for the surrender by the Festiniog Railway of its lease of the Welsh Highland Railway . . .' (By then of course, the track for the most part had gone and there was little left of the high hopes which could be traced back to the early 1870s.)

The sections of railway retained have been referred to; it was also intended to leave in use a section for about 1½ miles north of

J. M. Lloyd

Contractor's railway consisting of Croesor-type materials in a water-logged and unfinished section of the P.B. & S.S. north of Beddgelert. 1958.

Locomotive Publishing Co.

Beddgelert before official opening, with Russell *on N.W.N.G. coach train and before the stock was cut down. Erstwhile bookstall at right. 1923.*

f.p. 320

F. Frith

Beddgelert from the south, showing additional coal siding to right, and coal merchant's Ford lorry behind the bookstall (later removed).

H. F. Wheeller

Festiniog-lease period of the W.H.R., with multi-coloured train at Beddgelert, 1935.

F. Frith

The deep cutting immediately north of Nantmor Halt, looking north towards the main Aberglaslyn tunnel, in the early years of the W.H.R.

H. F. Wheeller

Leaving Portmadoc 1935, the Baldwin starts away from the compulsory stop at the High Street crossing.

H. F. Wheeller

Passenger's view of a northbound train nosing its way over the High Street, Portmadoc, en route for Portmadoc (New) station. 1935.

R. W. Kidner

Portmadoc train crossing the Glaslyn river at Port Croesor in 1934, with Welsh Pony *– Festiniog locomotive, Welsh Highland coaches.*

H. F. Wheeller

The Baldwin on a short train, makes its way towards the south end of the Aberglaslyn tunnel, with maintenance trolley 'tied' on behind. 1935.

P. M. Gates

Dinas in 1934, looking south; the Welsh Highland main line curves away top left, for Portmadoc and the L.M.S. line (on the Nantlle Railway site) disappears towards Afon Wen on the right.

P. M. Gates

Dinas in 1934, looking north towards the exchange sidings and with the L.M.S. platforms to the left.

R. W. Kidner collection

Beddgelert-bound Welsh Highland train in lush country west of Tryfan Junction; note the differing colours of carriage.

F. Frith

Looking westwards above Nantmor and a northbound train of Festiniog engine and stock. 1923.

L. & G.R.P.

Bryn-y-felin Bridge from the west bank, 1923.

F. Frith

Short tunnels in the Aberglaslyn Pass, 1922, looking north. This length was left unfinished between 1909 and 1922.

Locomotive Publishing Co.

The railways' crossing, Portmadoc New, with new station beyond after installation of water tank. The gates were to keep animals from straying onto the standard gauge; G.W.R. cabin right.

R. W. Kidner collection

Brave new world, Portmadoc, 1923. The New Station with corrugated iron waiting room, wooden refreshment room to left and G.W.R. rail crossing beyond.

Portmadoc (New) station of 1931 with Beddgelert Siding transfer yard beyond. The use of this station reduced the number of movements over the G.W.R. crossing.

L. & G.R.P.

C. E. Lee

General view of Beddgelert: Little Giant *on Portmadoc train with newly-built Van No. 4 next to engine.* Russell *on train from Dinas Junction, with 'The Gladstone Car' observation carriage in rear. Note also Station Mistress in Welsh national costume, bogie coal wagons (ex-W.D.) in foreground siding, and coal merchant's lorry. 1930.*

H. B. Tours

Beddgelert – the 'frontier post'. Trains from Dinas and for Portmadoc caught in an afternoon interlude.

H. B. Tours

'The Baldwin' still carrying its WD number awaits the 'right-away' at Nantmor: 1930.

Waenfawr in 1924 with Palmerston *on train of Festiniog stock en route for Dinas Junction.*

L. & G.R.P.

Special train for Scout Party at South Snowdon, with the Baldwin about to add an additional coach to the train.

J. I. C. Boyd collection

Southbound train with Russell *approaching Pitt's Head on the summit section, 1935.*

I. A. Higgon

Five Valley's Tour, with Festiniog engine detached and the Baldwin coupled on for the Welsh Highland run, at Portmadoc Harbour 1934.

G. H. W. Clifford

Dinas engine shed (with Baldwin within) water tank and signal box on 31 August 1926. The vehicle left is No. 24 (ex N.W.N.G. No. 12)

H. C. Casserley

Flour Mill loop, former junction of Gorseddau line to left and abandoned Welsh Highland tracks retained for revival of slate trade, Portmadoc. 1946.

J. I. C. Boyd

The north end of the Flour Mill loop, Portmadoc, with overgrown Portmadoc (New) station of 1923 beyond. 1946.

J. I. C. Boyd

High Street, Portmadoc 1946, with Festiniog link line crossing the street on to Britannia Bridge, and weed-grown Harbour lines off to right. 1946.

J. I. C. Boyd

The last year. Russell *on Dinas-bound train and Buffet Car next to engine. Beddgelert 1936.*

Demolition train at Glanrafon sidings with vehicles composed of slate, mineral and W.D. bogie coal wagon chassis. September 1941.

J. F. Bolton

Croesor Junction, rainswept and overgrown in the winter of 1946. The Croesor tramway struck off from the right-hand loop and was still intact, as was the railway into Portmadoc behind the photographer.

J. I. C. Boyd

Locomotive Publishing Co.

An example of the extensive use of Festiniog England-built engines on the Welsh Highland in its earlier years; Little Giant *at Dinas in 1923.*

C. E. Box collection

Russell *on the Portmadoc Harbour station link line, about to leave for the north. c. 1924.*

Baldwin Locomotive Works

Maker's photograph of the Baldwin engine for the War Department, London. The Welsh Highland example differed in various details from this engine which in turn, differs from the official drawings.

W. A. Camwell

Russell *and the Baldwin moulder in Dinas shed, amid collapsing beams and general decay following closure of the line in 1936. September 1938.*

J. I. C. Boyd/R. W. Kidner

Remains of N.W.N.G.R. wagon used as temporary water tank at Pont Croesor until Portmadoc New tank was installed in 1924.

Welsh Highland Railway Bagnall-built contractor's engine after moving back into England on Stockport Corporation reservoir construction at Fernilee in the Goyt Valley.

A. C. Baker collection

Kerr Stuart tractor on test at Dinas Junction 1928.

L. T. C. Rolt collection

G. H. W. Clifford

Former N.W.N.G. Observation and Corridor coaches at Portmadoc New, 1923. Note temporary dual brake fittings.

Cut-down Pickering coach at Dinas, 1935.

H. F. Wheeller

H. F. Wheeller

Cut-down semi-open carriage running without serial number, Dinas 1935.

Covered vans Nos. 2 and 4 at Dinas, 1935.

H. F. Wheeller

Derelict goods stock at Dinas in August 1935, showing Road Van No. 2 and (second from left) side tipping wagon.

H. F. Wheeller

Large mineral wagon No. 12. 1935.

H. F. Wheeller

Ex W.D. bogie open wagon in use at Beddgelert for coal traffic, 1924.

R. R. J. Plummer

Locomotive Publishing Co.

Goods stock at Dinas with second Road Van, frame and wooden sided slate wagons and covered van. The first wagon is a Festiniog Railway specimen.

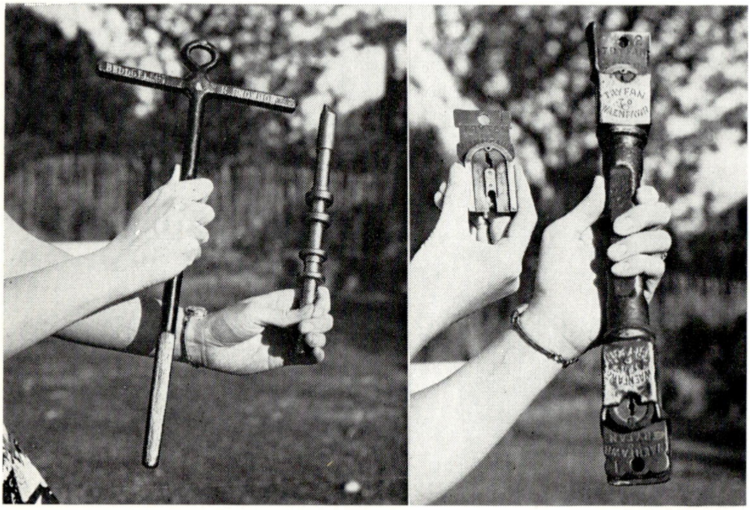

J. I. C. Boyd

Welsh Highland Railway single line staffs from 1924 involved (1) Boston Lodge-made 'crucifix' with key at bottom (2) ex-Festiniog Railway Miniature Electric Staff (3) Wise's Staff & Ticket (left to right).

Beddgelert for 'storage of stock in magazines situated on the route of your railway about one mile north of Beddgelert station, where the loops are most distant from the road', according to an Air Ministry letter to the Company of 16 November 1939. The Ministry's enquiry was evidence of their interest, as in the present case, of a railway 'out of commission but available for immediate use'. As an alternative, the Ministry suggested to the Company they might take over 'the total railway length from the Portmadoc transhipment platform to the site to be used, either by your Company or possibly by the Air Ministry separately from the present operations of your Company'. Alas, these suggestions came to nothing, though even if they had, the demolition of the line could hardly have been but deferred.

Messrs. George Cohen, Sons & Co. Ltd. were responsible for lifting the track etc. and they started work in August 1941. The Ministry of Supply had requisitioned all the material for £1,280 paid to the Receiver. Cohen's purchased the lot in July of 1941 and arrived at Dinas next month with petrol tractors and equipment. Lying there were *Russell* and the Baldwin, eight coaches and 104 wagons. The exercise produced ultimately 1,200 tons of rails suitable for further use, and a good quantity of sleepers with life still in them. York Railway Museum received the original name, number and works plates off the engines.

The 'Gladstone Car' seems to have been favoured by the contractors for taking up the line by tractor. At first progress was difficult as cuttings had been engulfed by trees and undergrowth. Ultimately at 10.45 a.m. a tractor, an ex-W.D. bogie wagon converted into a flat wagon, and a slate wagon chassis left Dinas on 13 August, the first train since July 1937. Barricades put up by the local Home Guard had to be dismantled en route. Aberglaslyn tunnel was reached, and then the train returned to Dinas; on the following day it broke through to Portmadoc New (1931) station. After this, the demolition worked north and south from South Snowdon, the northern party finishing at Dinas and the southern working to Pitt's Head, then from a point below Hafod-Ruffydd to Croesor Junction.*

The northern gang reached Tryfan Junction in January 1942 and then lifted the Bryngwyn branch; in May Dinas was reached and an auction of the coaches was made in June. These now stood on the only surviving track. The coaches were disposed of complete with running gear; the Baldwin was cut up outside the shed in August. The southern gang reached Croesor Junction in June 1942.

* See also 'Festiniog Railway', Vol. 2, p. 329.

All portable buildings in corrugated iron were removed, but the stone ones were left. Materials were stacked for standard gauge trans-shipment at Dinas and Beddgelert Siding . . . it was not possible to work south of here as the G.W.R. had lost no time in lifting the rail level crossing and removing the signal box as far back as October 1938!

The section of track at Pitt's Head commenced under about 3 ft. of water beneath the road bridge, and in December 1945 the track to Hafod Ruffyd was in excellent condition and free of undergrowth; on either side it was littered with derailed slate wagons of Festiniog origin, most of which had left the rails as their tyres had been shot away. There was a score of them.

Messrs. Shanks & McEwan Ltd. demolished this section and then passed onto the remainder of the Croesor Tramway for which any hope of traffic had now passed. The materials were again stacked at the Beddgelert Siding. This work was done between August 1948 and the following August. Their Motor-Rail petrol tractor No. 14 was abandoned at the New (1931) station afterwards, and not cut up until 1955.

The section between the G.W.R. rail crossing and the Harbour was not removed until May 1949, presumably by Shanks & McEwan, and far away from here it seems that some locals, seeing that authority presumed the Croesor tramway to be dead, illegally lifted most of the rails between the head of the Upper Parc Incline and Croesor Village.

A compulsory Winding-up Order on the Company was made by Mr. Justice Uthwatt on 7 February 1944 and a liquidator in Alwynne Aubrey Thomas of Llandudno appointed.

The engine *Russell* was purchased by the Ministry of Supply and sent to work at the Hook Norton Ironstone Mines (Oxfordshire) of the Brymbo Steel Company, Wrexham. Still in existence, the career of the engine after leaving North Wales may be followed elsewhere.*

In reply to a question in Parliament on 27 April 1965, it was stated that the Treasury had an outstanding debt in the Welsh Highland of £28,172.

In 1961 a Society was formed with the intention of restoring a portion of the W.H.R., the line in the Beddgelert and Nantmor areas seeming to hold out most promise, with the possibility of working north to South Snowdon. The Official Liquidator was very sympathetic to any idea of re-opening even a part of the line, but

* 'Introducing Russell' (P. Deegan). Published Welsh Highland Light Railway (1964) Ltd.

problems of environment, use of trackbed (which is used as a footpath for much of the length intended for re-opening as a railway) and lack of agreement among members of the County Council between a desire to see this part of Snowdonia unspoiled by tourist development or otherwise, and the problems of planning, road bridges and crossings (to give but a sample of associated questions) have prevented much evidence of activity being visible. The present body with such intent is now termed the Welsh Highland Light Railway (1964) Ltd., but because of some doubt about prospects with consequent difficulties of showing uniform purpose, negotiations for acquiring the trackbed and raising the capital, though at an advanced stage, are not yet complete. The engine *Russell* has been acquired and overhauled, and the current figure officially given for the re-instatement of services over about two miles of track is £60,000.

The Route described—new Welsh Highland sections

P.B. & S.S.R. works had taken that unfinished railway route southwards from Rhydd-ddu to Hafod Ruffydd. The 1922–3 work carried this on down the flank of the mountainside at 1 in 40, 48, 45 in a south-easterly direction until the course was swung round anti-clockwise on a 3-chain curve to bring it below Hafod Ruffydd once more. The extreme tip of the previous curve, involving an embankment in Coed Mawr, had been finished by the previous contractors. The line now ran north for 500 yards, as if returning to Rhydd-ddu, but was now crossing pastureland without any earthworks. At the end of this stretch however, came another full half turn of 3 chains, clockwise and easterly which, beginning with a cutting ended in carrying the line southwards again on a considerable embankment and now just above the rushing waters of the Afon Colwyn on its east side. Open ground ending, the line entered Coed Mawr for the third time! It then fell mainly at 1 in 40 in a straight length, part embankment and part cutting, over a mountain flank containing much broken and rocky ground, crossed the Afon Meillionen to enter Parc Tyn-y-coed, where details of P.B. & S.S. work have already been noted.

Beyond the house here, whilst the P.B. & S.S. course fell steeply and slightly eastward, the Highland built a steady straight fall of 1 in 40, carried above the top of the steep cutting which would have contained the older railway below to the east. The W.H.R. then curved westwards before beginning a long curve which carried it through Coed Cwm-cloch, over the Afon Cwm-cloch by a 10 ft. girder and concrete bridge and then, erupting out on to the bare

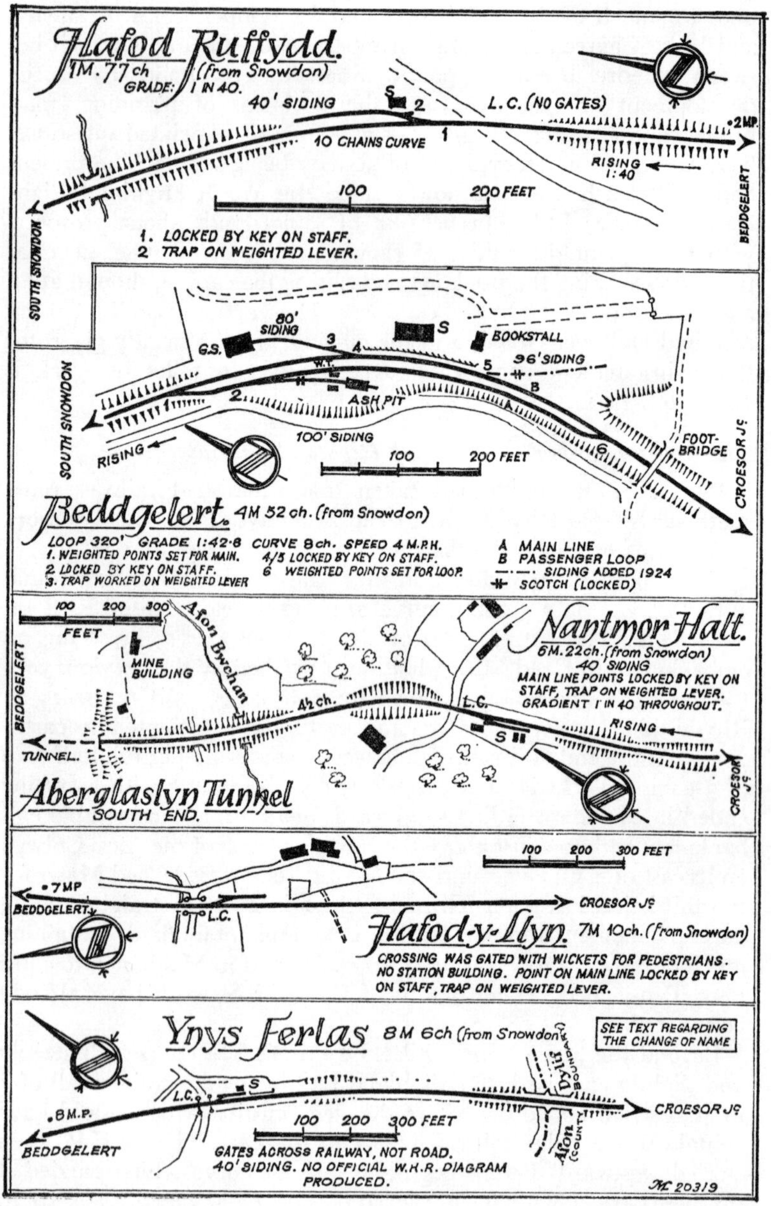
Hafod Ruffydd.
1M. 77 ch (from Snowdon)
GRADE: 1 IN 40.
40' SIDING
S 2
L.C. (NO GATES)
10 CHAINS CURVE
1
2MP.
RISING 1:40
BEDDGELERT
SOUTH SNOWDON
100 200 FEET
1. LOCKED BY KEY ON STAFF.
2 TRAP ON WEIGHTED LEVER.
80' SIDING
G.S.
3 4
S
BOOKSTALL
5 96' SIDING
W.T.
B
ASH PIT
A
SOUTH SNOWDON
RISING
100' SIDING
6
FOOT-BRIDGE
CROESOR JC
100 200 FEET
Beddgelert. 4M 52 ch. (from Snowdon)
LOOP 320' GRADE 1:42·8 CURVE 8ch. SPEED 4 M.P.H.
1. WEIGHTED POINTS SET FOR MAIN.
2 LOCKED BY KEY ON STAFF.
3. TRAP WORKED ON WEIGHTED LEVER
4/5 LOCKED BY KEY ON STAFF.
6 WEIGHTED POINTS SET FOR LOOP.
A MAIN LINE
B PASSENGER LOOP
SIDING ADDED 1924
SCOTCH (LOCKED)
100 200 300 FEET
Afon Bwchan
MINE BUILDING
BEDDGELERT
Nantmor Halt.
6M. 22ch. (from Snowdon)
40' SIDING
MAIN LINE POINTS LOCKED BY KEY ON STAFF, TRAP ON WEIGHTED LEVER.
GRADIENT 1 IN 40 THROUGHOUT.
4½ ch.
L.C.
RISING
S
TUNNEL.
CROESOR JC
Aberglaslyn Tunnel
SOUTH END.
100 200 300 FEET
7MP
BEDDGELERT
L.C.
CROESOR JC
Hafod-y-Llyn. 7M 10ch. (from Snowdon)
CROSSING WAS GATED WITH WICKETS FOR PEDESTRIANS. NO STATION BUILDING. POINT ON MAIN LINE LOCKED BY KEY ON STAFF, TRAP ON WEIGHTED LEVER.
Ynys Ferlas 8 M 6ch (from Snowdon)
SEE TEXT REGARDING THE CHANGE OF NAME
L.C.
S
Dylif (COUNTY BOUNDARY)
CROESOR JC
8M.P.
100 200 300 FEET
BEDDGELERT
GATES ACROSS RAILWAY, NOT ROAD.
40' SIDING. NO OFFICIAL W.H.R. DIAGRAM PRODUCED.
Afon (COUNTY)
MC 20319

mountain flank once more, the curve reversed and entered a formidable cutting 45 ft. deep in the centre. In passing through this, a left-hand 3-chain curve took over and on leaving this impressive defile, the line once more rounded into a northbound direction on a 25 ft. embankment. The track on which the line had entered this last cutting may be seen close by, but 40 ft. above on the left. This was a most impressive piece of civil engineering and kept the gradient at 1 in 48 on 3-chain curves and steepened it to 1 in 40 on the straighter sections.

The route then fell in front of Cwm-cloch-isaf and bending right and east once more, in a shallow cutting crossed the Cwm-cloch again and came up alongside the abandoned P.B. & S.S. earthworks, so that they completed the curve together to merge at the end of it and run southwards into Beddgelert station, bridging the river for a third time.

There were corrugated iron buildings here comprising the station building itself and a warehouse. A water tank for locos was mounted on concrete pillars, and an engine siding alongside with pit. Occasionally an engine was stabled in the goods warehouse. A coal siding was subsequently added. Beyond the station the line curved at 5 chains and entered another deep cutting, followed by a 132 ft. tunnel, behind the Goat Hotel. Here the old P.B. & S.S. roadbridge going south and east was abandoned and a new route falling at 1 in 40, 48, 54 was built along the hill contour, running south and east but above and to the west of the Portmadoc road. It entered a cutting and 3-chain curve behind Bryn-y-felin farm and emerged running eastwards, passed under the Portmadoc road by a concrete and steel girder bridge and, almost immediately crossed the Glaslyn river from west to east by means of the steel bridge previously described. On the east bank a sharp 3-chain right-hand curve with a low embankment of slate spoil, brought the railway on to the already-existing P.B. & S.S. works on the east bank of the river.

The route through the Glaslyn Pass, with its sheer sides and naked rock involving tunnelling and a ledge above the rushing stream, has already claimed attention. This is certainly a famous place and with a fine concert of fir trees, precipitous mountain flank and jagged rock was the *piece de resistance* of Welsh Highland scenery; the river falls in a series of cascades and rapids below, until the gorge is so narrow that the railway was obliged to lose its path and tunnel into the side of Craig-y-llan. It was usual to slow the train along this section to allow passengers more than what would otherwise have been a fleeting glimpse of the gorge. The steepest fall here was 1 in 119.

At the south (Cwm Bychan) end of the final tunnel the railway emerged on an embankment over the end of Cwm Bychan, and just before the Nantmor road crossing there was a long cleft dug for the railway. Rock spoil embankments carried the line after Nantmor, the high wooded ground to the east forming the foundation along which the railway gradually fell to the flood plain of the Glaslyn, now away to the west and flowing beyond meadowland. On its further side, the escarpment behind the Portmadoc road rises summit upon summit to the peaks which slowly reveal themselves against the skyline, as the Glaslyn valley widens out and the railway turned to the east. The fall from the last tunnel was 1 in 40 and 67, and after a 35 ft. cutting the Llanfrothen road was crossed on a ferro-concrete bridge; the line ran down at 1 in 67 and 391, thence almost level along the escarpment foot, following it south and eastwards, over the two further river bridges and past the three small halts (no more than two existing at one time), Hafod-y-llyn (7 m. 10 ch.), Hafod Garregog (7 m. 50 ch.), and Ynysferlas (8 m. 7 ch.). The foot of the escarpment dwindles away—this is the old coastline before the receding of the sea—at a point between the two river bridges, and gradually the lush pastureland with its backcloth of some of the finest hills in North Wales, turns into flat wasteland, that part of the Glaslyn estuary reclaimed by Madock's embankment. By the time the railway, running due east, had curved at 4–6 chains on a low embankment into a junction with the Croesor tramway, the beauty of the surroundings was all on the fringes of the scene rather than in the immediate vicinity of the railway.

The remainder of the journey into Portmadoc is described under the Croesor Tramway.

In Portmadoc, the route of the Croesor was followed along the east fringe of the town and apart from improvements to alignment and clearances, and the building of New station the coming of the Welsh Highland made little alteration to the surroundings.

Locomotives

WHR/ FR No	*Name*	*Type*	*Builder*	*No*	*Date*	*Withdrawn*
11	*Moel Tryfan*	(see N.W.N.G. Railways for earlier details)				Scrapped 1954
12	*Russell*	(see P.B. & S.S. Railway for earlier details)				Extant
13	—	4-6-0 PT	Baldwin	45172	1917	Scrapped 1942

(The above numbers, additions to the Festiniog Railway series, were applied after the Railway was leased to the Festiniog in the summer of 1934)

Moel Tryfan

Moel Tryfan and *Russell* lay side by side in the Dinas shed during the birth of the Welsh Highland. The story of *Moel Tryfan* between then and 1954 is outlined on p. 352 but a few details are appropriate. Boston Lodge returned *Russell's* wheels and axles in June 1922, having made but not fitted vacuum brake gear for the engine the previous month. *Moel Tryfan* was in a poor condition and at the time, *Russell* was used for the goods workings whenever available. When passenger working on the N.W.N.G. section was resumed on 31 July 1922, *Russell* did most of the work. By the November *Moel Tryfan* was quite out of use, with a number of tubes plugged up; as soon as *Palmerston* became available for Welsh Highland work, and the track permitted connection, *Moel Tryfan* was only used in emergency. In July 1923 it was at last sent into Boston Lodge for fitting the new brakes and a patch on the tube-plate. Boston Lodge's Engineer (who had been sent to Dinas on 7 June 1923) reported; 'In working condition. Requires retubing; tubes on order, will be seen to in the near future, centre piece much worn (this was the driving bogie cradle), new smokebox required. Axle boxes, side rods and bogie brasses much worn, require re-turning. Tanks have been patched and are much worn. Slide valves require examining. Working pressure 115 lbs . . .'

This report followed an anxious time on the old section before the engine could be spared; it was worked in emergency between April and June and in the earlier month, Boston Lodge's Williams had been sent to Wake's to see the ex-N.W.N.G. *Gowrie*, so serious was the locomotive shortage. On 3 May 1923 Dinas reported that another tube had burst in traffic on 30 April and 10% of the tubes were now plugged. Lloyd Williams at Port Dinorwic was asked to quote for tubes and do the work at Dinas shed during May 1923; however it was 17 June before Port Dinorwic Dry Dock Ship & Boiler Repairing Works (i.e. Lloyd Williams) had the tubes and could go to Dinas. When the work was done, the engine ran under its own steam to Boston Lodge. The Boiler Inspector at Dinas had said 'there are other defects that could be left until later' but Williams added on 22 June 'they are defects that will have to be speedily seen to'. After overhaul her roster included a daily run up to Blaenau Festiniog and back; coaling up for such workings was done from baskets or wagons whilst the train stood at Harbour or New stations.

The above are the only records available until 1937, when having run until passenger workings ceased, the Festiniog lost no time in acquiring the engine as a useful unit for the future. The engine was dismantled for firebox and boiler repairs, but the work was not commenced and the Second War intervened. The main portion was towed from the engine shed at the Lodge and scrapped at the Harbour station in 1954.

Regrettably, Williams's report on *Gowrie* was as follows: '... it appears the engine has not been working since 1918 when it was sold by the Disposal Board, previous to which it had been repaired and overhauled by Mr. Wake and tested by the Insurance Inspector to 225 lb. per sq. inch. I may say that I have not previously seen the engine, but judging from enquiries made regarding it at Dinas, I conclude that no structural improvement have been made to it compared to what it was when working on the N.W.N.G. Railway. I consider that the engine is badly designed and whatever defects were originally in it, are still there. I had the engine under steam for about an hour and although it has been standing for a long time in the open the working parts are in good order . . . I observed when working the engine that the steam pressure was very rapidly going down for no apparent cause, unless the great length of the steam pipe which is 8 to 9 ft. long caused the steam to be condensed before reaching the cylinders . . . I may add the price asked is very reasonable . . . but do not consider it the most suitable. It would do for light work but would require a lot of attention to keep it in order'. And that was the end of it.

Russell

Williams inspected this engine under steam at Dinas in early 1922 (no date given). It required general overhaul, the flanges were thin and new tyres were needed. Boston Lodge supplied these and the engine was out of service for some weeks, *Moel Tryfan* being used instead. It had been re-tubed in steel in 1917 and Williams suggested it should work the intended summer service—which it did. Pressure was only 120 lb.

The engine ran to Boston Lodge in the winter of 1923 and had the vacuum brake, previously made by then for it, fitted. It was Jack who had insisted that N. Wales' engines should be altered for through running between Blaenau Festiniog and Dinas and though the cutting-down of *Moel Tryfan* had been successful, *Russell*'s was disastrous. The work was actually done at Dinas, the chimney cap being removed and a section cut from the dome and the top of the cover replaced. Hunslet supplied a new regulator fitting. The cab was reduced in height. The sandpot had been removed from the boiler top earlier. It was now only possible to stand upright in the centre of the cab. For hot weather, the reduced back sheet could be removed in the upper part. No effort was made to repaint either of the two foregoing engines.

Russell was tested over the Festiniog, but nothing could reduce the width over the side tanks and the engine stuck in the Moelwyn Tunnel (full account, 'Festiniog Railway', p. 271). The butchery was all for nothing, and *Russell* returned to Welsh Highland metals, only to come to Boston Lodge for repair.

Russell spent her working life in very mixed duties. Between 1924–5 the Bryngwyn branch train was her livelihood; by then a newly-acquired Baldwin-built engine could help out on the main line and the engines borrowed from the Festiniog at the initial period, had gone back home—the service had until then required the two N.W.N.G. engines and an England Festiniog engine. The Bryngwyn service was two trips a day but with slate business falling off, one became sufficient. Coal traffic was also fair. When the timetable demanded, *Russell* would work a late-day trip to Portmadoc and back on the passenger.

The engine was off duty at Dinas by the end of the 1929 season, the tyres needing renewal. The wheels had been sent to Hunslet but the Railway Company could not pay for the work. Ultimately the Caernarvonshire County Council did so. At this time *Moel Tryfan* worked the thrice weekly passenger train (she was not powerful enough for the goods) and on the Tuesday and Thursday between —when there was no passenger service—the Baldwin worked the goods.

In 1934 the engine was painted light green under Festiniog leasing, but both *Moel Tryfan* and Baldwin were N.W.N.G. (or Festiniog?!) red, the latter sporting it in replacement for the original black. *Russell* and the Baldwin went into Boston Lodge before the summer 1934 timetable, hence the new paintwork.

Having worked the last trains to collect W.H.R. rolling stock, *Russell* and the Baldwin were incarcerated in the Dinas shed until 1941.

The Baldwin

Colonel Stephens could not resist a bargain. Some Baldwin-built 4–6–0 tank engines were on offer from the War Department Disposal Board and the Colonel bought a number for use on his railways. One came to the Welsh Highland and there would have been a second if he had had his way. It was purchased after inspection of *Gowrie* proved unsuccessful, and came through E. W. Farrow & Sons of Spalding, Engineers' Merchants. It was realised that the

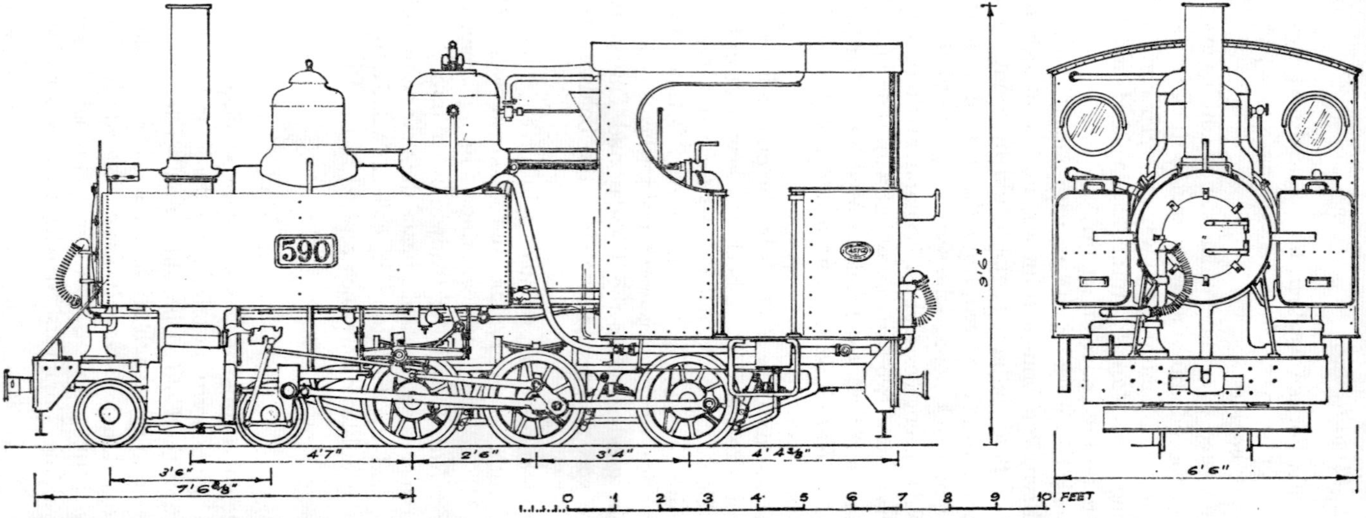

WELSH HIGHLAND RAILWAY BALDWIN 4-6-0 LOCOMOTIVE "590" CLASS 10 12 D 13 WORKS Nº 45172 OF 1917.

AS USED ON W.H.R. THE LOCO. DIFFERED IN DETAILS SO DRAWING BASED ON MAKERS DRAWINGS AMENDED BY VARIOUS PHOTOGRAPHS.

20423

engine's bulk would prevent it from being used over the Festiniog, but the price was only £240, and the engine arrived at Dinas on 4 July 1923. Boston Lodge fitters were sent there to fit the vacuum brake. The engine had carried R.O.D. No. 590 on a plate on the tank sides; it was of Class 10–12–D, 13, Indent D.R.T. 887 of 1 March 1917, the builder's title being The Baldwin Locomotive Works, Philadelphia, U.S.A. Main dimensions were: cylinders 9 in. × 12 in. stroke; driving wheels diam. 1 ft. 11½ in.; rigid wheelbase 5 ft. 10 in.; total wheelbase 12 ft. 2 in.; heating surface 254.5 sq. ft.; grate area 5.6 sq. ft.; pressure 178 lb.; tank capacity 496 gallons; weight in working order 14½ tons. Many engines of this type found their way onto the Western Front; this was the only one to have a second career in North Wales. Confined because of its size to Welsh Highland duties, it would be found working over the Cob to Boston Lodge at times, for coaling or stabling or shunting duties. Tractive effort was 5,429 lb.

As built these engines had large acetylene lamps front and rear, stove-pipe chimney with damper on top, sand dome on boiler, pop valves and whistle on top of steam dome, pull-out type regulator and open backed cab. There was a guard rail front and rear which extended across both rails, built up in girder section. Small brushes were suspended over each rail from it. The frames were bar type and in anticipation of trouble, a jack was carried on each side of the smokebox. The bogie wheels were solid, 1 ft. 4 in. diameter. The firebox was of copper and radially stayed; there were 83 1½-in. diameter brass tubes in a boiler of 2 ft. 9 in. diameter. In contrast to the other engines, she was huge, being 9 ft. 3 in. to top of chimney and 6 ft. 11 in. wide across the footplate. (Unlike later railways in Wales, the early lines' engines were somewhat small.) On delivery, 'the Baldwin' (as everyone knew her), was placed chimney-first from Dinas and given a coat of black paint. Her habits however soon became suspect. Evidence of this was that whilst the other two engines retained their places in the shed, 590 was left out in the open. Her riding qualities were rough, and from time to time the men succeeded in having her confined to goods traffic, where speed was lower.

As supplied, the cab roof did not extend the full length of the footplate. Nor was there a backsheet. Dinas extended the roof and fitted a low back sheet. When the engine went to Boston Lodge in 1934 for refit, red paint was applied, an upper cab rear sheet in wood with spectacles was fitted, and the engine turned to run chimney first to Dinas. Following the last passenger service in 1936, she went into Boston Lodge for cover; she was collected from there and taken to Dinas on 19 June 1937, being ultimately cut up by Cohen in August 1942. Repair records for Dinas have not survived, and it is not known why the Ministry did not requisition the engine for further use as they did *Russell.* Perhaps her reputation had reached their ears!

This bad habit of rough riding was not the fault of the W.H.R. track nor the engine in particular. The Ashover Baldwins behaved exactly the same; from the lineside they lurched in a terrifying way, though it has never been said they actually left the track! Train crews just refused to endure the ride. The summit level at Pitts' Head, always a rough place, was no joy on the Baldwin. The makers' steam brakes and injectors were fitted, the latter being held somewhat in awe. Tom Davies, who fired the engine quite often, came to Towyn in 1953 and was shown a similarly reluctant injector on Talyllyn Railway No. 4. To the delight of bystanders, he flicked it into action saying, 'I know all about that pattern, we had one on the Baldwin'! The poor reputation of W.H.R. timekeeping was laid at the Baldwin's door; maintenance became sketchy and the sanding gear was unreliable. The way she slipped on a wet day was a byword; once with only a bogie coach and a van she was 55 minutes late into Dinas and the connection was missed; on the following day both injectors failed at Hafod Ruffydd and the train had to gravitate back to Beddgelert. The engine was taken from traffic and Col. Stephens informed. Boston Lodge received a telegram in reply, 'Baldwin engine should not slip if sand used. Sand box on top of boiler. Only part of the general humbug, I suppose. Please tell Williams to use sand and send me report.' Williams then rode the engine himself, taking Captain May, then Manager, with him. May reported to the Colonel, '. . . today I went with the train to Dinas myself and they had plenty of sand, but the engine was a nuisance, it stopped here and there, Williams with a spanner and Enginemen with something else. Fiddling with the injectors. We lost the connection, fortunately there were not many passengers and they caught the charabanc.' The next day May sent Stephens a plaintive telegram: 'Baldwin engine disabled again today. Cancel instructions given Williams and give me an engine to work the train.' This brought a letter from Jack at Buckingham Gate suggesting the men were prejudiced against the engine. No doubt they were! The trouble was that the rostering was based on Boston Lodge at the time and the crew was a Festiniog one; the only man who could work the injectors had handled the engines during the war, but he was at Dinas. On this diagram, the engine was stabled overnight in the goods warehouse at Beddgelert, then known as 'the small engine house'.

Passenger services were much reduced in December 1923, and whilst working the goods, the engine burst a tube at Quellyn Lake on 19 January following. It had not been a happy time for the engine. Relegated to the goods workings, a few days before it had 'refused' to enter the Beddgelert Siding and when forced, fell off the rails; this happened twice. Stephens blamed McAlpine for poor pointwork; in fact, he alleged that all McAlpine's turnouts were faulty, laid with 1 in 6 frogs and irregularly curved. After the tube burst, a Festiniog engine was loaned and the Baldwin laid off.

Making the Baldwin steam freely was another problem. The ashpan was removed with beneficial effect, but on windy days the fire might be blown from the firebars and twice in one week sparks so caused had set the underside of carriages alight.

Baldwin turned out a total of no less than 495 of these engines between the latter part of 1916 and the spring of 1917, a remarkable output. The dimensions given above are the most recent available and differ from previous ones; Baldwin's supplied leading measurements, but these do not always agree with a metric blueprint in French in the possession of Colonel Stephens' which has 'Too high for Moelwyn Tunnel might be used on W.H.R.' pencilled across it. 'The Locomotive News & Railway Notes' for 10 September 1919 (p. 11) in describing narrow gauge engines then lying at Purfleet, gives dimensions as quoted and adds that 590 was one of eleven similar engines rebuilt by Messrs. W. G. Bagnall Ltd. in 1918. The accompanying diagram gives fuel capacity at ¾ ton; weight on the bogie was 3¼ tons and on each driving axles averaged 2½ tons empty or almost 3½ tons in working order.

Colonel Stephens was planning to buy a second Baldwin to replace the weak *Moel Tryfan*, but after the 1923 experiences, Dolgarrog would not sanction a purchase.

On 21 April 1936 Austen instructed Morris Jones at Boston Lodge to 'go through the stays on the Baldwin and put her right for the summer service on the Welsh Highland . . . there is very little work required . . . do not take the stays out for the sake of doing so . . . bear in mind the financial position is very acute indeed, and time and money cannot be wasted'.

Miscellaneous Motive power

Between March 1922 and May 1923 McAlpine used three contractor's engines for rebuilding the N.W.N.G. section and the unfinished W.H.R. link. At the south end, the Festiniog's *Palmerston* was in service from 9 May 1923 until sometime in the following month. On this length they had earlier used a Motor Rail petrol tractor No. 2193 of 1923 which was obtained specially for the contract. It later service is not known.

Shedded at Dinas they had a small standard four-coupled saddle tank by Messrs. W. G. Bagnall Ltd. of Stafford, No. 2080 of 1918. This engine had been new to the Ministry of Munitions and then sold to Thornton & Co., of Swansea, who were simply agents. They handled several Ministry engines and this one was purchased by McAlpine. After the Welsh Highland was finished, it was sold to Messrs. Lehane, McKenzie & Shand Ltd., for their Stockport Corporation contract at Fernylea Reservoir. It passed to Messrs. Twigg & Co. of Matlock in 1944 where the Author found it along with other reservoir contract engines. No buyer was found and Twigg scrapped it in April 1946. Dimensions were cylinders 6 in.×9 in.; driving wheel diameter 1 ft. 9 in.; wheelbase 3 ft. 6 in.; pressure 150 lb.; tank capacity 100 gallons; weight in working order 5½ tons; tractive effort 2,174 lb. Walschaert's valve gear was fitted, and inside frames.

Apart from the contractor's engines, there were a number of internal combustion machines, almost all second-hand, which were bought or tried variously for use as shunting engines on the Festiniog, for the Croesor run or for winter work on the Welsh Highland. Most of them were failures and they are listed with details on p. 391 of 'Festiniog Railway'. Directly connected with the Welsh Highland amongst this list were :

(No number or name) : 'Simplex' four-wheeled petrol tractor by Motor Rail Ltd., of Bedford, built 1917 for the War Department and being an earlier version of the same type as used by McAlpine. It could be loaded to 4 tons on a Croesor trip and was used from time to time on this work between July 1923 when purchased, and the closing of that line. These workings were arranged between its duties as Bottom Shunter.

No. 11 *Moelwyn* (name not carried in the period of this book). A class 4–50/1 four-wheeled petrol tractor by Pittsburgh Model Engine Co. of 1918 under sub-contract for the Baldwin Locomotive Co. Purchased by the French Government for War Department use as built; purchased February 1925 and vacuum brake fitted 1928 in connection with proposal to use it as a light and economical unit for a winter passenger service with one coach on the Welsh Highland.

(No number or name) : Austro-Daimler tractor of about 20 horsepower purchased by Colonel Stephens specifically for use on the Welsh Highland, in July 1925. Previously utilised by contractors for North Devon & Cornwall Light Railway. A very light machine and put to the Croesor tramway job by early 1926, where it was more suited than the Baldwin tractor. On this it displaced the horse haulage. The tractor was tested on 25 January 1928 with a single coach between Portmadoc and Croesor Junction with the idea of once again, seeing what might be done on the Welsh Highland during the winter. The coach in question was one of the light ex-W.D. pattern Hudson bogies which had been recently bought new. All the same, the weight was too much for the engine, and the journey took 45 minutes. After trials as a shunter it was stored in Boston Lodge paint shop from 1929 and not used again. No dimensions are recorded.

The Aluminium Corporation, Dolgarrog, owned a Muir-Hill four-wheeled paraffin tractor with a Fordson engine. Whilst not actually tested on the Welsh Highland it was sent to Blaenau Festiniog for trials on the Festiniog with a view to withdrawing all steam locomotives and working the combined W.H.R./F.R. system with these tractors. It was so light that the wagons attached to it would run away with the tractor. It was returned to Dolgarrog.

A much more extensive test was made with a six-wheeled Diesel tractor built by Kerr, Stuart & Co. Ltd. No. 4415 built in 1928. It was the maker's first Diesel tractor and had a McLaren-Benz 4-cylinder engine with a J.A.P. auxiliary engine for starting purposes. There was a chain drive and with 2 ft. diameter wheels on a 5 ft. 2 in. wheelbase, the 60 hp engine was bigger than anything tried formerly. It appeared at Dinas Junction in July 1928 and worked the Bryngwyn branch for a time, being transferred for trial on the Festiniog Railway on 29 March 1929, returning to Stoke and the makers in the following August. Colonel Stephens found the machine extravagant on fuel when compared with his standard gauge petrol Ford-engined railcars. Throughout the loan period the engine was driven by a maker's employee, named Philips, and mechanics were sent by them for repairs. The gearbox was an all-welded steel casting, one of the first of its kind. The starting engine was housed in the cab (this was before the days of 24-volt starting equipment). Apparently the weight was disappointingly high, 5–6 tons. The engine on test had the teak shuttered cab fitted to similar engines supplied to the Sudan. It worked on the East Lancashire road contract at Fazakerley later. At Dinas it was painted flat grey, and a development of the design was sold to the standard gauge section of the Ravenglass and Eskdale Railway in 1929.

By reasons of its dimensions (14 ft. long, 6 ft. $2\frac{3}{4}$ in. wide and 9 ft. 1 in. high) its trial on the Festiniog was limited and the cab was cut down. Nevertheless, it would not pass the Moelwyn Tunnel.

Passenger Stock

Robert Williams, the Boston Lodge Locomotive Superintendent, was sent by Colonel Stephens to inspect the N.W.N.G. stock lying at Dinas Junction in early November 1922. He reported, 'They have 11 Bogie Carriages, 4 Summer Carriages, 2 Corridor Carriages, 2 Composite Cge., 1 Inspection Saloon, Nos. 3 & 7 3rd Class closed carriages, woodwork in poor condition require heavy repairs. Bogies and wheels in fairly good condition. Nos. 4 & 5 Composite closed carriages, No. 4 requires heavy repairs to woodwork. Bogies and wheels fairly good. No. 5 in good condition requires light outside repairs, also cleaning and painting inside and out. Bogies and wheels good. Nos. 9 & 10 Corridor Carriages, No. 9 3rd Class, No. 10 Composite 1st and 3rd Class. In good condition, require scraping and painting, inside and out. Wheels and bogies good. Nos. 11, 12, 13 & 14. Summer Carriages. Nos. 11 & 12 partly glazed. Nos. 13 & 14, open. Nos. 11 & 13 have been recently painted and only require cleaning. Nos. 12 & 14 require painting woodwork. Bogies and wheels in good condition. No. 8 Inspection Saloon. In good condition, would advocate using this as an Observation Car.'

The last remark suggests that no one was at hand during his visit to explain it *was* an Observation Car! Williams concluded by recommending that as 'the carriages had been standing idle for years, give the bogies an overhaul before sending them out again'.

The new owners added to the existing Festiniog carriages numbers' series, by continuing with No. 23 upwards. Some coaches, as previously noted, were not acquired by the Dolgarrog Regime, so the position became:

WHR/ FR No.	*Old N.W.N.G. No.*	*Type and Date*	*Nickname*
32	3	'Closed Coaches' ex-Workman's Cars of 1891	'Closed Coach'
8	4	Guard's Brake/Composite of 1907	—
9	5	Guard's Brake/Composite of 1874	—
34	7	As 3	'Closed Coach'
29	8	Observation Carriage of 1891	'The Gladstone Car'
35	9	3rd Class Saloon 1878	'Corridor Coach'
36	10	As 9 but by 1923 1st/3rd Saloon 1878	'Corridor Coach'
23	11	Semi-glazed 3rd; 7 compartment 1894	'Summer Coach'
24	12	As 11	'Summer Coach'
27	13	Open 3rd; 7 compartment 1894	'Summer Coach'
28	14	As 13	'Summer Coach'

This totals the 11 bogie vehicles listed by Williams; apparently the fifth 'Summer Coach' which was allocated new number 26 and was probably N.W.N.G. No. 16, was not at Dinas or was missed.

It was in the sale of vehicles in June 1942. Its body was returned to Portmadoc in October 1958 and the number 26 was visible. It is now in service again.

Williams had to send another report to Colonel Stephens in June 1923 which may be summarised :

No. 4 Guard's Brake/Composite. Fitted new set of cast steel wheels. Vacuum brake fitted; Westinghouse removed; roof reduced in height and recovered.

No. 10 'Corridor Coach'. Fitted vacuum in place Westinghouse; roof reduced. Wheels require re-turning.

No. 9 'Corridor Coach'. Has flats on all wheels due to skidding.

No. 8 'Gladstone Car'. In good order.

Nos. 11–14 'Summer Coaches'. 'Have only been running a few summer seasons and always kept in carriage shed over the winter, and are in good condition.'

No. 5 Guard's Brake/Composite. 'Cast-iron wheels. Has been skidding and has flats on wheels.'

Nos. 3 & 7 'Closed Coaches'. 'These two carriages are in a rather dilapidated condition; the woodwork needs overhauling, 1 set of new cast steel wheels required and 1 set could be made up out of the old wheels.'

'All carriages have been painted inside and out this year except Nos. 3 & 7 which have only had one coat outside.'

It is unlikely that all the stock had had its brake gear changed by this date, and it seems the trains were kept in rakes of different brake to enable them to be operated by N.W.N.G. or Festiniog engines as required by their brake gear. To allow the carriages onto the Festiniog, they were lowered on their bogie bolsters and had their sides lowered above the windows; this reduced internal headroom and spoiled their neat external lines.

No illustration of No. 5 exists during the W.H.R. period though Williams writes of it as in good condition; it was in the 1942 sale (probably inside the shed) carrying its new number. Other stock was given the number as it went through the works, and certain carriages (including 26 & 27) were given cast-iron lettering screwed on to the waist reading 'WELSH HIGHLAND RLY'; Brake Compos 8 & 9 had 'W.H.R.' (numbers relating to lettering refer to W.H.R./F.R. series given at Boston Lodge).

No. 4, the Pickering Brake Composite, behaved like all the other N.W.N.G. stock when on Festiniog metals : it was likely to leave the rails. No. 4 was an especially indifferent performer. During June 1923 it went off at Portmadoc on the 9th, at Snowdon Ranger on the 14th and at Hafod Ruffydd and just north Beddgelert (on the same train) on the 20th. Hadfield's No. 10 cast steel wheels, 19⅛ in. diameter (as used on the Festiniog) cured this.

There was also a great deal of trouble over couplings, the matter coming to a head when N.W.N.G. stock was expected to engage with Festiniog. Trains were kept in separate rakes to avoid complication and many ingenious devices were used to couple odd coaches together; sometimes this resulted in odd coaches refusing to couple or worse, refusing to uncouple!

On 1 July 1924 a passenger train of mixed stock in the Festiniog's Moelwyn Tunnel incurred a break-away on the Down run. The N.W.N.G. Brake Composite at the rear of the train became detached and applied the brake on both halves of the train. *Moel Tryfan* with *Palmerston* as pilot were on the front, they stopped at about the middle of the tunnel. The driver of *Palmerston* was overcome by smoke, but his fireman uncoupled the engine and drove it out of the tunnel. Meanwhile the driver of *Moel Tryfan* squeezed between his engine and the tunnel wall and found his way back to the detached portion of the train whose guard had walked out of the tunnel behind, to protect it. *Moel Tryfan*'s driver returned to his engine and backed the train onto the detached van with such force that the coupling was broken, so he crawled back to couple the van to the train once more by hand. This accomplished, he walked out of the tunnel at one end, over the top, and rejoined the train from the other—this was easier than trying to pass along his engine and enter the cab. It proved that the Festiniog guard in charge of the train did not understand the N. Wales 'Chopper' type coupling, nor the eccentric action of the pendulum of this form of Norwegian coupler, which drew the buffing heads together. Luckily *Moel Tryfan*'s driver was an ex-N.W.N.G. employee and knew the action. Most stock from this Company had side chains also, but the breakaway van, though having links, had no hooks, so was not coupled up; the men disliked these hooks as they tended to pick up point blades. After a great fuss by the Board of Trade, a new all-purpose coupling was devised which would take the choppers or a plain hook if the chopper was taken out and a hook lifted into the chopper pin.*

There must have been other N.W.N.G. stock at Dinas which Williams did not list . . . in any case, his list was only of bogie stock. It is recalled that all the passenger stock was brought from Dinas which would run! Some of the six-wheeler bodies were used for stores and station outhouses; some other bodies became disused and lay about the Lodge before being broken up. Robert Evans agreed that the Statutory Returns for stock on the W.H.R. were meaning-

* See also 'Festiniog Railway', Vol. 2, pp. 287–8.

less and no record was kept of vehicle numbers. By the end of the Welsh Highland, the stock that stood on the main running line at Dinas, together with its individual colour (a scheme adopted when the F.R. took over the running and gave each coach an individual livery), and the stock stored inside the carriage shed, was:

On the running line:		*In the carriage shed:*	
8	Green	9	Grey (probably primer)
26	Blue	28	Green
27	Pink	35	Green
29	Red		
36	Green (Buffet Car)		

Of this collection, the carriages in the shed are thought to have been there for repairs which were not completed, especially Brake Compo. No. 9 which as noted, does not seem to have been seen in use during the post-1926 period and was probably left in grey primer.

Festiniog Railway No. 4 was a conversion made in September 1922 from a Quarrymen's Coach into a Brake Van without balcony ends, being fitted with dual brake gear for use on the Welsh Highland section, but only used on it during the first years of working. It was returned to Boston Lodge and scrapped before 1939. A second Quarrymen's Coach was stripped and a new van body with sliding doors built; it was painted grey with 'No. 1', and put to use as a Meat Van on the W.H.R.

The Festiniog purchased six open bogie carriages to War Department design in July 1923 from Robert Hudson Ltd. of Leeds. They had no doors, were narrow and open above the waist. Of course they were known to all as 'The Toastracks'. They had similar underframes and running gear to the ex-W.D. open bogie wagons which Stephens purchased for coal traffic on the W.H.R., and at first it was suggested these opens be converted for passenger use. In the end Hudson's quotation for new carriages at £155 was so cheap that new ones were ordered. Vacuum brake was included, and delivery made in three weeks! Delivery began on 23 August 1923 and to save time, they came in grey primer paint; after the season was over they were given a coat of 'lake', the then official name for Festiniog Railway 'brick-red'. They seated 30 persons and to prevent them falling out, chains were hung across the openings; they carried numbers 37–42, following the W.H.R. stock. It was intended to share the cost of the carriages between both railways, but in the event, the Festiniog bore the bill. They had a short life and a photograph of them in traffic has never been seen by the Author; they were used on both systems. Four were converted into flat wagons during 1926–8 and some of their parts were used to keep the W.H.R. open coal wagons in service as they were better revenue-earners in this form than as coaches.

No. 36 was converted into a licensed Buffet Car in late 1927 and was a very popular asset on the section. It was one of the 1878 'Corridor Coaches' which had begun life as a 3rd Class, but into which the N.W.N.G. put a partition and enclosed a small 1st Class section. This became the 'Kitchen Area'. Small destination boards hung under the cant rails of passenger stock were a feature of this period (black lettering shaded orange on a white ground) and 'Buffet Car' was painted up similarly—unfortunately a much older lettering showed through the paint, 'Gentlemen'; some wag nailed this to the bargeboard of Dinas station building, where it hung long after the Welsh Highland track had been lifted.

The carriage stock between 1923 and 1934 was painted a dark green,* and the Festiniog added enamelled plates on the doors like those fitted on their own stock, showing Class.

N.W.N.G. stock was lit by carbide gas, the cylinder being in the Guard's Van. The connecting pipe was led over the roofs and rubber hoses connected the carriages. When the winter service was suspended, the equipment was allowed to fall into disrepair, but not removed.

Goods Stock

It may be wise to begin by quoting the official N.W.N.G. Return for 1921 and showing the initial W.H.R. Return for 1922:

	1921	1922
Open Goods Wagons	82	9
Mineral Wagons (slate)	13	94
Rail & Timber trucks	18	13
Granite Wagons	—	—

against which Robert Williams, on his stock-checking visit in 1922 recorded:

Slate Wagons	82
Goods & Coal Wagons	19
Goods Vans	0
Timber trucks	12
Slab trucks (runners)	11

from which last list it is once again clear that Williams put his own interpretation on the use of the wagons and was not accompanied by

* 'Kentish Green' was the Tonbridge term.

any member of the N.W.N.G. staff to explain their function. Thus the Goods Wagons in his eyes were Slate Wagons and in his Report he used different terms from his stock-list viz: 'Iron Crate Wagons (these were iron slat-sided slate wagons) 29, Box Wagons 46, Coal Wagons 13 (bottoms very bad), Goods Wagons 5, in fair condition. Timber trucks 12 Bolsters, the whole in bad state, solebars broken and roughly patched. Check trucks 11. The 11 are in a very dilapidated state as far as the woodwork is concerned, but several good wheels and axles. A large proportion of the wagons with bad wheels much worn, flanges too high, flats, and require re-turning and new wheels. There are 15 Iron Crates, tops minus bottoms, and wheels in good condition' (June 1923).

Another stock list dated 31 December 1922 (source unknown) can be compared with the Official Return for 1922 (above). This list gives vehicles which existed in 1922 but did not appear in the Returns until later years, presumably because their condition did not make them fit for use in 1922 and they were later repaired.

Slate Wagons in Iron or Wood	106
Open Coal Wagons in Iron or Wood	9
Bolster Wagons	12
Goods Brake Vans	2
Miscellaneous	1

There is such variation that reconciliation is impossible. Like Williams' list, each depended on the interpretation of vehicle use!

Whatever the interpretation, the fact was that practically all the N.W.N.G. rolling stock lay at Dinas and it was in a wretched state. Most of the goods vehicles had been surplus to requirements and had lain out of use in the open. Earlier casualties during traffic had not been repaired. All the Welsh Highland did was to repair and paint such stock as was required, and that was little enough. The Returns made by the W.H.R. were useless, witness an extract from a letter to Evans at the time of the Festiniog lease. . . . 'So far as the Welsh Highland stock is concerned, this no doubt is a hopeless confusion, no stock was taken when the line was taken over and from what I have seen, especially of the wagon stock, there are dozens of vehicles which are absolutely scrap, apart from a number which would never pay to have repaired.'

Among the vehicles used by the Welsh Highland were two covered vans which like all N.W.N.G. goods stock, continued to carry their original numbers 2 & 4. Repainting was done in lake (brick-red of the Festiniog fashion) with black ironwork and white lettering which was done by stencils 'W H R' with the number below. There was no standard method of lettering etc. These vans had had corrugated iron sheets to replace the original roofs; they do not feature in any of the Returns of c. 1922, even in that of Major Spring (see p. 228) who at least embraced the fitted Brake Van which the others missed!

The W.H.R. reckoned it had something over 100 open wagons in existence up to 1933 (when all Returns cease); the 12 timber bolsters continue to be shown (they must have been patched up if Williams' Report is accurate), 2 Brake Vans appear out of the blue in 1924 and continue thereafter; one must have been the original N.W.N.G. fitted van and the other a second van built up locally; both survived to the end, out of use. The 2 Covered Vans are not shown until the last four years, from 1929 onwards. In odd years 'Miscellaneous' and 'Railway Service Vehicles' are given. Of the 100-plus open wagons, these were divided into 'Mineral Wagons under 8 tons' of which there were variously 91–96, and 'Open Merchandise Wagons' of which there were 9 at the start and 21 in 1933; these would include the 13 coal wagons some of which had no bottoms in 1922.

All this stock was burned at the end and the iron sold as scrap.

Bogie Coal Wagons

In October 1925 Colonel Stephens bought four ex-W.D. open wagons (5 tons capacity) from Honeywill Bros. of Ashford, Kent, purely for Welsh Highland coal traffic. This was virtually run between Dinas Junction and Beddgelert, where a new coal siding was put in. Ex-W.D. lorries were used by the Beddgelert merchant for road deliveries. This trade blossomed and in March 1926 when the Festiniog bought five similar wagons for the Brookes' Quarry traffic into Blaenau, they found there were too many on that work, so three were taken to Beddgelert, making seven in all on the Welsh Highland, and two on the Festiniog. No cash passed at this transaction, the ex-N.W.N.G. Ashbury-built bogie coach now No. 23, being brought onto the Festiniog in exchange. This carriage remained at Boston Lodge, so in consequence was the only Welsh Highland carriage to remain in use (nominally) after that line's closure; it was not of course, at Dinas for the sale of rolling stock. In the colourful repainting of all W.H.R./F.R. stock in the mid-1930s, it received a coat of yellow paint, as did Festiniog Nos. 21 & 22, thus becoming —so far as the staff was concerned—one of their own 'Yellow Coaches'.

The woebegone state of goods stock on the Highland line had the customary effect on the Festiniog's own stock—it gradually found its way into regular use on the Welsh Highland . . . just as the quarries found F.R. wagons most suited to their internal use! When Tonbridge wrote sharply to both the Receiver at Caernarvon, and D. O. Jones the factotem at Dinas, asking that Festiniog stock should be 'handed back at once', neither gentleman deigned to reply.

Permanent Way

This has been fully discussed in connection with the conversion of the N.W.N.G. and the building of the W.H.R. Clearly it was not necessary to give more than routine maintenance to it during the life of the W.H.R. though the Festiniog leasing period came to recognise the economic advantages of using ex-mainline standard gauge sleepers, suitably cut-down, for replacements. Until then, special sawing orders had been given. After 1928 the cost of Way and Works dwindled to a few hundred pounds each year; latterly less than 50 tons of ballast was laid in seven years and Festiniog backing apart, sleeper replacements after 1929 (with slight expenditure in 1930) were minimal.

Signalling and Staff Working

This has also been fully covered, but it remains to look adequately at the railways' crossing in Portmadoc, and the method of single line working over the South Snowdon–Portmadoc section. Of the old N.W.N.G., the signalling (semaphore) had all been removed by 1924 and the only Signal Box which remained was at Dinas; this became virtually a Ground Frame.

The regulations for the Portmadoc Crossing were dated 28 May 1923:

1. All trains to stop at the Stop Board and whistle;
   Up trains: 1 long 2 short.
   Down trains: 2 long 1 short.
2. The G.W.R. signalman will show a green flag by day and green light by night as an Allclear signal.
3. On seeing this, the driver will see that the points are set for him and take his train over the crossing without delay.
4. Drivers must use the greatest caution when approaching and crossing the G.W.R. line.
5. The Stationmaster or person in charge of Portmadoc New Station must personally see each train in both directions over the crossing and report any irregularity in working.
6. The Stationmaster or person in charge must see that lamps on the Stop Boards are lighted whilst trains are running during the hours of darkness.

In the G.W.R. Cabin, the 6-lever frame was responsible for Up and Down signals to protect the crossing itself, the former being added specially for the purpose. It also worked a slot in the Up starter (worked from Portmadoc East Cabin—beside the road crossing) and the Down distant. When the crossing was set for the Welsh Highland, a gong sounded beside the level crossing which could be heard by the station staff and the East signalman. Permission for the crossing signalman to allow a narrow gauge train over the G.W.R. was obtained by telephone link with the East Cabin.

There was a telephone link throughout, the N.W.N.G. section being carried on cast-iron poles and the Welsh Highland on wooden ones. Siemens equipment was fitted.

The Staff sections were divided (period *c.*1927–on):

1. Dinas Junction–Tryfan Junction. Wise's Patent Staff & Ticket. Key of Bryngwyn Branch attached. Lettered 'Dinas & Tryfan Jct'.

This Staff was kept either at Dinas booking office in the Stationmaster's charge, or in 'the appointed place' at Tryfan Junction.

2. Tryfan Junction–South Snowdon. Wooden Staff coloured Blue. Lettered 'Tryfan Jct. & South Snowdon'.

This Staff was kept either in South Snowdon booking office in the Stationmaster's charge, or in 'the appointed place' at Tryfan Junction. The keys of 'the appointed place' to be in the possession of guards of passenger and goods trains while they were on duty. The keys were kept by the Dinas Stationmaster when the guards were off duty.

Only 'One Engine in Steam' was to run on the Branch. No Staff would be required after the branch points had been re-set for the main line, the points locked and the Dinas–Tryfan Staff deposited in 'the appointed place' at Tryfan Junction.

Should work be required to be done during the night on the line the Dinas Stationmaster was to satisfy himself from the ganger or watchman that the line was safe for him to issue a Staff. In all cases the Staff had to be shown to the Guard first, who would satisfy himself it was the correct one. The Stationmaster would hand it over, plus key attached, and he too would satisfy himself it was correct. Alternatively he would do as foregoing and then remove a Ticket with the aid of the attached key to give authority to the driver to start. A Branch train could not proceed beyond Tryfan Junction if started on a Ticket, as he required the Staff to unlock the branch points; they were not in fact, allowed to travel with a Ticket.

The Guard was responsible for setting down the Wise's Staff at Tryfan Junction and taking up the wooden staff, which he showed to the driver who then took it. Before leaving, the Wise's Staff was locked up in 'the appointed place'. At South Snowdon (where the next staff member was employed) the driver gave the staff to the Stationmaster who entered the fact and time in the Train Book. Arrangements at Waenfawr (which was unstaffed) were in the hands of the Guard but of course, there was no Staff exchange to be done there.

Precisely converse directions applied to Down trains from South Snowdon. From the Regulations, it appears that the Wise's Staff only carried one Ticket at each end as, if any train was to work on that section by means of a Ticket, it had to be established that the following train was in fact capable of returning with the complete Staff and Ticket. This arrangement is believed to be done to avoid confusion among the operating staff.

Stationmasters at Dinas and South Snowdon were responsible for seeing the points were set correctly; at Tryfan Junction the drivers were responsible. At all other places on the line, the Guard was responsible for point setting (this was infrequently required, of course). At Tryfan Junction, to allow drivers time to examine the setting of the road, all trains had to stop short of the Junction points. Whilst standing at the Junction, the Guard had to enter up the Train Book there to show he had carried and was about to carry the correct staff, and in what position the points were found, and the time.

Up trains on a Ticket from Dinas had to report arrival at Tryfan before the following train could leave. Tryfan arrivals from Branch or Main had to check with Dinas before proceeding there.

The Staff arrangements described above applied to most of the life history of the Welsh Highland; they enabled the N.W.N.G. section to be worked with minimum of expense and personnel. The initial Regulations for working (dated May 1923) were quite uneconomic. Under these the N. Wales' section was in fact, Staffed entirely by Wise's Patent. The arrangements for this period were Staff Sections:

2. Tryfan Junction–Waenfawr
3. Waenfawr–Rhydd-ddu (sic)

A footnote explained that Rhydd-ddu 'is now known as South Snowdon'. As soon as it was seen that changing staff at Waenfawr involved time and equipment, and that only because of the junction at Tryfan was it necessary to have Wise's Staff and Ticket available between there and Tryfan, the timetable was ultimately adjusted to having only one train between Tryfan and South Snowdon, and the working on that section to be on an alternate basis, there being no Ticket for that section.

The remainder of the line had Staff Sections:

3. South Snowdon–Beddgelert: Wooden Staff coloured Red; Tickets Red. Staff lettered 'South Snowdon and Beddgelert'.
4. Beddgelert–Portmadoc New: Wooden Staff coloured Green; Tickets Green. Staff lettered 'Beddgelert and Portmadoc New Station'.

'The appointed place' at unstaffed stations is ultimately revealed as the Telephone Room. The Ticket Boxes were unlocked by a key on the Staff. Oddly, the Regulations on the above sections are more normal in that Staffs or Tickets were to be handed to the driver, and not via the Guard as on the N.W.N.G. section.

The key on the Staff unlocked the points in that section; guards were responsible for point setting where there was no one in charge. In the diagram illustrating how points were to be set at loops, the point at each end was to be set for left-hand running. In practice however, and possibly influenced by the Festiniog who used the system, trains often used the right-hand line, as this was often the running line; or at Beddgelert, for instance, the other side of the loop might be occupied by a train proceeding in the same direction. Probably this Regulation was honoured in the breach. Guards had a busy time; they might have to move the points at the far end of a loop before the train could leave, call it forward and stop it beyond the points, lock up the points again and, if proceeding on the Ticket from an unstaffed station, return the Staff to the Telephone Room before walking forward to the train. No wonder the service was lethargic!

Reporting of crossings, arrival and departures was done by telephone; boxes were provided at Dinas, Tryfan, Waenfawr, South Snowdon, Beddgelert, Nantmor, Croesor Junction, Pont Croesor, Portmadoc New, Portmadoc Old. There was an extensive code of calling signals.

Drivers were urged to use their whistles frequently to announce arrival at stations, level crossings and on sharp curves or other places where the view was restricted.

In the event of breakdowns on the line, an assisting engine, might, with permission, enter the section without a Staff and travel at 8 m.p.h. to the accident.

Working of Bryngwyn Incline:

1. The first pass of four wagons worked down the Incline must contain at least two wagons with good brakes which must be examined and tested before being brought to the top of the Incline.
2. The Drum, brake and gear must be examined each day before the Incline is used, and all defects put right.

3. The rope must be examined each week and greased if necessary. Any defects to the rope, drum or brake gear must be reported to Dinas as soon as possible.
4. The loaded wagons must not be detached from the rope at the foot of the Incline until they are under control by means of the brakes.
5. At least four efficient sprags must be kept at the foot of the Incline and used as required.
6. The weighted catch points at the level crossing must be examined and oiled before any traffic is worked on the Incline. They must not be propped or fastened up on any account whatever.

The Regulations for working the Railway end : 'The Instructions must be re-read not less than once every month'.

Working over the Junction Railway; Portmadoc New to Old Stations:

There are ten sections in this special appendix. Drivers were to stop their trains before crossing the public roads and keep a good lookout. On them speed must not exceed 5 m.p.h. and elsewhere 10 m.p.h. Staffs were exchanged at Portmadoc Old 'when trains are expected and . . . (the man on duty) . . . must use his discretion in passing trains onto the Junction Railway'. (The man in question was to be arranged by the Stationmaster at the New station—the Old station had no staff and was closed.) Whistles were to be sounded across the public road and on blind curves and the local Bye Laws and Special M.O.T. Regulations applying to the Junction Railway were to be observed. The Staff was of wood and coloured Blue, as were the Tickets; points on the section were locked by the key attached to the Staff so trains wishing to enter any of several sidings must have possessed the Staff. There were special arrangements for a train which was proceeding onto the wharves; this had to clear the Junction Railway and be locked onto the wharf branch. The train driver could then walk back with the Staff and give it up (the Regulations do not say where or to whom, or to which end of the Junction Railway!) Whilst without the Staff, the driver of the wharf engine might not bring his train within 50 yards of the Junction Railway until he regained possession of the Staff.

In these initial years of the Welsh Highland when Portmadoc Old was closed, there was a curious instruction dated 1 June 1923. This read that all Down trains from Blaenau Festiniog must stop opposite the Old station goods shed for passengers to alight. Up trains however, were not to stop at all when passing the Old station. This must have made it very difficult for Blaenau-bound passengers, who might forget to walk up to Portmadoc New to catch their train and then see it pass by them at the Goods Shed. The answer probably is that as the Old station did not appear in the timetables at this time; the Down stop was a convenience which was not publicly admitted!

In the event of Dinas-bound trains running late, and with the risk of a missed connection there, the Guard was to telephone from Waenfawr. This frequently happened, due to bad steaming of the engine, or slipping on greasy rail. Less frequently the Guard had to 'phone from Croesor Junction to Portmadoc to report late running.

The use of Wise's Staff over the northern section has been referred to: the new Working Instructions for October 1925 show Wise's equipment in use as far as South Snowdon. No exact date is available for the disuse of it beyond Tryfan save that it would be logical for it to be discontinued during the 'pruning' period of staff and trains which followed the appointment of the Receiver in March 1927. It was in fact, intended to use the Wise Staffs between the newly-opened loop at Croesor Junction, and Portmadoc or Beddgelert but, having no spares, an order was put in for new ones (in March 1924). Second thoughts prevailed and to economise the order was cancelled and instructions given to use two Festiniog Staffs which were redundant. (These would be Miniature Electric type, but the intention was to use them manually without the instruments). Festiniog reported they had none to spare, so Boston Lodge turned out two Staffs from iron rod in the shape of a crucifix. The bottom was shaped into a key and the names were punched into the cross-stave.

Train Operating and Timetables

(To be read in conjunction with 'Locomotives')

1922

Passenger trains resumed working on the old N.W.N.G. main line on 31 July. *Russell* was used for this work but in emergency, *Moel Tryfan* came out. Either engine might be found on the goods/branch train and both received heavy repairs at Dinas. Trains left Dinas at 9.24, 11.40X, 12.53S and 5.32, returning at 10.40, 1.50, 3.55X, 6.40. Unless there was an omission of 'S' after the 1.50 departure, there was an unbalanced working out of Snowdon except on Saturdays, perhaps in connection with workmen, materials etc. A new service began on 2 October, much reduced. Departures were:

Dinas:	9.45	12.40	5.20
Snowdon:	10.50	3.30	6.30

the timetable carrying a footnote 'Work is now actively proceeding on the remainder of the Railway from South Snowdon to Portmadoc. The whole Railway will be in operation in the early Spring of 1923.' The stations on the branch were placed in the table and against them it read 'Branch not yet opened'. Yet another table came into force on 1 December, carrying the same notes yet a much greater service—perhaps locomotive shortage had been the cause of the previous one? Departures were:

Dinas:	9.45	12.00S	12.40X	2.55S	5.20	7.40S
Snowdon:	10.50	1.00S	3.55		6.30	8.45S

and this lasted into 1923.

1923

Moel Tryfan was out of service for almost all the foregoing period; *Russell* continued on passenger work, and when connection was made at Portmadoc, *Palmerston* or some other England engine came to assist. The Baldwin, acquired on 4 July, was tried on various turns with indifferent results so far as passenger traffic was concerned. The new full table for the full-length railway began on 9 July; times were:

Dinas	—	9.45	12.00	3.10	5.40	8.00
Beddgelert	9.33					9.33
Portmadoc	10.18	12.22	3.05	5.30	8.05	—
Portmadoc	8.45	10.35	1.30	3.55	6.30	—
Beddgelert					7.15	8.25
Dinas	11.42	1.55	4.55	6.20	—	9.55

On 15 September, setting up a pattern which was to follow in later years when the Summer service was reduced in the late season, the 8.0 p.m. from Dinas became Saturdays only and the 8.25 p.m. from Beddgelert was taken off. There were further alterations in October and November, and the minimal Winter table started in December:

Dinas	9.50	—	4.25	5.25
Beddgelert		3.15	SX	SO
Portmadoc	12.15	4.00	6.52	7.55
Portmadoc	9.35	2.00	5.15	6.30SX
Beddgelert		2.45		7.15
Dinas	11.47	—	7.32	—

1924

During much of the year the Baldwin was relegated to spare engine, and *Russell* was commonly to be found on the goods and solely the branch engine. *Moel Tryfan* had begun her long spell of duties working between Dinas and Blaenau. Extra help came from Festiniog engines and occasionally double Fairlie engines worked through to Dinas.

WELSH HIGHLAND AND FESTINIOG RAILWAYS

14 January 1924 until further notice

		am	am	am	am	am	pm	pm	SX	pm	SO	pm
Dinas Junction	dep				9 50				4 25		5 25	
Tryfan Junction	,,				10 3				4 38		5 38	
Waenfawr	,,				10 15				4 50		5 50	
Bettws Garmon	,,				10 20				4 55		5 A55	
Quellyn Lake	,,				10 37				5 12		6 12	
South Snowdon	arr				10 46				5 21		6 22	
	dep				10 59				5 25		6 42	
Pitt's Head	,,				A				A		A	
Beddgelert	arr				11 24	SX	SO		5 52		7 7	
	dep					11 30	12 18		6 7		7 18	
Nantmor (Aberglaslyn)						11 42	12 30		6 19		7 30	
Ynysfor (Llanfrothen)						11 58	12 46		6 A35		7 46	
Pont Croesor (Prenteg)						12 4	12 52		6 A41		7 52	
Portmadoc	arr					12 15	1 3		6 52		8 3	SO
,, (Old Station)	dep	6 15	8 15	11 10		—	—	2 30	—	6 0	—	9 0
Minffordd	,,	6 25	8 28	11 25				2 45		6 9		9 15
Penrhyndeudraeth	,,	6 31	8 33	11 30				2 51		6 18		9 21
Tanybwlch	,,	6 53	8 55	11 51				3 11		6 39		9 45
Tanygrisiau	,,	7 14	9 15	12 11				3 31		6 58		10 5
Bl. Festiniog (L.M. & S.)		7 20	9 20	12 17				3 37		7 3		10 11
,, (G.W.R.)		7 22	9 22	12 19				3 39		7 5		10 13

		am	am	am	pm	pm	pm	pm	pm
Bl. Festiniog (G.W.R.)		7 30		9 30		12 36		4 25	7 10
,, (L.M. & S.)		7 33		9 32		12 38		4 28	7 13
Tanygrisiau	dep	7 38		9 37		12 43		4 33	7 18
Tanybwlch	,,	7 58		9 54		1 3		4 54	7 39
Penrhyndeudraeth	,,	8 16		10 12		1 12		5 13	7 58
Minffordd	,,	8 30		10 16		1 25		5 20	8 4
Portmadoc New Station		8 38	SX	10 30	SO	1 40		5 30	8 15
,,	dep	—	9 35	—	11 25		5 15	—	—
Pont Croesor (Prenteg)			9 A46		11 36		5 26		
Ynysfor (Llanfrothen)			9 A52		11 42		5 32		
Nantmor (Aberglaslyn)			10 8		11 58		5 48		
Beddgelert	arr		10 20		12 10		6 0		
	dep		10 24		12 25		6 5		
Pitt's Head	,,		A		A		A		
South Snowdon	arr		10 54		12 55		6 35		
	dep		10 56		1 0		6 39		
Quellyn Lake	,,		11 8		1 13		6 52		
Bettws Garmon	,,		11 19		1 26		7 A3		
Waenfawr	,,		11 27		1 35		7 12		
Tryfan Junction	,,		11 38		1 46		7 23		
Dinas Junction	arr		11 47		1 55		7 32		

A—Stops if required. SO—Saturdays only. SX—Saturdays excepted.

From May the table was:

Dinas	—	9.50	1.15	3.10	5.35	—
Beddgelert	7.15					8.16
Portmadoc	8.00	12.58	3.56	5.24	8.15	9.00
Portmadoc	6.15	9.35	10.40	2.25	5.40	6.45
Beddgelert	7.05					7.30
Dinas	—	11.47	1.42	6.01	7.52	—

which ran until mid-July when on 14 July the service became:

Dinas	8.10	9.50	12.00	3.05	5.40		
Beddgelert	9.26	11.22	1.17	4.24	7.25		
,,	9.30	12.15	—	4.58	7.29	8.30*	
Portmadoc	10.12	12.58	—	5.39	8.11	9.12	
Portmadoc	9.38	11.25	1.25	2.25	4.13	5.40	7.35*
Beddgelert	10.20	12.07	2.06	3.07	4.53	6.20	8.17
,,	10.24	12.11	—	3.25	4.56	6.24	—
Dinas	11.44	1.48	—	4.45	6.18	7.45	—

* Thursday and Saturday only until 13 September.

During August the noon train to Beddgelert was extended into Portmadoc (arr. 2.5) and an additional train left Beddgelert at 3.15, due Portmadoc 3.57.

By the end of the season the cash crisis had hit the Welsh Highland to an exceptional degree. With this intensive service a reasonably high number of passengers were carried, but working costs were so great that losses were increasing all the time. Income from passenger traffic had been at its zenith in 1923, then it continued to fall; income from goods services reached a peak in 1925; loss on Revenue Account reached a peak in 1924. The Company's Annual Meeting of 12 April had shown how dissatisfied were the shareholders, and as soon as the financial position over the 1924 Summer services was clear, the axe fell. The Winter service was reduced to trains leaving Dinas at 9.42 and 4.20, and Portmadoc at 9.10 and 3.45. Lack of patronage proved fatal and on 15 December 1924 the passenger service was suspended.

1925

Russell and *Moel Tryfan* shared most of the passenger duties this year, sometimes aided by a small engine off the Festiniog, but this was only during the height of the season. This help from Boston Lodge came to be mostly a high-season effort and though England engines continued to run through to Dinas, it was only for a few weeks in the year. *Russell* also worked the goods and the Baldwin continued to be the Black Sheep of the fold. Most of the time it lay at Dinas.

Services were restored and in the period July–September the timetable was : :

Dinas	9.50		12.00		4.30	
Beddgelert	11.15		1.25		6.00	
,,	11.20		1.35	2.20XS	6.05	8.05 Fri only
Portmadoc	12.09		2.20	3.05	6.50	8.50
Portmadoc	11.20	12.45XS	2.25	4.00		7.10 Fri only
Beddgelert	12.10	1.30	3.10	4.45		7.55
,,	12.20	—	3.20	4.50		—
Dinas	2.00	—	4.50	6.20		—

and on 21 September a reduced timetable was introduced :

Dinas	—	12.45	—
Beddgelert	—	2.11	—
,,	11.20	2.15	5.55 (Daily to 2 Oct; Fri only thereafter)
Portmadoc G.W.	12.04	3.02	6.38
Portmadoc G.W.	10.35	2.19	5.10 (Daily to 2 Oct; Fri only thereafter)
Beddgelert	11.14	3.05	5.42
,,	—	3.08	—
Dinas	—	4.35	—

A curious feature of this table was that all trains into Portmadoc were shown arriving at the 'New (G.W.R. link)' station, but in the converse direction departure times of 10.30 and 2.10 from 'Old Station' are shown for the first two trips of the day.

It will be noted how emphasis on a better train service on the southern half of the line was being built up. The whole main line was proving uneconomic and did not lend itself to through trains. The above table continued through the Winter but the morning short-turn to Beddgelert became Fridays Only.

1926

The Winter train was now a single bogie coach and an England engine. (The coach was often the ex-N.W.N.G. brake composite, now No. 8). Engines on this service included *Palmerston* and *Princess. Russell* took over again in the Summer. *Moel Tryfan* and the Baldwin do not appear to have been on Highland passenger trains.

For the Summer the service was :

Dinas	—	12.55	4.40
Beddgelert	—	2.25	6.03
,,	12.20	3.00	6.10
Portmadoc	1.05	3.46	6.56
Portmadoc	11.20	2.14	5.16
Beddgelert	12.11	2.58	6.01
,,	—	3.01	6.05
Dinas	—	4.25	7.30

and from 20 September this was drastically reduced to a train from Dinas at 12.45 arriving Portmadoc 3.0 and returning from there 3.10, due Dinas at 5.20. This skeleton table lasted through the Winter and led to the experiments with tractors and single coaches to see if the England engine with one coach could even further reduce running costs.

1927

The above table continued to the end of May 1927 when from 1 June the table was:

Dinas	—	1.00	4.45
Beddgelert	12.20		
Portmadoc	1.05	3.46	6.55
Portmadoc	11.26	2.14	5.16
Beddgelert	12.11		
Dinas	—	4.25	7.31

On 11 July a much more complex table followed; a northbound train from Portmadoc turned back at Beddgelert and another Boston Lodge-worked turn reversed at South Snowdon—the only season when this was done. In addition there were two through services which allowed some flexibility in the locomotive rostering, as engine changes could be made at Beddgelert, and units confined, with their crews, to their parent sections. The engine mileages on the Welsh Highland for May and August are fortunately available, and are quoted alongside their Festiniog mileages together with coal consumption. This is the most complete record to survive:

Loco.	*May 1927* *Miles run*		*Coal lb/mile*		*August 1927* *Miles run*		*Coal lb/mile*
PRINCESS	413	FR	25·14	FR	673	FR	31·26
	257	WHR	34·97	WHR	993	WHR	
PRINCE	1153	FR	26·95	FR	1947	FR	26·90
	18	WHR	46·66	WHR	181	WHR	
PALMERSTON	1215	FR	23·16		1082	FR	27·68
	126	WHR	43·33		1229	WHR	
WELSH PONY	43	FR	45·58		168	FR	35·49
	36	WHR	38·88		183	WHR	

and the following figures were applicable to those engines which did not run on the Festiniog at all during the two months:

RUSSELL	1627	23·42	932	27·87
The Baldwin	50	44·80	703	27·00
MOEL TRYFAN	—	—	135	31·31

From the above may be seen that the Summer table which follows was worked from Boston Lodge by England engines, *Princess* doing the 'lioness's' share of the work immediately prior to the introduction of the table and whilst continuing to do duty, giving way to *Palmerston* during August. The coal figures show that England engines were not so economical on coal on the Highland run, perhaps because of standing time or that their firemen were not used to the route. *Welsh Pony* was exceptional during the May, but possibly this was poor coal or steaming when on the Festiniog duty, as the consumption figures are better in the August. *Russell* compares favourably with an England engine and oddly, the Baldwin, after limited mileage at high consumption during May, was less hungry for coal during August when the figures were slightly better than *Russell*. One or more of many unknown factors may have accounted for this; separate figures are not available for the Bryngwyn goods train. *Moel Tryfan* was little used.

Dinas		12.00		4.20
S. Snowdon	12.04	12.58		5.21
Beddgelert	12.27	1.22		5.45
„	12.30	1.27	3.05	5.48
Portmadoc	1.10	2.08	3.43	6.30
Portmadoc	10.45	12.36	2.14	4.00
Beddgelert	11.30	1.21	2.58	4.44
„	11.33	1.30		4.47
S. Snowdon	11.59	1.59		5.16
Dinas		2.55		6.12

Extraordinary measures were taken on 26 September. The railway as a through route was abandoned, one working from Dinas to Beddgelert taking place daily at 12.45, arriving and departing from Beddgelert at 2.5 and 3.8 to arrive Dinas at 4.23 p.m.

Croesor Junction now appeared in the public tables for the first time and on Fridays the Croesor goods trip had a coach attached which the public was invited to patronise. This equipage left Portmadoc at 11.45 and arrived Croesor Junction at 12.5 p.m. The return working was 4.10 and arrival 4.29, and as Croesor Junction had virtually no connections (even by foot) with the outside world, passengers were probably taken unofficially to the Llanfrothen road crossing, or dropped off at various points between Portmadoc and Croesor Junction. The goods was allowed four hours to pick up its train and sort the wagons before starting from the Junction again; this allowed the Bottom Shunter to do 'the Croesor turn' between its other duties. The Croesor horse could collect the empties and take the loaded wagons to the Junction if required—in this way hire of the horse might be limited to one day a week. It will be recalled that the tramway was suitable for locomotive haulage to the Llanfrothen road, so the permutations of the day are almost endless, and way out of sight of Authority at that!

In December the daily Dinas–Beddgelert working became Tuesdays, Thursdays and Saturdays and because of the weekly pick-up to Croesor, it was not necessary to run any train between Beddgelert and Croesor Junction, which length lay in suspended animation.

1928

Trains ran through again from June, the service being increased on 11 June when the Fridays only was extended to Beddgelert, the Junction stop being retained.

Dinas		12.45
Beddgelert		2.05
,,	12.15	3.00
Portmadoc	1·00	3.43
Portmadoc	11.20	1.42
Beddgelert	12.04	2.26
,,		3.00
Dinas		4.25

During the Winter Dinas shops had been busy converting a coach into a Buffet Car and this worked between there and Beddgelert in the new table beginning 9 July. It was attached to the noon train from Dinas and returned there on the 3.5 from Beddgelert. It will be seen that the 'interval' idea of detaining certain trains at Beddgelert for a period, was now in force. The table, which showed through working with the Festiniog, is detailed in full on p. 357.

There followed numerous minor alterations during the Summer and on 2 September the two South Snowdon workings were discontinued. By 24 September, the Winter train was back again, running to Portmadoc at 12.30 from Dinas and leaving there at 3.0; by October it was cut back to Beddgelert on Mondays, Wednesdays and Fridays.

The Baldwin was working most of the goods services early in the year with *Russell* working out from Dinas on the northern section passenger duties. From July to Spring of 1929, the Kerr Stuart tractor worked many of the Bryngwyn trains, so for the high season the Baldwin was available if required on passenger trains.

1929

The tractor left the Welsh Highland in March, but otherwise, the same pattern of locomotive duties continued at first. The Winter train service was re-extended to Portmadoc in May on the same week-days. Then a crisis occurred. *Russell* required heavy repairs and new tyres; Boston Lodge was expected to do this work but in the event failed to do so. The wheels were sent back to the makers who would not release them until payment was made. Meanwhile, a

FESTINIOG & WELSH HIGHLAND RAILWAYS.

Time Tables—From July 9th, 1928, and until further notice.

DOWN TRAINS (Weekdays only)

				SX	SO	E			
	a.m.	a.m.	a.m.	p.m.	p.m.	p.m.	p.m.	p.m.	p.m.
Duffws ... ... dep.	6 28	9 15	July 23rd to Sept. 1st, 1928, inclusive.	12 2	*12 20*	1 33	3 50	4 23	7 0
BlaenauFestiniog(G.W.R.) „	s	9 16		12 3	*12 21*	1 34	3 51	4 24	7 1
BlaenauFestiniog(L.M.S.) „	s	9 18		12 5	*12 23*	1 36	3 53	4 26	7 3
Tanygrisiau ... „	s	9s23		12s10	*12 30*	1 41	4 1	4s31	7 8
Dduallt ... ... „	s	s		s	s	s	s	s	s
Tanybwlch ... „	s	9 43		12 29	*12 51*	2 1	4 20	4 52	7 29
Penrhyndeudraeth .. „	s	10s 5		12s50	*1 11*	2 22	4 42	5 13	7s50
Minffordd (for G.W.R.) arr.	s	10 10		12 55	*1 17*	2 28	4 47	5 18	7 55
„ „ dep.	s	10 21		12 56	*1 18*	2 29	4 50	5 20	7 58
Boston Lodge Halt	s	s		s	s	s	s	s	s
Portmadoc (Old Station) arr.	7 40	10 31		1 6	*1 28*	2 39	5 0	5 30	8 8
„ „ dep.		—		1 7	*1 44*	2 44	—	—	—
Portmadoc (for G.W.R.) arr.				1 11	*1 48*	2 48			
„ „ dep.	July 23rd to Sept. 1st, 1928, inclusive		10 40	1 16	*1 54*	2 50			
Pont Croesor ... „			10s49	1s25	*2s 4*	2 59			
Ynysfor ... ... „			10s54	1s30	*2s10*	3s 4			
Croesor Junc. ... arr.			s	s.	*2 16*	s			
Hafod Garregog ... „			s	s	s	s			
Hafod-y-Llyn ... „			s	s	s	s			
Nantmor ... ... „			11s13	1s48	*2s33*	3s22			
Beddgelert ... arr.			11 25	2 0	*2 45*	3 34			
„ ... dep.			11 28	3 5	*3 5*	3 35			
Hafod Ruffydd ... „			s	s	s	s			
Pitts Head ... „			s	s	s	s			
South Snowdon ... arr.			11 56	3 34	*3 34*	4 4			
„ ... dep.			—	3 40	*3 40*	July 23rd to Sept. 1st, 1928, inclusive.			
Quellyn Lake ... „				3s51	*3s51*				
Plas-y-Nant ... „				s	s				
Salem ... ... „				s	s				
Bettws Garmon ... „				4s 3	*4s 3*				
Waenfawr... ... „				4 11	*4 11*				
Tryfan Junc. ... „				4 21	*4 21*				
Dinas Junc.(forL.M.S.R.) arr.				4 30	*4 30*				

UP TRAINS (Weekdays only)

						SX	SO		
	a.m.	a.m.	a.m.	p.m.	p.m.	p.m.	p.m.	p.m.	p.m.
Dinas Junc.(forL.M.S.R.) dep.						12 0	12 0		
Tryfan Junc. ... „						12 13	12 13		
Waenfawr... ... „						12 25	12 25		
Bettws Garmon ... „						12s30	12s30		
Salem ... ... „						s	s		
Plas-y-Nant ... „						s	s		
Quellyn Lake ... „						12s45	12s45	K	
South Snowdon ... arr.						12 53	12 53	—	
„ ... dep.				12 2		12 56	12 56	4 7	
Pitts Head ... „				s		s	s	s	
Hafod Ruffydd ... „				s		s	s	s	
Beddgelert ... arr.				12 27		1 22	1 22	4 32	
„ ... dep.				12 28		2 5	1 52	4 34	
Nantmor ... ... „				12s40		2s17	2s 4	4s46	
Hafod-y-Llyn ... „				s		s	s	s	
Hafod Garregog ... „				s		s	s	s	
Croesor Junc. ... „				s		2 31	2 16	s	
Ynysfor ... ... „				12s55		2s36	2s22	5s 3	
Pont Croesor ... „				1s 0		2s41	2s28	5s 9	
Portmadoc (for G.W.R.) arr.				1 10		2 51	2 38	5 19	
„ „ dep.				1 11	K	2 52	2 43	5 21	
„ (Old Station) arr.	—	—	—	1 15	—	2 56	2 47	5 25	
„ „ „ dep.	*5 15*	7 55	10 10	—	1 17	3 0	3 0		5 45
Boston Lodge Halt	s	s	s	July 23rd to Sept 1st 1928, Inclusive.	s	s	s	July 23rd to Sept. 1st, 1928. Inclusive	s
Minffordd (for G.W.R.) arr.	*5 25*	8 5	10 20		1 27	3 10	3 10		5 55
„ „ dep.	*5 26*	8 7	10 26		1 30	3 12	3 12		5 57
Penrhyndeudraeth ... „	*5 31*	8s12	10s31		1s35	3s17	3s17		6s 2
Tanybwlch ... „	*5 55*	8 35	10 58		2 2	3 40	3 40		6 27
Dduallt ... ... „	s	s	s		s	s	s		s
Tanygrisiau ... „	*6 15*	8s55	11s13		2 22	4 0	4 0		6 47
Blaenau Festiniog (LMS) arr.	*6 20*	9 0	11 18		2 27	4 6	4 6		6 52
BlaenauFestiniog(G.W.R.) „	*6 23*	9 2	11 20		2 29	4 8	4 8		6 54
Duffws ... „	*6 24*	9 3	11 21		2 30	4 9	4 9		6 55

NOTES. S.—Stops if required. E-Leaves Duffws 1-43 p.m. & runs 10 mins. later throughout to South Snowdon on Sats K-Runs 12 mins. later on Sats.

shortage of suitable engines was evident and the Summer timetable was curtailed to that of being the Winter through train, leaving Dinas 12.22, Portmadoc times being 2.28–2.38 and Dinas at 6.10. Even this did not run on Saturdays. By October, the same train ran on the week-days of Autumn 1928.

1930

With *Russell* still *hors de combat*, *Moel Tryfan* re-appeared on Welsh Highland metals and shared some duties with the Baldwin, which itself was off for repairs during the year. In April the daily working included a 'Ghost Train' on the Portmadoc–Beddgelert trip, the reason for which is not clear;

Dinas	12.24	Portmadoc	—
Beddgelert	1.46	Beddgelert	—
,,	1.51	,,	3.30
Portmadoc	2.30	Dinas	4.56

No improvements in the situation taking place, the Summer service was as minimal as it could be, in fact it is doubtful if it really performed any really useful function except that the Baldwin was still on a twice-daily goods run, so the July–September passenger train continued on three days a week hauled by *Moel Tryfan* running between Dinas and Beddgelert only! On 22 September this shadowy service ceased and Winter trains with it. Also it is apparent that running over the G.W.R. crossing effectively stopped with the curtailment of trains at Beddgelert, but one source (unconfirmed) avers that even the daily train of Summer 1929 did not proceed beyond the Beddgelert Siding.

1931

The locomotive—and the cash—shortage was no easier and it was 20 July before a single through train to Portmadoc and back (now *officially* terminating north of the G.W.R.) re-appeared. Of course, this pattern of train only suited those originating at the north end of the line and was useless to holiday makers in Portmadoc as a there-and-back railway service. More especially use was made of it in connection with through tours, and it was the 2.45 return trip from Portmadoc (due Dinas 6.20) which conveyed most passengers on the round trip. Now both the Baldwin and *Russell* were laid up after the season closed, and *Moel Tryfan* had been responsible for the daily passenger train. In June an extra fitter was taken on at Boston Lodge to complete *Russell.*

The daily goods train was next to be hit—from 2 November this ran only twice a week (a circular of 2 November says, '... Railway is to be re-opened for parcels, goods, etc. . . .) and from 31 December goods traffic apparently ceased altogether. After nine years, the Welsh Highland had given up the struggle for life.

During this period no attempt had been made to designate the customary terms 'Up' or 'Down' to trains, and following the services of its predecessor, no Sunday trains operated either then or since . . . in fact, for the Welsh Highland/Festiniog system and with many small companies at this time, as regards train services the Sabbath was a 'dies non'.

1932

The season was extremely short, a service operating between 16 July and 9 September, consisting of one train leaving Dinas 12.28, Portmadoc arrive 2.37—depart 2.45, Dinas arrive 6.20, the return trip languishing at Beddgelert between 3.39 and 4.45 and at South Snowdon 5.14 to 5.30, refreshments now being advertised at South Snowdon and being provided by an outside contractor. *Russell* was now back in service (Caernarvonshire County Council having paid Hunslet's account), and shared this light duty with the Baldwin.

1933

The pattern was repeated for 1933, the basis being the circular tour rather than giving any sort of return trip. Dates were 17 July–10 September. This year the return working did not leave Portmadoc until 3.10 and the Beddgelert stay-over was reduced to under an hour. Arrival at Dinas 6.20 allowed three minutes for the change-over into the north-bound L.M.S. connection and this was often missed. Locomotives duties continued as for 1932.

1934

Under the Festiniog lease, a better service was introduced on 9 July–20 September:

Dinas	11.25	2.50	6.15 W & Thurs only	
Beddgelert	12.45	4.05	7.25 ditto	
,,	12.55	4.55	7.30	
Portmadoc	1.30	5.30	8.05	
Portmadoc	10.45	1.40	4.00	6.20
Beddgelert	11.20	2.15	4.35	6.55
,,	1.15		4.50	8.00 W & Thurs only
Dinas	2.30		6.05	9.10 ditto

No record is available of what goods services operated following the total stoppage at the end of 1931. The slump was at its height but obviously some requirement became necessary again, to meet the dying Moel Tryfan output (before it finally began to load at Pen-y-groes, perhaps because of the uncertainties of the branch goods train availability?) and the short-lived Bettws Garmon trade. Certainly there was a path for two trips on the branch during 1933–34 and when required, the Baldwin was on this job. It was the need for repairs which stopped the service on 31 December 1933 and during the year under review (1934) goods services must have been disordered, both engines being through the Dinas shops for repair. On the passenger side, 1934 began by *Moel Tryfan* based on Boston Lodge, thus accounting for the service being worked from the south instead of the north end.

1935

Some workings were taken by *Russell* and the Baldwin in the 1934 season's end and by the start of the 1935 season on 8 July the process was continued, with *Moel Tryfan* being phased out from the northern end of the run, but sharing the Beddgelert–Portmadoc workings with an England engine, much as had been done in earlier years. *Russell* worked the northern end. This arrangement continued for 1936 too.

The table was similar to that of 1934 and was in force 8 July–15

FESTINIOG AND WELSH HIGHLAND RAILWAYS

6 July–26 September 1936

Down Trains (week-days)

			a.m.	p.m.	p.m.	p.m.	p.m.
Bl. Festiniog (G.W.R.)	dep.		11.50	1.49	4.22	5.27	8C0
Bl. Festiniog (L.M.S.)	,,		11.55	1.50	4.25	5.30	8C3
			p.m.				
Tanybwlch	,,		12.20	2.15	4.50	5.55	8C25
Penrhyndeudraeth	,,		12A40	2.35	5.10	6.15	8C45
Minffordd	,,		12.50	2.43	5.18	6.21	8C52
Portmadoc	arr.		12.59	2.52	5.26	6.30	9C1
		a.m.					
,,	dep.	10B45	2.0	3B55			
Aberglaslyn	,,	11B9	2.24	4B19			
Beddgelert	arr.	11B20	2.35	4B30			
,,	dep.	11B30	3.15	4B50			
South Snowdon	,,	12B25	3.50	5B35			
Dinas Junction For L.M.S. Rly	arr.	1B15	4.35	6B15			

Up Trains (week-days)

				a.m.	p.m.	p.m.
Dinas Junction	dep.			11.25	1B30	4B50
South Snowdon	,,			12.15	2B15	5B35
Beddgelert	arr.			12.45	2B45	6B3
,,	dep.			12.55	2B55	6B5
Aberglaslyn	,,			1.6	3B6	6B16
Portmadoc	arr.			1.30	3B30	6B40
		a.m.	p.m.			
,,	dep.	10.20	12.30	3.10	4.15	6C50
Minffordd	,,	10.35	12.38	3.20	4.25	7C0
Penrhyndeudraeth	,,	10A40	12A53	—	4A30	7A5
Tanybwlch	,,	11.0	1.13	3.45	4.55	7C25
Bl. Festiniog (L.M.S.)	arr.	11.23	1.35	4.7	5.17	7C47
,, ,, (G.W.R.)	arr.	11.25	1.38	4.10	5.20	7C50

A—Stops if required. B—Runs to 12th September only. C—Runs August 3rd to 29th inclusive.

The above Services form suitable connections with the L.M. and S. and G.W. Coys in both directions at Blaenau Festiniog, also at Dinas Junction with the L.M. and S. Railway. Time is allowed at Portmadoc for break of journey in each direction.

The Company give notice that they do not undertake that the trains will start or arrive at the time specified on the Time Tables, nor will they be accountable for any loss, invonvenience, or injury which may arise from delays or detentions, but every endeavour will be made to ensure punctuality as far as practicable. Passengers booking at intermediate Stations can only do so conditionally upon there being room in the train.

September. This was reduced between 16 and 28 September, a dual Welsh Highland/Festiniog handbill (one railway on each side) proclaiming the final alterations.

1936

This proved to be the valedictory year for the Welsh Highland. The last table is given in full from the Pocket Timetable of Snowdon Mountain, Festiniog and Welsh Highland Railways, and operated 6 July–26 September.

The tables of the Welsh Highland have been given in some detail to illustrate that the demands of traffic were often secondary to the motive power position, and the sort of timetable offered was based on engines available. A traffic pattern which calls for intensive services for a short period is hopeless for an operator, and obviously the quarry users were not going to support a meagre goods service if it tended to disappear during the holiday season.

Some fascinating glimpses of everyday working can now be set against the background of timetable and locomotive rostering already given. On a day when the Kerr Stuart tractor was not on the Bryngwyn working (28 December 1928) the Driver's Daily Return reads: 'Engine Baldwin; delayed knocking off duty. Coal yard at Dinas blocked with mud over the rails. Mud over journals of engine.' In the previous January another reads: 'Worked on points at Tryfan. Very slippery to Bryngwyn. Worked incline. Pumping water at Tanycoed. At Nanmor loading flower (sic). Stop at Tanycoed to unload flower. Late starting from Dinas; went home to change clothes, wet through coming from Bryngwyn.'

Certain days involved running to Bryngwyn and back during the morning and Croesor Junction and back in the afternoon. Another Return says: 'Working Incline Bryngwyn. Three slate off track under high road bridge want lifting at bottom of incline impossible for one man to push them.' And another: 'Standing at Bryngwyn waiting for quarry engine. Did not come. Delayed with sheep on line from Tryfan to Wernlas-ddu.' Yet another note concerning *Moel Tryfan* reads: 'Steam pipe joint bursted at bottom. Had to turn back from Salem Halt.'

A typical make-up on the branch at this time would be 19 loaded slate, one load slab, 7 coal trucks, 2 empty slate wagons and a brake van. On such a day, one and a half hours would be spent working the incline. The staff were called upon to drive and repair engines, and to assist in unloading all sorts of commodities, including manure.

A passenger, booking at Portmadoc New in 1925 and wanting to go to Hafod Garregog, had some difficulty with pronunciation; he had to point to the name on the timetable for the booking clerk to understand. On alighting at the Halt he was about to set off when the Guard had the train brought back and addressed him to the effect there was a dangerous bull further along the footpath. The Guard suggested he and his friends continue on the train to Hafod-y-llyn, but they declined, and did not meet the bull.

Because of the 1926 coal strike, Boston Lodge was supplied with soft Belgian coal and the England engine had great difficulty in keeping steam on the Portmadoc–Beddgelert run. Several unofficial stops were made in the Aberglaslyn Pass, with clouds of billowing yellow smoke rising from the engine. Luckily, engines were changed at Beddgelert and *Russell*, fuelled at Dinas, seemed to have better coal.

On a typically wet day in 1934 *Welsh Pony* stood at the head of a four-coach Beddgelert train on the Harbour avoiding line, Portmadoc. The semi-open coaches were not very popular, as the rain was driving through them. This was a typical working, with an England engine for the southern section and *Russell* for the remainder. *Moel Tryfan* was working elsewhere, hence the *Welsh Pony*. The front coach had just left shops and was a bright pink in colour, and made matters no easier as its brakes tended to seize. All was well until the Pass, where slipping started and the fireman crawled onto the front of the engine and dropped handfuls of ash onto the rails. The blonde Welsh 'stationmistress' at Beddgelert did little to relieve the gloom and the steady rain. The train for Dinas had but two passengers already on it and only two more from Portmadoc joined it. The Dinas-bound train was strengthened to five coaches by adding the pink coach to its head, and *Russell* had some difficulty in starting owing to slipping on wet rail; as it crawled away in the driving rain two men ran up pushing a 'Pump Car' which they roped onto the back of the last coach. Then accelerating, they jumped into the train. At Dinas Junction custom in the refreshment room was limited to the two passengers off the train from Portmadoc and the tea girl, even though hailing from traditionally-wet Manchester, had some hard things to say about a Welsh summer in Llanwnda.

Another impression was of riding up to Bryngwyn on the footplate on the goods train that year (in the July), when the Baldwin was on duty. It had just returned from Boston Lodge in what was described as 'chocolate brown or light brown' colour. After Bryngwyn was reached, the Guard and unofficial passenger walked up the Incline where the quarry loco *Cadfan* was waiting; it was apparently on loan to the Alexandra Quarry because their own engine was 'in shops.' *Cadfan* looked very queer, as it carried the tall stovepipe chimney off the Spooner engine 'Kathleen'—this chimney proved too tall for the tunnels and was later taken off.*

The use of petrol-driven gangers' trolleys, which were introduced by Colonel Stephens, seems to have impressed itself on travellers as much as anything. Perhaps it was the way in which these (or a pump-handle car) were attached to the train by a length of rope and then detached in the manner of a slip-coach, complete with men, which so impressed passengers. '. . . a petrol gangers' trolley was a permanent part of the W.H.R. In 1932 or '33 one was attached to the train I travelled on and was hauled, plus four or five staff, as far as South Snowdon. It was then detached, the motor started, and disappeared rapidly back towards Dinas with an impressive fusillade of pops and bangs.'

There seemed also to be confusion on inter-departmental instructions; the bookstall at South Snowdon was to be sent via Beddgelert Siding to Dolgarrog, who presumably wished to use it for their own purposes. They referred to it as 'the small shed' and sent instructions in mid-October 1923. On 8 November Portmadoc reported it still stood on a W.H.R. wagon at the Siding awaiting the G.W.R. stationmaster's attention. Meanwhile Dinas Junction sent a complaint to Portmadoc. '6.5 p.m. train Beddgelert 2 November. This train was delayed 29 minutes owing to the fact that instruction was received at South Snowdon that a carriage trolley loaded with a hut must be taken to Portmadoc on the 4.25 p.m. from Dinas; however when arrived at Beddgelert it was found the trolley could not be coupled to Portmadoc train owing to different shackles and had to be shunted into a siding with Portmadoc engine and Dinas engine had to stand waiting on the platform while the shunting was done as there was no room for the train to pass out. Train Dinas 7.57 too late for the L.M.S. train 7.37 for Afonwen there being no passengers for Afonwen only for Bangor.'

The through line at the Portmadoc Harbour station was used as a stopping place for through trains between the two railways; during the waiting time, engines would coal up here. For the purpose a staging was built and coal from Minffordd unloaded from Festiniog wagons onto it. It was put onto the engines in wicker baskets. Before long the local residents in Britannia Terrace had a great deal to say about smoke nuisance, especially about Colonel Stephens' purchases of continental coal with its high smoke content. Ultimately the coaling point was moved beyond the engine neck west of the Harbour station. Now the prevailing wind blew the smoke all

* Extended details of quarry locomotives will be included in the 'North Caernarvonshire' volume.

over the passengers and the complaints continued from a different source!

The key to Welsh Highland/Festiniog holiday promotion of the early 1930s, was the Five Valleys Tour. L.M.S. and G.W.R. also co-operated, the Tour being a clockwise all-rail day's outing from the N. Wales coastal resorts, down the Blaenau Ffestiniog branch from Llandudno Junction and thence by an easy run, so far as the Festiniog enginemen were concerned, a downhill spin to Portmadoc. Here passengers changed onto the Welsh Highland not, as of yore, from one train into another drawn up alongside, but by being shepherded from the Harbour station (now fully restored to its original purpose) through the back streets, over the G.W.R. and to the waiting train at Portmadoc New (1931). The problems of working the W.H.R. often led to missed connections at Dinas Junction off this train, and the standard gauge connection to the north coast would not wait. A small fortune was spent in satisfying passengers who had missed the connection. It was a gruelling day for the tourist, and a constant worry to the Welsh Highland staff. For two years however (1931–2) there was equal emphasis on the reverse tour, the mid-day departure from Dinas connecting with a Festiniog train due to stand at Portmadoc New by 2.35. The Festiniog took no chances, and always sent a member of the staff to meet the Highland train; they escorted them over the G.W.R. metals and bundled them on their way so that Blaenau should be reached on time. Portmadoc station was instructed '. . . as soon as passengers have walked over the G.W.R. crossing and joined the F. Rly train, for it to run to Portmadoc Old Station. Passengers can then be allowed to get out of the carriages, to wait until 3.10 p.m. By the F. Rly train meeting the W.H. train at the crossing, it will ensure all the passengers joining the train, which will certainly be better than letting them walk across Portmadoc on their own, as it is quite likely some of them might take the wrong road and arrive at the Old Station after the F.R. has left . . . the crossing is not to be opened of course . . .' (Tonbridge; 16 July 1931). The problem of this direction of working was the arrival of the L.M.S. train at Dinas from Caernarvon: this did not arrive there until 12.25 p.m. and the W.H.R. could not depart before 12.30. To reach Portmadoc and return with the other tourists in time to catch the 4.55 L.M.S. train at Dinas was the constant wish of the Festiniog-orientated staff at Portmadoc. A connecting departure from there at 2.45 would easily make such a connection at Dinas. Griffiths the Receiver would have none of it. He insisted that the northbound train spend time at Beddgelert, and the 2.45 from Portmadoc in 1931 for instance, did not reach Dinas until 6.20 when, as commented, only three minutes were allowed for the connection. This made too long a day for most travellers, who would have preferred no delay at Beddgelert and to be back in their lodgings by 6 p.m. The Festiniog connection left Blaenau at 12.10, reached Harbour at 1.15, and passengers had 1½ hours before the Highland train left; they did not especially want another stay-over exceeding one hour at Beddgelert. Clearly the railways' level crossing was in use again during 1935 and 1936 and the leasing period. The 'clockwise' Five Valleys Tour stopped at the through line at the Harbour but not at the first New station; it crossed the G.W.R. and halted in New (1931) before proceeding.*

The late Professor C. L. Mowat, who knew the district well when the Welsh Highland first opened, suggests there were a number of curious workings which the timetables did not disclose. One was to extend Festiniog trains through Portmadoc and up the Highland to Croesor Junction (where there were no proper run-round facilities at the time) . . . 'northbound passengers changed into another train which had worked down that far from Dinas Junction. I remember the Guard giving out a great "spiel" to the general effect—"Croesor Junction. Change for Dinas, Caernarvon, Liverpool, Crewe, Manchester and the North!" '

Bradley, in 'In Praise of Wales' (1925) says: 'When reduced to realities, one's notions of time and mileage as represented by the ordinary railway timetable, don't come in. In other words, this rather humorous little train with its diminutive box carriages takes two hours and a half to make the through trip (23 miles) . . . I was puzzled to think how it could pay over this newly constructed section, for if on the one or two occasions I was not quite the only passenger, I was very nearly so'. Of waiting for trains to pass at Rhydd-ddu, he writes 'If one of them fails to be up to time, passengers on the other must possess their souls in patience until its arrival. I put in fifty minutes here one evening after a long day in Caernarvon, and missed my dinner at the hotel. Not even the fine view from this point . . . quite made up for this unexpected blow'. And doubtless many passengers shared his experience. Bradley says passengers might get out to wait for trains to pass, sit on the turf beside the line and while away the time singing Welsh songs and eating chocolates.

To save time and make connections more dependable, the Guard collected tickets before the terminus, by walking outside and along the footboards between coaches.

Although administration of the Welsh Highland was directed from

* The term 'New (1931)' instead of New (1933) used in other descriptions underlines the earlier use of this station now apparent.

no less than five different addresses—to its eternal disadvantage—the day-to-day affairs of the railway were administered by a clerk-in-charge at Dinas Junction who was responsible directly to Dolgarrog in early days. Oddly, his empire, though in reality stretching into Portmadoc, seems to have had a border of sorts at Croesor Junction for many of his instructions have an atmosphere suggesting that beyond here was the responsibility of the Portmadoc Harbour office. This may have been due to Portmadoc-based trains working up to the Croesor Tramway and back, from which Dinas deduced that anything awry with the Croesor Junction–Portmadoc section should be known about down there, and if not, it wasn't Dinas' worry!

Dinas was instructed to send slate and coal wagons to Boston Lodge for repairs, and to note the wagon numbers. By 1924 the paintwork of stock was so bad that complaint was made; reference numbers could not be quoted unless they were legible. From this stemmed a quick paint-job, using stencils for numbering. At Colonel Stephen's orders, '3 sets of timber trucks' went to the Lodge in March 1926 and among other varieties so consigned were (wagon numbers):

Coal Wagons	*Slate Wagons*			*Other Wagons*
6	10	35	9	511
	20	100	61	512
	40	106	63	
	88	131	121	

and in the following July their return was still awaited whilst Dinas complained of the shortage of wagons. By then Boston Lodge had too much work of Festiniog account and a man was sent from the Lodge to Dinas to help restore N.W.N.G. wagons lying out of service. Wagons Nos. 511–2 were lying at Beddgelert; their category is not known.

During early 1927 Dinas reported that 'slate box wagons are getting out of order with brake gears and axle brasses . . . consequently we are short of wagons suitable to carry coal to the quarries the following are out of order; 2, 57, 37, 27, 59, 30, 52, 155, also Crate Wagons Nos. 120, 127, 386'. This plea went unanswered and was followed by an urgent '. . . we are getting short of slate box wagons to load coal for the quarries, as Crate Wagons do not hold the coal. The position is the same as reported last time.' In the following July the wagon shortage began again . . . 'there are four wagons out of action through derailment on Incline and are still on the side of the Incline'. In view of the lack of stock returns, the above wagon numbers are a slender record of what must have been an impressive fleet of goods-wagonry.

The telephone seems to have been most temperamental; almost every week the lineman had to be out. In November 1925; 'The telephone is very unsatisfactory this week, some calls had to put thro over P. office Telephone as a result. Baldwin Engine broke a spring on the 19th and messages had to be telephoned to Portmadoc over the P.O. telephone. Also resulting from this mishap to the engine, Moeltryfan was put on and she could not move the traffic, there are some Coal Wagons, sand etc. left at Dinas untill next week, also some slates at Drumhead, as the engine could not take sufficient number of wagons to Bryngwyn to work the Incline'. (A matter of balancing the 'run'—Author.)

Welsh Highland trains were not the only ones which ran amok with the timetable; the Down L.M.S. train which connected with the 12.55 Highland departure was always a bad timekeeper in the Summer and this threw all W.H.R. trains out of step for the remainder of the day. Dinas also tartly referred to 'delays awaiting . . . F.R. trains at Beddgelert' (!) confirming that the former N.W.N.G. section considered it now worked only to Beddgelert and Festiniog administration was responsible for the remainder of the railway . . . an attitude of mind which was well-founded and made matters a little difficult with which to live! Again in August 1926 it was noted '. . . delays at Beddgelert waiting Festiniog Rly. train at 2.58 p.m. which causes holding up L.M.S. train 4.50 and re-acting on the 4.46 up and the 7.30 down.'

Trains running late, especially the 2.55 p.m. Dinas arrival, did more than miss the L.M.S. connection almost every day—there was no time for its engine to shunt Dinas yard, with chaotic results, as the sidings showed. In January 1928 emphasis of delays shifted somewhat: 'Some delays happened on Bryngwyn section. Enginemen say they are having difficulties in working the trains with Baldwin, also some delay occurred on Beddgelert section having to pump water for the Loco out of the river but there is now water supply at Beddgelert matters will improve I hope.' (This suggests the W.D. water-lifter fitted to the Baldwin had not been taken off.)

Reverting to plans to restore the passenger service to the Bryngwyn line, and the careful wording on early timetables to the effect the service was merely suspended, tests with the Festiniog's 'Simplex' tractor were made on both main and branch line. It was found it could haul two bogie coaches, but when the Ministry was approached on 4 January 1924, they would not allow a Guard's Brake/Composite coach and tractor to work the Bryngwyn line even if every wheel was fitted with a handbrake; 'in view of the gradients and other special features existing on this light railway', the Ministry insisted that continuous brakes be fitted (29 February 1924). It was not feasible to fit the tractor with a suitable exhauster.

Working the engine round the train on the north side of the railways' crossing, Portmadoc, tended to derail the engine if the loop was used. In consequence, especially following the Baldwin's derailments at this place, *Russell* usually worked around the train by attaching the end of it to a wire rope hitched to the engine; the carriages themselves were then pulled past the engine, through the loop. By and large, working for the W.H.R. could not have been easy. So bad had the reputation of bad timekeeping of northbound trains become, and so regular the missed connection at Dinas, that the Company soon had few passengers to convey north of South Snowdon. The 'delights' of the journey were not increased during winter darkness when mixed trains were obliged to shunt after nightfall, wherever necessary. And there was no steam heating. The fencing of the line was not all that it might be and speed after dark was reduced to reduce risk of collision with straying livestock. Blocked drains and ditches caused flooding, and animals were as wont to be drowned on railway property, as be run over by the train. The Forestry Commission, always much to the fore in the mountainous area where the Highland ran, was vociferous about the number of fires started by passing trains. Management sent every employee circulars from time to time, stressing the need for economy in everything. When the W.H.R. foreman ganger was approached by a farmer who had lost a sheep and said he had found blood on the line, the ganger removed the body and advised Portmadoc that the farmer could not prove the matter . . . 'as I have removed it and if he says that the train killed it where is the lamb's body and that he could not do anything until he will produce the lamb . . .'

So the Welsh Highland fought falling traffic, the new competition of the roads, changing public tastes in travel, the decline of the slate trade as well as the problems of working a railway which had no real beginning or end, relying on others to feed it, and many other lesser cares. Perhaps its worst enemy was itself; it never really operated as one unit, and its administrative staff never worked as a team. A weakly child with more guardians than it could obey it could never grow into a thriving youth.

Finally, from the surviving Advice Notes, a few samples of traffic carried by the labouring goods train will serve to remind of the days when the railway was common carrier to the community. Whilst slates were still the main Dinas-bound traffic, south from there were conveyed saws, grease (from Dublin of all places) for rope lubrication, and coal for the quarries. The local grocers took in sacks of vegetables, casks of sauce, earthenware, pig meal, soap from Port Sunlight, trusses of drapery, casks of vinegar, rolls of wire netting, bales of wall paper, 'bags' of bacon and hams, buckets, a typewriter (this for the Police Station, Beddgelert) and chests of tea. The local Holiday Homes and landladies used vast quantities of apples, cheese, milk in churns and linen. The Bryngwyn Slab Co. sent '12 Setts Grave Covers' to Hughes at Valley and the 'Saracen's Head' used many drums of disinfectant. But the gold medal of salesmanship went to the traveller from the Llandilo factory which made 'Queen Bee Polish'; his sales, together with barrels to and from the brewers, made the strangest bedfellows among the most frequent items found aboard the Welsh Highland goods.

PERSONNEL

At most times during the late 1920s, the line was staffed as follows:

Stationmasters: Dinas, Tryfan Junction (Waenfawr), South Snowdon, Beddgelert—later, Dinas and Beddgelert only.

Administration: (Dinas) 2 (later 1), (part-time) (Portmadoc) 1. Guards 2 (by 1930 1). Enginemen (1930) 2. Permanent Way 5 (later 4, finally 1). Croesor horse haulage costs, variably £3–£5 (the last entry is December 1931).

The Dinas employee was paid latterly £1 a week, and part time officials at Waenfawr, South Snowdon and Beddgelert received between 2s. and 3s. 6d. a week. The Guard was given £1 2s. 6d. and the two enginemen's wages totalled £2 9s. od. The solitary permanent way employee had 14s. and a ton of Loco coal cost £1 5s. 10d. In a typical latter-day week the total wages and stores bill was £15 6s. 8d.

Income from goods train services for week ending; (samples only) 7 July 1934 £4 16s. 9d., 13 October £10 17s. 9d., 19 January 1935 £3 2s. 8d., and during this time goods and coal, as against slate traffic, were averaging about the same income weekly, with preponderance in favour of the former. Hire of Festiniog engine during 1934 cost £54.

Against these may be set the initial 1922 (August) employee strength; Dinas 4, South Snowdon 1; Guards/Shunters 2; Enginemen 4; Fitter 1; Blacksmith 1; Carpenter 1; Painters 2; Loaders 4.

Directors

1923 Sir John Henderson Stewart (Bart)
Henry J. Jack
Evan R. Davies
M. E. Nee (solicitor of Caernarvon)

1925 H. F. Stephens
Evan R. Davies
George Westall (surveyor of London)

Tickets and Fares

An appendix covering all the narrow gauge railways in Caernarvonshire will be found in an appendix to the North Caernarvonshire Volume.

COSTS

	1922	1923	1924	1925	1926	1927	1928	1929	1930	1931	1932	1933
Maint. Works & Way	496	1180	1618	1045	936	1498	801	472	375	254	—	164
Loco Power Cost (inc. horse)	973	2483	2879	1636	1200	1367	606	509	324	267	—	270
Repairs & Renewals (Locos, Carrs & Wagons)	511	717	318	153	213	292	229	26	103	190	—	78
Traffic Expenses	1734	1795	1737	1661	1779	1778	1415	1133	870	419	—	218
Profit/loss on Working	(599)	(1573)	(2331)	(742)	(787)	(3304)	(339)	(52)	(474)	(742)	—	(278)
Merchandise Tons	1442	2513	2453	705	565	762	412	334	218	116	—	67
Minerals Tons (slate, etc.)	10,068	10,761	12,601	13,462	12,660	11,741	10,132	8160	6682	1632	—	1935
Coal, etc. Tons	4252	3903	4694	4548	3067	3897	3153	2303	1844	1965	—	796
Class 1st	24	562	337	112	101	84	23	27	—	7	—	3
3rd	4959	57,641	50,148	24,541	12,803	12,933	7404	5069	1343	2459	—	4324
Engine mileage (totals)	16,850	42,666	55,546	31,306	21,874	26,813	15,574	10,827	8389	6454	—	5140
Locos (tank)	2	3 (for remainder of period)										
Carriages of Uniform Class	6	6	6	6	6	6	6	5	5	5	—	5
Carriages of Composite Class	3	3	3	3	3	3	3	3	3	3	—	3
Merchandise & Mineral Wagons	103*	103	115†	115	116	117	117	115	114	114	—	114
Special purposes Wagons	—	—	1	1	1	1	1	1	1	1	—	—
Rail & Timber trucks	12 (throughout period)											
Miscellaneous Wagons	1	1	—	—	—	—	—	—	—	—	—	—
Brake Vans	—	—	2 (for remainder of period)									

* This total was made up of 9 open coal wagons, 94 slate & box wagons;
† This total was made up of 19 open coal wagons, 96 slate & box wagons; Returns continue in approx. proportion.

NB. An exceptional expenditure for 1927 was £1,395 (Law Charges) i.e. expenses of Receiver's appointment—in other years charges averaged £50.

STATIONS AND HALTS

Miles	*Chains*	*Original name*	*Open all Traffic*	*Closed Goods (official date)*	*Closed Passenger (last train)*	
00	00	South Snowdon	31.7.1922	31.5.1937	26.9.1936	(previous names in NWNG list)
1	00	Pitt's Head	9.7.1923	—	,,	
1	76	Hafod Ruffydd	,,	31.5.1937	,,	
4	52	Beddgelert	,,	,,	,,	
6	10	Aberglaslyn	,,	—	?.7.1934	
6	22	Nantmor (for Aberglaslyn)	,,	31.5.1937	26.9.1936	became Aberglaslyn 7.1934
7	10	Hafod-y-llyn	,,	,,	,,	
7	50	Hafod Garregog	,,	—	,,	Name given to Ynysferlas
8	7	Ynysferlas	?.7.1924	31.5.1937	,,	Became Hafod Garregog—7.1924?
8	58	Croesor Junction	26.9.1927	,,	,,	Not always shown in timetables
9	7	Ynysfor (for Llanfrothen)	9.7.1923	,,	,,	
10	13	Pont Croesor (for Prenteg)	,,	,,	,,	
10	69	(Pont Rhyddin loop)	—	—	—	Several spellings used; see text for lifting
11	55	(Sand Siding)	—	—	—	Installed by W.H.R. Closed 31.5.1937
11	60	(Beddgelert Siding)	—	—	—	Closed 31.5.1937
11	79	(G.W.R. Crossing)	—	—	—	Closed 31.5.1937
12	1	Portmadoc New (for G.W.R.)	9.7.1923	Not open goods	26.9.1936	See notes below
12	38	Portmadoc Old (Harbour)	dates apply, but not to Festiniog station.			

Notes

All stopping places were Halts except Beddgelert and Portmadoc stations.

Portmadoc New referred to variously as Portmadoc (G.W.R.). Not used by all W.H.R. trains by Summer 1929 but connecting F.R. trains utilise. By 1931 timetable the north side of the G.W.R. Crossing was the admitted terminus of W.H.R. passenger trains, and duly fitted with crude nameboards.

Portmadoc Old (Harbour) station; stops were made alongside Goods Shed, not in Festiniog's station.

ACKNOWLEDGEMENTS

In some previous publications within the Series, the Author's task has been eased by the existence of those who had made a special study of certain of their contents. Caernarvonshire, whilst enjoying the well-earned interest it deserves from railway historians, has produced no such specialists. Worse than this, past accounts have been sketchy and repetitive so that the task of collecting material apart, the manuscript has involved exactly seven years' work.

The demanding job of unearthing and collating archive material is a time-consuming and extremely expensive pursuit; material is not always available without prior notice and is often not on the premises. I am convinced that the collection and treatment of available material is now beyond the time and means of the average historian, unless he is professionally involved, subsidised—or his objects are limited. The cost of publication, too, is more than most publishing houses is prepared to risk.

My thanks therefore, extend firstly to my good friend and publisher Roger Kidner; his support for this Series continues unbounded. Secondly, in Jeremy S. Wilkinson this book has found a gifted historian who has sifted through masses of often-irrelevant material in North Wales, Manchester and London which enabled the Author to take a smaller share of this part of the work and saved an enormous amount of time. John M. Lloyd and I have covered the fieldwork not once but many many times these last twenty years, and this groundwork has on many occasions proved that what may be found in the archives is not necessarily what actually happened! Such matters make up the love of the chase! John Lloyd's drawing and maps are drawn and redrawn with loving care and patience; he accepts my last-minute alterations without comment; 'nothing but the best' is the book's good fortune to enjoy in this respect.

I recall with gratitude the companies who have come to my assistance, including Messrs. R. Y. Pickering & Co. Ltd., The Hunslet Engine Co. Ltd., The Metropolitan Cammell Railway Carriage & Wagon Co. Ltd., Messrs. Beyer Peacock & Co. Ltd., The Vulcan Foundry Ltd., Messrs. Freeman Fox & Partners and many others too numerous to mention. A list of kind contributors is appended.

Groundwork for this book began in Portmadoc in 1944; my wife has been a constant assistant out on the site, in the nursery, the kitchen and the study . . . to mention some places where for a quarter of a century we have plotted together to give the neglected narrow gauge railways of Caernarvonshire the sort of book we thought they deserved. I also acknowledge:

The County Archivists of Caernarvonshire and Merioneth.
The Archivist, University College Library, Bangor.
The National Library of Wales.
The Librarian, Manchester Central Reference Library.
The Librarian, Manchester Law Society Library.

E. Boydell & Co. Ltd.	(Tractor details)
The Baldwin Locomotive Co.	(Locomotive details)
A. C. Baker	(Contractor's locomotives)
J. L. H. Bate	(Biographical notes; mining details)

D. E. Bick	(Mining details)
J. F. Bolton	(Welsh Highland demolition notes)
C. R. Clinker	(Recollections and closure notes)
B. E. Crompton	(Beyer Peacock references)
R. W. Chaney	(Illustrations)
late Thomas Davies	(Welsh Highland material)
late J. M. Dunn	(Unpublished material on railways of county)
A. Michael Davies	(Welsh Highland material)
Robert Evans	(Material and recollections)
M. D. Greville	(Extracts from Bradshaw)
A. G. W. Garraway	(Loan of Festiniog Railway material)
F. M. Gates	(Illustrations)
C. C. Green	(Illustrations)
S. H. P. Higgins	(Newspaper references)
Frank Hewitt	(Gift of large personal collection)
the late W. Hayward	(General information)
G. E. Hughes	(Personal recollections)
Robert Hudson Ltd.	(Manufacturers' records)
R. Y. Honychurch	(Material and illustrations)
R. W. Kidner	(Recollections and illustrations)
Dr. Jean Lindsay	(Slate Quarrying)
the late T. S. Lascelles	(Spooner family; signalling)
Charles E. Lee	(General information)
David M. Lee	(Materials)
W. J. Milner	(Loan of source materials)
E. Mellowes	(Source material)
the late Professor C. L. Mowat	(Recollections; signalling)
the late Donald Mackereth	(Gift of personal collection)
Professor G. H. Platt	(General information and illustrations)
R. R. J. Plummer	(Illustrations)
G. Parker	(Illustrations)
L. T. C. Rolt	(Tractor details)
A. E. Rimmer	(Welsh Highland materials)
Douglas Rendell	(Photographic services)
Bernard Roberts	(General information and illustrations)
Michael Seymour	(Archivist, Festiniog Railway Society)
Trustees of Narrow Gauge Railway Museum	(Archive material)
R. E. Tustin	(Materials, illustrations, drawings)
Colin Wilson	(Contractors' locomotives; slate quarries)
Colonel Dudley West	(The Huddart Family)
P. B. Whitehouse	(Illustrations)
H. F. Wheeler	(Illustrations)
the late W. H. Whitworth	(Illustrations)
Welsh Highland Light Railway (1964) Ltd.	(Loan of Publications' materials)

The Author is also indebted for the loan and use of illustrations duly credited individually.

BIBLIOGRAPHY

(Dates recent unless given otherwise where known)

General

Madocks and the Wonder of Wales: E. Beazley, Faber 1957.
History of Caernarvonshire: A. H. Dodd, Caerns. Hist. Soc. 1968
Slate Quarrying in Wales: Morgan Richards, 1876
Snowdonia: Various, Collins 1949
Cambrian Travellers' Guide (2 Edn.): George Nicholson, 1813
Topographical Dictionary of Wales (4 Edn.): S. Lewis, 1850
Mines, Mills and Furnaces: Morgan Rees, H.M.S.O. 1969
British Mining: R. Hunt, 1887
Steamers of North Wales: Frank C. Thornley, Stephenson 1968
Industrial Revolution in N. Wales: A. H. Dodd, University of Wales 1950
Tours in Wales: Pennant, Humphreys 1883
Anglesey and North Wales Pilot: Henry Glazebrook, Yachting Monthly 1961

Railway

Chester Division of the Great Western Railway (official): G.W.R. 1924
Great Western Railway—Running Powers (official): G.W.R. 1924
Industrial & Independent Locomotives & Railways of N. Wales: Bradley & Hindley, Birmingham Locomotive Club 1968
Railway Reminiscences: G. P. Neele, McCorquodale 1904
How Ffestiniog got its railway: M. J. T. Lewis, Railway & Canal Hist. Soc. 1965
The South Caernarvonshire Railway (unpublished): J. M. Dunn, (per Prof. Platt)
The Chester & Holyhead Railway: J. M. Dunn, Oakwood Press 1968
Light Railways: Mackay, Crosby Lockwood 1896
Etude Technique sur le chemin de fer Festiniog & quelques autres chemins de fer a voie etroite de l'Angleterre: M. E. Vignes, 1878
The Festiniog Railway: J. I. C. Boyd, Oakwood Press 1959
Report of Investigation Committee on Light Railways: 1921
Hand Book of Railway Stations (Railway Clearing House): McCorquodale Various

Among other sources consulted:

Index to Parliamentary Papers on Railways, The Engineer, Engineering, The Locomotive Magazine, Railway Magazine, Bradshaw's Railway Manual, Journal of Transport History, Stock Exchange Year Book, Skinner's Register of Defunct Companies, Universal Directory of Railway Officials, Directory of Directors, Official Returns—Ministry of Transport, British Transport Commission Historical Records, House of Commons Sessional Papers, House of Lords Record Office, Registrar of Companies, National Library of Wales (especially collections; Longueville, Glynllivon, Henry Robertson and Davies Brothers), County Record Offices Caernarvon (especially Collections; Breese Jones & Casson, W. A. Madocks and J. W. Greaves), Dolgellau (especially Collection;

Taylor & Francis re. Croesor United), Library of University College North Wales (especially Collections; Carter Vincent, Searell and Cynhaiarn), Manchester Law Society Library, Narrow Gauge Railway Society, L.N.W.R. Earlstown records, G.W.R. Swindon records, Liverpool Museum, Ordnance Survey, *The Times*, Geological Survey & Mineral Statistics of Great Britain, Archaelogia Cambrensis for 1968 (D. M. Rees: 'Copper Mining in North Wales'), Quarry Managers' Journal, Archives of the Narrow Gauge Railway Museum Trust. The house journals and private publications of about one dozen enthusiast and professional bodies have been searched, together with surviving copies of short-lived monthly publications now defunct.

INDEX

Note: Collective headings in the text for each Part ('Locomotives, Signalling, Timetables', etc.) enable a complete index to be foreshortened. Information should first be sought under collective headings; the remaining principal references under the various general headings are indexed below.

Scattered references to stations will be found under signalling, permanent way, timetables, accidents; these also contain miscellaneous references to personalities, stock, finance, etc.

The North Wales Narrow Gauge Railways and The Welsh Highland Railway.

Examples of Freight Rolling Stock.

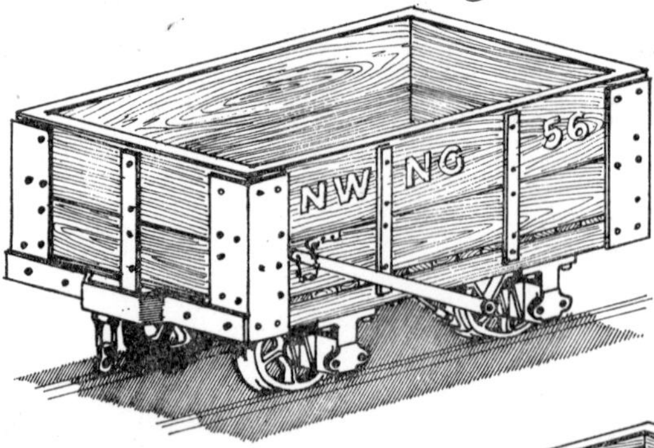

2-plank Merchandise Wagon №56 in original form.
Brake on one side only.

Body Length	7'
Body Width	4'
Body Height	2' 9"
Height above Rail	4' 3"
Wheel Diameter	1' 6"
Wheel Centres	3' 6"

Coal & Mineral Wagon №3 Lift-up door one side only, coil springs, heavy duty axleboxes brake lever on opposite side.

B.L.	10'
B.W.	5'
H.R.	5'6"
W.D.	1'6"
W.C.	6'

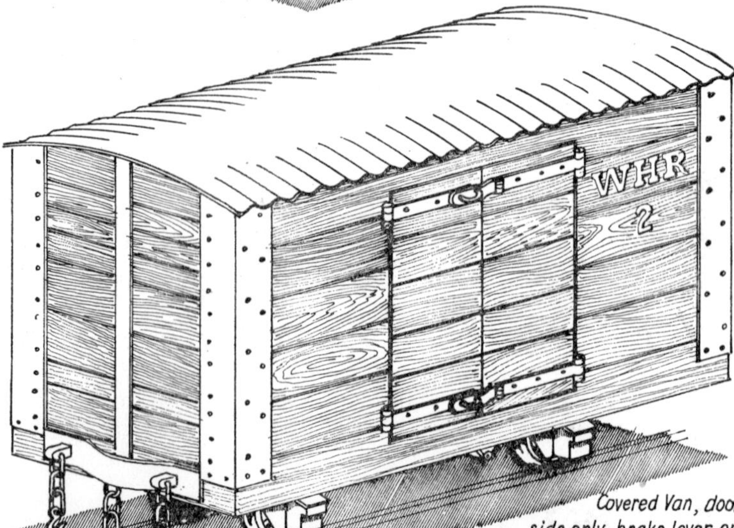

B.L.	11'
B.W.	5'
B.H.	7'
H.R.	8'6"
W.D.	1'6"
W.C.	6'

Covered Van, doors on one side only, brake lever on othersid running gear as coal & mineral wagons. corrugated iron roof.